Collecting Political Americana

Edmund B. Sullivan

THE CHRISTOPHER PUBLISHING HOUSE, HANOVER, MA 02339

To my father, who introduced me to Finley Peter
Dunne's immortal commentator on the American scene
Mr. Abner Dooley of Archery Road. My father taught me
that politics is an honorable profession; from Mr. Dooley
I learned never to turn my back on a politician.

*Unless otherwise indicated, all items pictured are in either
the author's collection or in that of the University of Hartford.*

Inquiries should be directed to:
The Christopher Publishing House
24 Rockland Street
Hanover, MA 02339

Printed in the United States of America

Library of Congress Card Number 90-83146

ISBN: 0-8158-0462-8

Contents

Acknowledgments

SEVERAL PEOPLE HELPED to make this book possible. First on any list must be J. Doyle DeWitt, pioneer collector of political Americana, who stimulated me—as he did so many collectors—to become a serious student of that uniquely American event, the political campaign. In time, his collection became the property of the University of Hartford, and I am grateful to its president, Stephen Joel Trachtenberg, for permission to photograph many pieces from it. Herbert Collins, Curator of Political History at the Smithsonian Institution, read part of the manuscript. Larry Krug, former president of the American Political Items Collectors, gave me permission to quote from APIC publications, and current president Robert Fratkin offered several helpful suggestions. My good friends and fellow collectors U. I. "Chick" Harris, Richard Maxson, and John Drost provided several important photographs and insights. I appreciate the long hours of labor put in by photographers Norman Pastor and my son Geoffrey, and I am especially indebted to my editor, Kathryn Pinney, for holding me to a high level of expression. I could always count on my wife Marie's happy combination of patience and thoughtfulness for the times when both were needed.

Introduction

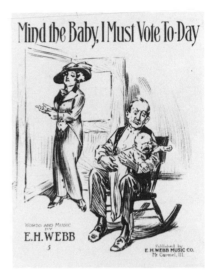

A. Popular Collecting Subjects. The women's rights movement is a traditional favorite among collectors. Song sheet ca. 1915.

PERHAPS NO OTHER institution is so typically American as a presidential campaign. It can be rowdy and raucous, emotionally moving and boring, dignified and intensely pragmatic. It is a popularity contest on a grand scale. Over the years presidential campaign style has evolved into a blend of serious purpose, hokum, and inevitable controversy. It is a style that accommodates aristocrats, farmers, generals, professors, editors, lawyers, and the occasional eccentric. Each nominee of a major party must be able to convince voters that he is humble, urbane, a true believer, a clear alternative to the incumbent, and in favor of peace, prosperity, and progress.

The advent of the two-party system and the merging of ideologically similar local and national candidates into a single "ticket" by the 1830s, along with the expansion of the franchise, generated an increasing need for candidates to seek support directly from voters. It seemed a natural next step for candidates to advertise their own availability and their virtues—while condemning their opponents' "vices"—and to promise what they would do if elected. Sparsely at first and later in torrents, a tremendous variety of objects have been made, all of them intended to persuade voters to vote for a candidate and not for his opponent.

The design, the function, and the materials of campaign artifacts or "political Americana" are limited only by their makers' imaginations. Artifacts are known manufactured in ceramic, tin, common and precious metals, textiles, gutta-percha, tortoiseshell, glass, wood, ivory, and several other materials. In the earlier campaigns highquality imports (mostly ceramics and medals) from England and France, plus traditional regional American arts and crafts, provided the contexts for whatever messages a candidate wanted to get across. Later campaigns were, like those today, dominated by mass-produced pieces, some of which, despite their large production, are now frequently difficult to find, simply because so much campaign material is ephemeral—meant for a specific use and then discarded.

B. Personalities: John F. Kennedy is one of the most popular of all collectible subjects. This brochure is from the 1946 Massachusetts congressional primary campaign.

Either a good general collection or a specialized one will reflect its owner's taste. At one extreme in political Americana are artifacts that can only be described as tawdry, banal, and grotesque—kitsch, in German, meaning commercially made objects with a low level of aesthetic appeal and intended for a mass market.* My own favorite kitsch includes bubble gum cigars from the 1960 campaign, hollow pot- or base-metal clocks depicting Franklin Roosevelt (see Ill. 282), and modern plastic campaign hats. At the other extreme are superb examples of America's rich folk art and craft traditions, such as Washington inaugural buttons, tin lanterns and torchlights, early campaign banners and other political textiles, and early prints and cartoons. But most artifacts, obviously, fall between those extremes, so it is reasonable to say that the quality of a collection is only as good as its owner's taste.

Because of its scope, political Americana includes many kinds of artifacts that figure in other fields of collecting as well. Political collectors need to have basic information and be reasonably well informed about price trends in historical glass and china, paper ephemera, and nineteenth-century photography and numismatics—from the

---

*Cf., Jan von Adlmann, "Kitsch: The Grotesque Around Us." *Museum News* (vol. LII, no. 1), September 1973.

viewpoint of collectors in those other fields. It has been my experience that few political collectors bother to keep themselves this widely informed. As a result, they are likely to pay too much for some items or, worse, not recognize the value or historical significance of others. At least some awareness of the literature of other hobbies is a matter of self-protection for political collectors.

DEFINING POLITICAL ARTIFACTS.   For collectors, the term "political artifacts" includes material that originates under different circumstances. First is campaign-related material, artifacts used in actual campaigns—from the moment the first hopeful declares his candidacy to the inauguration itself.

Second is commemorative artifacts. Political material dating from before the 1820s falls into this category, since aspirants for the presidency did not campaign before that period. Material associated with the early presidents, George Washington through James Monroe, marks inaugurations and later events occurring during their administrations. (Note that early inaugural material can be placed in either of these two categories, however.) The best known of all early presidential commemorative artifacts are Washington inaugural buttons. Other examples of early commemoratives are Liverpoolware, patriotic textiles, numismatic issues of the period, and broadsides and similar paper material.

C.   A cobalt plate commemorating the opening of the Lewis and Clark Exposition in Portland, Oregon in 1905. Collecting political glass and ceramics is increasing in popularity.

Some modern commemoratives also deserve a place in a political collection. The Watergate pitcher (Ill. 145), Washington Stevengraphs, modern Washington and Lincoln medallic items, and certain buttons are examples. Beginning collectors should note that, generally, modern commemoratives are not considered as valuable as modern campaign artifacts, but early commemoratives sell at prices reflecting the effect of supply and demand because there is nothing else to collect from the early period.

The third category is mourning artifacts, such as certain lapel ribbons, several pitchers depicting James A. Garfield, and a variety of cards and ribbons marking Lincoln's assassination. Generally, mourning material is not as desirable as actual campaign material and early commemorative artifacts, but some mourning items, such as ribbons marking the nearly simultaneous deaths of John Adams and Thomas Jefferson, can bring high prices.

A few artifacts defy exact classification. Andrew Jackson material inscribed "The Hero of New Orleans" was probably issued some time before he became president. Yet such material was certainly used in later campaigns. This inexactness also characterizes some early numismatic issues and occasional modern artifacts, such as a banner I know of that pictures Theodore Roosevelt and says "Welcome Roosevelt." Was it produced during the 1904 campaign or later, when Roosevelt—as do all presidents—made a special visit to some part of the country? Most collectors do not worry about this kind of vagueness, but if that Roosevelt banner, for example, also said "Our Choice for President," or had a similar inscription indicating actual campaign use, it might well sell at a higher price. Obviously, such a fine distinction is not relevant with material related to Andrew Jackson or other early presidents—collectors consider themselves lucky to own even one artifact associated with them.

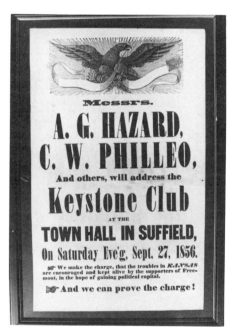

D.   James Buchanan's native state of Pennsylvania, the Keystone State, lent its nickname to the Democratic grassroots organization which supported his candidacy in 1856.

The emphasis in collecting political Americana is on campaign artifacts and early commemoratives; there is less emphasis on modern commemoratives. But the careful collector tries to attribute or otherwise identify every artifact in his collection. Not only should he do this for the sake of historical accuracy, but because the actual value of an artifact may be affected.

No book can provide a totally comprehensive knowledge of political Americana, but I hope this one will introduce the reader to a provocative and always timely hobby, which can also be intellectually, emotionally, and financially satisfying.

Introduction to the Revised Second Edition

NEARLY A DECADE has passed since publication of the first edition of this book. During those years the hobby has attracted thousands of new collectors and many scholars; both groups see in political Americana rich grass roots expressions of the presidential election process.

The collecting and study of political Americana has come of age with a maturity distinguished by several noteworthy accomplishments. Among the publications in this decade: Both my revision of J. Doyle DeWitt's classic study retitled *American Political Medals and Medalets, 1789-1892* and my collaboration with Roger Fischer, *American Political Ribbons and Ribbon-Badges, 1825-1981*, compiled and standardized these specialized subjects. Fischer's *Tippecanoe and Trinkets, Too* was the first work by a professional historian to demonstrate the historical significance of political material culture. Button collectors, beginners especially, profitted from Marc Sigoloff's *Collecting Political Buttons* and H. Joseph Levine's *Collector's Guide to Presidential Inaugural Medals* was a major advance in the study of political numismatics. Several collectors contributed illustrated compilations of campaign material associated with such candidates for the White House as John Anderson and John F. Kennedy.

During the 1980's membership growth in American Political Items Collectors nearly doubled in numbers from the previous decade. Its bi-annual national "convention" and frequent local chapter-sponsored meetings attract annually thousands of collectors and members of the general public.

The auction of the Warner collection in 1982 was the occasion for the highest price ever paid for a political campaign button. The winning bid of $30,000 has not since been surpassed. This auction set the precedent for what are now commonplace "blockbuster" prices— for campaign buttons, especially. Extraordinarily high prices represent the union of investing, speculating, and collecting, and is an inevitable result and a mixed blessing at best, when hobbies reach a certain level of growth.

Rounding out the evidence for the widespread popularity of political Americana is the University of Hartford's recently opened Museum of American Political Life. Here in a comprehensive exhibition, expanded from the nuclear collection of early A.P.I.C. member J. Doyle DeWitt, are displayed provocative arrangements of subjects and themes essential to understanding and appreciating the sometimes mysterious ways by which we Americans choose our presidents.

Preparing this new edition has been a genuine pleasure due mainly to the considerable support from fellow collectors and scholars, especially from members of the A.P.I.C.'s DeWitt/Connecticut chapter. I am grateful to President Humphrey Tonkin of the University of Hartford for permission to illustrate objects from the Museum of American Political Life. My good friend and colleague Roger Fischer was always available for insightful comments. On the University of Hartford campus, Nancy Swain of the News Bureau, Susan Harrington the Museum secretary, and Christine Scriabine the Museum historian, has each in her own way helped channel my passion for political Americana in productive and imaginative directions. To my family, I reaffirm what I said about my wife Marie in the first edition and for Geoffrey, David, Maura, and Mark, your good-humored support is deeply appreciated by your proud father.

1
Campaigning for the Presidency

E. An early figurine of Washington, possibly from the Staffordshire pottery of William Adams and Sons.

FROM THE VIEWPOINT of collectors, presidential campaign history is best divided into eras for a number of reasons. Some eras are characterized by the prominent use of certain artifacts; thus ferrotypes were used most frequently in the 1860s and bandannas in the 1880s; buttons have dominated every campaign since 1896. Other eras are popular with collectors because of the availability of material and the frequency with which it comes on the market. Certain candidates who are collectors' favorites—such as Abraham Lincoln, both Roosevelts, and John Kennedy—are often a stimulus for widening the scope of one's collection to include representative material of other candidates from the same era. Themes and issues that dominate an era are also an attraction for collectors: This is particularly true of the "Common Man" era, when political campaigning was beginning to assume its modern form, and the "Jet Age" era, in which recent campaigns are marked by an interesting assortment of protest material.

There is also historical consistency in presidential campaigning, which can sometimes be highlighted in a collection by bringing together artifacts from several eras: cartoons, buttons and other devices bearing campaign slogans, and artifacts carrying both a commercial advertising message and a political message are examples. Or collectors may wish to build a collection that demonstrates the consistency with which some political themes dominate eras—the prosperity theme is an example. Historical consistency can also be indicated by assembling artifacts used in different eras that exemplify aspects of the campaign process itself. For example, consider collecting material that demonstrates the evolution of the national party convention from its beginning in the 1830s, or material that illustrates the gradual emergence of the state primary election as an indicator of candidates' popularity with voters.

F. For most collectors the rare, expensive and drab Cox and Roosevelt jugate buttons are too costly. Here is a neat colorful window decal, usually available at reasonable prices, which will serve as an acceptable substitute. See plate #12 for the mate.

Eras provide a focus for collecting. Historical consistency is a focus also, but, more important, it is a reminder to collectors that presidential campaigning is a continuously evolving process that began with the Founding Fathers.

1

1.   An attractive brass button commemorating George Washington's first inauguration in 1789. For other examples of Washington inaugural buttons, see Illustration 36.

2.   Andrew Jackson's two terms were stormy ones. This early 1800s broadside of an 1828 poster depicts him as "King Andrew" who rules by whim rather than adhering to constitutional principles.

Campaign Eras

ERA OF THE FOUNDING FATHERS: 1789–1830.   The first five presidents were remarkable men. All had been active in seeking separation from Great Britain. George Washington was the great general and the presider at the Constitutional Convention. John Adams was an early colonial agitator and negotiator of the Treaty of Paris. Thomas Jefferson was the author of the Declaration of Independence. James Madison was the chief architect of the Constitution. James Monroe gave his name to the young nation's first significant foreign policy statement. All were presidents before the two-party system had emerged clearly—when candidates did not actively seek votes—when, in fact, the franchise was generally restricted to propertied white males.

Politicking was a dignified affair. Party stalwarts would wait upon their choice; he, in turn, felt himself humble, chosen by Providence and committed to reason, justice, and moderation in all things. That pattern survived through only the first quarter of the nineteenth century. The advent of "frontier democracy," widening of the franchise, choosing of electors by popular vote, and —above all—the inevitable emergence of the two-party system meant eventually that the earliest presidents, especially George Washington, became idealized models. Washington would be forever "first in the hearts of his countrymen" and the paragon of truth for children of later generations.

Political material from this period commemorates presidential inaugurations and the highlights during a president's term of office. Related artifacts from the period can be quite expensive; nevertheless, the collector should try to add a representative piece of such material if at all possible. First choice would be a George Washington inaugural button (Ill. 1) because these handsome buttons mark the first term of our first president. The collector on a more limited budget can turn to paper material, such as contemporary newspapers containing accounts of presidential elections and other political events; or broadsides, ballots, and song sheets; or contemporary books concerned with a president and his administration.

Another possibility is building a specialized collection of the Washington material that has appeared in association with the material issued for candidates in later campaigns. Washington became the model for later candidates to emulate, and a specialized collection would demonstrate this. There is much to choose from, as the subsequent chapters of this book will clearly show.

ERA OF THE COMMON MAN.   The nearly simultaneous deaths of John Adams and Thomas Jefferson on July 4, 1826, marked the formal ending of the era of the Founding Fathers. But already the forces were in motion that would not only alter drastically how a president was elected, but also determine what kind of personality was most likely to be elected. Historians have termed the first decades of the nineteenth century the National Era, characterized chiefly by the emergence to political power of the "common man" — i.e., those citizens born on the frontier or in the row houses of the industrializing cities. In their behavior these Americans developed a strong sense of egalitarianism, patriotism, confident optimism in the future, and social activism that would forever stamp the American character.

Their hero was Andrew Jackson. He had been a general too, but there his resemblance to Washington ended. Jackson was our first authentic folk-hero president. His log cabin origins, his unconventional victory over the British at New Orleans, and his controversial adventures in Spain's Florida territory helped propel him into the presidency. He possessed all those qualities that Americans have usually admired in presidential candidates ever since: He was a fighter born in humble or socially average circumstances; an outspoken man, not overtly intellectual; a plain dresser—in fact, a candidate with whom most voters could easily identify. To his detractors he was "King Andrew the First" (Ill. 2); always a center of violent emotions, he was the first president upon whom an assassination attempt was made.

Andrew Jackson represents the arrival of the common man to national political leadership. William Henry Harrison represents the consolidation of that triumph. What General Harrison lacked in military prowess and stature his campaign strategists more than made up for in their brilliant exploitation of the common man theme in the justly famous 1840 Log Cabin campaign (Ill. 3). A descendant of the Harrisons of Virginia was hardly likely to be poor. But the Whigs managed to convince enough voters that a log cabin and a jug of cider were Paradise. Harrison himself spoke not at all, a campaign first. With great hoopla, an incredible array of campaign material, and blunt smears of the Democrat, Martin Van Buren (all of which seem very modern), the Whigs sent their first successful candidate to the White House.

The Log Cabin campaign was without a doubt the wildest, the most exciting, colorful, and nonsensical of all political campaigns in American history. It saw the beginning of street parades for candidates and the transformation of catchy slogans and phrases—"Tippecanoe and Tyler too!"—into campaign music. Genteel politics had given way completely to hard campaigning. Parades and rallies were numerous, and often culminated in the emptying of several barrels of hard cider by thirsty partisans. Large balls bearing slogans were rolled across the country from one community to another—thus the origin of the phrase "keep the ball rolling."

The presidential electioneering process was beginning to assume the form that modern Americans would recognize, although they might have trouble identifying most of the presidents who came between Harrison and Lincoln: John Tyler, James Polk, Zachary Taylor (Ill. 4), Millard Fillmore, Franklin Pierce, and James Buchanan. Only Polk proved to be a decisive and imaginative president. It seems in retrospect as if the stage was being set for Abraham Lincoln.

The Common Man Era is an exciting period for collectors. Many artifacts from the period are expensive—but many are not. There is an abundance of material from William Henry Harrison's campaign. The Whigs' use of the log cabin symbol in this campaign was brilliant; and collectors can build a specialized collection that demonstrates the use of symbol—and later, image—in presidential campaigning. Some artifacts associated with Henry Clay and a few Jackson, Taylor, and Buchanan medalets are fairly low in price. Polk, Tyler, and Pierce artifacts are generally scarcer and more expensive. But, again, much paper material can be bought cheaply. In fact, so much fine collectible material has survived that no collection need lack something associated with this very important and influential period in American political history.

3. *Above*: An 1840 brass Log Cabin button; it was responsible for the origin of the term "political button." *Below*: A glass-encased lapel brooch from the same campaign.

4. These portrait lithographs measuring about 3 inches in diameter are known in both color and black and white. They were enclosed in glass within a pewter frame, and usually were looped for suspension. Most of them contain a vice-presidential candidate's picture also or, less often, a mirror on the opposite side. They are scarce, expensive, and desirable.

ABRAHAM LINCOLN.   Despite their overwhelming victory in 1840, the Whigs could not maintain their popular support. In 1856 the Republican party was founded by dissident Whigs. It lost with its first nominee, the explorer-general John C. Frémont. But the second Republican nominee was Abraham Lincoln.

In a book published in late 1859 describing the background of politicians likely to seek the presidential nomination in 1860, Lincoln was not mentioned. Many voters thought his given name was Abram as did some manufacturers of campaign material even after he became the Republican nominee. Given his later deification, it is difficult for modern Americans to imagine the abuse and vilification heaped upon Lincoln throughout his tenure: "Ape" and "ugly caricature" seem the least offensive epithets.

The consensus of most Washington citizens was that he was the homeliest man in the city. He was 6 feet 4 inches tall, spoke in a high voice, seemed awkward physically, and took a rather laconic view of people and events (Ills. 5 and 6). He was perhaps the most complex personality ever to occupy the White House. To this day he is the subject of books, monographs, and an occasional film; and he is the focus for thousands of collectors of "Lincolniana." His White House tenure coincided with that new phenomenon, photography; his face became a classic study for photographers. He achieved a fairly easy electoral victory, becoming the first president to have been nominated by the new Republican party. (In 1860 the Democrats split themselves into three slavery and antislavery factions.) Despite the vicious opposition of the Copperheads, Lincoln also easily defeated the popular Civil War hero, General George McClellan, in the 1864 campaign (Ill. 7).

5.   An 1864 cartoon critical of Lincoln. Here he is portrayed as indifferent to the many dead and wounded Union army soldiers on the Antietam battlefield.

Lincoln's southern counterpart, Jefferson Davis, elected the first (and only) president of the Confederacy in 1861, presided over seven states based upon a slave economy. In the closing days of their defeat, Davis was captured as he attempted to flee Richmond (Ill. 8).

Lincoln's log cabin origins, a superb sense of humor, the rail-splitter image, his courage during the Civil War, and his assassination just after victory all combined to make him an outstanding figure in American history, ranking alongside the great Washington in the American pantheon.

There is plenty of Lincoln-related material to satisfy collectors. Lincoln artifacts are more expensive than most of those related to other candidates of the period simply because the subject is Abraham Lincoln; fairly common Lincoln artifacts will often sell for more than scarcer Douglas, Grant, and McClellan material. Lincoln ribbons and ferrotypes are among the most desirable of all campaign items, and are priced accordingly. The competition from Lincolniana collectors is also a factor in maintaining high prices. The political collector should consider broadening the scope of the Lincoln component in his collection by adding political material from campaigns of later candidates in which Lincoln is used as a symbol. He is, of course, a continuing inspiration for the Republican party—the collector can begin with that approach. How one collects "Lincoln," especially, is a good indication of whether one is an accumulator or a collector. An accumulator's two dozen Lincoln ferrotypes are valuable, but they tell us next to nothing about Lincoln's political significance in future campaigns, or Lincoln the campaigner, or Lincoln the "martyr" president.

BOOM AND BUST: 1872–1892.   His military prowess helped elect Ulysses S. Grant to the White House. He was a superior general, but an inept president whose final months in office were marked by the first of the great scandals that have plagued the presidency—Teapot Dome and Watergate would follow. America was changing too fast for many politicians to comprehend: Sprawling tenements and soot-grimed neighborhoods spoke of a new force in American politics. At first, presidential candidates were slow to appreciate the significance of the shift of power from town and farm to city and factory. Garfield material (Ill. 9) pictures him as a robust farmer and Rutherford Hayes material pictures him as a gentleman farmer. But by 1884 candidates were campaigning as the champions of the workingman; much 1884, 1888, and 1892 campaign material shows a concern with tariff problems, "living" wages , and, for the first time in American campaign history, with "prosperity," that so overworked word beloved by candidates ever since (Ill. 10).

6. A famous cartoon that appeared shortly after Lincoln's victory over George McClellan in 1864. The caption reads "Long Abraham Lincoln a Little Longer."

7.   A McClellan campaign badge with a paper photograph of "Little Mac."

7A. An interesting lapel piece indicating some of U.S. Grant's political history.

8. One of several versions of a cartoon lampooning Jefferson Davis's attempted escape from Union troops by disguising himself in his wife's clothes (an incident, by the way, that is not true). In this version Mrs. Davis protests the invasion of a "lady's" privacy.

9. James Garfield did work briefly as a farmer in his youth, so the allusion here is correct.

10. Benjamin Harrison and Levi Morton were pictured on an 1888 lapel badge with a slogan advocating domestic tariffs.

Campaign literature by this time was being printed in a dozen or more languages—Polish, Turkish, Greek, Italian, Yiddish, to name a few—in recognition of the hundreds of thousands of southern and central European immigrants who were a new source of votes. The ideologies of the two major parties were beginning to assume a recognizable contemporary cast. The torchlight parade had become a national institution. The satirical weeklies *Puck* (Ill. 11) and *Judge* were publishing the best political cartoons of the period. A host of third parties were emerging, including Prohibitionists, Socialists, and Equal Righters; most spoke for a single issue and were largely ignored—but their time would come.

Some artifacts of the period reflect the rococo aesthetics of that day: florid embossed lettering on inaugural programs and flourishes, curlicues, and floral designs of all sorts dominating other paper material. The simplicity of most kinds of torchlights is in stark contrast to the overdecorated political ceramics. Some collectors find such contrasts endlessly fascinating. A plain homemade tin campaign torch placed beside the attractive Garfield Wedgwood pitcher illustrated in Chapter 6 makes a startling aesthetic impression; it is the sort of contrast to consider when preparing a public display.

There is much from this period for collectors. All major party candidates can easily be represented, but material for some third-party candidates may be more difficult to obtain. Many different artifacts from the period are available in moderate amounts: delightful shell badges, handsome glass and ceramic pieces, bandannas, torchlights, and other fascinating novelties such as marching canes and toys. A good general collection can be made better with some representation from this period.

GOLD, SILVER, AND INTERNATIONALISM: 1896–1916. The nineteenth century ended with one of the great campaigns in American history, the silver and gold "Full Dinner Pail" campaign of 1896. William Jennings Bryan, the "Prairie Populist," won his party's nomination with his extraordinary "cross of gold" speech at the Democratic National Convention: "Thou shalt not crucify mankind upon a cross of gold/Thou shalt not press upon his brow a crown of thorns . . ." Many Americans saw their first presidential candidate, as Bryan crisscrossed the country in the first whistle-stop campaign ever. But William McKinley won the election—and he never left his front porch in Canton, Ohio! The country came to him. Thousands of other Americans got up special trains and made a "pilgrimage" to Canton to hear their favorite expound on the issues of the day: full employment; a gold or silver standard for our monetary system; America's involvement in Puerto Rico, Cuba, and the Philippines.

10A. A foreign language leaflet from a later day. By 1936 the ethnic vote was a solidly entrenched factor in party strategy planning.

11. A typical cartoon from *Puck*: "The Cinderella of the Republican Party and Her Haughty Sisters." Rutherford Hayes as Cinderella is left behind as the sisters, Ulysses Grant and Roscoe Conkling, leave for a gala party (the Republican National Convention). But Hayes ultimately received the nomination.

12. This 1895 newspaper cartoon pictures Eugene Debs as "king" of America's railroads shortly after he led his railway workers "brotherhood" in a successful strike against the owners.

13. A scarce 1896 linen banner showing McKinley and Hobart in exaggerated campaign poses, surrounded by statements from the Republican party platform. This banner also exists in paper.

14. An original 1908 drawing by cartoonist Kirk Russell picturing Teddy Roosevelt as "A Specter in the Canebrake"—in other words, the Republican party prepared for the 1908 campaign under the threat of not knowing what to expect from the unpredictable Teddy.

Voters were inundated with the newly invented campaign buttons: Among the hundreds of different designs are some that collectors rate highly because of their imaginative graphics. Mechanical brass pins were also a popular novelty: The wings of gold or silver bugs, an eagle's wings, a flag—and other fanciful designs—snapping open to reveal candidates' pictures. All such mechanical pins are highly prized today. Cartoons hostile to both candidates picture McKinley as a strutting Napoleon or a lackey of business interests and Bryan as a loudmouthed buffoon intent on destroying the nation's economy. Not even twentieth-century campaigns with all the benefits of mass production can match the immense variety of campaign gadgets and novelties that were issued for the 1896 campaign! Prints, cartoons, buttons, mechanical brass pins, lapel ribbons, torchlight parade accessories, ceramics, and glassware—there is something for every collector and for every budget.

When Teddy Roosevelt became president following McKinley's assassination in 1901, the country expected a drastic shift in presidential style—and they got it! "That damn cowboy" (groaned Mark Hanna, McKinley's campaign manager) and apostle of the strenuous life provided more newspaper copy, it seemed, than all previous presidents combined (Ill. 14). He was one of the most cartooned of our presidents. An unabashed jingoist, he gave that very visual word "muckraker" to the American vocabulary; and his own self-assessment, "I feel as strong as a bull moose," has entered the folklore of politics. Soldier, cowboy, policeman, big game hunter, with an active and well-publicized family—the artifacts associated with Teddy Roosevelt are noted for their whimsical humor. Understandably, he is a collector's favorite.

William Howard Taft entered the White House in 1908. He carried the most magnificent paunch in presidential history, but his presidency was singularly uninspired. Later he became a distinguished chief justice of the United States Supreme Court, but collectors remember him best for the humorous campaign artifacts that were inspired by his rotundity (Ill. 15).

This era in campaign history closes with the two terms of the austere Princeton professor Thomas Woodrow Wilson. His election to a first term was helped considerably by the deep split between Taft Republicans and Teddy Roosevelt's Bull Moose Republicans. Wilson was returned to office in 1916 after winning a squeaker over Charles

Evans Hughes (Ill. 16). Democratic literature in that year made much of the slogan "He Kept Us Out Of War," but within a few months following his inauguration American doughboys were fighting in France. Wilson died a mentally and physically broken man; his plan for America's participation in the League of Nations was in shambles. During his second term women's suffrage became a reality, although militants made him a figure of scorn before he agreed to support what eventually became the Nineteenth Amendment. But Woodrow Wilson is a popular collecting subject, perhaps more because he was president in a perilous time than for distinctive personal achievements. He stands in sharp contrast to his immediate predecessors. Campaign material associated with him is not particularly noteworthy, although certain buttons can be quite expensive.

15. William Howard Taft was the first White House golfer. He is shown in this 1912 cartoon as worried about the contest against his two opponents, Roosevelt and Wilson. Taft's caddy is James Sherman, Republican vice-presidential nominee in 1908 and 1912.

FOR PRESIDENT — FOR VICE PRESIDENT

CHARLES E. HUGHES — CHARLES W. FAIRBANKS

16. An uncommon Hughes and Fairbanks poster from the 1916 campaign.

"NORMALCY," DEPRESSION, AND THE NEW DEAL: 1920–1945.

17. One of several varieties of 1920 campaign posters showing James Cox and Franklin Roosevelt. All varieties are scarce.

One of the more interesting bits of trivia from the 1920 campaign was the fact that an Ohio Republican newspaper editor defeated an Ohio Democratic newspaper editor. Warren G. Harding is one of the presidency's tragic figures; he died before his term was completed and before the Teapot Dome scandal was fully exposed. History has forgotten the man he defeated, James M. Cox, but Cox's running mate, Franklin Delano Roosevelt, never again lost an election (Ill. 17). Calvin Coolidge, "Silent Cal," completed Harding's unfinished term and went on to defeat Democrat John Davis in 1924. Coolidge's habitual dour expression hid a sly Yankee humor, which comes out best in some of the crazy camera poses that candidates can never seem to avoid. One in particular comes to mind: It shows Coolidge looking more than a little lost in an elaborate Indian headdress. Another shot depicts him appearing properly bucolic in a farmer's smock at his Vermont homestead.

A fact all collectors learn early is that Democratic material from the 1920 and 1924 campaigns is very scarce. Cox and Davis material is the most difficult of all twentieth-century candidates' material to locate. Most collectors dream at one time or another of finding a button bearing pictures of Cox and Roosevelt; the sale of one should finance a round-the-world cruise. Material picturing John Davis (Ill. 18) and Charles Bryan

AMERICA FIRST

PRESIDENT — VICE PRESIDENT

18. A campaign leaflet used in 1924.

19. A poster similar to this one, with the same slogan, pictures Smith with his running mate Joseph Robinson.

20. Herbert Hoover is shown looking properly solemn in this red, white, and blue celluloid window hanger from the 1928 campaign. Other similar examples pictured Al Smith and Franklin Roosevelt.

INTRODUCING OUR NEXT PRESIDENT

JOHN W. DAVIS

"In place of him who says 'I doubt' I place my confidence in the man who says 'I believe'; for him who says 'I fear' give me the man who says 'I trust'; for him whose first thought is 'is this course expedient?' I prefer to follow him who says 'is this course right?' "

—Speech at Wilmington, Delaware.

(brother of William Jennings Bryan) is almost as scarce. Even longtime collectors can count on one hand the number of Cox or Davis artifacts that they own. I consider myself fortunate to have even one item in my own collection.

When Coolidge declared that he did "not choose to run for president in 1928," the eventual choice of the Republican party was Herbert Hoover. Hoover had been a successful mining engineer on overseas projects, a famine relief administrator during World War I, and a member of President Coolidge's Cabinet. The Democrats countered with Alfred Emmanuel Smith (Ill. 19), the ebullient former governor of New York. His friend Franklin Roosevelt dubbed him "The Happy Warrior" in a nominating speech at the Democratic National Convention. But Al Smith's flat New York accent, his strong stand against Prohibition, and his Roman Catholicism were too much for many voters. Hoover entered the White House, a Republican's natural prerogative, it seemed. There is a steady demand for Hoover material (Ill. 20), but certain buttons associated with Al Smith sell for several hundred dollars each.

Franklin Roosevelt's victory in 1932 was the beginning of a long love-hate relationship with the American people. The New Deal and Franklin Delano Roosevelt are synonymous. For a good many older Americans today he was the president of their childhood. His death in April 1945, ending twelve years in office, is one of those national events that becomes a landmark in one's own life. Roosevelt could be ruthless and arrogant and he was an adept political manipulator, yet he had a touch with ordinary people that helped elect him to four terms, on each occasion against very capable Republican opponents: Herbert Hoover, Alfred Landon (Ill. 21) (from the sunflower state of Kansas), Wendell Willkie (one of the rare dark-horse nominees), and Thomas Dewey. In his first inaugural address he promised a "new deal," and within the next three months he got through a willing Congress the most sweeping social and economic reform legislation ever experienced in this country. During his long tenure he put together a voting coalition of blue- and white-collar workers, ethnic and racial minority group members, and intellectuals that has dominated the Democratic party ever since. He led the United States out of the Great Depression and through World War II, oversaw the birth of atomic power—and he was the husband of Eleanor Roosevelt, the choice of many of us for the most outstanding First Lady.

Campaign pieces from the Roosevelt years are many and varied. Like his distant cousin, Teddy, FDR was a favorite target of satirists and a cartoonist's delight. Republicans spent millions of dollars in 1940 attempting to deny him a third term. Buttons were made with such slogans as "Dr. Jekyl of Hyde Park," "Out! Stealing Third," "Third Term Taboo/23 Skidoo!" and "We Don't Want Eleanor Either!" The Democrats' reply became a classic, a button saying simply "A Pauper for Roosevelt" (Ill. 22). In one of my own favorite cartoons of the period, a little girl runs into the house to tell her mother that brother Albert is writing a dirty word on the sidewalk. The word? "Roosevelt." A satirical booklet (Ill. 23) issued during the 1936 campaign pictured Roosevelt dressed as

Mother Goosevelt . . .

> Who lived in a shoe,
> She had a lot of children, but she knew what to do:—
> She gave 'em a hand-out, they were all easy marks,
> A farm for to live on, some trees for their parks;
> A concreted highway, a maid and a car;
> A boondoggled bungalow equipped with a bar,
> And three meals a day of breakfast-food oats—
> The smiling old lady was after their votes.

There is an abundance of material associated with Franklin Roosevelt's four campaigns, and most of it sells at respectable prices. Roosevelt is the subject of some of the finest specialized political Americana collections. Of course, a visit to his home and the museum in Hyde Park, New York, is mandatory for all collectors of Roosevelt campaign artifacts.

FROM A TYPICAL PRAIRIE STATE

ALF M. LANDON OF KANSAS
Republican Nominee for President

21. Alf Landon carried only Maine and Vermont in 1936; it was the worst defeat ever experienced by a Republican party candidate.

22. Anti-Roosevelt slogan buttons from the 1940 campaign. There were many different ones, and most of the buttons are easily obtained. Note the pro-Roosevelt button at upper left.

23. This amusing booklet cover—done in several colors—and the satirical verses inside made no dent in Roosevelt's popularity with voters.

THE JET AGE: 1948—. Three themes dominate contemporary campaigning for the presidency: violence, jet aircraft, and television. Consider: President John Kennedy was murdered in November 1963 while on a political visit to Dallas, Texas; his brother Robert, in Los Angeles just after his California primary election victory in June 1968; Alabama's governor George Wallace was paralyzed permanently by a bullet while campaigning in Laurel, Maryland, in April 1971. Martin Luther King's death on the eve of a protest march he was to lead in Memphis, Tennessee, must also be counted as a political murder. And there was violence of a different kind when delegates and police confronted each other in the Chicago streets surrounding the Amphitheatre, site of the 1968 Democratic National Convention.

VOTE THE WINNING TEAM IN NOVEMBER!

DWIGHT D. EISENHOWER   RICHARD M. NIXON

YOUR LAST CHANCE!!

END THE KOREAN SLAUGHTER	KICK OUT THE COMMIES
1000 killed and crippled every week.— our war production is the wounded and dead. Is this what you want?	Truman's "Red herrings" and Stevenson's "phantoms" are still betraying America.
CLEAN UP TRUMAN'S MESS	STOP CRAZY SPENDING
Stevenson can't throw out the cronies and grafters who are trying to put him in.	$260,000,000,000 in debt—your $1.00 is worth 50¢—your income is phoney—record taxes for everyone

END OUR HIT-OR-MISS FOREIGN POLICY
Restore our National Self-respect. No more Acheson—No more Appeasement —No more Apologies.

24. A 1952 broadside showing candidates Dwight Eisenhower and Richard Nixon in what was to become a familiar victory pose throughout the 1950s.

25. This delightful red, white, and blue wall decoration measures about 3 by 2 feet; it is assembled by inserting tabs into slots.

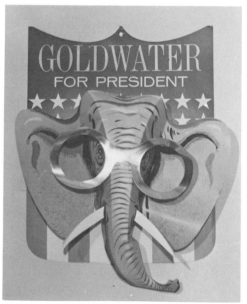

GOLDWATER FOR PRESIDENT

In 1948 Harry Truman traveled the country by rail to achieve his upset "give 'em hell" victory over Thomas Dewey. He was actually seen by perhaps 20 percent of the number of people who saw Richard Nixon in 1960 when Nixon campaigned by jet aircraft in all fifty states. Jets are the new campaign headquarters for major party candidates. Each has at his disposal a sophisticated travel system that ties him into every community in the country with at least a medium-size airport available nearby. A candidate can "do a state" in one day if need be.

Winners and losers in these years were all nationally known before their campaigns. The 1950s were dominated by affable Dwight Eisenhower (Ill. 24) (whose slogan "I Like Ike" became a campaign classic) and Adlai Stevenson, the intellectual's hero, who raised campaign oratory to a fine art. The 1960s were dominated by six United States senators: John Kennedy, at forty-three the youngest man and first Roman Catholic ever elected to the presidency; Richard Nixon, secretive, innovator in foreign policy, disgraced; Lyndon Johnson, the brash self-assured Texan, destroyed by the Vietnam War (Ill. 26); Barry Goldwater (Ill. 25), jet pilot, and nowadays Senate spokesman for conservative Republicans; Hubert Horatio Humphrey, early leader for civil rights and never at a loss for words; and George McGovern who could not hang on to the Roosevelt coalition and thus gave Richard Nixon the single largest percentage of the popular vote ever achieved by a winning candidate.

In 1973 Gerald Ford (Ill. 27), another of our "accidental presidents" (vice-presidents chosen as a result of political compromise, with no thought that they might unexpectedly fill their president's unexpired term), entered the White House. Gerald Ford and George Washington—for his first term—are the only presidents not elected to the presidency. In 1976 Jimmy Carter became only the second southerner elected by popular vote to become president (Wilson was the first) since Andrew Johnson's brief term—but Johnson was an accidental president also.

Among collectors, artifacts associated with the campaigns of Harry Truman and John Kennedy are most eagerly sought after. But the modern period is so rich in campaign material that collectors can branch out in a variety of directions. A specialized collection might focus on the Kennedy brothers, Martin Luther King, or George Wallace's three attempts at the presidency. Or campaign material can be combined with antiwar material, as exemplified, for example, in Eugene McCarthy's 1968 campaign. Some collectors have chosen to focus on the congressmen involved in the Watergate impeachment hearings; others are interested in the unusually large number of hopefuls in this period. And for young collectors, the modern period with its abundance of inexpensive material is the best place to begin.

How a Modern President Is Elected

Understanding the process by which a candidate for the presidency eventually attains that office is fundamental knowledge for collectors. Knowing what kind of material is available at each step along the way and where it can be found is equally fundamental. For collectors, the campaign season—that period beginning about two years before an inauguration—is, naturally, a busy time. Collectors need to be alert to local campaign activities such as the opening of candidates' headquarters, area visits by candidates, and the staging of parades, rallies, and similar events. The general rule: Wherever a candidate is at any moment on the campaign trail, collectible material will be there also.

Campaign season is the time when buying, selling, and trading among collectors will be most intense. The first material to look for is leaflets and buttons in one or two different designs. As a hopeful's prospects continue to look good, bumper stickers, posters, and more buttons become available. By convention time, if a hopeful is still in the race, there will be a considerable amount and variety of novelties, jewelry, and still more buttons and paper material in circulation.

ENTER THE HOPEFULS. As much as two years before Election Day, would-be candidates—or hopefuls—for their party's nomination declare their availability. Before long a campaign committee will be formed, which will be responsible for publicizing the candidate through public appearances with the party faithful, commissioning campaign materials, and raising funds. At this stage a hopeful is both attempting to build a national image and seeking party delegate support for the forthcoming national party convention (Ill. 28).

A hopeful's home-state headquarters will probably have some material available to collectors in return for a contribution. Further sources of material are his headquarters in other states, if his candidacy is that far advanced, and if a state coordinator has been appointed in a collector's own state.

CHOOSING DELEGATES. About a year before the election, party members in each state will begin the process of selecting delegates. The rules vary by state and between the two major parties, but generally party delegates to a state convention will listen to the various candidates, draft a "platform" (a statement regarding the issues of the day), and choose a slate of delegates to attend the national convention.

THE PRIMARY ELECTION. In some states, which slate goes to the national convention will have been determined by party voters at a state primary election. These elections begin in early March of the election year and continue around the country through the following summer. Because rank and file voters—in some states—are registering their preferences among the candidates, the "primary" can be an extremely important indication of how particular candidates are faring. This is the point at which some candidates will drop out of the race, having read the writing on the wall. No one candidate

26. Socialist Labor party candidate Clifton DeBerry and President Johnson are pictured on this 1964 leaflet, an early protest against American involvement in Vietnam.

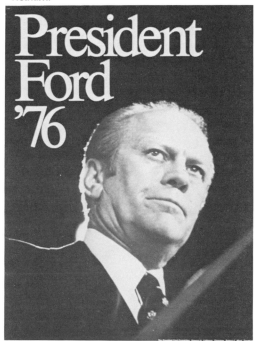

27. This 1976 Gerald Ford campaign poster is the one most often found.

28. An amusing and colorful placard showing Senator Eugene McCarthy prepared to challenge President Johnson for the Democratic party's presidential nomination in 1968.

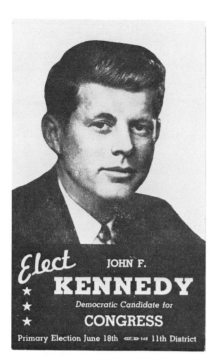

29. This card was distributed in the spring of 1946 during Kennedy's first try for national political office. He beat several other contenders for his party's nomination in the June primary election, and went on to defeat the Republican party nominee in the fall.

30. Canvas banner measuring about 5 by 3 feet.

will enter all the primaries; each will choose to enter those in which he thinks he has the brightest prospects. Depending upon party and state rules, delegates may or may not be bound by the results, but in any case the primary election will provide direction to those delegates who are selected.

This is the stage for the parties' first heavy use of material. New England collectors are especially fortunate in that the New Hampshire primary, the first in the nation, occurs early in the year. Party incumbents and hopefuls usually make a big push in this state in order to estimate their appeal to voters, take advantage of the free television coverage, and gain momentum for the primaries coming up shortly after in other states. For a few weeks, at least, there are likely to be a dozen or more different candidates' headquarters in operation. Contributions are expected.

PREPARING FOR THE NATIONAL CONVENTION.   Meanwhile, party representatives from each state's central committee will be meeting for the purpose of writing convention procedural rules; hearing arguments brought by conflicting slates of delegates, if necessary; and drafting a national platform, any plank of which may generate controversy. Candidates are sometimes present to speak to the various issues. The platform is important because it indicates how the party will present itself to the voters and what the eventual party nominee will be expected to be in favor of and opposed to. Decisions made at this time are subject to ratification by the assembled delegates at the national convention.

THE NATIONAL CONVENTION.   By the time the Democratic National Convention begins in early July (the Republicans will follow in August) some candidates will have dropped out, some delegates will be committed to one candidate or another, other delegates will be holding off to see what happens next, and perhaps a dark horse will be quietly politicking for his party's call. There will be a bonanza of tourist dollars and national publicity for the city that hosts the convention. America's greatest quadrennial extravaganza is about to begin (Ills. 30 and 31). If everything occurs according to plan, which never happens, the entire affair will take no longer than four days. The first day: checking delegate credentials, arbitrating delegate seating disputes, electing presiding officers. The second day: voting acceptance of the platform. The third day: balloting for the presidential nomination by roll call of each delegation. If there are no problems, the process is quite rapid; if there are problems, the time can be interminable (103 ballots and two weeks were required to nominate Democrat John Davis in 1924). The third or fourth day: balloting for the vice-presidential nominee, which is usually a routine matter because the presidential nominee, with rare exceptions, chooses his running mate and expects the convention to endorse his choice. In the evening nominees will give their acceptance speeches—statements of gratitude, intention, and inspiration. The convention is adjourned immediately afterward.

No description in words can begin to convey the sense of excitement and anticipation that dominates every moment of most national conventions: the cajoling of delegates to switch their votes, state delegations holding their voting strength for a favorable moment, floor demonstrations for each candidate (the louder and longer, the better), and the eternal politicking in hotel corridors, candidates' suites, and on the convention floor itself. Some conventions prove to be more exciting than the campaign following later.

For collectors of political Americana, the week of a national convention is the only time during the entire election process when so much different material will be available. State delegations will have their own particular issues; hopefuls may be making last-ditch efforts, so this is the collectors' last firsthand opportunity to acquire their material; spontaneously generated material, perhaps made on the convention site, for a dark horse will be briefly available; cause groups will be circulating their material, as will the single-issue nonparty candidates, who always seem to be hovering around the action at national party conventions; each major party will be selling material from its temporary headquarters; and ubiquitous button peddlers will be hawking their wares from tables and vest pockets.

THE CAMPAIGN. By early September, traditionally on Labor Day for Democrats, each major party nominee will have begun his arduous and intensive two-month campaign that will culminate on Election Day, the first Tuesday after the first Monday in November. The populous states with their large blocs of electoral votes will be visited repeatedly. Each nominee will suffer through innumerable barbecues and fish fries; will raise calluses, if he has not already, from shaking hands; smile as his carefully planned schedule goes awry; and generally exude confidence, optimism, and boundless energy no matter what public opinion polls may be showing. Every community in the country with any claim to self-importance will have its campaign headquarters. Most party workers in local headquarters will never see their favorite during the campaign, but nevertheless they will work long hours for him and for local and state candidates with whom the presidential candidate will be paired in the local publicity.

Collectors will be at their busiest during this stage: buying and trading material by correspondence and through visits to regional meetings of hobby groups, visiting local party headquarters at least weekly, and keeping themselves informed of local political events at which material is likely to be distributed.

ELECTION DAY. The polls in eastern coastal states will open at 6:00 A.M.; three time zones later the polls will open in the western coastal states. Voters will enter their neighborhood precincts and vote either by marking a paper ballot or pulling the appropriate levers on voting machines. The candidates will inevitably be televised voting in their precincts, although they will otherwise maintain a low profile. In most elections the result is predictable by late evening, at which time the loser will congratulate his opponent, and the winner will thank the voters, his wife, God, and his workers in about that order. If the election is close, the results may not be known until the following day or, as in the 1960 Kennedy–Nixon contest, not for several days. The loser enters that special limbo reserved for most also-rans; the winner goes on a vacation while the press speculates on the content of his inauguration speech and his possible Cabinet choices.

Collectors should make a final visit to headquarters, if they are not already working there. Help clean the place. Some headquarters workers collect their candidate's material or want a few pieces as souvenirs. Arrange to trade with them, since collectors are likely to have relevant material from other parts of the country.

THE INAUGURATION. In late January, usually on a cold and dismal day, the new president is sworn in by the chief justice of the Supreme Court in a by-now-hallowed ceremony outside the Capitol. The president's inaugural speech is always anticipated both for its forensic style and for the clues it provides to possible direction in the new administration. Following the speech come an elaborate parade, an evening banquet, and an inaugural ball. For a few months there will be a "honeymoon" while press and critics abstain from the usual criticism. But within the year after inauguration, some politician will decide that he can do a better job than the incumbent, and will declare his availability. And the race is on again.

Inauguration time is the last opportunity for the collector to acquire material firsthand. Thereafter the campaign and the election are history, and collectors must turn to dealers and other collectors for material they missed earlier. There is usually a good variety of inaugural material available commemorating special events such as inaugural ball programs and the oath of office ceremonies. There will be plenty of souvenir buttons, programs, and pennants to choose among; artifacts issued in limited numbers such as inaugural badges will not appear on the market until shortly after the inauguration.

31. A placard used at the Democratic National Convention in 1964.

31A. James Garfield, the second president to be assassinated, and debonair Chester Arthur are pictured on this very decorative inaugural ball program.

32. Thomas Nast, the great cartoonist
of the Civil War era, portrayed the 1864
election as a matter of soldiers giving
their lives for the right to vote. Very small
print at the lower right makes it evident
that Nast supported Lincoln's reelection.

33. Miguel Covarrubias, "Painter Extraordinary and Historiographer to the Court on the Potomac," depicted Franklin Roosevelt being crowned with the victor's wreath by Chief Justice Charles Hughes while former President Herbert Hoover and a distinguished audience looked on. In an identification key (not shown) an almost obscured figure at the far right was described as "The Forgotten Man."

33A. A potpourri of things political.

34. The Rosenthal Group of West Germany produced this china plate to commemorate the inauguration of Jimmy Carter and Walter Mondale.

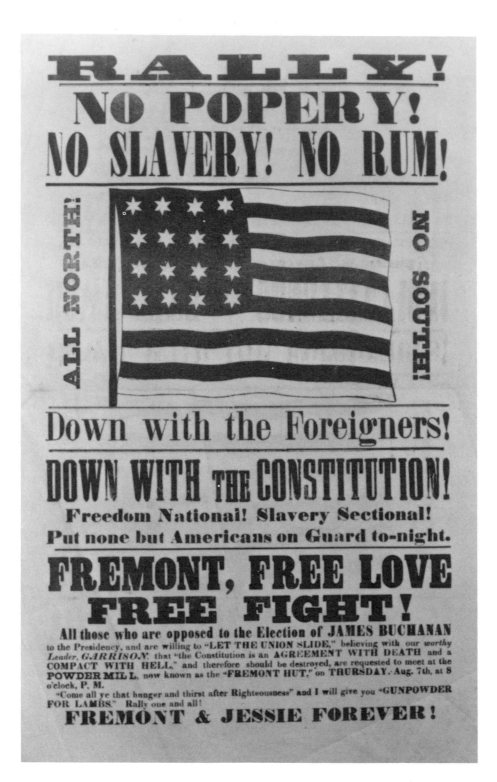

34A. One of those great broadsides that is a history lesson in itself, a super commentary on the 1856 campaign.

2
What the Collector Needs to Know

BEGINNING COLLECTORS SHOULD collect indiscriminately at first—as motivation and whim dictate—while simultaneously learning as much as they can about political campaign history. Experienced collectors know that a solid base of knowledge is the best protection one can have. At one level, this includes a broad understanding of campaign history and a fund of information about the many issues and personalities. At another level it encompasses a vast amount of factual detail about events, symbols, and the thousand and one incidents that make a campaign and, in many cases, are the motivation for campaign material.

A good illustration of the need for this kind of detailed knowledge is a small cast-iron statue of a dog, which occasionally comes on the market. On the base of the statue is inscribed "Laddie Boy." The experienced collector knows that that was the name of Warren G. Harding's pet dog, and that the statue is an artifact from the 1920 campaign. Another example is a small tin lapel piece, otherwise unidentified, in the shape of a broad-brimmed hat with suspended clasped hands (Ill. 35)—obviously a Horace Greeley artifact from the 1872 campaign. A white Quaker hat and hands clasped behind the back are Greeley attributes familiar to voters of that day and to knowledgeable collectors today. Collectors virtually do need to know the names of presidents' pets and to be aware of candidates' personal habits.

I consider the following suggestions, therefore, as basic to developing both levels of knowledge. There are no priorities among these suggestions—all are important—and can be initiated as soon as one begins collecting.

1. *Maintain a reference shelf.* Included in the Bibliography are sources that I have found particularly valuable in my own collecting. The ability to recognize obscure campaign slogans or references to long-forgotten political events and personalities is essential. I know of more than one collector who has added important pieces to his collection—pieces unrecognized by other collectors—simply because he had done his reading and hence knew what to look for.

2. *Maintain a clipping file.* For much the same reasons that one keeps at hand a shelf of background reading, the collector should keep a supply of newspapers and

34B. Wide Awake club pin is probably from the 1860 campaign.

35. Horace Greeley "hands and hat" lapel pin from the 1872 campaign.

19

magazines available. These sources, especially during campaign season, can be quite informative. Look for anecdotal accounts, newspaper fillers, and news and articles about local politics. So-called in-house publications also frequently contain political material during a campaign. I paste clippings on pages that can be inserted in three-ring binders; this way, the information is easily arranged and is readily accessible.

3. *Consider joining a collectors' group, such as American Political Items Collectors.* (See Appendix.)

4. *Develop plans for displaying and protecting your collection.* This is not a matter that can be delayed for very long. Once one becomes serious about collecting, material can accumulate rather quickly. Plan early, unless you want to trip over boxes full of artifacts and spend your time searching for a particular item buried in one box or another. Several suggestions are offered in Chapter 10.

5. *Develop a system for coding or numbering your treasures.* Again, this essential action cannot be long postponed. Distinguishing among several hundred buttons, for example, can be a problem. The numbering systems used by political collectors are described in Chapter 10, but remember that most material other than buttons is not presently numbered, although the systems I describe are designed to accommodate additional material.

6. *Learn early how to detect fantasies and reproductions.* Being able to distinguish this material from original campaign and commemorative material is a skill new collectors must work to acquire from the outset. It is a mistake to purchase fakes, no matter how showy they may appear.

7. *Read auction catalogs and dealers' lists.* Here is still more required reading. Not only does one need to acquire a knowledge of prices; it is also useful to learn of the frequency with which different artifacts come on the market, the relationship between the price and condition of an item, and the relative popularity among collectors of certain artifacts. I have listed a number of auctioneers and dealers in the Appendix; ask to be put on their mailing lists.

8. *Attend antique shows and flea markets.* Good finds can still be made wherever Americana is sold, and once one knows what to look for the search can be rewarding and frustrating. Recently, shows called Papermania by their sponsors, specializing in paper Americana, have begun to appear in some cities. Plan also to visit shows sponsored by bottle collectors and stamp and coin clubs. In my experience, these kinds of hobby shows often do have something of interest to political collectors.

9. *Upgrade your collection.* Aim at building a collection that you can be proud of. Be discriminating in what you add to your collection and try to improve, whenever you can, the quality of the individual artifacts.

CHOOSING AMONG CANDIDATES.   Starting from the first impulse to become a collector of political Americana, one needs to know the relative ranking of candidate popularity among collectors because popularity—demand—plus availability of material—supply—is the basic factor in setting prices. Collectors' enthusiasm for candidates may wax high or low at any given point in time, but over the years a discernible pattern is evident.

The reasons for one candidate's popularity with collectors and the lack of collector interest in other candidates are too complex to be easily summarized. Certainly these factors are significant: admiration for a candidate; extent and cost of material pertaining to a particular candidate; a candidate's status in political history; nostalgia; a collector's personal experiences with candidates; a collector's political orientation; and financial speculation. The following lists, therefore, simply provide a relative ranking of candidates' popularity among collectors. There is considerable demand for artifacts related to candidates in category A—and the prices reflect that demand. Candidates in the B list have their following among collectors, but the demand generally is not as intense as for those in the A list; hence prices are generally lower.

The most noteworthy feature of the C list is the large number of candidates for whom little material is available; there is not enough there to attract collectors. But prices are not necessarily lower; indeed, prices for Greeley, Cass, and Davis items can be astronomical!

A good general rule is: A scarce or rare artifact usually sells high, and the greater the popularity of the candidate to whom it is related, the higher the price for that artifact.

A. Candidates judged highly popular among collectors:

The Founding Fathers Presidents	Harry Truman
Abraham Lincoln	Al Smith
Theodore Roosevelt	John Kennedy
Franklin Roosevelt	Andrew Jackson
William Jennings Bryan	Eugene Debs

B. Candidates with moderate popularity among collectors:

Henry Clay	William Henry Harrison
Grover Cleveland	James Cox
William McKinley	Benjamin Harrison
Woodrow Wilson	Richard Nixon
Calvin Coolidge	Wendell Willkie
Herbert Hoover	William H. Taft
Ulysses Grant	James Polk
Gerald Ford	Dwight Eisenhower
Hubert Humphrey	Jimmy Carter
Barry Goldwater	George McGovern
Lyndon Johnson	Adlai Stevenson
	Alton Parker

C. Candidates of less interest among collectors:

John Tyler*	John Quincy Adams*
Zachary Taylor	Chester Arthur*
Martin Van Buren*	Andrew Johnson*
George McClellan	Horatio Seymour*
Horace Greeley*	Alfred Landon
Thomas Dewey	Charles E. Hughes
Winfield Scott*	Winfield Hancock*
James Buchanan*	Franklin Pierce*
James Garfield	Levi Cass*
John Breckinridge	John Bell*
Stephen Douglas*	John Davis*

FORMING A SPECIALIZED COLLECTION.   Beginning collectors should start by forming a general collection if for no other reason than the education that one receives while doing so. As they become more knowledgeable about political campaign history, and more experienced in buying and trading material, however, there will be the urge to specialize. A good specialized collection often provides the depth that a general collection, by its nature, cannot, but a general collection forms a broad context into which a specialized collection can fit. Each kind of collection should complement the other. The following ten suggestions demonstrate the diversity of worthwhile collectible specialties.

1. *Campaigns.* Material is most abundant from the 1840, 1884, 1888, and 1896 campaigns in the nineteenth century, and in the twentieth century, from the 1952 campaign onward. Material representing third parties and issues in any campaign year should be included.

*Candidates for whom related material ranges from nearly nonexistent to barely adequate.

2. *Campaign Themes.* Specialized collections can be built around such themes as the log cabin (1840), gold and silver (1896), prosperity (1888, 1892, 1932), and peace and war (1920, 1944, 1952, 1964, 1968, 1972).

3. *Campaign Images.* William Henry Harrison, the log cabin candidate; Lincoln, the rail splitter; Teddy Roosevelt, the outdoorsman; Barry Goldwater, champion of conservatives; Jackson, Taylor, Eisenhower, Grant—military heroes. A collector may want to demonstrate by means of artifacts how a candidate was presented to voters.

4. *Campaign Issues.* Consider collecting artifacts representing the great issues that divided parties and voters. Since this topic is the subject of Chapter 8, it will not be discussed further here.

5. *Third Parties.* This subject is always popular with collectors, especially the material associated with the Prohibition party, the different Socialist parties, George Wallace's American party, and the Bull Moose party. Of less interest are the American Communist party, Henry Wallace's Progressive party, and various "states' rights" parties from 1948 on. Material associated with most nineteenth-century third parties is nearly impossible to find, and so they have been given little attention by collectors.

6. *Specialized Artifact Collections.* I know of several outstanding collections of ribbons, ceramics, glassware, paper ephemera, and textiles. There is plenty of room for expansion in this area.

7. *Campaign Graphics.* Look especially for posters, broadsides, buttons, banners, and other objects that are aesthetically pleasing. There is potential here for framing an exciting collection.

8. *Political Folk Art.* Material in this category may be too expensive for many budgets, but consider having at least a few pieces of nineteenth-century folk art on political subjects.

9. *Women in Politics.* Material from the women's movement, past and present; campaign material related to contemporary women in politics; equal rights amendment material, and certainly material opposing women's involvement in politics.

10. *Specialized State and Local Collections.* Collectors who choose this area tend to concentrate on buttons only, which is unfortunate because so much more is available. This specialty has been gaining recently in popularity, so we can expect some new directions to emerge.

Additional possibilities are suggested within the context of the subjects discussed in the following chapters.

35A. Examples of eglomise or reverse paintings on glass. This kind of artwork was most popular in the 1830s-1850s period and usually originated in central Europe and China for the American market. Paintings of all the early presidents and other White House candidates are known.

3
Lapel Devices

THE SINGLE ITEM most associated with political campaigning is, of course, the campaign button. Many thousands flood the country every four years, and nearly as many are issued annually touting state and local candidates. The modern campaign button is produced very cheaply and says much in a small space. Although having given ground in recent campaigns to television advertising, the ubiquitous button still enjoys a priority status in candidates' budgets and continuing popularity with voters. Yet, on the day after an election, most voters casually dispose of the button they wore so proudly, or else put it away as a "souvenir." Years later, the souvenir is discovered in grandmother's sewing basket or trinket box or in a long unopened trunk in the attic. Once the discovery is made, a new collector is born.

Despite its generally ignoble end the campaign button has an illustrious history. The story begins with the simple metal clothing buttons of the Washington era, continues with the handsome cameo brooches from early nineteenth-century campaigns, then the later tintypes or ferrotypes and the imaginative shell badges from the latter part of the century, and explodes in a deluge of the celluloid buttons that first appeared in the 1896 campaign. In this chapter, each of these lapel devices and the modern evolution of the campaign button itself will be discussed, and suggestions will be given for building and maintaining a campaign button collection.

The Washington Era and the Nineteenth Century

WASHINGTON INAUGURALS. The first political buttons were actual buttons in that they were looped, or shanked, for attachment to clothing. March 4 was the day provided by the Constitution for organizing the new government. By April 6, 1789, the electors had cast their votes for Washington, and a messenger was sent to Mount Vernon to duly inform him. Washington at once set out on his triumphal trip to New York, the site of the inaugural ceremony. Dewey Albert, the foremost authority on these buttons, says that Washington wore a set on his coat at the ceremony. Beyond that fact, not much is known about them, especially about their origin. It is possible that they were also worn in celebration of Washington's trip through the New England states later in his first ad-

34B. For those collectors fascinated by the adversarial relationship between the White House and the nation's press, think about building a collection on that subject.

23

36.   Washington inaugural buttons. *Top*: Linked states type; *bottom (left to right)*: monogram; "Memorable Era" variety.

ministration. Albert believes that the approximately twenty-seven varieties (Cobb lists thirty) all date from Washington's first inauguration or from his first term.

All Washington inaugural buttons are of relatively unsophisticated workmanship, consisting simply of a flat copper or brass disk and a soldered shank (Ill. 36). The buttons range in diameter from 15mm to 36mm. They were worn on breeches, waistcoats, and outercoats, but the only original article of clothing ever found with inaugural buttons actually attached was a pair of seaman's breeches. These breeches, now in the University of Hartford Collection, have a row of six of the smaller buttons on each leg.

The most often found patterns are the linked states varieties—i.e., those patterns decorated with a "wreath" of incised circles around the outside, each containing the abbreviation of one of the thirteen colonies; the monogram "G W" in a depressed center encircled by "Long Live the President" around the outside; and a spread eagle, the most striking variety of which is inscribed "March the Fourth/1789/Memorable Era." Scarcer patterns depict a bust of Washington, a sunburst added to the spread eagle motif, or a sunburst only with the inscription "Unity, Prosperity, Independence."

Washington inaugurals range from scarce to rare. They were treasured by their owners over the generations, and the discovery of another one today usually rates a story in the local newspaper. Reproductions are very common. Many were made in 1889 for the centennial celebration of the first inauguration, and they are still being made and advertised today. The genuinely antique Washington inaugural buttons are very expensive; $950 would be the minimum price for a linked states or monogram pattern in good condition. Nevertheless, the serious political collector hopes eventually to own one or two examples to round out his collection.

THE TWO-PIECE BUTTON.   For a few years the flat, or one-piece, button was popular with voters. From these early elections, perhaps through 1832, buttons are known with a blank front surface (obverse) and a shanked reverse bearing such inscriptions as "Jackson Huzza," "Jackson's Victory," "Andrew Jackson/March 4, 1829," and "Martin Van Buren/Excelsior." The last named exists in a brilliant gold wash with an elaborate surface design.

Eventually, manufacturers produced a two-piece brass button (Ill. 37). This usually had either a shallow or deep convex obverse bearing a device in raised relief; the obverse was attached to a flat shanked back piece. Similar buttons are worn today on military uniforms and blazers. Political themes of the day were represented on two-piece buttons. On one button a comical figure is portrayed thumbing his nose; above is the inscription "You Can't Come It, Matty . . . . " This button suggests, in the slang of the day, that Van Buren would not be reelected in 1840. On another button Justice with her scales stands beside a large safe upon which perches a spread eagle. This button refers to the dominant issue of the 1830s, the question of a national bank. On still another button from the 1840 campaign a man is shown setting fire to a log cabin while opening a safe; two decanters and letters spell out "Hard Cider"; over all is a spread eagle and "Tammany."

That very busy button, however, is not typical; simplicity of design was more characteristic. Typical of the 1840 campaign is the justly famous "log cabin" button showing a relief of a log cabin with, usually, a waving flag and a cider barrel nearby. William Henry Harrison's partisans wore the button sewed on the lapel, thus giving rise to the phrase "campaign button." The log cabin button is, at least, a direct ancestor of the modern pinback. Over sixty varied 1840 campaign button designs are known, most bearing the familiar log cabin motif, but a few bear the likeness of General Harrison either in profile or on horseback. A very few designs are carved from animal horn.

A smaller variety of two-piece buttons features General Zachary Taylor, "Old Rough and Ready," the hero of the Mexican War and the successful Whig candidate in the 1848 campaign. Other nicknames found on these Taylor buttons are "Old Zach" and "The Hero of Buena Vista."

37. Early political brass lapel buttons, 1824–1840. *Top (left to right):* "Van Buren/Excelsior," 1836; "Huzza/Jackson,"1824. *Bottom:* All are two-piece buttons: eagle and safe design; one of the many log cabin variants; and "You Can't Come It, Matty . . ."

BROOCHES.   The most aesthetically appealing lapel levices used during the first half of the nineteenth century were exquisitely fashioned cameo, or sulphide, brooches imported from France, although possibly a few were made at Greenpoint, Long Island (Ill. 38). These measured no more than 1¼ inches by 1 inch. They consisted of three parts: a white cameo likeness of the candidate set on an enameled surface, usually black but occasionally orange, green, or blue; an encasing glass with beveled edges; and a plain or chased brass frame into which the cameo and its glass cover were mounted. A clasp was on the reverse. Most varieties from the 1840 campaign bear a cameo log cabin and the appropriate slogans. An earlier black and white design shows Andrew Jackson astride a rearing horse. Martin Van Buren's profile appears on a pale orange surface in an 1840 issue. Some few brooches have hand-painted log cabin scenes rather than cameos, and are quite possibly of American origin. An impressive two-sided brooch exists with a white cameo bust of William Henry Harrison on the ob-

38. Brooches and shell medalets. At top is the beautiful and scarce Taylor shell medalet; the medalet at bottom pictures James Polk. In the center are three brooches: The Van Buren brooch is flanked by one at left depicting Andrew Jackson and, at right, a Harrison design.

39. Lewis Cass shell medalet. Contrast this bust of Cass with the almanac one of him—a more realistic picture—in Illustration 101.

verse and a log cabin on the reverse; both sides are enameled black and the piece is holed for suspension from the lapel (Ills. 40 and 41). If a collector is lucky enough to add a brooch to his collection, he can be reasonably sure of having it in good condition. Campaign brooches were treasured by their owners and were frequently passed down through a family. They are very scarce.

FERROTYPES. Probably the first presidential photographs—daguerreotypes, specifically—appeared during the 1848 campaign. For the few photographers of the time, presidential campaigns were a major occasion for publicizing their talents. As daguerreotypes, ambrotypes, and tintypes made their successive appearances on the market, photographs of presidential candidates became a customary means of familiarizing voters with their names and faces. (Photographs were especially important in making Abraham Lincoln known to eastern voters.)

The breakthrough in presidential photography occurred with the invention of the malainotype process in 1856. The photographic surface was a japanned sheet of iron, which was coated with collodion, exposed, washed, and varnished. The result was the "tintype." Among political collectors, tintypes bearing the likenesses of various candidates are known as ferrotypes, referring to the iron base (Ills. 42 and 43). With the arrival of the ferrotype, two-piece campaign buttons no longer remained in vogue, although they appeared occasionally in campaigns as late as 1912.

Ferrotypes were encased in either a solid or hollow circular—or occasionally an oval brass—frame with an appropriate slogan, such as the Republican party's "Constitution and Union/1860" in raised letters around the rim. A few are known framed in plush cloth of various colors. The presidential nominee's picture appeared on one side, the vice-presidential nominee's picture on the reverse. Rarer varieties picture both candidates together on one side with a pin on the reverse. Ferrotypes were holed for sus-

40. Obverse of the two-sided Harrison brooch, one of the very best nineteenth-century lapel artifacts.

41. Reverse of the Harrison brooch.

42. Typical ferrotypes, 1860 campaign. At top is one of John Breckinridge. Bottom row *(left to right)* shows John Bell and Stephen Douglas.

43. Three "doughnut" ferrotypes and one that is oval.

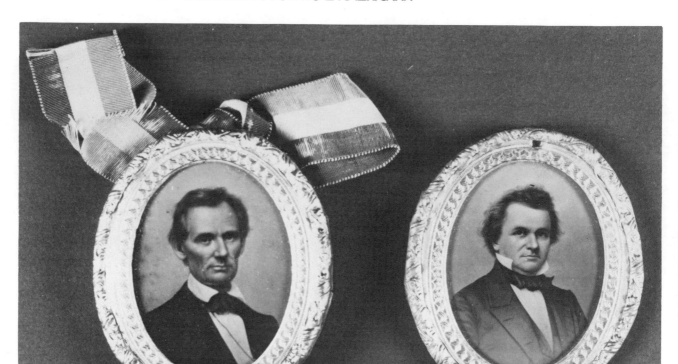

44. These framed ambrotypes of Abraham Lincoln and Stephen Douglas are approximately actual size. The Lincoln piece has an attached pin and a red, white, and blue rosette; the Douglas piece is holed for suspension.

45. A "bearded" Lincoln albumin shell badge, 1864.

pension from the lapel, and occasionally one turns up with its colored ribbon intact. Most ferrotypes are about an inch in diameter, but a few 1½ inches in diameter are known; several very rare varieties, known as "doughnut ferros" (Ill. 43) because of their unusually large frames, are 1¾ and 2¼ inches. And several designs, all rare, from the 1860 campaign are oval in shape.

Something over three hundred varieties of ferrotypes for all candidates in the 1860s campaigns exist. All are precious and extremely fragile. Ferrotypes should never be exposed to natural light, especially sunlight. Do not attempt to clean the picture or touch it with your fingers; handle it only by the rim edges, between thumb and forefinger. Always treat a ferrotype like a rare coin, with tender love and care.

The new popularity of the ferrotype coincided with perhaps one of the most interesting campaigns, from a collector's viewpoint, in American history. With their party split hopelessly over slavery, three Democrats vied against one Republican, Abraham Lincoln, for the White House. Because there were so many candidates, plus vice-presidential candidates, the 1860 campaign is a happy hunting ground for collectors. As would be expected, the great demand and the small supply guarantee high prices for ferrotypes. An additional factor that helps keep prices high is the competition from Lincolniana collectors, a group that has been active almost from the day of Lincoln's death.

There are approximately 120 different known photographs of Abraham Lincoln dating from his frontier lawyer days in Springfield to just four days before his death. Only certain ones of his photographs have appeared on ferrotypes, and collectors must be able to assign these to the proper campaign. First are the beardless photographs, which date a piece from the 1860 campaign. Second are the beardless photographs to which a thin beard has been added. These pieces are usually derived from romanticized prints, such as those produced by Currier and Ives, and should be assigned to the 1864 campaign. Third are photographs picturing Lincoln with a full beard, which also dates them as from the 1864 campaign (Ills. 45–48). And just to complicate the process, any photograph used on a ferrotype might have been retouched or be a reversal of the original.

SHELL BADGES. During the 1864 campaign manufacturers produced ferrotypes set in a variety of frames bearing in relief patriotic motifs such as shields, scrolls, and spread eagles. The frames were also widely used in the 1868 campaign and subsequent campaigns to the end of the century. These are known as shell badges because they were usually stamped from thin sheets of copper or brass into which the ferrotype was set (Ills. 49 and 50). Among the many designs, collectors should look for knapsacks with a ferrotype of Ulysses Grant (1868); pine trees showing the state of Maine's James G. Blaine (1884); a hand and a rooster showing W. S. Hancock (1880); a torchlight showing Grover Cleveland (1884); or perhaps whisk brooms showing various candidates, recalling that old political wheeze, "Sweep the rascals out!" One of my own favorite badges pictures the 1872 Democratic nominee, journalist Horace Greeley, on a brass quill pen with the inscription "The Pen Is Mightier Than the Sword."

In this period the albumin print became popular. It was the first paper photograph, and because of its low material cost and simpler developing process it eventually replaced all other types. This print gets its name from the fact that egg white was used to ensure a permanently bright and protective glaze. Albumin prints are invariably sepia and tend to fade very easily, and so they should be kept out of natural light of any intensity. By the 1880s albumin prints had virtually eliminated ferrotypes in presidential photography, although ferrotypes showed up occasionally in shell badges as late as the 1904 campaign.

46. A "bearded" Lincoln ferrotype; Andrew Johnson is pictured on the reverse.

47. Another "bearded" Lincoln badge. He is pictured here on a tintype in the sort of frame that is sometimes found with black enameling around the edge and mounted on a black ribbon for use as a mourning badge.

48. This large Lincoln ferrotype has a solid brass frame. It is uncommonly scarce, but the portrait is the "bearded" one most likely to be found on 1864 issues.

49. Shell badges. *Top row:* Harrison broom (1888); Hayes and Wheeler and Tilden and Hendricks jugate albumin prints (1876); Blaine "Plumed Knight" (1884). *Middle row:* Grant knapsack, which opens up to show his picture (1868); Garfield flag and eagle (1880); Seymour ferrotype (1868). *Bottom row:* Greeley quill pen (1872); Grant and Wilson ferrotype (1872); Cleveland torchlight (1884); Hancock rebus puzzle (1880).

50. An 1876 shell badge linking the candidates with the centennial of the nation's birth. A similar piece pictures Samuel Tilden and Thomas Hendricks.

51. A manufacturer's advertisement picturing one of the several varieties of Hancock rebus shell badges.

52. Mechanical shell badges. *Top row:* "The Presidential Chair/Who Shall Occupy It?" (snaps open to reveal a picture of Cleveland—or another candidate); when the devil's tail is pulled the hand goes to the nose on these 1880 Garfield (closed) and Hancock (opened) lapel novelties. *Middle row:* The wings on these 1896 eagles snap open to reveal pictures of McKinley (closed) and Bryan (opened) and their respective running mates; a picture of Bryan is hidden beneath the inscription on this 1896 skeleton pin (a similar one pictures McKinley). *Bottom row:* A colored enameled flag snaps open to show pictures of McKinley and Hobart as does the elephant blanket on these 1896 shell badges.

The wonderful array of nineteenth-century lapel devices ends with perhaps the most marvelous designs of all, the mechanical shell badges (Ill. 52). They were prominent in only one campaign, that of 1896, but a few are known from the 1892, 1900, and 1904 campaigns. Made usually of brass or silvered brass, mechanical shell badges depended for their novel effect upon a tiny spring. The best-known mechanical badges are the 1896 gold and silver "bugs," which have the shape of beetles. When a catch at the bottom of either badge is touched, the wings snap open to reveal either pictures of McKinley and Hobart on the "gold" (brass) bug or pictures of Bryan and Sewall on the "silver" (silvered brass) bug. Another 1896 variety is in the shape of a hand holding an American flag, which snaps open to reveal the candidate's picture. One of the very rarest 1896 designs, in brass and silvered brass, shows a large eagle holding a silver (or gold) bug in its beak; the wings snap open to reveal the candidate's picture. My personal favorite is a "dancing" skeleton attached to a string pin and bearing a shield on its chest reading "Death to Trusts." The shield snaps open to reveal a picture of William Jennings Bryan.

All the mechanical shell badges are ingenious. Collectors should be aware that many of these badges exist in pairs. Most range from scarce to extremely rare; shell badges with parts intact and in working condition command considerably higher prices than those that are damaged.

OTHER NINETEENTH-CENTURY LAPEL PIECES. Two other kinds of lapel pieces were in popular but short-lived use at different times during the nineteenth century. Foremost in this category are the beautifully fashioned brass shell medalets (see Ills. 38 and 39) bearing embossed busts of a presidential candidate on one side and the vice-presidential candidate or, less often, a slogan on the other side. These scarce and highly desirable pieces are made of two thin shells joined together; they are attached to

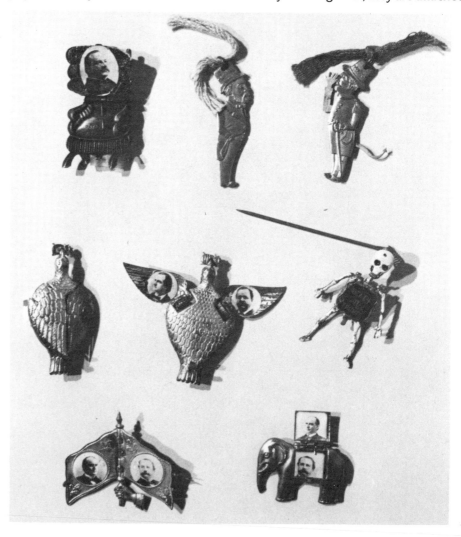

a lapel by means of a loop. With one exception, shell medalets range in diameter from ½ to about 1 inch; they seem to have been used exclusively in the 1844 and 1848 campaigns. About twenty to twenty-five examples are known, including variants, and most of them depict Henry Clay and James Polk; fewer are known for Martin Van Buren, Lewis Cass, and Zachary Taylor. The one exception is strikingly different: Taylor is pictured on the front of a glass-enclosed brass shell frame 1½ inches in diameter; the reverse lists in embossed letters the names of several of his victories during the Mexican War. This piece is considered by collectors to be one of the more exceptional nineteenth-century lapel pieces; I know of only two specimens. Shell medalets sell in the range of $400 to $800, and the rare Taylor example would probably sell for over $500 should one ever come on the market.

The second kind of nineteenth-century lapel piece was made in an abundance of varieties and was widely used in the 1884–1900 period. Lapel studs, in fact, are an embarrassment of riches for collectors (Ill. 54). They are so-called because of the attached peg by which the piece was inserted into the buttonhole of the lapel. Several hundred different examples are known; they range in size from about ½ to 1 inch in di-

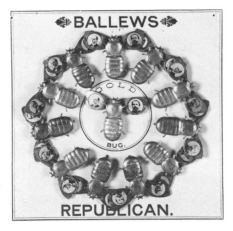

53.   A salesman's card displaying 1896 mechanical "gold bugs" picturing McKinley and Hobart. A similar card is known with "silver bugs" picturing Bryan and Sewell.

54.   Lapel studs. The group includes a matched pair depicting Harrison and Cleveland (1892), an 1896 McKinley "gold bug," a Harrison silhouette (1892), and other typical examples. The stud backs are shown at bottom.

55.   Images of Harrison and Morton carved from smoky quartz—more commonly called "moonstone" by collectors. Examples of these attractive and desirable lapel pieces show either Harrison or Cleveland alone or with their running mates; all known varieties apparently date from the 1888 campaign.

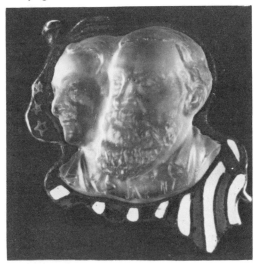

ameter, although the great majority are less than ¾ inch in diameter. A few were made in the shape of a hat, which was Benjamin Harrison's campaign symbol in 1888 and 1892; a beaver hat motif was used in many ways to signify his candidacies. Other studs were shaped like flags, shields, and in the likenesses of candidates. A copper Cleveland stud is shaped like a bass drum, and is inscribed "Ta-Ra-Ra-Boom-Deay/Cleveland/He Has Come to Stay." Political lapel studs were made of copper, brass, white metal, celluloid, and porcelain; some were cloth covered. Probably well over five hundred different types exist, most of them associated with the campaigns of Grover Cleveland, Benjamin Harrison, and William McKinley; William Jennings Bryan is represented by somewhat fewer types.

Of special interest to collectors are the well-executed shield-shaped enameled copper studs and those portraying Cleveland and Harrison on silk surfaces; other collecting favorites are small porcelain studs made by the O'Hara Company in Waltham, Massachusetts, for the 1896 campaign. Studs are a first-rate collecting opportunity, but in the past they have not proved as attractive to collectors as shell badges and portrait pins from the same period. Because of the low demand for them, lapel studs can be found at reasonable prices, and the many interesting kinds make them an excellent subject for beginning collectors.

55A. Examples of the uncommon and marvelous porcelain O'Hara studs, all from the 1896 campaign.

The Modern Campaign Button

Campaign buttons are generally the most popular of presidential Americana artifacts—for several very good reasons. Brooches, ferrotypes, and shell badges are too expensive for many collectors, but a fine collection of campaign buttons is simple to assemble because there are so many available at very little cost. Adequate display space is a serious problem for many collectors, but the small size of most campaign buttons makes it possible to display a great many in a limited area.

Of course, in the past few years, the prices of the rarer campaign buttons have skyrocketed — to over $6,000 and up in several instances. However, "better" buttons, the classics especially, have considerable investment potential, a fact that has attracted quick-money operators to the hobby and made the buying, selling, and trading of buttons a rather hysterical activity whenever collectors get together.

Buttons are also the most reproduced of campaign artifacts. At times the deluge of fakes and fantasies seems overwhelming; even experienced collectors are occasionally fooled. Almost every flea market has its array of reproductions, albeit usually offered unknowingly. Beginning collectors must be very cautious about the so-called "good buys."

CELLULOID BUTTONS. The modern campaign button is truly an ingenious device. All that was needed to spread the message, once the custom of displaying a candidate's picture on one's lapel was established, was a transparent substance more durable than albumin. The invention of celluloid in the 1870s provided the stimulus. A few campaign lapel pieces were made of solid celluloid in various colors, but they tended to crack and split very easily. Solid celluloids are known for Grover Cleveland, James Blaine, Rutherford Hayes, Samuel Tilden, and Benjamin Harrison. All these are fairly scarce.

Although solid celluloid was impractical, celluloid sheets were not. Just as the 1860 campaign had given a boost in popularity to the ferrotype, so the 1896 campaign popularized the celluloid button. The design of the button was simplicity itself: A thin metal disk was covered with a paper picture and a thin piece of celluloid, both of which were curled around the edge of the disk and held in place with a metal ring, which also held a spring-wire pin for attaching the button to the lapel. The arrangement was patented in the 1893–1896 period by Whitehead and Hoag of Newark, New Jersey, the

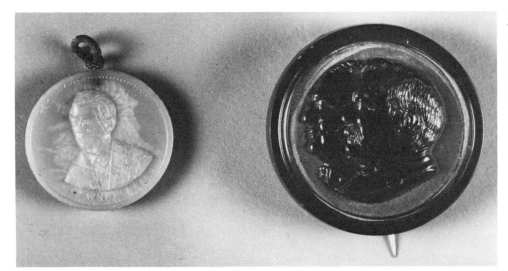

first prominent manufacturer in the field. Actually, several other designs preceded the Whitehead and Hoag type (Ill. 57). For a while, two in particular were popular: 1) the solid, or "filled," back into which a length of wire pin was soldered for attachment to the lapel; 2) the clasp back, which had an attached metal piece with a slot on each end to accommodate a hinged clasp. Note the illustrations carefully because both the filled and clasp designs were fairly common in the political campaigns of the period. However, both are scarcer than the Whitehead and Hoag type, a fact some collectors and dealers have tried to publicize as adding to their value. But this should not add to the button's value. It is what is on the front that counts.

57. Examples of early button attachments. The upper row shows clasps and pinbacks; the lower row shows filled backs.

THE GOLDEN AGE OF CAMPAIGN BUTTONS: 1896–1920s. The success of the Whitehead and Hoag design is immediately apparent in the immense number of celluloid buttons distributed across the country during the 1896 silver and gold campaign. Although the company produced many thousands of buttons picturing sports heroes, actresses, warships, national flags, and other devices that gum and tobacco manufacturers could give away with their products, it is for their campaign buttons, which were frequently imaginatively designed, that they are best remembered. By the end of this period, well over two hundred companies were involved in the manufacture of campaign buttons. Some, such as the St. Louis Button Company and Boston's Ehrman Manufacturing Company, likewise produced designs of consistently superior quality.

Today, collectors view the period from 1896 through the 1920s as the "golden

57A. The hinged lower jaw of this super brass shell lapel pin opens to reveal, on a paper label, "Give 'Em Hell, Boys!"

58. Collectors tend to become excited about matching or "paired," buttons. This pair have the added appeal of being novelties and on their original cards.

age" of campaign buttons. In this quarter century manufacturers produced a wonderful array of designs combining pictures, slogans, and brightly colored inks that have never since been matched in graphic quality. This peak in campaign button design ended in the 1920s with the introduction of the more cheaply produced lithograph button.

In the golden age it seemed that all kinds of organizations wanted to get into the act and to issue their own button designs. Among the organizations that come to mind are the Princeton McKinley Club, the Overseas Americans Club, Farmers for Bryan, Rough Riders for Roosevelt, Commercial Travelers Republican Club, the Bryan League, American Republican College League, the Parker and Davis League, and the Taft League of Massachusetts (and other states). It was not unusual for a business firm to couple its product with the candidate (as was done with trade cards), such as "Lucas Paints for McKinley" and a "Full Dinner Pail" or "Smoke Hartford Times Cigars" above a picture of Teddy Roosevelt. On a 1904 button Teddy is pictured with a bar of Zig-Zag soap, and from the same campaign a button urges votes for his opponent, Alton Parker, as well as asking voters to use Maple City soap!

With a few exceptions from later campaigns, buttons from the golden age are the most prized by collectors. Those that express a campaign theme in an imaginative way, humorously or seriously, are a collector's pride. If these buttons are also scarce, so much the better.

CAMPAIGN BUTTON CLASSICS. This section might well be titled "Author's Choice," since one collector's preference is not necessarily another's. But certain buttons, such as the 1896 McKinley and Bryan "hobby" designs (Plate 2), would doubtless be on every list, as would the 1900 McKinley factory design.

In any case, buttons that are especially appealing graphically and perhaps also carry an uncommon message are considered classics. Most date from the golden age and range from scarce to extremely rare; hence they can be quite expensive. And if

such buttons are associated with candidates popular with collectors—e.g., William Jennings Bryan and Theodore Roosevelt—prices can be even higher. Note that classic buttons are not limited to the Democratic and Republican candidates; buttons of some third-party candidates such as Eugene Debs, the perennial nominee of the American Socialist party, are just as popular—and just as expensive.

The "hobby" pair well illustrates why some campaign buttons are classics. McKinley is likened to Napoleon (a favorite Democratic theme in that campaign) and is shown riding his hobbyhorse, imperialism, on to greater glory. Bryan's hobbyhorse is a bird, perhaps a plucked chicken, perhaps typical of his crusade against the gold standard—or is Bryan's head in the sand, as typified by his riding a hobby ostrich? Or can this pair be interpreted in other ways?

A 1908 button (Ill. 60) pictures an early phonograph and bears the inscription "His Master's Voice," after the famous Victor advertisement of that era. Viewed right side up, the button shows a donkey looking at Bryan's face inside the horn; turn the button around, and an elephant is looking at Taft's face inside the horn. On the popular 1904 Parker "white elephant" button, an elephant is standing on a football in front of goalposts, with his legs bound by a ball and chain inscribed "Protection/The Trustees/ The Trusts." Around the rim and in just about all other available space the following is inscribed:

'Its' Game/Uncle Sam's "White" Elephant/
'Its' Finish/
Goal/Rooseveltism/Grand Old Pirate/
"A Safety" Standpatism/

Rah! Rah!! Rah!!!
A Safety's the Score
Parker & Davis/1904

We cannot ask for more.

59. Collectors value these buttons highly. Note, especially, the political advertising buttons in the middle, the button punning Landon's name in the lower row, and the attractive 1932 Roosevelt and Curley button.

60. An unusual 1908 campaign button. Look carefully at the donkey and the horn's opening. Then turn the book sidewise. Now what do you see?

A few classic buttons are necessary for any collector who wants quality in his collection. And collectors who want only one or two representative buttons of a candidate infinitely prefer these to be classics.

LITHOGRAPHED BUTTONS.   During the 1920 campaign there appeared for the first time campaign buttons with the design printed directly, or lithographed, on a tin sheet. These buttons were punched from a large sheet, then curled sharply around the rim, thus allowing the spring wire to sit snugly inside the rim without benefit of a collar. In one stroke, celluloid, paper, and collar were eliminated.

Lithographed buttons become scratched and chipped very easily, and the quality of design possible with celluloids is simply not possible with "lithos" (Ill. 65). Nevertheless, since lithos are cheaper to produce, in later elections many more of them are likely

61.   A card of Coolidge–Dawes buttons. Individually, these buttons sell for very little, but the price is much higher when such buttons are found on their original card.

62.   A selection of premium buttons. Note the number of jugates. The Roosevelt button was used in his unsuccessful 1918 senatorial campaign; Barker and Donnelly were People's (Populist) party candidates in 1900; the Stevenson-Kefauver button is the only lithographed one in this group.

63. Good modern buttons. "FMBNH" on the tiny button at the bottom means "For McCarthy Before New Hampshire." The Willkie button is important because of a community tie-in; the McGovern button is one of the very best for his candidacy, which is also true of the small Nixon button at upper left center.

64. More good modern buttons. With the exception of the 1948 Henry Wallace button—at center right, which is quite scarce—all these buttons are easily obtained.

to have been in circulation than celluloids. In recent years some political groups have purchased and distributed lithos only, a practice that will probably increase in the future. Note, too, that although some lithos command fairly high prices, none would be considered a classic.

65. Some of the most common buttons. No button here should sell for more than $109. All are "lithos" with the exception of the Bryan, Taft, and McKinley buttons.

66. Modern 3-inch buttons. The McGovern button is rated highly. Several of the designs pictured here are also known in smaller sizes.

PREMIUM BUTTONS.   Buttons in this category range in price from about $100 on up. Many are scarce and a few are exceedingly rare—but so are many classic buttons. The difference between classic and premium buttons is mostly a matter of graphic appeal. Premium buttons are, in effect, those buttons in demand primarily because of their scarcity and/or because they interest collectors specializing in a given button subject. The rarest and most valuable premium buttons are the 1920 Cox-Roosevelt jugates, most of which are lacking in graphic appeal. They do picture the young Franklin D. Roosevelt in his second try for national political office (he had lost a contest for the United States Senate in 1918), which makes them an attraction for FDR collectors. But these jugates are rare and they are valuable (one dealer advertising in a hobby publication offered to pay up to $6,000 for certain designs), so, if nothing else, they are a good investment. Premium buttons can be celluloids or lithos; they are associated with every campaign from 1896 to the present.

"MAKE YOUR OWN" BUTTONS. In the past few years a small and highly efficient hand-operated button-making machine has been selling very well in retail stores. Usually the buttons produced by this machine have a diameter up to about 2¼ inches. They consist of four parts: *a*) a tin disk with two holes for inserting a clasp pin; *b*) a similar disk, without holes, which provides the surface for *c*) the paper design and *d*) the plastic covering (Ill. 67). All parts are brought together properly under pressure. The colors on these buttons are usually pastel hues, and the designs, including 1976 buttons, are singularly uninteresting.

67. The back of a "make your own" button.

Although such machines have proved to be a boon to groups selling buttons as a fund-raising scheme, they have become a thoroughgoing nuisance in the hobby. Unfortunately, the existence of these buttons raises the specter of fantasies and reproductions. Many nonprofit political groups sell them quite legitimately— i.e., for actual use in a campaign. But there is nothing to prevent unscrupulous collectors, dealers, and speculators from doing the same and passing off their products as legitimate. In my opinion, a large percentage of "make your own" buttons from the 1976 presidential campaign are suspect for just that reason. (More will be said about this problem in a later chapter.)

Building a Campaign Button Collection

SOURCES OF BUTTON ISSUES. Beyond button manufacturers, campaign buttons are issued by several quite legitimate sources:

1. National, state, and local party organizations of both major and minor parties.
2. Nonprofit groups with a particular message to publicize. In 1976, for example, these groups, among others, issued buttons: University of Illinois Alumni in support of Gerald Ford, the New York State Educational Association in support of Jimmy Carter, and the Arlo Guthrie concert tour in support of Fred Harris. (These were legitimate because all proceeds were donated to the Harris campaign committee.)
3. Individuals who are themselves bona fide candidates for public office. Usually, such candidates are seeking support for a particular cause; their seriousness of intent is measured by the extent to which they obtain legal candidate status in various states. Recent examples that come to mind are Ellen McCormack, an antiabortion advocate in 1976; Willis Stone, who advocated repeal of the federal income tax during the 1968 campaign; and, one of my favorite candidates, "Farmer" Henry Krajewski, the self-styled pig farmer from Secaucus, New Jersey, and the driving force behind the Poor People's party in the 1952 and 1956 campaigns (Ill. 68). Sometimes these individuals will incorporate their position into a political party, as did Krajewski. Thus, there are likely to be political "parties" all over the landscape and ranging across the entire ideological spectrum. Very often the "party" will consist of just one candidate and a few supporters, a typewriter and copy machine, a minuscule budget, and a fine sense of public relations.

On the borderline between obvious legitimacy and unverifiable suspicion are the issues of individuals who take advantage of the presidential campaign to publicize their own serious or humorous message. Among the latter were Will Rogers, who seemed almost serious about his candidacy during the 1928 campaign, and Pat Paulsen, who held his 1968 kickoff campaign dinner in a Los Angeles automat. In 1964 there was

68. Fringe candidates, serious and not so serious, whose buttons belong in a collection.

68A. A selection of buttons from recent campaigns. In my opinion, the Anderson button is the best single design of the 1980s. The Jackson button is one of a series with provocative slogans; it was issued by the Boston Jackson headquarters.

Dan Gurney, publisher of *Car and Driver Magazine,* with his Car and Driver party. In 1976 Democrat George Rodin of Waco, Texas, staged his own one-man campaign to publicize his concern about the nation's well-being. And there were Eric Sebastian of the "Hamiltonian party," perennial candidate Stanley Arnold, and the grass-roots movement for Ralph Nader. Many more names could be added to the list.

Which buttons should be included in a collection? One collector may insist on purity and accept only buttons issued by recognized major and minor parties. Another will include buttons from one-issue candidates as well. This is a gray area in campaign button collecting; the decision is pretty much a matter of individual taste and preference.

THE SELECTION CRITERIA. Once a collector is satisfied with the legitimacy of an issue, there are five other equally important criteria to be considered: scarcity, design, condition, size, and demand.

1. *Scarcity.* Obviously, buttons commissioned for local and state distribution will be fewer in number than those commissioned for national use. Sometimes rank and file party workers' disaffection with their party's choice means fewer buttons are ordered from manufacturers. At other times a budget may be practically nonexistent. Until recent years, manufacturers' overstocks were destroyed (now they are sold to collectors). But most campaign buttons are easy to locate; many are so common as never to be worth more than a dollar or two. A good many, however, including even buttons from recent campaigns, are elusive, showing up only occasionally on dealers' lists. A few are known to exist in very small numbers, and when they appear on the market they set off a flurry of comment and high bidding. Once in a great while a hitherto-unknown design of superior quality, a "superbutton," will appear, causing considerable excitement and perhaps a story in one of the hobby publications.

2. *Design.* The general attractiveness of a button (i.e., the graphic quality—colors, picture, and letter style, and the arrangement of these elements) is extremely important. As mentioned earlier, buttons from the golden age are superior partly because of their graphic quality. Note that almost every classic button pictured in this book has an interesting design. Generally buttons picturing both the presidential and vice-presidential nominees together (jugates) are the most desirable, followed by designs picturing only the presidential nominee. Name and slogan buttons ("I Like Ike"; "Nixon's the One!") are the least desirable, but also underrated.

Frequently buttons with a clever theme are more popular than picture buttons. Examples are the 1904 Parker "white elephant" issue; the very popular 1900 McKinley factory design; several from Theodore Roosevelt's campaigns (particularly those with the Rough Rider association); the 1944 Franklin Roosevelt groundhog issue; the 1940 Willkie "chemurgy" button; plus several associated with third-party candidates, such as the 1948 Henry Wallace "Seamen for Wallace" issue. I should mention also the very imaginative, and very scarce, embroidered and silk-screen designs advocating Eugene McCarthy in 1968.

3. *Condition.* A button in mint condition will not be rusted; the design will not be spotted; the celluloid will not be scratched, chipped, or peeled away from the collar. Colors will be bright, the design will be centered, the letters will be sharp. Lithographed buttons will not be scratched or dented. Defects can be tolerated, barely, in scarce buttons, but not in common varieties. In both cases, however, value will drop accordingly.

4. *Size.* Button diameters range from ½ inch to about 4 inches. The larger 3½- and 4-inch buttons began appearing in the early 1950s, although a few are known from earlier campaigns. Buttons in these larger sizes must have looked ridiculous hanging from a lapel, and today they require considerable display space. Hence, they tend not to be popular with collectors. Infinitely preferred are buttons in the ⅞- to 2½-inch range, which seems to be the best size. Obviously, larger and usually scarce buttons from earlier campaigns are highly prized.

5. *Demand.* Perhaps the best way to discuss this subject and its dramatic im-

pact upon the hobby is in terms of market values. Certain intangible factors may keep a button in demand either just briefly or consistently. First is the popularity of the candidate among collectors (to be discussed shortly). Second is collector enthusiasm itself, a built-in hazard of campaign-button collecting. In 1973 I discovered a hitherto-unknown McGovern slogan button saying simply "I'm a Teamster for McGovern." (Collectors, myself included, like to brag about their collections, however politely.) Suddenly this button was the hottest item on the market, selling at one point for $200 before settling back to a more respectable $25. That story can be repeated many times over about buttons from recent campaigns. There was a similar frenzy about certain Carter buttons in 1976. In effect, an artificial and inflated market is created. While it lasts, for perhaps six months or so after the election, quite unspectacular buttons sell for abnormal prices. So if you must have the particular button that everyone else wants at the same time you do, then be prepared to pay a high price. Wait a while and your patience will be rewarded. But remember, I am speaking here of buttons issued during the last two or three campaigns. Competition is intense, and always will be, for the better older and some few newer buttons.

A third factor related to demand is button speculation. Unfortunate, but true: Campaign buttons are the newest entry in the "blue chip" artifact category. Although nearly all political campaign items have risen in price, some quite rapidly, in recent years, button prices have increased the most. Better buttons seem to operate in their own market, quite independently of other kinds of campaign items. The situation is perhaps best described as an investment market. A very few individuals can afford to pay over $500 consistently for rarer buttons. These "superbuttons" so seldom appear on the market that it is difficult to make a definitive price for them; when they do appear, the sky is the limit. An example: The known 1920 Cox-Roosevelt jugates, the rarest of all buttons, as we have said, have bland and uninteresting designs. But late in 1977 four different designs of these jugates sold at private sale for $14,000, and in 1981 a previously unknown 1¼" variety sold at auction for $30,000! So, though they are not very attractive buttons, they do have enormous investment potential.

The market is bullish, and will remain so because better buttons are few in number and much in demand. The situation will not change because demand will continue to intensify as new collectors become addicted.

But a reminder: Most Taft buttons, most Bryan buttons, most McKinley buttons, most Truman buttons, most Kennedy buttons, and most other presidential campaign buttons can be obtained inexpensively, and they will provide the basis for an interesting collection. No collector need be scared away because of the high prices for a relatively few buttons.

ASSOCIATION. This refers to the popularity of candidates among collectors. Certainly both the value of a button and its educational importance are considerations, but just as immediate to many collectors is the appeal of the candidate himself. Obviously, some candidates are more popular than others. The most popular candidates (not necessarily in this order) are William Jennings Bryan, Teddy Roosevelt (especially as the 1912 Bull Moose party nominee), Woodrow Wilson, Al Smith, Franklin Roosevelt, Harry Truman, and John Kennedy. Other candidates' buttons may enjoy brief spurts of popularity, but those listed seem to have continuing appeal. All of which is not to say that other candidates are not popular; those listed just appear to be more so. Note, too, that those candidates are perhaps better known to the noncollecting public.

THIRD PARTIES. Collecting third-party buttons (Ill. 69) and other material can be a fascinating pursuit. Regardless of their ideologies, third parties usually lack the inhibitions of the major parties when it comes to publicizing unconventional and outrageous positions. With rare exceptions they seldom have an adequate budget, and most states make it very difficult for them to get on the ballot. But third parties represent a slice of American history that seldom appears in school history books. Often biased

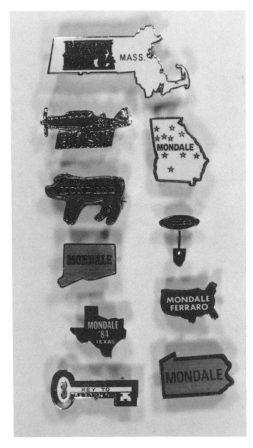

68B. A selection of colorful brass lapel pins from the 1984 and 1988 campaigns. Some are very difficult to find and, in my opinion, the enameled state silhouette pins are far superior to all political buttons from those campaigns.

election laws, shoestring budgets, lack of public awareness, and the deeply rooted acceptance of the two-party system make it very difficult for third parties to survive from one campaign to the next. Once in a while, however, they are strong enough to make major party candidates think twice. Third-party candidates do not win the White House, but they have denied it to the major parties, as the Bull Moose party did to the Republicans in 1912 and George Wallace's American party probably did to the Democrats in 1968. Most third-party candidates are legitimate contenders, and they deserve serious attention from collectors.

69. A representative selection of third-party buttons. All are fairly easily obtained.

Finding pieces from the more than seventy parties legally in existence in this century is not easy. Along with the reasons mentioned above, third parties do not usually have a grass-roots network, an important source of buttons. Their buttons, at least through the 1964 campaign, do not exist in large numbers. With few exceptions there is no great demand for them. However, these exceptions are very important. Bull Moose party jugates picturing Theodore Roosevelt and his running mate, Hiram Johnson, are quite rare and command very high prices. Eugene Debs jugates also bring healthy prices, as do early Prohibition party pieces. That party, in fact, has run candidates in every presidential election since 1872, and is one of the more popular third parties among collectors.

Collectors should attempt to obtain at least one button from as many third parties as possible, or perhaps add a third-party specialty collection to their general collection. (I myself have developed a particularly fine American Communist party collection.) Or a collector may specialize in third parties only, as an increasing number of collectors seem to be doing. However, to collect third-party buttons successfully, the collector will need to read widely and deeply.

COLLECTING HOPEFULS AND FAVORITE SONS.   For every major party candidate who attains his party's nomination, there will be several "hopefuls" who fell by the wayside along the state primary path or lost the nomination at the following national convention (Ills. 70–72). Generally, buttons for hopefuls are not in much demand. But buttons associated with hopefuls who were striking personalities, such as Huey Long (1936), or who commanded a zealous national following, such as Robert Taft (1952), or who dramatized a great national issue, such as Eugene McCarthy's anti-Vietnam War crusade in 1968, are always in demand.

Among other hopefuls whose buttons enjoy popularity with collectors are James "Champ" Clark (1912); William Randolph Hearst (1920); William "Alfalfa Bill" Murray (1932); Douglas MacArthur (1948, 1952); Harold Stassen (1948+); Estes Kefauver

70. Early "hopeful" buttons. The Long button *(top row)* is the most desirable. At lower right is a button picturing "Oklahoma Bill" Murray, whose campaign slogan was "Bread and Butter/Beans and Bacon."

(1956); Nelson Rockefeller (1964+); Robert Kennedy (1968); Edward Kennedy (1972); Morris Udall, Fred Harris, and Ronald Reagan (1976).

Early "favorite son" buttons are more difficult to find because they were available only at national conventions. Sometimes favorite sons receive spontaneous support at conventions, thus necessitating a quick and usually small order of buttons from a nearby manufacturer. But buttons from later campaigns, at least since 1964, are readily located. A favorite son is supposedly a nonserious candidate, usually a senator or governor, who hopes to place himself and/or his convention delegation in a favorable position to exert some influence over who is ultimately chosen as the candidate. At other times favorite son status is sought in order to gain media exposure, perhaps as a boost in a forthcoming reelection bid. Whatever the reasons, this category is a more whimsical part of campaign button collecting in that it is very difficult to define precisely who is a favorite son at any moment, and that makes this a rather interesting category.

There is little demand for favorite son buttons, although a few collectors do try to assemble, as some do with hopefuls, a representative button or two for each favorite son at different conventions. There is also considerable overlapping between these categories, since a favorite son may also be a hopeful. That was, in fact, the situation at the

71. These are 1968 McCarthy silk-screen designs on cloth. The smaller size has an embroidered edge. These buttons are among the most interesting of all modern issues—all designs are scarce.

72. Modern "hopeful" buttons. The significant buttons in this group are the Arlo Guthrie/Fred Harris button at lower left, the Margaret Chase Smith button at lower center, the seldom-seen Kefauver button at right of center, and the heart-shaped Reagan button (1976) in the center. (We can expect to see more irregularly shaped designs like it in future campaigns.)

1940 Republican National Convention when the delegates stampeded for Wendell Willkie, thus helping him win the nomination. A few of the more popular names in this category are favorite sons Hiram Fong, Strom Thurmond (also the 1948 nominee of the "Dixiecrat" party), Orville Faubus, W. Averell Harriman, Robert Kerr, and Stuart Symington.

COLLECTING STATE AND LOCAL CANDIDATES.   In the past few years there has been a surge of interest in buttons associated with candidates who have campaigned for Congress or governorships. Implicit in collecting this kind of material is the hope that the state or local candidate may someday run for the White House. Buttons advocating Harry Truman for district judge and Truman and Lyndon Johnson for the Senate bring very high prices. Also popular, but far less expensive, are buttons advocating Hubert Humphrey for mayor of Minneapolis and Richard Nixon for governor of California. John Kennedy buttons from his House and Senate campaigns are very much in demand. This category also attracts collectors who cannot or will not pay the higher prices for presidential campaign buttons. Generally, button prices in this category are very low—many interesting buttons sell for ten dollars or less. The subject is wide open; the demand is not great, but it is steady. There are periodic auctions and sales lists; and a newsletter is published occasionally—all of which suggests the likelihood of increasing demand and rising prices.

Among the currently popular types are buttons associated with the House Judiciary Committee members who dealt with the impeachment charges against Richard Nixon; governors from one's own state; "sets" of buttons from all fifty states and possibly for each congressman as well; and mayors and third-party candidates from the larger cities. And political bosses: Personally, I am quite proud of my collection of

73. A grouping of buttons for state and local candidates: John Kelly, a candidate for mayor of Philadelphia, is the father of Princess Grace of Monaco; "Big Bill" Thompson was a mayor of Chicago; most of the other buttons picture candidates for state and federal offices.

James Michael Curley material; Curley's colorful career spanned nearly fifty years of Massachusetts politics. The potential of this category is interesting and well worth investigating.

HOUSING YOUR BUTTON COLLECTION.   To me, it has always seemed that the way a collector treats his collection is a good indication of his respect for what he owns.

A collection of buttons can be housed in commercially made display frames with glass fronts, which can be mounted on the walls or stacked on end in a bookcase. The most reliable and attractive of these frames are usually made of walnut or hard pine; they are commonly used also by the collectors of regular clothing buttons. The frames measure up to 10 by 14 inches, and are from ½ to 1 inch in depth. They can also be ordered in custom sizes and shapes.

Biological specimen frames, known as Riker mounts, are also popular with collectors. These are made of heavy black paper-covered stock and packed with cotton batting, on which specimens are placed. The weight of the glass front presses the specimen into the batting. Despite their popularity with political collectors, I do not recommend Riker mounts as permanent housing for button collections. These mounts are made of stock cardboard, which is susceptible to moisture; the glass is clear, thus allowing fading to continue; and a solid white background tends to give a harsh appearance to multicolored buttons. Because the glass covers of Riker mounts are attached only by common pins to the containers, the covers are easily removed and the contents just as easily stolen.

Also available are Carter mounts. These measure 9 by 12 inches, and are heavy stock covered with styrofoam-padded cloth and enclosed in acetate sleeves. They do not particularly enhance the appearance of a button, but they are suitable for displaying duplicates and for storage. Duplicates can also be enclosed in 2- by 2-inch coin "huggers" and inserted in acetate pocket sheets that are holed for three-ring binders. Huggers and sheets are available from any coin dealer.

A quality collection deserves quality housing. In the belief that buttons should be exposed as little as possible to dust and both natural and artificial light, I recommend a coin cabinet. Such cabinets stand anywhere from 18 inches to perhaps six feet in height, and contain shallow drawers about ¾ inch deep. Large numismatic collections are housed in this manner, and these cabinets with hinged and locked doors are equally fitting for a button collection. For the handyman-collector, building a special cabinet is a worthy project. My collection is housed in such a cabinet, each drawer being lined with deep blue velvet that shows off the buttons to maximum advantage. Most important, it keeps them in total darkness when they are not being viewed.

A NOTE ON THE CARE OF CAMPAIGN BUTTONS.   As already explained, light of any kind, but especially natural light, is extremely damaging to buttons, as it is to all nineteenth-century lapel picture items; it should be avoided at all costs. Although wooden wall frames do show off buttons very well, the natural light entering through windows is sufficient to cause buttons to fade—imperceptibly at first but quite noticeably over a period of time. Leave a deeply colored sepia button near a window for a while and watch what happens.

Water or dampness, however slight, can also be destructive. If buttons must be cleaned of surface film, a gentle touch with an ever-so-slightly-dampened soft cloth will suffice. But first inspect the button surface with a magnifying glass to check for cracks in the celluloid. The slightest trace of dampness beneath the celluloid will trigger an irreversible staining. A very gentle rubbing with #0000 steel wool will remove light rust from the spring pin and the back of the button. Never use steel wool or any other abrasive material on the front of lithographed buttons. And sometimes it is better not to touch the button at all!

Buttons should be stored and housed at room temperature. When they are in storage, it is a good idea to place a small bag of silicon crystals nearby, to counteract dampness.

74.   Examples of damaged buttons. The Roosevelt/Fairbanks button is badly faded although that condition is not evident in the picture. The McKinley/Roosevelt button shows serious water damage, and the celluloid of the 1900 Bryan button is badly cracked.

4
A Treasure in Political Paper

74A. One of the most desireable of all political trade cards, this whimsical and colorful example is a mechanical. When the card is flexed slightly, Teddy's mustache flips open to reveal "Delightful."

THERE IS SOMETHING impressive about the quality and the variety of paper items having to do with presidential campaigns. Probably thirty or more different kinds are collectible, from attractive examples of political graphic art and unusual novelties, to common modern leaflets and cheap lapel stickers. Here we will discuss (A) items most in demand, such as prints and cartoons; (B) those not in great demand but that do enjoy a small and consistent interest, such as sheet music and postcards; and (C) items for which there is now little demand—the sleepers—that are well worth collecting and likely to increase in value in the future.

Political paper is perhaps the one category that the collector who wants to be well informed cannot afford to ignore. Reading issues of campaign newspapers, for example, provides insights into campaigns and clarifies the significance of other political artifacts. Political prints, posters, and cartoons are not only a part of American graphic history; they provide succinct comments on the affairs and personalities of the day.

Most political paper has been undervalued, and so the beginning collector has a good chance to assemble a very fine collection. Prints and cartoons, however, can be very expensive. Dealers who specialize in them are likely to have outstanding stock at any time. The Swann Galleries in New York occasionally include political prints and broadsides in their frequent book auctions. Dealers in a general line of paper Americana are also a fairly good source. And, of course, in antique shops and at flea markets, always take the time to poke through boxes of books and papers.

75. A book engraving. Note the early use of the Liberty cap.

Political Prints

The political portrait print enjoyed a long and reputable career in Europe. A fine etching or engraving, epitomized in the work of Albrecht Dürer, was as much an art form as the finest painting or sculpture. With the emergence of George Washington into international prominence, European printmakers, especially those in England and France, began exporting quality folio-size engraved portraits of him to this country. Many of these prints were copies or variations of paintings by Gilbert Stuart, Charles Willson Peale, and John Trumbull, among other American painters. Also popular were engravings of Thomas Jefferson and John Adams (Ill. 76), who were both members of Washington's first Cabinet. These prints were usually purchased by wealthier Ameri-

76. A British engraving of President John Adams, c. 1796.

cans, set in elaborate frames, and hung in sitting rooms or foyers. And they were frequently hung in public buildings, a custom that continued well into this century in our public schools.

The quality of these earliest presidential prints varied considerably. European printmakers sometimes had no idea of what Washington looked like. The results of their ignorance were amazing, but Americans bought their prints anyway, strong testimony to Washington's popularity. Prints by such engravers as Juste Chevillet and Noel le Mire in France or the Americans Joseph Wright and William Wooley are superb creations, historically accurate and aesthetically attractive. These prints are all difficult to find, though usually reasonably priced by most dealers. Many prints are folio size. However, collectors should note that much smaller prints taken from contemporary books are also collectible. Often prints of this period were embellished along the margins with appropriate scenes and/or events from the subject's life or perhaps with a patriotic motif instead.

All nineteenth-century presidents were portrayed on engraved prints, as were most vice-presidents and defeated candidates. And as the century advanced, printing techniques improved, as did design, mechanical processes, varieties of paper, and color. In fact, it is most important that collectors know something about the history of printing. Recognizing different engravers' styles, types of paper, and printing processes is basic knowledge.

Lincoln, of course, is well represented (Ill. 77). Many of his portraits are copies of photographs by Brady and other photographers of the day. There is also a variety of prints engraved by British and French artists. Actually, a collector could devote much of his time to collecting nothing but Lincoln prints—and still lack many.

Columbia's noblest Sons

77. Lincoln is joined with Washington in America's Pantheon in this 1865 print.

With the development of stone lithography in the 1820s, prints for the first time became available at low cost to the larger American public. This technique does not allow for the subtlety of line that is possible with etched and engraved prints. But the lack of subtlety contributes to the charm of stone lithographs. They were immensely popular with the public from the beginning, and through the early 1880s they were perhaps the single most important art form for many Americans.

The noted authority Harry Peters wrote, in his *America on Stone,* that American lithographs were successful because they were made by those who knew what the people wanted, who liked it themselves, and who expressed their ideas quickly and ade-quately, for sale at the lowest price possible to as many people as possible. In those years before the mass production of books—indeed, before widespread higher literacy (i.e., education beyond the common school)—prints, broadsides, and cartoons were frequently a major means of quickly disseminating knowledge about candidates, how-ever exaggerated, distorted, or sentimentalized that knowledge usually was.

Many lithographs of the day were unashamedly patriotic, even maudlin. Horses are depicted as long-legged and nimble-footed. Generals astride their favorite steeds wave their swords grandly or stand in a Napoleonic pose contemplating their stirring deeds (Ill. 78). One colorful Kurz and Andersen print depicts General William Henry Harrison putting Chief Tecumseh and his obviously disorganized braves to rout at the "Battle" of Tippecanoe. George Washington is well represented; always he appears no-ble—whether he is at Valley Forge or strolling through his Mount Vernon acres or taking the oath as president. But he is positively godlike as he lies on his deathbed. Indeed,

78. A Baillie print depicting Zachary Taylor in a heroic equestrian pose. Most candidates from Jackson through Buchanan were pictured in this manner by the different printmakers.

79. General Taylor dies serenely while surrounded by relatives and political cronies. This subject was popular from about 1840 to the 1880s.

long after the battles, the campaign, and the election—at the end of life itself—the great man, whoever he may be, is pictured dying serenely in bed surrounded by his family, cronies, and every statesman of note at the time. Thus, there are some rather crowded bedrooms in these "death scene" prints (Ill. 79).

Collectors prize two particular series. One, produced chiefly by the Kelloggs and by Currier and Ives, illustrates the party's presidential and vice-presidential nominees in wreath-enclosed ovals or circles surrounded by appropriate symbols of the day, per-haps a spread eagle, a cornucopia, wheat sheaves, and agricultural, commercial, and maritime scenes. On a scroll below may appear such titles as "Grand National Whig Banner," "Grand National Banner of the Radical Democracy," or "Grand National Union Banner for 1864." The other desirable series was issued by Currier and Ives from about 1858 to 1861. It pictures the party's presidential nominees from Washing-ton to Lincoln, with either a red or a green drape in the background (Ill. 80). It is possible to put together a set of these, but if the collector wants a set in which all the drapes are red or all of them green, then the search will be long indeed.

Other subjects worth collecting are presidential birthplaces; events in the life of the candidate; various interpretations of Washington taking his first-term oath of office; Lin-coln's assassination (there is a fine Currier and Ives series portraying the whole se-

80. An example of the Currier "draped curtain" series of presidential prints, a series published about 1860.

quence of events from the assassination to Booth's death in the burning barn); U. S. Grant, portrayed with familiar Civil War battlefield scenes; and Zachary Taylor, portrayed similarly but with Mexican War scenes.

An unusual type is that in which the portrait of a president is created with Spencerian script, that elaborate penmanship so beloved of the nineteenth-century educated class. A mark of one's skill was one's ability to draw animals, birds, and other objects with the script. Presidents were often portrayed with some appropriate text—the Emancipation Proclamation (longer than the Gettysburg Address) most often shapes Lincoln's portrait. The custom continued into the early twentieth century.

One can also collect the prints of a particular publisher. A biographer of Currier and Ives described them, rightfully, as "printmakers to the American people." But there were other publishers who produced prints with political themes, and collectors should be aware of them too: James Baille, John Bufford (with whom Winslow Homer began his career), the Endicotts, the Kellogg brothers, Louis Prang (the first popularizer of the valentine), Henry Robinson, and Napoleon Sarony. Very often the productions of some of these publishers were superior aesthetically to Currier and Ives's work.

Campaign Cartoons

It is cartoons, however, rather than prints that most grip collectors' interest and imagination. The art and history of the American political cartoon have received considerable attention from scholars, but here we will simply discuss some of the highlights of the subject and mention the specific cartoonists and the publications in which they appeared that are most interesting to collectors.

A political cartoon is a strong, exaggerated rendering—with or without humor—of a topical, political, or moral issue. William Murrell, in his *History of American Graphic Humor,* says that such a cartoon is intended for a wide audience and hence makes liberal use of popular symbols and slogans. He adds that a cartoon is often more grotesque than comic because the intention is ridicule rather than laughter. A caricature is a more subtle form, Murrell continues, "a satiric exposing of individual physical peculiarities and idiosyncracies of manner . . . diminution and exaggeration . . . shot through with irreverence . . . a form of graphic mimicry [that] victimizes and pillorizes its subjects."

Both cartoons and caricatures have a short life. The passions of one year are forgotten the next. The national convulsions over the Vietnam War that inspired considerable cartooning, often very imaginative, seem not even a conscious memory less than a decade later. Cartoons and caricatures highlight the immediate moment in a way that perhaps no other art form can. They generate an instant response. Certainly for these reasons, at least, they were very popular throughout the first three-quarters of the nineteenth century. Many are easily obtained, and a fine collection is possible. Most collectors use the term "cartoon" to include caricatures as well, and I shall do the same here.

A really fine political cartoon collection should span, approximately, the years from 1750 (or earlier!) to today's creations by Herblock and his contemporaries. Such a collection is obviously impossible for most people because of the scarcity and cost of the material. A more rewarding starting point is the presidency of Andrew Jackson. Literally an explosion of mostly anti-Jackson cartoons resulted from the popularity of the new stone lithographic process and the widespread hostility to many of Jackson's policies. And "Old Hickory" was a marvelous subject for the caricaturist. The cartoons printed in several colors through the 1860s are more desirable, hence more expensive, than those in black and white. Few cartoons were printed in color before the 1860s, but from that period on color cartoons predominate.

Cartoons were sold across the publisher's store counter or hawked in the streets, but many more appeared in publications of the day, particularly in comic weeklies and almanacs such as *Peter Porcupine's Gazette* and *The Tickler.* By the Civil War era cartoons were a common feature of weekly newspapers such as *Frank Leslie's Illustrated Weekly* and *Harper's Weekly,* and later in the century in the pages of *Puck* and *Judge* political cartoons reached their zenith. Collectors should also be alert for foreign cartoons of American subjects. The best known are the strong anti-Lincoln cartoons by Sir John Tenniel (better known as the original illustrator of *Alice in Wonderland*) for the London *Times.* And a few appropriate caricatures from the inimitable pages of *Punch* will enhance any collection, as will a selection of Franklin Roosevelt cartoons by David Low.

But to appreciate the great diversity of themes and styles, collectors must be familiar with those American cartoonists who dominated the art. First is David Claypool Johnston (1798–1865), sometimes referred to as "the American Cruikshank." The fact that he was a well-read man is sometimes reflected in his title quotations drawn from Milton, Shakespeare, Cowper, and Swift. However, he did not take himself too seriously: Many of his cartoons are signed with a pseudonym such as "Hassan Straightshanks," "Gebolidus Crackfardi, M.D.,LLD," and "Busybody." Absolutely necessary in a political paper collection is his bank-note-size caricature of the Radical Democrats (better known as the Locofocos) and their policies. The subjects are Andrew Jackson and the members of his Cabinet (including Martin Van Buren). This scarce caricature note issued in 1837 has an obvious tie-in with "Hard Times" tokens, and is the best of its kind.

Johnston is also responsible for a unique form of caricature. On a two-ply 4- by 2½-inch folder is drawn a color caricature bust with slotted openings at the mouth and eyes (Ill. 81). When a tab at the bottom is pulled, the facial expression changes from a smirk to a grimace. One example from the 1840 campaign pictures a smiling Martin Van Buren with "A Goblet of White House Champagne" below; when the tab is pulled his expression changes to a grimace and the caption then reads "An Ugly Mug of Log Cabin Hard Cider." Another example pictures a rather big-nosed, smirking, low-browed character, "A Locofoco"; the caption "Hurra' for Cass" changes to "What! Old Zack

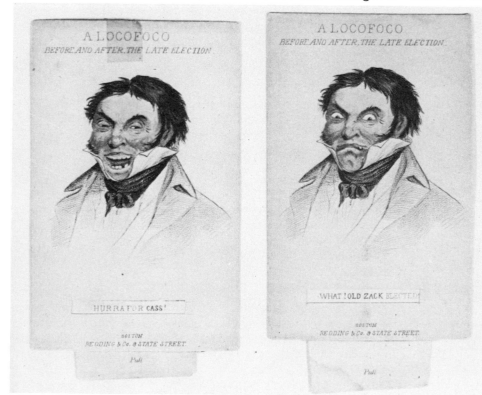

81. One of David Johnston's caricature mechanicals. Pulling or pushing the tab at bottom opens or closes the eyes and mouth.

Elected!" (1848). On an 1856 campaign folder the same character appears but as "A Frémonter Before and After the Presidential Election." Similar folders exist for James Buchanan (1856) and Jefferson Davis (c. 1863).

Other cartoonists in the pre-Civil War era with whom collectors should be familiar are James Akin, Amos Doolittle (best known for his superb propaganda piece "The Boston Massacre"), and William Charles, all of whom flourished in the 1770 to 1820 period, and Elkanah Tinsdale, creator of the immortal Gerrymander. Edward Clay, Johnston's contemporary, who was most prolific from 1836 to 1850, probably enjoyed a wider distribution of his work than did Johnston.

Best of all the great nineteenth-century cartoonists, German-born Thomas Nast stands well above the others, not because he was more imaginative or technically superior (he was not necessarily), but because a) his career encompassed the fall of Fort Sumter in 1861 and the subsequent Civil War as well as the ugly postwar excesses of urbanization and industrialization; b) he flourished at a time when newspaper publishers were "beginning" to use wood pulp, thus ensuring cheaper production costs and wider distribution, and c) he was a fervent patriot of the Union cause, expressing in his cartoons what many northerners passionately believed. Nast was hostile to Irish Catholics; he was a 101 percent American with a consuming hatred of slavery and the Confederacy, and he was an uncritical admirer of Lincoln and Grant. His savage cartoons of Boss Tweed and the Tammany ring were an important factor in their eventual downfall. Nast was the creator of the Democratic donkey and the Republican elephant (Ill. 82). He was a Radical Republican progressive, nationalistic Protestant cartoonist described by one of his biographers as unerringly hostile to whatever he perceived as a threat to the Republic (Keller, 159). Unlike his contemporaries, Nast preferred wood engraving to lithography, and wood engraving is distinguished by its greater variety of shading and the countless fine lines that are not possible with the more common method. Many of his cartoons are florid in style and saturated with sentiment, but his best are emotionally powerful, humorless statements that have never since been matched.

There is perhaps a brief hint of humor, however, in the work of his southern contemporary, the German-born Adalbert Volck. Nast's vitriol was easily matched by Volck, a Baltimore dentist who drew only occasionally and in secret. Some 130 carica-

82. The first appearance of the Republican elephant (1874, above) and the Democratic donkey (1879, at right) as created by Thomas Nast.

tures of Northern personalities and attitudes published in a folio volume entitled *Confederate War Etchings* (1863), a few scattered cartoons, and a brief series satirizing Union General Benjamin Butler, published as *The American Cyclops* in 1868 under the pseudonym Pasquino, make up the bulk of Volck's production. His distinctive style is most noticeable in his judicious use of line; little else was needed, not even captions. His favorite subject was Lincoln (Ill. 83).

As would be expected, Volck cartoons are extremely difficult to locate. Nast's cartoons appeared in the major New York City newspapers of the time, especially in *Frank Leslie's Illustrated Weekly* and *Harper's Weekly,* in either single- or double-page form. Most are easily obtained.

The satirical weekly *Puck* burst (the best word) upon the literary scene in the late 1870s. Much of its humor about country bumpkins, city dudes, drunken Irishmen, rapacious Jews, and illiterate blacks would be considered tasteless and racist today, as would that of its similar contemporary, *Judge.* But, whatever the reasons, *Puck* was an immediate success. Joseph Keppler, its founder and chief cartoonist (like Nast, a frequent user of Shakespearean allusions in his work), was quick to utilize the new photomechanical process of reproducing color drawings. This process permitted lavish use of color relatively cheaply. Nearly every issue of *Puck* carried three large colorful cartoons, one each on the front and back covers and a double-page centerfold. The foibles of politicians and political parties were satirized in elaborate detail. The magazine's

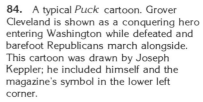

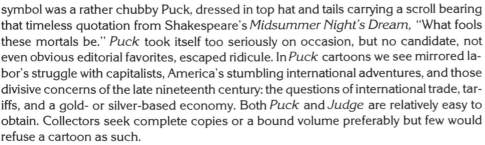

83. One of Volck's caricatures of Lincoln, who is portrayed as a court jester manipulating puppets—his generals and Cabinet members.

84. A typical *Puck* cartoon. Grover Cleveland is shown as a conquering hero entering Washington while defeated and barefoot Republicans march alongside. This cartoon was drawn by Joseph Keppler; he included himself and the magazine's symbol in the lower left corner.

symbol was a rather chubby Puck, dressed in top hat and tails carrying a scroll bearing that timeless quotation from Shakespeare's *Midsummer Night's Dream,* "What fools these mortals be." *Puck* took itself too seriously on occasion, but no candidate, not even obvious editorial favorites, escaped ridicule. In *Puck* cartoons we see mirrored labor's struggle with capitalists, America's stumbling international adventures, and those divisive concerns of the late nineteenth century: the questions of international trade, tariffs, and a gold- or silver-based economy. Both *Puck* and *Judge* are relatively easy to obtain. Collectors seek complete copies or a bound volume preferably but few would refuse a cartoon as such.

The *daily* newspaper cartoon arrived in the early twentieth century. With the need to meet almost immediate deadlines, there simply was not time for the precise delineations that characterized the satirical magazines. Simple pen-and-ink drawings with a minimum of captioning and detail became the standard. But the better cartoonists were not fazed by these limitations. Some who come to mind are Rollin Kirby of the *New York World,* known best for his exemplary creation of Mr. Dry, a stern, humorless satire of Prohibition in frock coat, top hat, and always with a rolled umbrella; Homer Davenport of the *Cleveland Journal,* who invented perhaps the epitome caricature of capitalists (viz, a bloated Mark Hanna in a suit covered with dollar signs trampling the skeleton of labor while standing on a pedestal in Wall Street once occupied by George Washington, whose statue is being hauled away to make room for Hanna); and Gluyas Williams for the old *Life,* portraying Calvin Coolidge on the eve of Herbert Hoover's inauguration, sitting in the White House foyer beside a monumental pile of luggage and a solitary rubber. As servants scurry about, one whispers to another, "Mr. Coolidge refuses point blank to vacate the White House until his other rubber is found."

From more recent decades, collectors should be aware of Miguel Covarrubias's Art Deco style in the pages of *Vanity Fair;* and later, Bill Mauldin for the *St. Louis Post Dispatch*; Conrad, and Gary Trudeau, who broke successfully from the traditional single illustration with his political comic strip "Doonesbury." But, above all the contemporary cartoonists, we must place Herbert R. Block (Herblock), who seems a direct descendant of Thomas Nast in the serious intent of his cartoons and in his capacity for moral outrage. Richard Nixon, shortly after receiving the 1960 Republican party nomination, is reported to have said, "I have to erase the Herblock image." We must also mention David Levine, whose superb and sometimes savage caricatures of politicians, especially the Vietnam War and Watergate principals, have no contemporary equal.

For collectors, then, there is a rich heritage of American political cartooning to investigate. Interestingly enough, earlier cartoons, before the 1870s, are easier to acquire. Once cartoons became almost exclusively a feature of magazines and newspapers, just one master copy was needed for printing. And once wood pulp replaced rag as the basis for newsprint, then later cartoons had even less chance of surviving. Collectors will have to settle for an occasional master copy—i.e., an original black-and-white pen-and-ink drawing. Cartoonists frequently inscribe their creations for friends, or for a charity auction, or for a gallery display; in such ways do modern cartoons come on the market. Occasionally a newspaper will "clean out"; and lucky is the collector who may be on hand when and where that happens. In any case, consider yourself lucky, indeed, to possess an original pen-and-ink cartoon by Thomas Nast. Surely some have survived (Ill. 85).

85. This original Nast cartoon was drawn in 1892. Uncle Sam is shown pinned down by a Republican Congress dawdling over the need to reform tariff laws. Penned on the back in what may be Nast's hand is the inscription: "The White Quadruped on Uncle Sam's hands. We hope the Pan-American visitors will not notice it." Possibly that was Nast's first choice for the inscription.

Advertising Cards and Broadsides

For a brief period, 1880–1920, manufacturers issued—and boys and girls collected—colorful cards of various sizes that advertised a product and were embellished with fairy tales, animal characters, historical personages, famous events, sport heroes, and just about any other motif that might enhance the product's sales potential. Although these trade and advertising cards eventually gave way to cheaper newspaper advertising and radio commercials, they are just as fervently collected today—by adults. Many cards are found loose, but probably just as many, if not more, are found mounted in scrapbooks. Either way, for the political Americana collector the results are worth the search.

All winning and losing candidates, hopefuls, and some minor party candidates as well are found on trade cards in association with some product. Nothing seemed sacred. On one card Grover Cleveland is pictured apparently touting a brewery's special ale; on another card Mrs. Cleveland praises the virtues of a bolt of cloth; on still another, 1892 Republican candidates Benjamin Harrison and Whitelaw Reid, in beautifully toned sepia, bless a particular sewing machine, of all things! The same candidates, and the same color and design, turn up also on a card advertising mincemeat, which is what Democrats Cleveland and Stevenson made of them in that campaign. Some companies preferred the middle of the road—for example, the Wilcox Organ Company, which issued a card picturing 1888 Democratic candidates Cleveland and Thurmond and Republican Harrison and Morton with a red, white, and blue waving flag for a backdrop—an unbeatable combination.

86. A selection of political advertising cards. At upper right is one of the Duke "Presidential Possibilities" set; at the lower right is a Blaine and Cleveland mechanical—a flap picturing Blaine's head lifts up to show Cleveland's head.

86A. One of the rare and immensely popular Honest Long Cut tobacco cards. All 1888 presidential and vice-presidential candidates are pictured in various baseball scenes.

Besides the usual single cards there are various novel cards with some unusual feature; all are considered desirable and many are exceedingly rare. First are the "metamorphics," cards that have a movable part. The best-known example (Ill. 87) pictures the 1876 Democratic candidate, Samuel J. Tilden, with an easily forgettable verse above:

> Come all you true born Democrats,
> You hardy hearts of oak,
> Who know a thing when it is good
> And BLACWELL'S [sic] DURHAM smoke,
> Gaze on this face and you will see
> Your presidential nominee
> The sage and statesman S. J. T.

When the lower flap is lifted a picture of Ulysses Grant is revealed, with an appropriate verse. A Blackwell Durham two-flap card pictures the unlikely combination of George Washington, Chancellor Bismarck of Germany, and 1884 Greenback party candidate

Benjamin Butler. A rather dandified James. G. Blaine and Grover Cleveland are pictured on an 1884 card, which urges the voter to "Take Your Choice of Men But Buy the Mitchell Wagon." A four-flap variety picturing various 1888 hopefuls predicts, correctly, Benjamin Harrison as the people's choice.

Other novel cards were made in sets. There might be as few as two cards or as many as twenty-five. The most common are sets picturing the presidential nominee on one card and his vice-presidential nominee on the other. Most likely to be found are the 1884 candidates, Democrats Cleveland and Hendricks and Republicans Blaine and Logan. Collectors should look particularly for the scarce two-card set (the cards measure 3 by 1½ inches) advertising "Between the Acts" cigarettes and picturing 1880 Democratic candidates Winfield Hancock and William English. One of the most interesting sets consists of twenty-five colorful cards issued by the Duke Tobacco Company; they picture "Presidential Possibilities" for the 1888 campaign. Some of these cards are very difficult to find. This same company issued a sepia-colored set in 1888 featuring the major party candidates as baseball players. On one card Grover Cleveland deftly tags out a sliding Benjamin Harrison, and on another Senator Allan Thurmond strikes a menacing pose at the plate. There are believed to be six cards in this set, but variations of each one are known.

A third novelty is the puzzle card. These are very scarce and seldom appear on the market. The rebus type is particularly rare. The one shown here (Ill. 87) was issued by a Republican newspaper in 1880, but it supported Democrat Winfield S. Hancock! Prob-

87. At upper left in this selection of political advertising cards is an 1880 rebus puzzle supporting Winfield Hancock; below that card is a tonic card picturing Frances Cleveland and a mechanical flap-type card picturing Samuel Tilden and Ulysses Grant. At upper right, Hancock and English are shown on "Between the Acts" cigarette cards, Ben Butler appears on a card advertising a Baltimore saloon, and— below—President and Mrs. Cleveland admire a yard goods manufacturer's products.

88. James A. Garfield is pictured on an unusual palette-shaped card that has an advertisement for the Great Atlantic and Pacific Tea Company on the back.

ably no more than four or five copies of this card are known. Even more ingenious is an extremely rare, colorful twelve-card puzzle set from the 1888 campaign issued by the Victory Tobacco Company. Each card pictures a hopeful, an appropriate verse and scene, and a portion of a human face. When the cards are arranged properly a large picture of Grover Cleveland emerges together with the words "Cleveland's Victory" and the verse:

> On the wings of time comes eighty-eight,
> The year of presidential fever.
> And for "Victory" the candidate
> Applies his presidential lever.
>
> The public called on this man of brains,
> Who arose and thus he spoke:
> "The 'Victory' now before your eyes,
> Is the best on earth to smoke."

I like to think that verse helped contribute to his defeat in 1888.

Much scarcer than most trade cards are advertising broadsides. They were usually printed on cheap newsprint, hence perished easily, and they were printed in far fewer numbers than trade cards. Some were printed in several colors. My favorite is an unusually large and colorful example (23 by 16½ inches) issued by the Nazareth Manufacturing Company (Ill. 89). In the foreground the 1896 campaign hopefuls are

89. The 1896 presidential "hopefuls" are off and running in a fine political advertising broadside that is done in several colors.

racing toward the finish line. McKinley is in the lead. In the background Uncle Sam and John Bull are sparring, Sandow (the strong-man celebrity of the day) is hefting a barbell, the nation's favorite actresses Cissy Fitzgerald and Lillian Russell are crossing foils, and a few European leaders are doing their thing. All are suitably garbed in Nazareth shirtwaists: "When Children Wear the Nazareth Waist They Grow Right and Keep Healthy." Presumably actresses and politicians did too.

More typical of broadsides are those issued by clothiers. Illustration 90 shows president-elect James A. Garfield posing with his sartorially elegant Cabinet. At the far left wearing a fur-trimmed velvet evening coat is James G. Blaine, the unsuccessful Re-

90.   President Garfield poses with his sartorially elegant Cabinet in a clothier's advertisement.

publican candidate in 1884. Standing at far right is Robert Lincoln, President Lincoln's only surviving son, attired in a finely tailored morning suit. A colorful broadside shows candidate Benjamin Harrison steering a horse-drawn threshing machine as a train moves past in the background. This particular piece exists both as a centerfold in a booklet issued by the company and on cardboard backing for counter display.

A number of paper Americana dealers around the country specialize in trade cards, and there are usually one or more dealers at most antique shows and flea markets who offer trade cards or broadsides. If a collector wants to take the time to pick through shoe boxes full of unsorted cards or thumb through foot-high stacks of paper items, the rarities will be found. Unfortunately, there is no published description or value guide to political-advertising artifacts.

Campaign Biographies

The "Man Who . . ." might be a better title for this subject. Or even better, "From Log Cabin to White House." But, either way, it is easy to recognize the fact that the campaign biography is tied more closely to American mythology than any other kind of political artifact. Important parts of that myth are the assumptions that every boy can aspire to become president and that the president is the embodiment of the hopes and aspirations of the American people. Thus, the campaign biography is to the would-be president what a Horatio Alger novel was to the would-be capitalist. An Alger title might also be appropriate: not "Luck and Pluck," although it takes some of both to get to the White House; more likely "Do and Dare." The hero of the campaign biography is always a doer and a darer who, from humble beginnings, has gained the highest reward the nation can offer—and we the people have given him that reward; in him we expect to see what we are and hope to become.

Or at least that was the message that the nineteenth-century authors of these biographies wanted their readers to get. And it was probably romanticism at its worst. But these authors were not striving for literary excellence. They were selling their candidates in the most palatable manner possible. Over the years, and only somewhat modified in the face of twentieth-century pragmatism, a number of ground rules developed for writing campaign biographies. Collectors of political Americana might do well to memorize these rules, for they reveal the assumptions behind the message and the tenor of many kinds of campaign artifacts.

Rule 1: Stress humble beginnings; parents must show initiative; a birth in a log cabin or on a farm is helpful, or in a small frame house in a small town; a small city is permissible in the twentieth century; if the candidate was ever associated with New York City, gloss over that fact.

Rule 2: Play down "too much" education; emphasize yearning for education. If a college graduate, stress athletic achievements rather than classroom performance; if that cannot be done, forget it.

Rule 3: Play down love of power; emphasize keen interest in participating in the democratic process.

Rule 4: Play down business ties, cronies, back room politics; emphasize human interests such as children and pets, wife's community involvement (wife should be a loving helpmate).

Rule 5: Play down specific religious beliefs; emphasize vague positive feelings toward religion in general.

Rule 6: Play down things intellectual; emphasize hard knocks, experience, love of the outdoors.

Rule 7: Emphasize patriotism, particularly if a veteran; if not a veteran, stress home-front contribution.

Rule 8: Emphasize previous leadership; if no examples, stress leadership when elected; but always compare to great leaders of history and/or great previous presidents, particularly Washington, Jefferson, Lincoln, or Franklin Roosevelt.

Rule 9: Emphasize ancestors' association with important historic events; if foreign born, emphasize how hard parents or grandparents worked to become good Americans.

Rule 10: Expand small achievements; recognize but gloss over damaging events.

Rule 11: Ex-generals must be basically men of peace.

Rule 12: Stress favorable nickname, if masculine sounding; invent one, if necessary.

Rule 13: Make the obvious profound and skip the profound altogether; avoid topics that require scholarly analysis.

With these thirteen basic rules, a collector should be able to write his own campaign biography. He will be in good company. Nathaniel Hawthorne wrote one of his Bowdoin College classmate Franklin Pierce; William Dean Howells wrote a campaign biography of Abraham Lincoln and one of Rutherford Hayes; Lew Wallace created a particularly unblushing one of Benjamin Harrison; and Franklin Roosevelt wrote one for his friend Al Smith. Despite the prestige of some of its authors, says one authority, "the campaign biography is generally a hastily and poorly written bundle of paradoxes loosely tied by platitudes . . . [but] it is an American institution" (Hart, 103).

The first campaign biography was probably written by Senator John Henry Eaton in 1817; the latest are probably being planned now for the 1980 hopefuls. Possibly Zachary Taylor was the subject of the most biographies in one campaign (at least seventeen in 1848), but William Henry Harrison and Abraham Lincoln (1860) would be very close behind. Several of the longest biographies go well over five hundred pages, but they are usually padded with speeches and convention proceedings. One of the smallest in size is a 3- by 2-inch booklet in both German and English versions written for Teddy Roosevelt in 1904 (Ill. 91). Some modern biographies are actually comic books. Broadside biographies, usually illustrated with scenes from the hero's life, were issued in the 1840s and 1850s. Campaign newspapers such as *The Log Cabin* (1840) always carried a biography in at least one of the issues. And everybody's standby, almanacs, usually had a few columns about the publisher's favorite candidate. Along with German

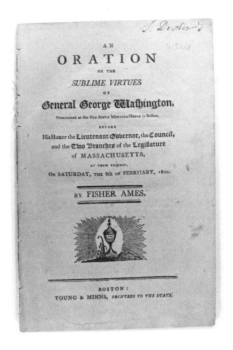

90A. A variation on campaign biographies. Mourning or commemorative orations were a popular form of adulation quite common in the earlier decades of the nineteenth century.

90B. A typical example of a campaign biography issued for German-speaking voters.

91. Typical campaign biographies: The Teddy Roosevelt one measures 3 by 2 inches and is also known in a German text.

and English, campaign biographies have been published in Yiddish and possibly a few other languages as well.

Collectors should also look into anticampaign biographies. These are a feature of most campaigns, but they tend to be more difficult to locate than sympathetic biographies. Probably Horace Greeley, during the 1872 campaign, was the butt of more anticampaign biographies than any other candidate. He had led a long public life, was well read and outspoken, and was prone to wear a white cotton knee-length coat wherever he went. One well-illustrated booklet entitled *The Comic Life of Horace Greeley* opens with a typical paragraph.

> Horace was young at an early period of
> his life, and his father, old Zaccheus,
> used to say of him, that when he was
> subjected to the rod, he was the most
> "promising" child he ever knew;
> although, on account of a very bad
> memory, he was not half so good
> at keeping promises as he was
> at making them.

Another anti-Greeley title is *Wreck-o-lections of a Busy Era.*

A favorite type of anticampaign biography dating from the 1850s was a small booklet usually titled *The Life of John Frémont* (or some other candidate). After the title page, all the other pages were left blank. Usually, however, anticampaign biographies said something even if it was a diatribe such as Davy Crockett wrote against Martin Van Buren in the 1830s. My own favorite is a tiny 1852 booklet, 1½ inches by 1 inch, about "Franky" Pierce, who was "elected to the Senate, looked wise and said not a word," and was later, during the Mexican War, "dangerously wounded in the rim of his hat." A similar booklet exists for Winfield Scott.

For collectors who lean toward book collecting, both kinds of biographies provide an interesting new direction. Despite their ubiquity in their own time, a good many of them are not easy to find today.

Underrated Political Paper

CAMPAIGN POSTERS. These are just now becoming popular with collectors, although finding acceptable storage and display space for them is a problem. Poster art

92. Jugate campaign posters from 1880 through 1908. Three of these posters are especially desirable because they are embellished with an abundance of decorative symbols.

is, of course, a subject in itself, and there are several great collections in America and Europe. With some exceptions, American political posters do not compare favorably artistically with other American poster art. The exceptions: McGovern posters created by Peter Max, several posters for Eugene McCarthy in 1968, and a scattering of posters for Teddy Roosevelt, William McKinley, William Jennings Bryan, and Grover Cleveland. Naturally Lincoln posters are the most desirable and the most expensive; some run into several thousands of dollars each. It would be a challenge to assemble at least one poster for each major party candidate from Abraham Lincoln onward. Possibly the most difficult candidates' posters to locate are those for Charles Evans Hughes (1916), Alton Parker (1904), William Jennings Bryan (especially the 1896 campaign), and Harry Truman (1948). But just about any poster in decent condition from the later nineteenth-century campaigns on would be a treasure to own.

POLITICAL POSTCARDS. Collecting postcards has been a popular American hobby for decades, so in this category political collectors can expect more than the usual amount of competition. Although postcards have been issued since the late

93. The figures cavorting in this unlikely scene bear no resemblance to the 1856 Republican nominee John Frémont or to his wife Jessie Benton Frémont—which adds to the charm of this campaign poster.

UNCLE SAM—MR BRYAN, YOUR ENEMIES ARE MINE ALSO.

95. A 1908 campaign poster showing William Jennings Bryan in his favorite stance—as an enemy of trusts and monopolies.

94. This unusual matched pair of 1884 posters shows Grover Cleveland and James Blaine "angling" for the presidency. Cleveland's small plurality in New York was a major factor in his victory.

96. A 1940 campaign poster for Wendell Willkie. His sudden death in 1943 robbed the Republican party of a potentially influential spokesman for its principles.

97. A selection of campaign postcards. At upper right is a mechanical card; a wheel in back revolves to position portraits and appropriate inscriptions in the hole in front. The Roosevelt card (1912) has attached animal fur; on the 1908 Bryan card beside it the vest, bow tie, and coat are felt. (A similar card pictures Taft.)

1890s, the most desirable political postcards date from 1900 to about 1912; thus, only a few candidates are involved. Collectors will find the many books about postcards and postcard collecting helpful for the necessary background information.

The most popular category of political postcards is the "mechanicals." Such cards have some kind of moving part, perhaps a revolving disk or a coiled-spring elephant or donkey tail or a "seesaw" cardboard strip. Another category includes cards made in whole or in part of some material other than paper—such as leather, bear fur, or fabric. Some cards defy classification: I have in my own collection a leather change purse in the shape of a pair of trousers; one side reads "Teddy's Pants/I Am Sending In Advance a Pair of My Old Pants"; on the other side, "PostCard" with space for the address and a postage stamp. Some cards form a series—e.g., a "Billy B" (Bryan) and "Billy T" (Taft) set from the 1908 campaign. Other cards exist in matched pairs. Collectors should look particularly for the embossed and gilt-trimmed red, white, and blue cards with pictures of major party presidential and vice-presidential nominees in the 1908 campaign. Several different designs are known. Also popular are humorous cards, especially those that ridicule William Jennings Bryan.

Topical cards such as those picturing women's rights, Prohibition subjects, the early Socialist candidates, and the labor "martyrs" are always in demand and often bring higher prices than those picturing major party candidates.

98. A 1908 postcard pictures William J. Bryan, "The Great Commoner," pitching hay, and likens him to Lincoln; in contrast, William Howard Taft is shown wasting his time playing golf with John D. Rockefeller.

98A. An uncommon example of a campaign poster, one showing the party's platform.

CAMPAIGN MUSIC. Perhaps the most striking thing about campaign music is that most songs would be better left unwritten. Much political campaign music is that bad! But the quality of the music as such is not the collector's primary concern. Collectors are attracted to the graphic quality of sheet music, the candidate that a song praises, and the lyrics. No catalogs or other listings of campaign music are available except for a "representative" selection in historical studies. Certainly there are hundreds of songs, most of which were published between 1824 and 1892. Many were written for some candidates and very few for others.

The first actual songs apparently date from the John Adams and Thomas Jefferson campaign in 1800. There were probably well over sixty songs for William Henry Harrison; nearly as many for Henry Clay; perhaps thirty or more for Ulysses S. Grant; a dozen or more honoring Jackson's victory at New Orleans (and later used as campaign songs), including one that is "Respectfully Dedicated to the Fair Sex of America." The songs reflect the musical taste of the day: grand marches, waltzes, and quick steps,

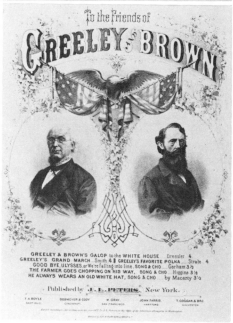

99. Hundreds of examples of campaign sheet music are available for collecting. The two shown here date from the 1856 and 1872 campaigns.

perhaps fewer schottisches, cotillions, and hornpipes in the nineteenth century. Twentieth-century music is barely represented. No rags, no blues; composers preferred familiar tunes. It was safer to put words to such popular favorites as "Old Rosin the Beau" (or Bow), "Old Dan Tucker," "Row, Row, Row Your Boat," "Wait for the Wagon," and "The Battle Cry of Freedom," among many.

Some of the early songs, such as "Fair and Free Elections" (Jefferson, 1800), seem better suited for a large chorus and orchestra; others are better sung by a male quartet—e.g., "A-Smoking His Cigar" (Grant, 1868). Others are a semantic mess, such as an 1876 song, "Roll Along, Shout the Campaign Battle Song," in which the campaign wagon goes to Washington with a "load of Hayes" where it is "Wheeler-ed" around. And some songs see the candidate as the devil himself, as in "King Andrew" (1832):

> [Who] had an itching palm
> To Finger the Nation's Cash . . .

and in "Van Buren" (1840)—

> Who, while but a little boy,
> Was counted crafty, cunning, sly
> Who with the wily fox could vie
>
> Who never did a noble deed,
> Who of the people took no heed,
> But followed worst of Tyrants' creed.

And on for many more verses. Perhaps some student of music and linguistics may be able to interpret the following line of nonsense words, which is part of the chorus in an 1840 piece called "Non-Committal Song": "Snapooter, snapeeter, philantro, kiksheeter, snapoo."

So, for grand themes, try "Jefferson and Liberty" (1800); for noble passions, "Honest Old Abe" (1864); for baser passions, "The Treacherous President" (Tyler, 1844); for a foot stomper, listen to "Ye Jolly Young Lads of Ohio" (Harrison, 1840); for the athlete, "Walking Down to Washington" (Kennedy, 1960); for the hero worshiper, "If He's Good Enough for Lindy, He's Good Enough for Me" (Hoover, 1928); and if you are a standpatter, then "Keep Cool and Keep Coolidge" (1924). I cast my vote for the titles better not written—"Get on the Raft with Taft" (1908); "Hurrah for Hayes and Honest Ways" (1876), and "Row, Row, Row with Roosevelt" (1932). What, then, is the best campaign song? In my opinion, "Happy Days Are Here Again." Interestingly, this piece was not intended to be a campaign song, but the words and music spoke so perfectly for the Democrats' outlook in 1932 that the song became Franklin Roosevelt's campaign theme music in all his succeeding campaigns. It continues to this day as the musical theme whenever Democrats get together.

A collection of sheet music could make a fascinating specialty. Important factors for the collector to consider, in choosing pieces, are rarity, the attractiveness of the cover, the particular candidate, the prestige of the composer (both Stephen Foster and Irving Berlin wrote campaign songs), the condition of the sheet music, and the demand for a particular piece. Modern sheet music will be found loose, but nineteenth-century campaign music will often be found bound in folio volumes with other music of the day. With rare exceptions, sheet music can be purchased for under $50. Early pieces with hand-colored covers may cost more.

100. Campaign "songsters," or songbooks. They are known for most candidates from the 1830s through the 1890s.

Political Paper Sleepers

The pieces that fall into this category have received very little or almost no attention from collectors, and are thus, with a few exceptions, very inexpensive.

ALMANACS.   The importance of almanacs to a political Americana collection is generally not recognized by collectors. Some almanacs were written by local persons concerned with local political issues. Thus, they often contain a fascinating variety of trivia—not easily found elsewhere—such as anecdotal accounts of parades, rallies, and conventions and grass-roots opinions about national candidates and issues. Most political almanacs contain at least one illustration—often located on the title page (the cover)—but a few may have as many as six or more. All such printed and pictorial information can be of considerable help to collectors when they are tracking down or attempting to attribute accounts of obscure events or trying to identify personalities. As a collectible category, almanacs are well worth investigating.

AUTOGRAPHED MATERIAL.   Generally, political collectors show only a mild degree of interest in collecting autographed political material. Occasionally particular items written by George Washington or Abraham Lincoln or an interesting letter penned by another presidential candidate—at the time or later—causes a brief flurry of interest and sells for a high price. But most political collectors simply do not bring the same level of enthusiasm to the subject as do autograph collectors, from whom tough competition for the better items can be expected.

For new collectors of political Americana, autographed material is a subject worth looking into. What does it matter if one cannot afford high-powered examples? There is so much available that is politically informative and sells for well under $100 that no collection need lack representation. Autograph books containing signatures of politicians are particularly interesting conversation pieces. These books are sometimes found

101. A selection of almanacs. The one at upper right is written in German. The almanac at lower left is pictured beside its publisher's prospectus. The almanac picturing Lewis Cass is quite scarce.

102. A superbly illustrated campaign song appeared on the back of the Cass almanac. In the illustration an impaled "same old coon," a cider barrel, and a log cabin—which would be only curiosities of the defunct Whigs once Cass was elected—are shown on their way to "the Chinese Museum" in Philadelphia.

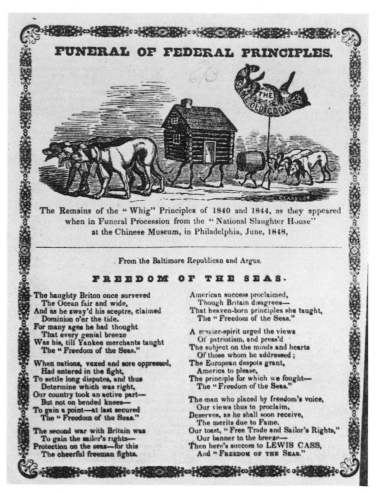

103. Cartes de visite. *Top row:* The Lincoln family in a composite photograph (i.e., there was no actual sitting); Lincoln as he appeared in an Alexander Gardner photograph in February 1861. *Middle row:* A studio photograph of John Wilkes Booth; a composite photograph of Lincoln and Davis. *Bottom row:* George Francis Train as he appeared shortly before his first try for the presidency in 1864; an 1866 Nast caricature of President Johnson.

filled with the signatures of senators and congressmen and, less often, those of a president and his Cabinet and members of the Supreme Court. Most of these books apparently date from the 1850s (and perhaps earlier) through the World War I era. The earliest example I have seen is dated 1858; it contains the signatures of a good many personalities who were to become nationally prominent and remembered to posterity for their roles in the Civil War and Reconstruction. Possibly these books were put together by the children of Washington politicians and other officials or by other persons who had considerable degree of access to public figures. Since these books usually contain the signatures of a future president or two and the current president, they can bring fairly high prices when they appear on the market.

Collecting political autographs is risky business for beginners who have not explored the subject. Forgeries, proxy and machine signatures, and facsimiles are dangers one has to be able to recognize. As a start, we recommend Charles Hamilton's *Collecting Autographs and Manuscripts,* second edition. The best sources of political autograph material are dealers whose advertisements appear in national publications concerned with antiques in general; Sotheby Parke-Bernet Galleries in New York City, which publishes several auction catalogs annually on the subject; and the Mail Americana Auction, which includes autographed material in its monthly catalogs (see Appendix).

Ballots. Old ballots range in size from a few inches square to as large as a single newspaper sheet. The larger ones were quite common through the 1930s, until they were replaced by voting machines. The more interesting ones illustrate the various party symbols. Ballots can be an important reference, since the names of local candidates are also listed.

Cartes de visite.   These small cards, usually sepia in color but occasionally black, with photographs of celebrities of the day were produced by many prominent photographers (Ill. 103). They were popular from 1860 to about 1885. Assembling a collection of Lincoln photos in this size would be a real challenge. However, it is necessary to beware of later copies, and so some knowledge of American photographic history is helpful.

Convention material.   This includes proceedings, tickets, posters, programs, buttons, and the like from both the state and national levels.

Inaugural material.   Included here are invitations to the various entertainments and swearing-in ceremonies, the special District of Columbia one-week-only license plates, programs, parade-related pieces, and so on. (Some inauguration material can be very expensive.)

Newspapers.   Although highly important as source material, campaign newspapers have not been appreciated by the majority of collectors (Ills. 104 and 106). Most campaign newspapers were, obviously, short-lived, many existing for less than a year. Several were printed for William Henry Harrison; the best known of these is *The Log*

104.   Two early campaign newspapers. Note the tie-in with state candidates on the 1840 newspaper *(bottom)*.

Cabin. The Young Hickory for James Polk is quite scarce; but even scarcer is Victoria Woodhull's *Woodhull & Claflin's Weekly,* a key newspaper for collectors of women's rights material. A campaign newspaper was a major item in the budgets of third parties well into this century.

Nineteenth-century examples usually consisted of four pages. Many carried an elaborately designed masthead that illustrated such campaign subjects or themes as a log cabin, or General Taylor on the battlefield, or portraits of a party's presidential and vice-presidential nominees. A particular issue may have contained one or more woodcuts picturing a candidate or some stirring scene associated with his career and perhaps a campaign song or two. Of particular interest to collectors are the occasional advertisements offering campaign medalets and other lapel pieces for sale. Standard features in these newspapers included biographies of candidates, news of campaign activities, and criticism of the opponents. The earlier newspapers ranged from about 9 by 6 inches in size to 12 by 18 inches; newspapers used in late nineteenth-century and early twentieth-century campaigns are usually the size of modern newspapers.

105. Campaign tickets. Lincoln and Johnson issues are especially valued by collectors. The Prohibition party ticket shown here was used in Rhode Island and the Greeley ticket in New Hampshire.

Pictorial envelopes.   These date from the late 1850s. As patriotic envelopes they became an important propaganda device during the Civil War. This category constitutes a hobby in itself, in that perhaps 15,000 different envelopes are known, including a few issued by Southern sources. Related political envelopes are known for each campaign from 1856 through 1896; most, however, date from the 1860, 1864, and 1868 campaigns. Envelopes from the 1860 campaign are the most desired; examples in good condition may be priced up to $50. Whether or not the envelope is postally cancelled makes no difference to the political collector.

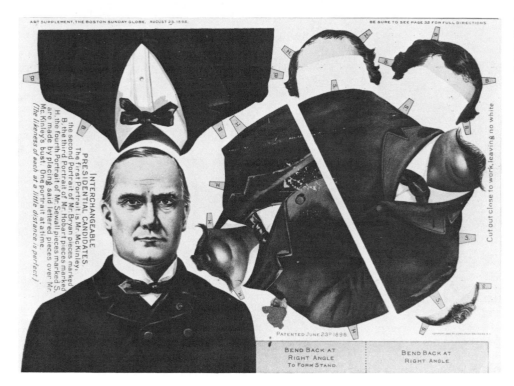

106.   When cut and folded properly, this 1896 newspaper supplement would reveal the likenesses of all four Democratic and Republican presidential and vice-presidential candidates.

TICKETS.   These are single-sheet leaflets, up to about 4 by 9 inches, that list the names of national, state, or local candidates for office (Ill. 105). A few tickets carry the names of the candidates for all three levels. During much of the nineteenth century—at least from 1824 on—tickets were distributed at polling sites to remind voters of the candidates' names. Sometimes a ticket was, in fact, used as a ballot: A voter signed his name to it, as evidence that he had voted, and gave it to the poll official.

Many tickets are fine example of printing and of the styles of design popular in their period. Those picturing a party's national candidates and/or having elaborate decoration are most in demand, but some collectors also seek tickets from state and local elections in order to have a more rounded representation. Third-party tickets are popular with collectors too, as are certain tickets distributed apparently only in California in the 1860-1872 period, which picture candidates on the front and have a historical scene or slogan on the back. Some of these California tickets were printed in two or three colors, a fact that adds to their value. Another ticket of interest to collectors is one listing Jefferson Davis for President of the Confederacy, along with the candidates for office in the various Southern states. These tickets are found frequently bearing voters' signatures; examples from Virginia seem to be the most numerous. Most political tickets sell for far under $75; a few sell for more than that amount.

106A.   A selection of recent campaign posters.

106B.   A fine example of a limited edition poster sold by Fairfield, Connecticut Republicans to raise campaign funds.

5
Political Numismatics

IN MY OPINION, medallic art is the highest aesthetic form to be found in political Americana. Numismatists have long appreciated the subtle tones and shades that enhance silver coinage and mellow copper and bronze, as well as the evident craftsmanship that can make medallic art a genuine creative expression. But more to the point is the fact that this category is one of the most underrated by political collectors—fortunately for political numismatists, there is not a great demand, inaugural medallions excepted. Very fine and often rare pieces can be acquired at reasonable prices. But a warning to anyone considering building a collection: Political numismatics is a highly complex subject; prices fluctuate widely; the condition of a piece is always important; and reproductions of various pieces are known to exist. Become familiar with the literature, the specialized vocabulary, and sale and auction prices.

Numismatics, of course, is one of the world's oldest and most popular hobbies. Political pieces were frequently an important part of some of the great nineteenth-century American numismatic collections. In fact, the first authoritative cataloging of Lincoln campaign pieces was published only a few years after his death. Modern collectors are as much attracted to political numismatics as their predecessors were because of the often sophisticated designs, the abundance of allegorical subjects and themes, the consistently high technical quality, and, in some primitive pieces, the rather charming naïveté of design and subject.

Political numismatists arbitrarily define as medalets pieces under 1¾ inches in diameter, and as medals, pieces with larger diameters. Occasionally pieces with diameters of 3 inches or more are called medallions. Because most political medallic issues are under 1¾ inches in diameter, they are referred to here as medalets. Some collectors use the term "medal" interchangeably with "medalet" and "medallion," but this practice causes unnecessary confusion. I use "tokens" to describe issues—the Hard Times issues, in particular—whose designs approximate copper pennies of the day. A few Lincoln and McClellan issues actually were used, along with hundreds of other designs, as substitutes for money during the Civil War, and so they are the only political medallic issues that can rightfully be called political tokens.

Throughout much of the nineteenth century political medallic pieces were often more popular with voters than the earlier two-piece buttons. Medallic issues held their

106C. This first medallic likeness of George Washington was struck by Jacques Manly of Philadelphia in 1789.

own with ferrotypes, but finally succumbed to the new and more cheaply produced celluloid campaign pinback (button) at the turn of the century. Many medallic pieces are found holed near the upper rim for suspension from the lapel. In no way does this affect the value or appeal of a piece to collectors. Some medallic pieces are well worn, evidence of their use as pocket pieces; occasionally, there will be tiny rim nicks, especially on white metal pieces. These indicate that test cuts were made by some collector attempting to distinguish white metal from silver.

Political numismatics is a wide-open field that offers considerable challenge to collectors. Among the more interesting types are nineteenth- and twentieth-century issues, inaugural medallions, and the satirical pieces, with their rich tradition.

Nineteenth-Century Medalets

106D. Refer to text at right.

Many nineteenth-century pieces are graphically superior to most twentieth-century issues. Numerous earlier designs bring unity to what is often a quite complicated arrangement of drums, flags, cannon, sun rays, spread eagles, symbols of commerce and agriculture, and perhaps a sailing ship or two. Some of the more desirable issues depict the candidate on the obverse (front) and an allegorical scene on the reverse (back). Other reverses have a stirring slogan such as "The Flag We Wear at Our Masthead Should be the Credentials of Our Seamen" (Henry Clay, 1844); or a direct appeal, "The Union One and Indivisable [sic], Buchanan, The Crisis Demands His Election" (1856); or the pietistic, "A Halo Shines as Bright as Day Around the Head of Henry Clay" (1844). One rather earthy 1864 anti-McClellan issue (struck in leather!) carries the slogan "The Great American Hesitator, Themor Ucri Theles U.P."

Nor is humor lacking, as is evident on two examples issued during the 1892 campaign. The Republican platform in that year echoed what was becoming a standard party economic stance—tariff protection for American industry and opposition to foreign imports at noncompetitive prices. (That stance is the dominant theme also in other Republican campaign artifacts of this period; it is especially evident in the "red" bandannas discussed in Chapter 6.) A Benjamin Harrison issue in tin states this familiar "protection and prosperity" theme in words aimed at "gullible" Democrats, who, Republicans said, were being misled by British economic policies: "Protection's Banner Guards Our Land from England's Greed and Pauper Pay/and When I Play Great Britain's Hand/Please Take Me for a Blooming Jay." Jay was an 1890s synonym for a naïve person. But Democrats seemed to take matters more casually in 1892, as an inscription on the reverse of a medalet touting Grover Cleveland suggests: "Grover, Crover/Four Years More of Grover/In We Go, Out They Go/And Then We'll Be in Clover."

A sentiment far more lofty than the usual slogan associated with Cleveland appears on his 1888 and 1892 issues: "A Public Office Is a Public Trust."

EARLIER ISSUES. Although a few large copper and pewter pieces, all very scarce, are known that commemorate the election to office of John Adams and Thomas Jefferson, the first widespread use of medalets dates from the 1824 campaign (Ill. 107). In that year supporters of Andrew Jackson wore small brass lapel pieces bearing his bust on the obverse and such slogans as "The Hero of New Orleans" or "The Nation's Pride" on the reverse. A virtual outpouring of medalets occurred in 1840. Over eighty designs are known in the usual metals, with most bearing a bust of the Whig candidate William Henry Harrison on the obverse and a log cabin on the reverse. As mentioned in the first chapter, the 1840 Log Cabin campaign was the first in which voters were deluged with an enormous variety of campaign devices and a great deal of hoopla. Most 1840 medalets, as a result, are among the easiest to locate; and if one also succeeds in finding the elusive pieces, the 1840 medalets make a very fine collecting specialty.

The most difficult to locate political medalets of any candidate in the pre-Civil War era are those issued for the 1848 Democratic nominee Lewis Cass. Only six designs are known, all of which are rare. Only five medalets are known for the 1852 Democratic nominee Franklin Pierce, but one or two of them appear quite often on the market. Among the more interesting medalets are several from the 1856 campaign. James Buchanan's name is easily spelled in a rebus puzzle; the obverse depicts a buck jumping over a cannon. This piece, along with a Buchanan issue displaying a spread eagle, the sun's rays, and the names of the thirty-one states, is considered by collectors to be one of the great classic issues.

107. These examples are typical of medalets issued before the Civil War: At top, second column, an 1856 issue says "Buchanan" in a rebus; in the third column, Henry Clay is shown standing by the flag on the obverse, and the reverse (fourth column) carries a Know-Nothing inscription; at bottom right, the reverse of a Martin Van Buren medalet glorifies the farmer. Most of these medalets exist in several metals.

MEDALETS OF ABRAHAM LINCOLN.   Several classic pieces are also associated with both of Abraham Lincoln's campaigns (Ill. 108). Because of his importance in American political history, pieces associated with him deserve special attention. Among the approximately 155 medalets issued for both campaigns is a small group of seven that were distributed in 1860. Some of the obverse busts are different, but on the reverse of each is a scene recalling the young Lincoln's brief career as a rail-splitter. Each of these medalets is heavy with allusions. On one reverse Lincoln swings a maul; in the background is a rising sun, a log cabin, and the White House—one of the most interesting "common man" designs of the era. On another reverse, a kneeling figure holds a wedge while Lincoln swings his maul. Whom this figure was intended to portray remains a mystery. Some authorities suggest Stephen Douglas, whom Lincoln defeated that year; others suggest John Hanks, Lincoln's cousin, who had split rails with him in their youth. A trivial matter, perhaps, but not to the political numismatist. Diesinkers and engravers seemed to take as much pleasure as photographers in working with Lincoln's features. All the many 1860 busts appear to have in common is an exaggerated shock of hair and a rather pronounced jawline. And despite his four years in office, the 1864 busts show similarly wide differences, but now with the addition of a beard. Building a good Lincoln political numismatic collection is possible if one is infinitely patient. Some of the rarer pieces are quite possibly unique or may exist in only a very few copies. Because of his enduring popularity, Lincoln pieces are always in demand; thus prices tend to be higher than for other candidates' medalets.

LATER ISSUES.   Pieces issued during the last quarter of the nineteenth century frequently show considerable imagination in the use of themes, especially if the candidate was a rather colorful figure (Ill. 109). This is particularly true of the 1872 Democratic nominee Horace Greeley, journalist, keeper of the nation's conscience, and espouser of causes whose time was still in the future. On the reverse of one Greeley medalet is a scroll and olive branch, symbolic of his profession and of his intent to reunite North and South if he was elected. On another reverse are the phrases "universal amnesty" and "impartial suffrage," indicating his desire to pardon all Confederate veterans and extend the vote to women and freed men. On various U.S. Grant reverses appears part of the famous quotation he penned in 1864 shortly after the battle of Spottsylvania, "I Intend to Fight It Out on This Line If It Takes All Summer."

108.   A sampling of Lincoln medalets from his 1860 and 1864 campaigns. Note the use of the rail-splitter theme on several reverses. The medalet at bottom center picturing Lincoln and Andrew Johnson is rated very highly by collectors. At lower right is a Hartford Wide-Awake medalet depicting members in torchlight parade regalia. Most of these medalets exist in several metals.

Significant episodes in the candidate's life are recalled on various reverses. An 1880 piece depicts James Garfield as a canal boy—i.e., the boy who rode or drove the mules that towed the barges; Winfield Scott Hancock's leadership as a general in the 2nd Army Corps is symbolized with a clover on another 1880 piece.

On several medalets great events of national importance appear in conjunction with a candidate. The 1876 centennial celebration is linked with the campaigns of Rutherford Hayes and Samuel Tilden. Benjamin Harrison's inauguration in 1889 also marked the centennial of Washington's first inauguration. Hence the first president's appearance on some issues. Collectors should not, by the way, confuse some 1888 and 1892 Benjamin Harrison medalets depicting a log cabin with 1840 medalets issued for the candidacy of his grandfather, William Henry Harrison. Among the most interesting reverses in this period are several from the 1892 campaign depicting the arrival of Columbus in the New World in 1492, an event duly celebrated during this campaign year. Interestingly enough, these medalets and a few others from the 1892 campaign were issued in aluminum, a new alloy just beginning to appear in American industry.

109. A selection of medalets issued in campaigns from the 1860s through the 1880s. The reverse of the McClellan medalet at top, second column, pictures the American eagle subduing the snake of rebellion. Reverses of the Grant medalets quote two popular statements he made during the Civil War. Note the "towboy" reverse of the Garfield issue and the army corps insignia on the reverse of the Hancock medalet. The reverse of the Blaine medalet at lower right depicts him as "The Plumed Knight." All these medalets exist in different metals.

Twentieth-Century Medalets

Perhaps the most noticeable aspect of political issues in this century is that there are so few of them—and mostly of such poor quality. Certainly, the popularity among voters of the new celluloid campaign buttons and their comparatively lower production costs were factors. Aluminum is also much cheaper to produce than copper and silver, but unfortunately it cannot accommodate the rich quality of design and relief that is possible with those metals. It is much more difficult to assemble an aesthetically appealing group of modern issues (Ill. 110).

Medalets issued during the 1896, 1900, and 1904 campaigns mark the end of the great nineteenth-century tradition in political numismatics. Most of these issues are beautifully engraved; the copper ones have rich, reddish brown tones that make them a pleasure to collect.

A few brass pieces, fairly unimaginative in design and theme, were issued between 1908 and 1928. Some were made with a loop, to wear suspended from a watch chain. A few exist in "pairs"—i.e., the same design on the obverse and reverse, but each with the appropriate bust and wording. Some brass issues are gilded, and gilding wears off fairly easily. In my opinion the only interesting piece issued during this period is a 1908 brass medalet with a bust of Taft and the wording "I'll Toss You" on one side; on the other is a bust of Bryan with the wording "I'll Match You."

Slightly better-designed brass and nickel medalets, or "prosperity tokens," were issued during Franklin Roosevelt's 1932 and 1936 campaigns. A pair in brass and nickel was issued for the 1960 campaign, but the facing busts of the candidates are so poorly done that they are unintentionally caricatures. One unusual design issued in the same campaign is a 33mm copper uniface (blank reverse) reproduction of the famous "Washington Born Virginia" medalet (Baker No. 60). To the left of Washington's bust in a semicircular channel is the surname of one of the Republican or Democrat hopefuls; to the right is the year "1960." In 1968 the Medallic Art Company issued a handsomely designed matched bronze pair portraying Hubert Humphrey and Richard Nixon with their respective running mates.

110. A few modern medalets. *Top:* Medallic Art Company's paired set from the 1968 campaign; *center:* A 1964 goldine medalet picturing Barry Goldwater; *bottom:* The well-executed Ford and Dole medalet issued by a Connecticut company in 1976.

During the 1950s there appeared on the market a gold-colored aluminum called goldine. It is very cheap to produce, and pieces in this material were generally distributed by the tens of thousands. The 1964 campaign between Lyndon Johnson and Barry Goldwater generated several varieties, as did the various campaigns run by George Wallace, who used them as a fund-raising device. Several aluminum and goldine designs were also issued in the 1968 and 1972 campaigns.

With a single outstanding exception, mediocrity was the rule in the 1976 campaign also. The exception, reminiscent of nineteenth-century quality, is a handsomely designed 38mm nickel-silver issue supporting Gerald Ford's candidacy. This issue, produced by the powder metallurgy process, shows Ford and his running mate Robert Dole in profile on the obverse. On the reverse are depicted various occupations and the inscription "With a Job a Person Has a Chance."

Inaugural Issues

111. Recent inaugural medallions. The Eisenhower issue was struck for his 1953 inauguration, and the Nixon issue marks his 1973 inauguration. Silver varieties are pictured here, but these issues also exist in bronze.

Mediocrity, however, has not been the rule with inaugural issues. Although not of uniformly superior quality in design and appearance, their general excellence and, most important, the scarcity of medals issued prior to 1950 make them extremely attractive to collectors (Ill. 111). They have been, in fact, the single "hottest" medallic presidential Americana item in recent years. The prices range from $30 or less for modern bronze issues to $1,200 or more for the 1929 bronze Hoover, 1933 bronze Roosevelt, and the 1953 silver Eisenhower; $4,500 for the 1917 Wilson; $5,500 + for the 1904 Tiffany Roosevelt; and $15,000 for a gold 1909 Taft issue.

Those prices are reasonable. Since the medals were not originally intended for dis-

tribution to the public, but only for circulation among inaugural committee members and other selected party members, the pre-1950 production seldom exceeded three thousand bronze pieces and often was far lower—seventy-five pieces, for example, for the 1924 Coolidge issue. The custom was to strike two or three gold ones for presentation to the new president and vice-president and perhaps the chairman of the inaugural medal committee. Few silver pieces were struck until the 1953 and 1957 Eisenhower issues.

Medals commissioned by an inaugural medal committee were first issued in 1896, although those issued by private individuals and the United States Mint date back to the earliest inaugurations. All these medals are eminently collectible, but here we will be concerned only with the medals (so-called "official" issues) sanctioned by the national party organization with the president-elect's approval. A subcommittee of the inauguration committee oversaw submission of sculptor's designs, the final choice, its production, and its distribution. A profit was not necessarily expected from the earlier issues, although one did result occasionally. Often the nation's top sculptors submitted designs. Augustus Saint-Gaudens, better known numismatically for his magnificent reverses on the eagle and double eagle gold pieces of the period, was selected at Theodore Roosevelt's urging to commemorate the 1905 inauguration. (There are two official issues for this inauguration.) On this medal, known as the Tiffany Roosevelt (because the famous New York firm handled the production), the ebullient Teddy is portrayed as a rather stiff-necked Prussian Junker. Although not one of Saint-Gaudens's better efforts, this medal is considered the most desirable in the entire series because of its very low mintage and the artistic status of its creator.

In my opinion, however, the medal designed by the sculptor Paul Manship to commemorate Franklin Roosevelt's first inauguration in 1933 is superior to all other designs. The high-relief bust of FDR is the result of twelve strikings. The reverse is a design chosen by Roosevelt himself: Surrounding a slightly stylized version of the U.S.S. *Constitution*, "Old Ironsides," are the familiar lines from Longfellow's poem, "The Building of the Ship": "Thou to sail on/O Ship of State/Sail on O Union strong and great." Manship also created the superior 1945 issue (and the 1941). For Roosevelt's fourth inauguration, he used a reverse similar to that on the 1933 issue, but the bust of Roosevelt cannot conceal the fatigue and illness of the president in the last year of his life.

The medals issued for subsequent inaugurations are generally bland in conception and theme. Most reverses portray the conventional presidential eagle or the new president's name within a wreath or inscription. The 1965 medal commemorating Lyndon Johnson's inauguration is perhaps the only imaginative issue struck in the 1950s and 1960s. The 1977 one depicting Jimmy Carter is similarly bland and uninspiring.

To commemorate Harry Truman's inauguration in 1949, the inaugural committee issued 7,500 bronze pieces, mostly for sale to the public; in 1953 they issued 25,685 pieces; in 1957, there was a slight drop to 21,705 bronze pieces. Over 1,000 silver pieces were issued to commemorate John Kennedy's inauguration in 1961. By that year inaugural medals had become a major source of income to the inaugural committee. In 1969 over 79,000 bronze and 15,000 silver medals in different finishes and diameters were struck to commemorate Richard Nixon's first inauguration. Well over 100,000 bronze and 23,000 silver medals were struck for his second inauguration in 1973. The figures are similar for Jimmy Carter's inauguration in 1977.

An ad hoc inaugural medal committee successfully marketed a medal commemorating Gerald Ford's ersatz inauguration in 1973. Not to be outdone, a vice-presidential inaugural medal committee was formed to commission an issue commemorating Nelson Rockefeller's elevation to that office. The result, by sculptor Frank Eliscu, was a pleasant surprise. A contrasting smooth and rough textured surface dominates both sides, thereby adding considerable character to the bust and to the defiant, perched eagle on the reverse.

111A. Collecting this set of medals marking Franklin Roosevelt's four inaugurations is a numismatic challenge.

Obviously, collectors will need luck, patience, and money to assemble an inaugural medal collection. New collectors should not confuse these medals with the United States Mint's Presidential Series, usually issued in an unlimited amount since 1865 for each inauguration, and available for a few dollars. Rather than attempt a complicated explanation of these, I urge would-be collectors to read the various studies by Julian, Dusterberg, and MacNeil; all are well illustrated.

Satirical Issues

Certainly one of the most interesting ways to appreciate the scope and sometimes the silliness of presidential campaign history is through the study of the many political satirical pieces issued from about 1796 to the present. Few of these are truly scarce, and most are of immense historical interest (Ill. 112).

THE PAINE MEDALETS. Historical interest is immediately apparent in these copper medalets. They were known in Great Britain, their country of origin, as Condor tokens (after the first authority to classify them). A few varieties began to appear in this country in the late 1790s. At that time there was considerable hostility between supporters of President John Adams and Vice-President Thomas Jefferson (the first and only time, by the way, that the two opposing parties were represented in the chief executive positions of the government) over how the United States should treat the new republic of France in her war with Great Britain. At the same time Thomas Paine, the great Revolutionary War polemicist, was a Jacobin refugee in France and the target of English Royalist gibes. Because Paine aroused equally strong feelings in this country, a few varieties of the British medalets were imported into the United States, for whatever political effect they might have.

Although most Paine medalets allude to British political events, as can be noted, several of the themes are perhaps universal in their implication. On a number of the medalets Paine is shown hanging from a gallows; on one reverse is the inscription "The Wrongs of Man . . ."; on another, "May the Knave [i.e., Paine] of Jacobin Clubs Never Get a Trick." Still another piece shows Paine's head mounted on a pole with figures dancing around; the reverse bears the inscription "Cain and Abel: The Beginning of Oppression." A favorable Paine medalet has on its obverse a pig standing on a crown, a scepter and shield, and the inscription "Pigs' Meat . . ." above. The reverse reads

112. Early political and satirical tokens. *Top row:* "Hard Times" issues depicting Andrew Jackson in different guises as the enemy of private banks. *Middle row, from left:* The obverse of this 1793 Paine medalet shows him hanging from a gallows, and the reverse mistitles his *Rights of Man* as the *Wrongs of Man.* The ship of state is depicted sailing smartly with Daniel Webster at the helm, but under Martin Van Buren it flounders. The antislavery token "Am I Not a Woman & a Sister?" *Bottom row:* Along with hundreds of other varieties, these Lincoln and McClellan tokens served as pennies for a brief period during the Civil War.

"Noted Advocates for the Rights of Man/Thos. Spence, Sir Thos. More, Thos. Paine." But the same inscription appears on the reverse of a medalet whose obverse shows three figures hanging from a gallows. On another piece the devil and a monkey dance while "Pain [sic] swings . . ."

Most pieces are of technologically superior quality; probably all are of copper, and—as would be expected—they are quite scarce, at least in this country. For the ambitious collector, therefore, assembling a Paine medalet group would be quite an achievement.

HARD TIMES TOKENS. These pieces, found usually in copper, were issued during the congressional elections of 1834 and 1838 (Ill. 112). One of the major controversies of the early 1830s was President Andrew Jackson's feud with the United States Bank. It was in these years, too, that the Whig party was formed. Pieces issued during the 1834 congressional election are dominated by themes critical of Jackson, often coarse as well as laudatory—rarely of Jackson but more frequently of New York City and state politicians and events. Some pieces nearly pillory Jackson: On one obverse, a fat hog (of corruption) represents the end of credit and commerce, and on the reverse Jackson is portrayed as destroying the nation's economy in order to enhance his own vanity; on another he is shown raiding the nation's treasury. Favorable tokens describe him as a hero who has deserved his reelection (in 1832).

112A. There are those today who may think that White had a good point.

The Whigs' major stronghold was New York City. William H. Seward, who would be better known to posterity as Lincoln's secretary of state, was their candidate for governor. Some pieces praise his virtues; others extol the healthy state of the nation under Whig leadership.

Martin Van Buren won the presidency in 1836. As happened to Herbert Hoover a century later, Van Buren too became the unfortunate scapegoat of a depression. The panic of 1837 and proposals for ending it caused a storm of ridicule from the Whigs (and helped cost him the 1840 election). Pieces issued during the 1838 congressional election show Van Buren's ship of state floundering—but sailing majestically under Daniel Webster's proposals; he was the leading Whig spokesman of the day. One fine satirical piece shows a very ugly head of Liberty with her headband inscribed "Locofoco," a blunt Whig gibe at radical New York Democrats, so-named because they had used the newly invented sulfur, or locofoco, matches to illuminate one of their meetings at Tammany Hall after a bit of Whig skullduggery.

112B. These late 19th century examples are typical of the many fine Washington pieces issued throughout our nation's history. Those pictured here were issued in the later decades of the 19th century.

Among their other beliefs, the Locofocos stood for equality of human rights. We are reminded that abolitionist sentiment was beginning to affect the conscience of many northerners with the issuing of two antislavery medalets. These pieces are both absolutely essential to a black history collection. One portrays a chained, kneeling female slave surrounded by the inscription "Am I Not a Woman and a Sister?" The companion piece, which is rare, portrays a male slave in a similar position and with a similar inscription. These antislavery medalets are not satirical pieces, of course, but like satirical pieces of the same period they call attention to a serious national concern. Collectors should not confuse these antislavery issues with very similar British pieces. The obverses are the same but the American reverses have only a wreath and the inscription "United States of America/Liberty/1838"; the British reverses show different designs.

Most Hard Times designs in copper are easily collected. Some tokens were made of brass, and these are fairly difficult to obtain. The few tokens known in silver and pewter are extremely rare. Hard Times issues have been popular with token and medal collectors for years; hence they have been cataloged extensively and can be found in the stock of many dealers in numismatic material.

THE AARON WHITE ISSUE. One of the few pieces that does not fit conveniently into our categories is the clever late-1850s issue by the Connecticut lawyer and iconoclast Aaron White. This piece, inscribed in four languages, publicized White's belief that the

United States government would sooner or later go bankrupt because of its reliance upon paper currency. The obverse shows a sow hanging from a hook and has the inscription "Sus Pendens/Never Keep a Paper Dollar/1837–1857." The reverse shows a fat sow rooting in a money bag and is inscribed "Sus Tollens/Deux Sous/Di Oboli/In Your Pocket Till Tomorrow." The White token is known in brass and copper.

BRYAN MONEY (OR "DOLLARS").   Of all the political satirical pieces, this one is the most extensive (Ill. 113). William Jennings Bryan won the nomination of the Democratic party in 1896, partly on the strength of his vehement opposition to the gold standard. He argued that the nation's monetary standard should be based upon a ratio of sixteen parts silver to one part gold. Republican opposition was derisory, especially as expressed through the nearly 150 varieties of Bryan money. To modern Americans it seems an overblown argument, and it all became academic when Franklin Roosevelt took the country off the gold standard in 1933.

113.   Examples of Bryan money. At the left is a cast-iron piece, 3¼ inches in diameter, designed like a 50¢ piece of the period. At upper right is a silver cartwheel design. (Most varieties are found heavily tarnished.) At lower right is an aluminum medalet picturing a donkey-goose, a characterization of Democrats who advocated a silver-based monetary system.

Despite their name, these pieces are actually anti-Bryan—a very few support his position; hence they are satirical references to the Republicans' position. Bryan money exists in base or type metal, cast iron, aluminum, lead, and silver, and ranges in diameter from 1 to 4 inches. Many pieces are technologically crude. Most of them portray on the obverse the same profile of Liberty that appeared on the regular coinage of the day; the reverses show a spread eagle. The combination of a cheap metal and an exaggerated diameter was intended to demonstrate what would happen to our coinage if Bryan were elected president: It would be debased and inflated. The reverses of these varieties frequently are inscribed "NIT (Not in Trust)/16–1," or "In God We Trust/With Bryan We Bust," or "In God We Trust for the Other 47 Cents."

Exceptions to those rather unimaginative designs are the sterling or coin silver ones issued by various jewelry firms. On the obverse of a typical issue are a cartwheel (historically, the common name of an American silver dollar) and the inscription "This [Size] of Government Dollar Contains 412½ Grains of Silver 900/1000 Fine"; on the reverse is the added inscription "This Piece Contains 823 Grains Coin Silver 900/1000 Fine/In Value the Equivalent of One Gold Dollar/September 16, 1896/Spaulding and Company/Goldsmiths and Silversmiths."

113A.   The decidedly grotesque image of Bryan adds to the appeal of this cast aluminum and fairly scarce example of Bryan money.

Some varieties show considerable humor. An aluminum piece displays on one side a figure with the body of a goose and the head of a donkey and the inscription "United Snakes of America/In Bryan We Trust." The reverse reads "Free Silver/One Dam/1896." The only mechanical Bryan money is a riveted two-piece type made of brass. On the obverse is a spread eagle and the inscription "I'm All Right"; the reverse reads "Sound Money/Means a Dollar Is Worth 100 Cents/McKinley, Hobart and Prosperity." When a loop at the top is moved, the eagle's head droops and the inscription "Where Am I At?" is revealed. The reverse now reads "Free Silver/Means a Dollar Is Worth 50 Cents/Bryan, Sewall and Adversity." A 1900 version of this design has different wording. A large base metal variety caricatures Bryan as a country bumpkin without a glimmer of intelligence.

Perhaps no more than a half-dozen or so pro-Bryan pieces were issued. The only interesting one is a 1908 brass piece depicting Mark Hanna (McKinley's astute campaign manager and a frequent target of Democrats' barbs) holding money bags and attired in a suit with a dollar-sign pattern. The surrounding inscription reads "Trade Mark Hanna/In Hanna We Trust/Gold Issue/ 1900." The reverse shows a prone Republican elephant with a protruding arrow reading "Imperialism."

Assembling a Bryan money collection would be difficult. I know of a few nearly complete collections, but some of the pieces listed and illustrated in Farran Zerbe's study (the major reference) are very elusive and perhaps only a few examples exist. One cause for the scarcity of some Liberty head designs was the rather ambiguous policy of the United States Treasury Department toward Bryan money. Because some of it did resemble coinage of the day, the department confiscated the pieces as counterfeit, along with the dies. But not everywhere. The zealousness or indifference of local Trea-

sury agents, rather than adherence to a policy or regulation, seems to be the important factor in accounting for scarcity.

TWENTIETH-CENTURY SATIRICAL PIECES.   The paucity of imagination and the lack of interest that mark twentieth-century medallic issues are also evident in the near nonexistence of satirical pieces. What does exist is summarized in a few paragraphs.

The famous coin dealer Thomas Elder is responsible for two half-dollar-size copper pieces issued during the 1908 campaign. One obverse emphasizes Bryan's three defeats (anticipating the third loss in the election) and asks "What Will the Great Commoner Do Now?" The other obverse cites Bryan's platform. The reverses are identical, almost exactly the same as the Spaulding Bryan money piece described previously. Both pieces are very scarce. On a 1912 aluminum piece Elder takes a few digs at the leading candidates of both major parties, naming them as "O-Hi-O! Bill Taft/Oyster B. Roosevelt/Wis(e) Pomp. LaFollette" on one side, and on the other "Harmonious Judson/Wouldrow/3 × 16 to 1 Bryan." And that is about it—until many years later, in connection with the 1960 campaign.

In that campaign Kennedy's Catholicism was an issue, perhaps the most important one. Although the Kennedy satirical piece is dated "1963," Rochette records that it was actually issued in 1961 to describe the direction of the country's leadership two years after the inauguration. On the obverse is a spray with the inscription above "Good for 1 Confession/By the Authority of Pres. Kennedy and John XXXIII." On the reverse is the inscription "Catholic States of America/In the Pope We Hope/1963."

The War in Vietnam and Lyndon Johnson's "Great Society" legislation generated a few pieces. An aluminum piece caricatures Johnson with an exaggerated nose, chin, and ears, and the inscription "The Great Society/He Poorhouse Ruined Em/1984." The reverse pictures a donkey's rear end and "Tyranny/Inflation We Trust/Nonsense." Not particularly in good taste, but there was not much that was tasteful in America in the 1960s. A few brass slogan pieces from the 1968 campaign are worth noting: "Support the Viet Cong/McCarthy for President"; "Keep America Humph-Free/Dump the Hump"; "LBJ Coin/No Gold/No Silver/Just Pure Brass." Others were made that ridiculed Richard Nixon and George Wallace.

The popularity of pinbacks over metallic pieces in this century is perhaps nowhere more evident than in this category. Literally hundreds of pinbacks with satirical statements, some quite humorous, have been produced since the early 1960s. No candidate, or president, or pet program has been spared. But virtually none of this satire appears in metal. Since there are so few of these metal satirical pieces and just about all of them are easy to come by, the collector should have no difficulty in completing such a collection.

Collecting Other Categories

As is evident from the previous discussion, it is still possible to assemble an outstanding political numismatic collection. There are several categories that, though not specifically related to presidential campaigning as such, can help extend our knowledge of the presidency and its incumbents. But before making any decisions, consider the following:

1. Candidates such as Washington, Lincoln, and Kennedy were commemorated during their lifetimes and have continued to be memorialized ever since they died, even up to the present day. There are, therefore, both an abundant variety of material and very few truly rare issues.

2. Some presidents, particularly the three just mentioned, have their own devoted following of medallic collectors who are not otherwise interested in political Americana. For these there is more competition, and many of the pieces are expensive.

3. Both private mints and individuals issue pieces specifically for collectors, a cus-

113B. These four medalets barely hint at the great variety of modern political numismatic material.

113C. A finely made medalet although in exceedingly poor taste.

tom dating back at least to the 1860s, and nowadays the business is booming. High-priced issues in singles or sets, in silver or gold, are selling well. Since there are no external criteria, collectors must judge for themselves what is or is not commemorative.

4. A surprisingly large number and variety of presidential medallic issues are of European origin, beginning with Washington pieces produced during his lifetime. Not all these issues did, or do now, necessarily appear in American dealers' stocks, and so it can be useful to establish contact with European dealers.

MEMORIAL AND COMMEMORATIVE ISSUES. These represent a very extensive category (Ill. 114). Collectors may wish to focus on specific events during a particular president's administration. Among the hundreds of such commemorative issues in large and small sizes are pieces (usually with the president's bust) marking such diverse events as the opening of the Panama Canal and the round-the-world cruise of the Great White Fleet (Teddy Roosevelt); the International Peace Jubilee (McKinley); the first Japanese embassy to this country (Buchanan); America's entry into World War I (Wilson); the twentieth anniversary of D-Day (Eisenhower); Richard Nixon's trip to mainland China; the Four Freedoms (FDR); John Kennedy's trip to Germany and his visit to the Berlin Wall. The list is nearly endless and, obviously, indicates a wide-open field for both collecting and researching.

Memorial pieces are known for most presidents as well as for many defeated candidates. Very often, medalists simply added a death date to campaign pieces; this was particularly true for Lincoln, Douglas, Grant, and Garfield. Occasionally, however, entirely new designs were created; the famous "broken column" marking Lincoln's assassination is perhaps the best example. More conventional designs depict a mausoleum on the revese or carry a eulogistic statement.

WASHINGTON, LINCOLN, AND KENNEDY ISSUES. This category is perhaps even more extensive than the preceding one. Certainly there is a greater variety of metals—in modern times silver, silver matte, sterling silver, gold, gold matte, and gold vermeil as well as several different copper and bronze finishes. Again, this is a wide-open category for collectors to investigate.

There are probably more than two thousand different Washington issues, beginning with the famous Manly medal in 1790 (Ill. 106C). Specialists in Washington numismatics divide the subject into several categories; the Revolutionary War period; the centennial of his birth in 1832 and bicentennial in 1932; the centennial of his inauguration in 1889; and 1976 bicentennial pieces. Along with the Manly medal, highlights of a Washington numismatic collection should include the Halladay and Sansom medals; the exquisitely designed funerary issues; the handsome Bushnell piece and certainly the huge (115mm) cast bronze medallion, which was designed by Augustus Saint-Gaudens to commemorate the centennial of the first inauguration in 1889; one of the early Washington-before-Boston issues, and an 1889 Washington-Harrison piece. And that lucky collector who obtains an original silver shell Indian "peace" medal can keep it as the capstone of his collection or sell it at any price he wishes.

Collecting medallic issues commemorating or memorializing Abraham Lincoln can also be a rewarding endeavor (Ill. 116). Robert King numbered over 1,040 pieces when he first published his listings forty-five years ago. He included over fifty or so badges and ferrotypes that political collectors would not consider numismatics. But the many—perhaps hundreds of—pieces issued since King made his list bring the number of items up to King's figure or more. Some of the better Lincoln pieces that collectors should look for are the 1909 GAR memorial issue; the Victor Brenner varieties (he designed the Lincoln penny); the earlier issues from the United States Mint; the 1909 design, on a rectangular plaquette, issued by the American Numismatic Society; and one or more of sculptor Jules Edouard Raine's handsome designs.

Issues commemorating or memorializing John F. Kennedy, of course, do not re-

114. Note the different shapes among these presidential commemorative issues. The ones pictured here are contemporary with a president's term, except for the Frémont piece, which was issued in the early 1900s.

115. Augustus Saint-Gaudens designed this cast-iron medallion, 4½ inches in diameter, to mark the centennial of George Washington's first inauguration.

flect the changing styles of medallic art that are evident in Washington and Lincoln issues. Nevertheless, Kennedy medallic issues are often attractively designed, especially some of the European pieces, and are usually reasonably priced and relatively easy to obtain (Ill. 117). There are no great rarities, ordinarily, in bronze or silver, but some issues in gold may exist in no more than two or three pieces. These are usually in the hands of the original recipient or in his family and out of circulation for the foreseeable future. Among the more difficult issues to obtain are the 1961 National Postmasters' Convention, in three metals; the 1962 Essay Commission (possibly restruck?); and several European designs.

COLLECTING THE WORKS OF A SPECIFIC MEDALIST.   Few collectors are aware of the challenge in trying to assemble the total production of a great nineteenth-century medalist. In many instances, unfortunately, such work is not easy to identify. Of all the categories discussed in this chapter, this one attracts the fewest collectors. But that circumstance can be viewed as an advantage.

There were perhaps more than three dozen medalists who each issued more than a few pieces in the nineteenth century. Some, such as Jacob Reich, are known for only a very few pieces; others, such as the Lovetts, father and son, and William Key, had a voluminous output. One medalist, John Adams Bolen, who was prominent during the Civil War era, devoted some of his work to personal messages extolling patriotism. Bolen's series depicting Washington, Webster, Jackson, and Jefferson is particularly well executed, and his 1868 medalet picturing Ulysses S. Grant is an actual campaign piece.

Many issues produced by the United States Mint and engraved by Charles Cushing Wright, Moritz Furst, Anthony Paquet, and William Barber rank high in quality of design and finish. This whole subject, so largely untouched by political numismatists, is well worth investigating.

116.   These examples of Lincoln medallic art range up to 3 inches in diameter and are typical of the wide variety available.

117.   Representative issues honoring John F. Kennedy. At left is an inaugural medal struck by a private mint; at right Kennedy is shown in the company of other assassinated presidents on a large brass medallion.

117A. This charming 1910 pitcher is a rare survivor of the Roosevelt Bears fad that became, which he wouldn't have liked, one of Theodore Roosevelt's lasting legacies.

6
Ceramics and Glassware

POLITICAL CERAMICS FROM the early years of the republic are almost entirely of European origin, although glassware from the same period is both European and American made. Generally, American-made ceramics and glassware with political subjects were in relatively common use by the 1820s. Up to that decade, both glass and ceramic pieces commemorated an inauguration or a president's term of office. Actual campaign pieces probably first appeared during the 1840 campaign. It was not until after the Civil War that American potteries dominated the American market. European potteries, however, continued to market their wares sucessfully in this country, and do so to the present day. In fact, the single most interesting political ceramic issued in recent years is a British-made pitcher commemorating the Watergate scandal.

Most political ceramics and glassware were made for the mass market and were intended to serve common household functions. The articles were not jardinieres, urns, perfume bottles, candelabra, or punch bowls but rather crocks, sugars and creamers, tumblers, whiskey flasks, and ordinary dinnerware. They were fashioned cheaply from whatever type of glass or ceramic was available locally, and were distributed widely. Items made abroad were, by contrast, generally of better quality, designed for upper-class households.

Much of the pre-Civil War ceramics and glassware is appealing aesthetically. Early patriotic whiskey flasks and stoneware crocks are starkly simplistic in design and decoration, and the unabashedly naive-sounding slogans that adorn many other pieces remind us of the uncritical admiration with which many Americans viewed the presidency in that age of fervent nationalism.

The style of the political ceramics and glassware produced after the Civil War is altogether different. The love of frills and flourishes so typical of Victorian Americans is evident in the ornate designs of trinket boxes, campaign plates, and the frosted glassware that, for example, looked more appropriate sitting on the living-room mantelpiece than on the kitchen table. There are many interesting pieces from this period that mark the ascendancy of American potteries. Although most ceramic and glass pieces were mass produced, many of them were of high quality in design and material right up into the campaigns of the early twentieth century. But quality has deteriorated in recent campaigns, to the nadir—plastic tumblers, abomination of abominations!

117B. A rather chunky Washington is the subject of this delightful Lenox Toby. ca. 1889. Known in several sizes.

85

In the descriptions of ceramics here, I have added the names of manufacturers when possible, as an aid for collectors who wish to track down sales catalogs. However, remember that even if a ceramic bears the name "Dresden" or "Sèvres" or the mark of a European pottery, that is not proof the piece was European made. In the days before protection was offered by tariff regulations, American potteries often marked their wares in such ways because the buying public had a high regard for the quality of European ceramics. Collectors are also advised to investigate some of the many fine books on American ceramics and glassware that are widely available in libraries and bookstores.

Political collectors should remember too that the collecting of historical (and that includes political) ceramics and glassware is a very enthusiastically pursued hobby, and that pieces with political themes were produced in far fewer designs and numbers than those with floral and geometric patterns. Glass items are generally more difficult to find than ceramic pieces; hence, political collectors tend to prefer ceramic pieces, and as a result they command higher prices even though glass pieces are generally scarcer. I know of only one political glass collection. I had the pleasure of appraising it before it was donated to the Smithsonian Institution. All of which suggests that for the persevering collector assembling a political ceramic and glassware collection could be an exceptional experience.

I have emphasized unusual and uncommon material in this chapter on the assumption that reading a few sales lists will show collectors what is most available—not what is infrequently available. Most collectors of political Americana have an inadequate knowledge of political ceramics and glassware, and I hope that the information given here will stimulate them into branching out into what I think is a highly challenging area of collecting.

Patriotic Commemoratives, 1789–1850

118. Liverpool jug, "America in Tears"; this is one of the designs most likely to be found by collectors.

WASHINGTON LIVERPOOLWARE.   This category is so titled because the pieces discussed are among the wonderful variety of English-made pitchers, jugs, tankards, and mugs that flooded the American market between 1789 and 1830. Each piece was transfer-decorated, in black or color, with a picture of a historic event in the America of that day or a national figure or some other motif that appealed to one's pride in his country. Most pieces were made from common clay and given a white glaze, although very occasionally pieces will be found with a light beige, blue, or green glaze. All these come under the general heading of Liverpoolware (less often, Herculaneum or creamware) from their place of origin. Among the most popular commemorative subjects were Commodore Preble's battle in Tripoli Harbor; allegorical scenes including Liberty, Justice, and Commerce; portraits of naval heroes during the War of 1812; sailing ships and coats of arms; and busts of Samuel Adams, John Hancock, and Benjamin Franklin.

A good many designs honored George Washington with either paeans to his statesmanship or eulogies on the occasion of his death in 1799. Washington commemoratives portray him in uniform, either full length or a bust, and usually surrounded by allegorical figures, cannon, or flags, with a verse, of which the following is typical:

> As he tills your rich glebe,
> The old peasant shall tell
> How your WARREN expired
> And how MONTGOMERY fell,
> And how Washington humbled
> yours foes.

That verse underscored Liverpoolware's European origin. No American farmer of the day would have thought himself a peasant.

On the magnificent tankard (Ill. 119) that probably commemorates his first inauguration, Washington is pictured with stylized figures of Liberty and Justice at each side. On the reverse appears this malediction!

> Deafness to the Ear that will patiently hear
> & Dumbness to the Tongue that will utter
> A Calumny against the immortal Washington
> Long Live the president of the United States.

Memorial pieces usually depict Washington, but some feature a weeping Columbia and a willow tree, or an urn and an obelisk, and always an appropriate sentiment, of which "Washington in Glory/America in Tears" is typical. Generally, collectors do not make a distinction between memorial and commemorative pieces— the pleasure of having one or two examples of Washington Liverpoolware in one's collection is reward enough.

There are also a few pieces that commemorate the inaugurations of John Adams, Thomas Jefferson, James Madison, and James Monroe, but all these are difficult to find. Most of them portray the president on one side and a ship or some other patriotic subject on the other side. (The picturing of a ship is perhaps the earliest use of the ship-of-state theme that would become so commonplace in later decades.) A more unusual piece from this period is a handsome 6½-inch slate blue and white rose jar, possibly a lovers' token from before 1800, and most likely of French origin. Below black transfers of John Adams and James Madison on each side is this charming sentiment: "Kindly Take This Gift of Mine,/Full of Love for Thee and Thine." There are also a few mugs, each about 3 inches in height, that are similar to children's alphabet plates and maxim mugs of the period. Some simply say "Washington" or "Monroe" (or occasionally "Munroe") and carry a floral decoration. Monroe portrait mugs in blue or black transfers turn up occasionally.

Liverpoolware pitchers and jugs with black transfers are not uncommonly scarce, but tankards and mugs are. Pieces with color transfers and in solid colors other than black are very difficult to locate. Several fine studies of Liverpoolware are available. The best source of the ware itself in this country is Sotheby Parke-Bernet Galleries in New York.

EARLY HISTORICAL CHINA. About the time that Liverpoolware was at its peak of popularity in the United States, enterprising British potters began shipping dinner sets made from cheap clay and colored in a rich deep blue that hid the many imperfections in workmanship. Pieces ranged in size from saucers to large platters and tureens, and were often sold in large sets sufficient for serving as many as twelve people. Among the most popular designs were American scenic views, state capitols, church and college buildings, Erie Canal scenes, state coats of arms, city street scenes, Lafayette's visit to this country in 1824, and medallion portraits of George Washington, Thomas Jefferson, and Governor DeWitt Clinton of New York. Most were decorated with scenes or portraits and elaborate combinations of flowers and seashells and various small motifs.

This pottery, known as Historical Staffordshire, is avidly sought by its own group of collectors, and many pieces bring very high prices. One or two pieces in a political collection make a striking eyecatcher and, as is also true of Liverpoolware, add a touch of class. The patterns that would interest political collectors include George Washington on the grounds of Mount Vernon, a seated Lafayette at Washington's tomb, Jefferson standing beside Washington's tomb, and several scenic and building views with medallion portraits of Washington and Jefferson.

One other kind of historical china—in this case finely made china, indeed—should be mentioned. I refer to the handsome copper and silver lusterware imported from En-

119. Washington inaugural tankard, c. 1789.

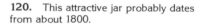

120. This attractive jar probably dates from about 1800.

121. A rust-red copper luster plate picturing Andrew Jackson, probably dating from before 1824.

122. Yellow copper luster teapot from the 1840 campaign; the cover is missing.

123. Examples of Ridgway's "Columbian Star" pattern. The size and scope of the pieces in this set are large: I have seen a platter about 20 by 13 inches and demitasse saucers about 3 inches in diameter, not to mention a wide variety of other dishes and containers.

gland and France in the period 1810 to about 1840. Most pieces make up tea sets, although pitchers and mugs appear occasionally. The decoration consists of portrait transfers in black or brick red, and wide or narrow bands of luster and glazes in deep blue, pink, or yellow. Andrew Jackson and William Henry Harrison are the presidents most frequently pictured (Ills. 121 and 122). There is a rare deep blue and copper pitcher with a transfer of Martin Van Buren in the Smithsonian Collection, and a few pieces are known with transfers of John Quincy Adams. Jackson pieces usually carry the inscription "The Hero of New Orleans" or "Our Country's Hero." Collectors should watch especially for pieces with the former inscription, but bearing a picture of a very youthful Marquis de Lafayette. Harrison designs are usually inscribed "The Nation's Choice," "The Pride of Our People," or something similar.

All political lusterware is so extremely scarce that the event is worthy of comment whenever a piece appears on the market. If I had the choice of adding just one piece of political ceramics to my collection, I would choose a Jackson lusterware design.

Mid-Nineteenth Century Campaign Pottery

LOG CABIN CHINA. During the 1830s British potters began coloring their production for the American market in soft pink, blue, brown, black, green (rarely), and a dark mulberry. The famous 1840 Log Cabin campaign provided the context for an outpouring of dinner sets and tea sets in those colors, produced by two or three potteries, most notably John Ridgway of Staffordshire.

The Ridgway design known as the "Columbian Star" pattern (Ill. 123) pictured a log cabin and usually a farmer and his horse plowing (or just a plow), a few figures, and a background of trees and shrubs. A wide band around the rim contained about 31 five-pointed stars and many very tiny stars. The pattern, very popular in this country, was undoubtedly produced for several years after the 1840 campaign. Political collectors should be aware that the "Columbian Star" pattern may bear several different marks. Of particular interest are children's tea sets, which are most often found in light blue.

One other British potter, William Adams of Tunstall, produced a few pieces of log cabin china in pink or dark brown (Ill. 124). The decoration consists of a log cabin scene and medallion busts of Harrison alternating with floral sprays and urns.

The Log Cabin campaign was also commemorated by the first substantive appearance of American-made pieces. Of particular interest is a large creamware milk pitcher with pink or black transfers made by the American Pottery Company of Jersey City, New Jersey. The transfer design on these pitchers varies in minor details, but all the pitchers seem to be decorated with large civilian portraits of Harrison alternating with log cabin scenes. More typical of American-made political ceramics from the 1840 campaign are pieces produced from cheap local clays, many of which are considered folk art today. Stoneware was popular: Crocks and cider jugs are known with short inscriptions—"Harrison," for example, or more rarely, "Harrison/1840/Ohio." Red earthenware was also a commonly used material. Deep dishes and soup bowls are known with crudely incised designs on the inside surfaces. Despite the fact that they must have been in widespread use, stoneware and earthenware pieces are almost impossible to find today. They were so ordinary that they were not valued.

In my own collection is an unusual Harrison salt-glaze cup plate in light blue, which is an exact duplicate of a Sandwich glass cup plate. A similar plate is known in dark blue depicting Henry Clay that probably dates from the 1844 campaign. Both cup plates are well made, unmarked, and must be considered exceedingly rare.

One of the oddest pieces from the 1840 campaign is a rather crudely made deep blue and gray log cabin, which has no functional use except, perhaps, to be admired (Ill. 125). This piece is possibly unique; certainly it was a labor of love for its unknown maker. On the peak of the roof is a cider barrel inscribed "Hard Cider Boys/Log Cabin, Tippecanoe/Hard Cider." On each side of the roof is an inscription that in choice of words is most typical of Harrison partisans. On one side is:

> Harrison the Hero of Tippecanoe
> Fort Meigs and the Thames
> Against Van Buren, the
> Demogogue of Kinderhook
> Hurrah for Old Tip, the
> Farmer of North Bend.

On the other side is inscribed:

> William Henry Harrison,
> President in 1841.
> With Tip and Tyler
> We'll Burst Van Buren's Boiler.
> Log Cabin.

There is nothing to add.

ISSUES FROM THE 1844–1868 PERIOD.

The comparatively large volume of pottery produced for the Harrison campaigns was not equaled during the next few campaigns. No candidate, not even Abraham Lincoln in 1864, excited voters as Harrison had. As a result, both the amount and variety of ceramics from the 1844–1868 period are strictly limited.

Most likely to be found from the earlier campaigns of this period are alphabet plates and an occasional tea set honoring Henry Clay. Undoubtedly ceramic pieces marking the campaigns of Franklin Pierce, Lewis Cass, James Polk, and Winfield Scott do exist, but they are seldom seen. One early authority mentions a "biscuit porcelain" bust of Clay made as a cane handle (Barber, p. 164).

The day is saved for political collectors because Zachary Taylor was a war hero candidate in 1848. He made few appearances, spoke not at all to the issues, and—in fact—he seemed hardly aware that a campaign was going on. But he had successfully

124. A typical piece by Adams of Tunstall.

125. Possibly a raccoon was mounted on the opposite peak of this unusual 1840 campaign novelty.

126. Later nineteenth-century mugs are contrasted with a well-made modern mug picturing Gerald Ford and Queen Elizabeth and commemorating the Queen's visit to the United States in 1976.

vanquished the Mexicans in a war that did not last long enough to produce heroes. Most ceramic issues, therefore, refer to or imply Taylor's military exploits rather than his candidacy. There is a particularly well-made shaving mug with a black transfer of "General Taylor" on one side and George Washington on the other and—in between, in gilt—the inscription "Gift from Boston." There are also several china plates, possibly a series, showing an equestrian Taylor at the center of various battle scenes in the Mexican War. Those plates are found in pink or light blue with floral borders, and are probably American made. One of the few presidential pieces is a deep dish that commemorates his inauguration. On the inside bottom surface Taylor is pictured together with the inscription "General Z. Taylor/Born Nov. 23,1781/Elected President of America/1848."

PARIANWARE. Zachary Taylor is also the subject, as were many of his contemporaries, of a handsome parian bust. Parianware is one of the more interesting ceramics of the period. The name comes from the likeness of this fine porcelain, which can be nearly translucent, to marble quarried on the Greek island of Paros. Parian busts probably made their first appearance in 1845 at the Copeland Pottery in England and in this country at the United States Pottery Company in Bennington, Vermont, one or two years later. There are two types of parianware, according to the composition of the porcelain: 1) soft paste or grit parian easily distinguished by its gritty surface and a certain vagueness in detail; 2) hard paste parian, which first appeared in the late 1850s and is distinguished by its smooth surface and very sharp details. Pieces of the first type are scarcer. Parian busts range in height from about 3 to 19 inches, but most busts fall within the 6- to 9-inch range.

The custom of honoring prominent persons of the day in parian busts continued throughout the remainder of the century, so it is possible to assemble a fine grouping of these political busts. Soft-paste parian busts exist for John Frémont, Daniel Webster, and Henry Clay, and probably for Franklin Pierce and Lewis Cass. Hard-paste parian busts exist for all major party candidates from the late 1850s at least through Theodore Roosevelt. The Lincoln bust (Ill. 127) is typical of those honoring presidential candidates. From the standpoint of appearance and historical significance, this fine bust from the 1860 campaign with "Constitutional Freedom" inscribed on the base should be the key bust in any such collection. Collecting parianware is popular in Europe, but the subject has not drawn much attention in this country. Because few political collectors are aware of parian busts, the category is a ceramic sleeper.

127. A bust of Lincoln, a superb example of parianware statuary.

CERAMICS OF ABRAHAM LINCOLN. Further comment is necessary on the subject of Lincoln and ceramics. Unhappy as the thought may be, fully 99 percent of all ceramics honoring him were produced after his death, a fact that should not deter the serious collector. The actual campaign pieces are few—I am not aware of any Lincoln ceramic that can be definitely ascribed to the 1860 campaign. His likeness, with a small beard, appears on an 1862 or 1863 alphabet plate (Ill. 128) and matching children's mug; both are part of a series that includes generals Winfield Scott (Ill. 129) and Ulysses

128. Children's alphabet plates from the early 1860s. Children's mugs with similar transfers are known.

129. One of the Fenton Pottery vases: The bust shows against a bright blue ground.

Grant, Vice-President Hamlin, and probably other Union leaders. From the 1864 campaign there are at least three attractive blue and white parian vases, 7 to 10 inches tall, produced by the Fenton Pottery in Bennington. There are also a rather unattractive 6-inch terra-cotta vase in muddy brown or white glaze, a few small plates, and perhaps a trinket box or two.

But there are many Lincoln ceramics available that were issued either during the nation's centennial in 1876, during Lincoln's centennial in 1909, or to commemorate highlights in his life. He is often pictured on Grand Army of the Republic items and other articles associated with veterans' organizations of a later day. One particularly interesting theme combines Lincoln, James A. Garfield, and William McKinley under such headings as "Our Martyred Heroes" on small flat plates, saucers and cups, and canteens. There is no shortage of Lincoln commemorative ceramics.

Later Nineteenth-Century Political Ceramics, 1872—1896

' There is no shortage, either, of political ceramics issued during the last quarter of the nineteenth century. Indeed, so much material is available, both in volume and variety, that collectors may elect to specialize. All major party candidates are pictured—on tea sets, pitchers, plates, vases, plaques, novelties (to be discussed in a later section), trinket boxes, and tiles. Probably most American potteries and a few British and French potteries as well issued at least one or two objects picturing a presidential candidate, and often as not the vice-presidential candidate as well.

Opportunities for collectors seem endless. For example, "paired" pieces—i.e., ceramics issued in the same design but differing in candidates' pictures—can be assembled. Or one can collect the wares of a particular manufacturer, an ambition that requires locating the appropriate catalogs and sales lists. Or the collector can concentrate on a particular candidate or campaign. Grover Cleveland, Benjamin Harrison, and William McKinley are the most frequently pictured candidates; the least often pictured ones are Horace Greeley, Winfield Scott Hancock, Rutherford Hayes, and Samuel Tilden. Most ceramics are associated with the 1888, 1892, and 1896 campaigns; the 1872 and 1876 have the fewest number and smallest variety of related ceramics. However a collector decides to build a collection of ceramics from this period, he should be able to build an outstanding one. A few pieces are very expensive, but a great many can be purchased for under $400, even under $200. Many pieces in the lower price range were standard houseware items in manufacturers' stocks, to which black or brown, and less often blue or green, political transfers were added, together with the appropriate wording.

130. Winfield Hancock is pictured on an 1880 ironware plate along with a ceramic example of the "martyred presidents" theme in political Americana.

PITCHERS. The volume of material available from the 1872–1896 period is too great to be discussed in detail here, and so only the more interesting pieces will be mentioned. Beginning with pitchers is not a difficult choice because it is a pitcher that is, in my opinion, the single most outstanding political ceramic produced during the entire period: the magnificent Wedgwood "Etruria" pitcher (Plate 14), 12 inches high, that commemorates the inauguration of James A. Garfield (or possibly it is a memorial issue). The pitcher is colored in rich shades of brown, olive green, rust red, and blue, with an added bit of gilding. On one side is an oval portrait of Garfield enclosed in a laurel wreath with the inscription above, "Garfield/Born 1831/President 1881." Decorating the opposite side is a large spread eagle, crossed flags, a shield and a scroll above inscribed "E Pluribus Unum." Fortunately for collectors this pitcher does appear on the market occasionally. At least three other fine Garfield pitchers, all memorial issues, are also known (Ill. 131). The first is stoneware with a white glaze and flecked gilt trimming. On each side is a raised profile of Garfield. Both the handle and the spout are in the shape of an eagle's head and neck. The second is glazed in a rich dark brown reminiscent of Bennington pottery, comes in two heights, 9 and 11 inches, and likewise bears a raised profile of Garfield on each side. The third pitcher

131. *Left:* The Garfield acrostic memorial pitcher. *Right:* Garfield is portrayed on both sides of this fine stoneware pitcher.

is a British-made memorial linking Garfield with Queen Victoria's deceased husband, Prince Albert. One side pictures Garfield in profile below draped British and American flags. The other side contains a treacly eulogy in the form of an acrostic:

<blockquote>
*G*arfield is dead—his memory blest,
*A*ngels have welcomed him home to rest.
*R*adiant his life—in suffering brave.
*F*riendship now weeps o'er a martyr's grave,
*I*ntwined in a bond of sympathy sweet
*E*ngland's and America's widows greet:
*L*ike Albert—was Garfield a nation's pride
*D*evoutly they lived, beloved they died.
</blockquote>

PLATES. The most ubiquitous form of political ceramics from this period is plates. Collectors can find a good variety of McKinley issues with smooth or embossed surfaces and elaborate floral designs (Ill. 132). Some are "souvenir" plates picturing the candidate and his boyhood home or events in his life. Among the more popular plates with collectors are standard stock pieces, frequently ironstone ware, bearing a transfer picture of a party's presidential and vice-presidential candidates, together with the appropriate symbols and wording. These plates are usually collected in pairs.

One of the more interesting plate designs from this period was produced by the Sarreguemines pottery in France. This firm, known for the superior quality of its patterns, issued a series in cream glaze commemorating every president from Washing-

132. Candy or bonbon dishes in fine china are found often with colorful decals.

133. Harrison and Reid (1892) and Bryan and Sewell (1896) are pictured on typical late nineteenth-century campaign plates. Plates with this kind of design are known in several pastel colors.

134. An example of the Sarreguemines presidential inaugural plates.

ton to McKinley. Each plate pictures a president in black with his surname and the dates of his presidency below. Surrounding the picture is a design in reddish brown consisting of an oak and laurel wreath, a spread eagle, flags, and the date "1779" ("1789"?) above. I have never seen a complete set, but individual plates do turn up frequently. Collectors should remember that these plates were made in the 1896–1901 period; no plate that I know of pictures a president after William McKinley—except for McKinley, therefore, no plate is contemporary with the president pictured on it.

Some other plates to look for: from the 1880 campaign, a striking red-clay piece with a pattern in the style of ancient Grecian pottery, picturing James Garfield, with his facsimile signature in black on a white and deep red surface (New Jersey Pottery); from the 1908 campaign, a deep dish in beige and gold with a high-relief outward-facing bust of William Jennings Bryan (possibly a similar one picturing William Howard Taft exists also); from the 1888 campaign, a matched pair of ironware bread plates with black or brown portrait transfers of Grover Cleveland and Allan Thurmond on one and Benjamin Harrison and Grover Cleveland on the other—around the rim of each is the embossed inscription "Give Us This Day Our Daily Bread"; again from 1880 a 10-inch blue spatterware plate bearing a raised profile of Garfield (Burford, East Liverpool, Ohio); from the 1884 campaign, an 8-inch ironstone plate with light sepia or black transfers of James G. Blaine or Grover Cleveland and matching pieces picturing their running mates John A. Logan (the founder of Memorial Day) and Thomas A. Hendricks, respectively (in effect, a four-plate set).

TEA SETS AND OTHER PIECES. Acquiring matched sugars and creamers is a particular challenge for collectors. Creamers, most often with prints of Harrison or McKinley, appear occasionally on the market, but for some reason sugars seldom do. Both Cleveland and Harrison creamers are known with their pictures on one side and their vice-presidential nominees on the opposite side. Look also for small pin trays picturing Blaine and Logan or Cleveland and Hendricks; two-handled mugs from the 1896 campaign depicting McKinley and Bryan; celery and other oddly shaped dishes for Cleveland, Blaine, Harrison, and McKinley.

Among the more interesting tankards and mugs from this period is a colorful thick clay mug commemorating Benjamin Harrison's inauguration in 1889 (Ill. 135). The medallion bust of Harrison on one side is matched by one of Washington on the other. Between the two busts are the dates "1789–1889," indicating that the mug also commemorated the centennial of Washington's first inauguration (L. B. Beerbower Company). Another inaugural mug, this one commemorating the inauguration of William McKinley, equates the gold standard with patriotism. A large spread eagle and a shield dominate the design; inscribed below the shield is "March 4, 1897/For Gold and Our Country's Honor." The scarcity of Rutherford Hayes ceramics has already been mentioned, and two rather large and crudely made tankards are no exception. Both, undoubtedly originating from the same source, are made of red earthenware with deeply incised inscriptions—"Hayes and Wheeler/The Spirit of '76" and "The Hayes and Wheeler Mug."

135. Colorful campaign mugs. The Kennedy mug dates from the 1968 campaign, and is easily obtained.

PORTRAIT TILES.   For a brief period during the 1880s and 1890s displaying decorative ceramic tiles was popular; the custom of using tiles in interior design remained in fashion until about the World War I period. Beautifully created designs in Art Nouveau style featured themes from mythology; American history, nature, and sporting scenes were among other subjects depicted on single tiles or on sets. These were not just mounted as fireplace borders, but were framed in wood or brass and hung; in better homes decorative tiles were used as a border between ceiling and wall.

Celebrities of the day, particularly from politics and the theatre, were often portrayed. Portrait tiles of major party candidates exist from the campaigns of the 1880s through 1912 (Ill. 136). Some tiles were issued as trivets for use with tea sets, and these

136.   Presidential portrait tiles: The Cleveland piece probably dates from 1884 and the Wilson piece from 1912.

will bear the same picture of the candidate as appears on other pieces in the set. A hexagonal tile, 3 inches across, styled in classic Wedgwood blue and white, portrayed Woodrow Wilson; a similar one portraying Abraham Lincoln was probably issued during the 1909 centennial (both were made by the Mosaic Tile Company, Zanesville, Ohio).

But the most interesting political tiles are the imaginatively designed intaglio portraits. The portrait was first molded below the surface level; the carved spaces were then filled with a colored glaze, which—when properly applied—created shadows and highlights at the surface level. The effect was that of a portrait on a flat surface, but actually suggestive of a relief portrait—almost like a photograph in clay. Grover Cleveland appears on a purple tile (as is also true of other colors, "purple" may range from very deep, almost black, to a soft shade such as lavender); Benjamin Harrison appears on olive green and rust red tiles: Theodore Roosevelt and Woodrow Wilson appear on black and gray green tiles. Most of the political portrait tiles are 6-inch squares, but a few are rectangles 6 by 4 inches. One particularly desirable four-tile set consisting of 3-inch squares portrays McKinley and Hobart and Bryan and Sewall. On the back of each tile is a brief biography of the candidate. (Encaustic Tile Company of Zanesville and C. Pardee Works of Perth Amboy, New Jersey, were major producers of intaglio portrait tiles.)

136A.   The crackled glaze adds to the appearance of these 1896 political tiles. The pale blue and white hexagonal tile picturing Lincoln shows up fairly often.

Twentieth-Century Ceramics

ISSUES OF THE 1904 AND 1908 CAMPAIGNS.   The high quality of late nineteenth-century political ceramics was continued into the early twentieth century. But there is a difference in the ceramics of the two periods. It is a difference due almost en-

137. On the left Taft and Sherman are pictured on a plate from the "Smiling Bill and Sunny Jim" series; at the right is, in my opinion, one of the finest campaign plates of the period—Taft is caricatured on translucent china.

138. One of a variety of designs in deep blue British-made plates picturing Teddy Roosevelt.

tirely to the appearance and personality of each of the Republican party candidates in the 1904 and 1908 campaigns, Theodore Roosevelt and William Howard Taft. Democrat William Jennings Bryan (1900 and 1908) appears in solemn poses on a few pieces, and Democrat Alton Parker (1904), the most forgotten of the forgotten candidates in this century, appears hardly at all. Surprisingly, most ceramic pieces, novelties excepted, of Roosevelt picture him in one serious "presidential" pose or another. But pieces caricaturing the rotund and affable Taft seem as frequent as those depicting him in serious poses.

The interesting plates from these campaigns are Taft associated. The most desirable is the "Smiling Bill and Sunny Jim" series picturing Taft and his running mate James Sherman facing each other (Ill. 137). One plate is inscribed "An Invincible Combination," another is titled "The Morning After," and a short verse appears on still another variety. Among the more popular serious Taft poses is a handsome deep dish in "Staffordshire blue" commemorating his inauguration that is bordered with scenes of Washington, D.C. (made by Rowland and Marsellus, England). Similar plates depicting Teddy Roosevelt are bordered with scenes from his eventful life or events in American history (Ill. 138). There are a number of tasteful Taft and Sherman and Roosevelt and Fairbanks plates picturing the candidates amid flags and shields with perhaps a simple floral design or a plain gold rim. Some of these plates are of German origin.

There are a very few Bryan plates, none of which is especially distinctive, that can be paired with Taft plates. Few though they are, there are more 1908 Bryan plates than from his 1896 and 1900 campaigns combined.

CERAMIC ISSUES FROM WOODROW WILSON TO JIMMY CARTER. Fewer ceramics have been produced in later campaigns, and much of what is in existence is of inferior quality and poorly designed. Plates are most often found, but a few pitchers and mug and cup/saucer sets are also available. There are no rare pieces, although a few pieces may be considered scarce; just about every piece described in this section will appear on dealers' lists at one time or another. Gift shops at presidential birthplaces often stock the same ceramics that appear on dealers' lists, which indicates that some pieces are kept in continuous production because of their appeal to birthplace visitors. In fact, many of the pieces described here could well have appeared first in gift shops.

Generally, the ceramic mementos of defeated candidates are harder to find. Although such pieces probably do exist, I have never seen ceramics associated with Charles Evans Hughes, James Cox, and John Davis. The ceramics most available are associated with Franklin Roosevelt and John Kennedy, and, as would be expected, most of the ceramics related to those two presidents are memorial issues. Kennedy pieces are still available in the Washington, D.C., area gift shops.

There are three categories of Franklin Roosevelt ceramics. First are the actual campaign issues, of which there are very few. Some pieces from the 1932 campaign also commemorate the repeal of the Volstead Act; there are two or three mugs displaying that dual theme. There is also a splendid, and scarce, pitcher and mug set in light brown or green with a low-relief caricature of Roosevelt, and there are a few unadorned picture plates. Second are ceramics honoring Roosevelt's role in World War II. Most desirable are cup and saucer sets, small pitchers, and plates with small colorful transfers of Roosevelt and Winston Churchill (Meakin, England)(Ill. 139). A plate series pictures Roosevelt and other contemporary American leaders, including General MacArthur and Admiral Nimitz; each portrait is surrounded by patriotic and military scenes. A similar series honoring Allied leaders pictures Roosevelt in light sepia (Plate 15); around the rim is a very colorful border consisting of flags of all the Allied nations (Salem China, Ohio). Third are the memorial issues. One of the best is a "historical blue" plate with an uncommon picture of Roosevelt and a floral border (Royal Staffordshire Pottery, England) (Ill. 140). The Salem China Company also produced a high-quality plate with a sepia sketch of Roosevelt and a wide cobalt border decorated in 24-karat gold.

139. Two pieces from the Meakin Pottery that are part of a dessert set.

140. These plates are British made. The one on the right is a memorial issue produced by the Royal Staffordshire Pottery.

Most political ceramics from the early 1950s through the 1976 election are inferior in design and workmanship. Many pieces were produced in large volume for sale in gift shops, and along with the ubiquitous Kennedy issues, one can also find Lyndon Johnson items and even the occasional Harry Truman plate. Very likely such pieces are still being manufactured. Nevertheless, there are a few modern political ceramics that are worth adding to a collection.

There is a handsome 10-inch creamware plate in black or brown that commemorates Dwight Eisenhower's first inauguration in 1953 (Ill. 141). A French-made plate of

141. Two of the better modern plates. On the left is a 1953 inaugural commemorative and on the right an uncommon design from the 1956 campaign.

142. This plate, almost 13 inches in diameter, was presented to convention delegates by the San Francisco Host Committee. It is attractively colored in deep blue, yellow, and red. An inscription on the back notes that the Republican party is holding its first national convention in a far western state.

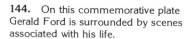

143. The very small production in both the black and white and color varieties makes this plate a tough item to locate.

144. On this commemorative plate Gerald Ford is surrounded by scenes associated with his life.

superior workmanship, but with a rather bland design, pictures Richard Nixon and other principals at the swearing-in ceremony for his second inauguration in 1973. A 9-inch plate in both color and black-and-white transfers honoring George McGovern was issued in very limited numbers by his supporters in Hamell, South Dakota (Ill. 143). Both types were sold at the McGovern headquarters in Miami Beach during the 1972 Democratic National Convention. Gerald Ford is commemorated in a rather attractively designed 10-inch plate in blue that was issued by a Grand Rapids, Michigan, public health group near the close of his presidency (Ill. 144). From the 1977 inauguration there is a handsome German-made 10-inch plate with a busy design depicting President Carter and Vice-President Mondale, an eagle, and the Capitol dome in the center; around the rim are gilt-outlined medallion portraits of all the previous presidents set within a wide, deep blue border (the Rosenthal china firm).

But the most noteworthy piece issued in recent years is a British-made 7-inch multicolored pitcher commemorating the Watergate scandal (Ill. 145). This piece is shaped similarly to the early Liverpool pitchers, and although a bit overdesigned, it would be a highlight in a political ceramics collection. On one side is a portrait cluster consisting of Richard Nixon, John Mitchell, and the major White House staff members involved in the scandal. On the opposite side is a picture of George Washington, a view of the White House, and the historic inscription "I Can't Tell a Lie" below. Above is the inscription "The Small but Corrupt Town of Washington" (presumably in imitation of the inscription that appears on a similar-size Liverpool pitcher, "Success to the Interesting but Crooked Town of Boston"; crooked streets, that is). Beneath the spout are transfers of the presidential eagle and Judge John Sirica. A design of magnetic tapes and reels lines the rim and the base (Honiton Pottery).

145. Both sides of the Watergate pitcher.

Ceramic Novelties

In political ceramics, all the silliness and seriousness of political campaigning seems to be represented among the fascinating variety of novelties that certain campaigns have inspired since the 1880s. There is not space here to describe all the mugs, pitchers, flasks, and novelties that are almost impossible to classify. I will simply describe some of the more ingenious and amusing pieces.

How, for example, would one classify the most imaginative of all political ceramic novelties? There is a saying dating from the early years of the nineteenth century that refers to inferior candidates as "weighed in the scale and found wanting." Two small bisque china figures of Benjamin Harrison and Grover Cleveland, each wrapped in the national flag, are suspended from a wooden steelyard (Ill. 147). The figures are so attached to the crossbar that Cleveland is "found wanting." That arrangement was a correct prediction of the outcome of the 1888 campaign, the year this piece was issued, for Harrison did defeat Cleveland.

One of my own favorite pieces is a whimsical little light blue flask that depicts William Jennings Bryan and Woodrow Wilson under the same bedcovers. On the reverse is the inscription "Strange Bedfellows." That phrase undoubtedly refers to Wilson's eyebrow-raising appointment of Bryan as secretary of state in his first-term Cabinet; the two men were far apart ideologically. The title was prophetic, as Bryan did resign before the end of the term because of a foreign policy dispute.

There is also a very scarce, well-made British flask in the likeness of Teddy Roosevelt, who is featured complete with his pince-nez and in politician's pose with his hands at his lapels (Royal Doulton) (Ill. 148). As he was in other kinds of political artifacts, Teddy (he detested that nickname and nobody used it to his face) is well represented in ceramic novelties. The teddy bear theme is highly popular with collectors. Roosevelt is pictured cavorting with little bears on wall plates, children's tea sets, and shelf bric-a-brac. The teddy bear pieces were probably most popular during the 1912 campaign; verses on various items usually describe how Teddy will save the "Grand Old Party," which he considered his holy mission in 1912.

One of the oddest novelties is the Knickerbocker shoe (Ill. 149). Its use is rather mystifying. It may have been intended as a planter or simply a shelf ornament. The only example I have seen is poorly glazed in deep, mottled olive green and brown. The inscription "Cleveland & Hendricks" on the horseshoe-shaped buckle is not very helpful.

A miniature 3-inch-high stoneware cider jug from the 1904 campaign pictures Alton Parker and his running mate Henry Davis. Davis, by the way, was a major financial contributor to the Democratic party; he was eighty years old when he was chosen as the vice-presidential nominee. The Al Smith stoneware mug shown in Illustration 150 is a good example of why collecting "locals" can be just as interesting as collecting presidential material, especially when the candidate concerned will ultimately become a presidential nominee. In 1915 Smith was a New York State assemblyman and still a few years away from the governor's office and his run for the presidency in 1928.

Other novelties worth looking for include a small 1944 chalkware statuette of Franklin Roosevelt wearing a hugely self-satisfied look that only a four-time winner could achieve (a matching figure of Thomas Dewey is known); thick, well-made, 6-inch decorative Delft plates in blue and brown, each with a deeply incised portrait of Dwight Eisenhower; and an attractive china beaker with black transfers of Gerald Ford and Queen Elizabeth II, marking her visit to this country in 1976 (Panorama Studios, Devon, England) (Ill. 126).

146. The 1976 Carter campaign is represented by a variety of ceramic pieces such as this tankard.

147. One of the most interesting of all campaign novelties; the position of the hook predicts a victory for Benjamin Harrison over Grover Cleveland in 1888.

TOBY PITCHERS. Al Smith was also the subject of a creamware toby pitcher issued during the 1928 campaign that is paired with a toby depicting Herbert Hoover (Ill. 151) (Patriotic Products, Syracuse, New York). Smith wears a happy Irish smile, but Hoover looks very forbidding. Drinking containers in the shape of a human face date from earliest times, but the tobies that most attract collectors today originated in seventeenth-century England. The origin of the name "toby" to describe these effigy pitchers is controversial. One theory holds that it refers to Toby Fillpot, a collective name describing topers who drank their local Yorkshire pubs dry on occasion. Another theory attributes the name to Shakespeare's Sir Toby Belch. Collecting tobies is an extremely popular hobby in this country; hence, political collectors will meet stiff competition.

The earliest American-made political toby is a flint-enamel face jug of Zachary Taylor produced by the Bennington, Vermont, potteries in the 1849–1858 period. This exceedingly rare toby is the only political toby known to me predating the McKinley tobies issued during the 1900 campaign. *Puck* and various newspapers of the day fre-

148. A whimsical German-made ceramic bottle depicting Wilson on one side and William Jennings Bryan on the opposite, ca. 1916.

149. The Knickerbocker shoe; its purpose is a mystery to me.

quently likened McKinley to Napoleon because of the president's jingoistic explanations for the United States' involvement in Cuba and the Philippines. Probably one or more New Jersey potteries produced the two different toby pitchers depicting McKinley in a Napoleonic uniform. The design most likely to appear on the market—and not often, either—is a multicolored standing figure on a 9½-inch pitcher. The same design is known on a smaller, 5½-inch size, multicolored and in yellow brown and yellow green glazes. A 9½-inch seated multicolored depiction of McKinley is also known. There are probably smaller versions in existence too. The larger tobies have one of two inscriptions: "The McKinley Jug" or "The American Napoleon Jug."

As might be expected, Teddy Roosevelt and William Howard Taft were popular subjects for tobies. Probably other Taft designs exist, but the one that collectors are most likely to see is a small 6-inch German-made torso toby known in both multicolor and light blue. Both varieties are inscribed "Souvenir of Washington," which suggests that they were sold during Taft's inauguration in 1909 and for a time thereafter. The most interesting Roosevelt toby is also a torso; it was designed by the artist Edward Penfield and is 7¾ inches high (Ill. 152). It depicts the twenty-sixth president as a Rough Rider. The handle is in the shape of an elephant's head and trunk (Lenox China). That toby is the very best that most collectors are ever likely to see—like the Watergate pitcher, it should be a highlight in a political ceramics collection.

A toby of similar quality, and exceedingly scarce, is a British-made one depicting Woodrow Wilson sitting astride a biplane. This multicolored toby is part of a set of eleven produced by the Royal Staffordshire Pottery to honor Allied leaders during World War I. The set was not distributed in the United States; it is considered scarce by British toby collectors. There are perhaps five or six face tobies of Franklin Roosevelt in cream and other solid colors. None are particularly outstanding, although they are nice to have; most of them appear on the market fairly often. There is also a small Carter caricature face toby in both cream and beige (peanut colored?) that is quite unremarkable. But there is one colorful 7¼-inch face toby made in recent years that is of superior quality (Ill. 153). It is of Dwight Eisenhower, and was produced in England, probably about 1948. This toby is well designed in rich brown, green, and yellow, and was probably issued on two separate occasions because the marks differ (Barrington Potteries).

150. This scarce mug marking an event early in Al Smith's career is strong evidence of why it pays to collect material associated with local candidates—some of them do become presidential aspirants.

151. These tobies from the 1928 campaign nicely capture the characteristic facial expressions that we associate with Al Smith and Herbert Hoover.

152. Two of the very best—but scarce—tobies.

153. The well-executed Eisenhower toby.

Political Glassware

This section on political glassware is divided into three categories, according to the function of the pieces. Within each category, both historical and contemporary pieces will be considered, beginning with the early historical flasks, the equal of Liverpoolware in their romantic appeal, and then moving on to later nineteenth-century flasks and bottles. The second category includes plates, tumblers, and other containers, with special emphasis on the popular Sandwich cup plates. The fascinating variety of glass novelties, which can be as appealing as their ceramic counterparts, makes up the third category.

154. This beautifully made Grant trinket box stands about 5½ inches high and probably dates from the 1868 campaign.

155. Sometimes a few political election artifacts from another country add interest to a collection. These colorful plates mark Prime Minister Edward Heath's forced retirement from British political life in 1975 and the parliamentary elections in the same year that made Harold Wilson Heath's successor. Conservative Margaret Thatcher and Liberal Jeremy Thorpe are also pictured.

154A. This rare Woodrow Wilson Toby, designed by Carruthers Gould in 1918, is part of a British set depicting Allied leaders.

Flasks and Bottles

EARLY HISTORICAL FLASKS.   First, the collector must learn to accept and appreciate the early nineteenth-century American glassblowers' preoccupation with the making of whiskey flasks. The kind of uncomplicated patriotism that is evident on so many other political artifacts of the day is the most striking feature of these flasks. If their number and variety are any indication, Americans believed firmly that the consumption of whiskey was a most patriotic act indeed.

Collecting early historical flasks has been a preoccupation for half a century or more. Despite the large numbers that must have been produced, they range (for obvious reasons) from scarce to unique—virtually one of a kind. Most collectors will have to content themselves with no more than one or two different examples in their collections; in a general political collection that is enough. But a warning to aspiring collectors: Assembling a collection of historical flasks with political subjects demands considerable knowledge, most especially the ability to distinguish between flasks produced by the different glasshouses and the ability to distinguish between variants of any one type. Deep and extensive reading and an opportunity to observe firsthand the marvelous variety of these flasks is mandatory before one proceeds too far into this specialty.

These early flasks are known in quart, pint, and half-pint sizes (Ill. 156), but not every type is represented in three sizes—the majority are known only in pint and/or half-pint sizes. The usual colors are green, aqua (the most common color), and different shades of amber, olive, blue, emerald, and purple; the last three colors are the rarest.

Flasks bearing political subjects first appeared in the early 1820s and continued in popular use through the 1850s. George Washington's bust—in uniform or toga—appears on about seventy-two flasks; the reverses of these flasks show an eagle, a sheaf of grain, a ship, a monument, or busts of Andrew Jackson, Henry Clay, or Zachary Taylor. About thirty-seven flasks honor Zachary Taylor. Those Taylor flasks that do not picture Washington on the reverse usually bear a likeness of Major Samuel Ringgold, who was supposedly the first American officer killed in the first battle in the first foreign war

156. Examples of early historical flasks: Taylor half-pint, pint, and quart sizes are pictured.

waged by the United States. On these Taylor/Ringgold flasks—and on some of the Taylor/Washington flasks also—are such stirring phrases as "General Taylor Never Surrenders" and "I have Endeavored to Do My Duty." A few flasks carry Taylor's nickname by which he was best known, then and now—"Rough and Ready." Perhaps no more than a half-dozen different Taylor flasks show up often enough to be collected relatively easily, and these are the flasks likely to be found in political collections.

All other flasks depicting presidential candidates of the period range from scarce to exceedingly rare. There are apparently twelve different flasks picturing Andrew Jackson, most of which are found in olive and amber. Some of the Jackson reverses also picture Washington. Four flasks picturing Henry Clay are known, and, again, Washington is represented on three of them. If any evidence were ever needed to dramatize the near deification that earlier Americans accorded Washington and the desire of would-be presidents to be compared favorably with him—we need only point to historical flasks. William Henry Harrison is depicted on one flask, and two other flasks with eagle or log cabin motifs are believed related to the 1840 campaign. This small number of Harrison-related flasks is surprising in view of all the hoopla and the abundance of other kinds of 1840 campaign material. John Tyler, who assumed the presidency at Harrison's death a month after the inauguration, may be represented by one flask—although McKearin and Wilson (see Bibliography) date it from the 1820s during the years when Tyler was United States senator from Virginia, rather than from the 1840 campaign. John Quincy Adams is represented by one very rare flask picturing our sixth president on one side and an eagle on the other.

FLASKS FROM LATER CAMPAIGNS. Early nineteenth-century flasks, of course, are simply a variety of bottles used exclusively for whiskey. As more sophisticated glass-molding machinery came into common use, thus leading to shape standardization, that distinction is no longer of any importance—at least to the political collector. By the end of the century, political flasks might have contained whiskey, cologne, a liniment, or a tonic of some sort. In the discussion that follows, bottles are round and flasks are flat; and irregularly shaped glass containers will also be referred to as bottles.

The single most interesting flask from this period is a small (5 inches tall) golden amber one depicting a youthful bust of Bryan and bearing the inscription "In Silver We Trust/Bryan and Sewall/1896" (Ill. 157). On the opposite side are a spread eagle and wreath and the inscription "United Democratic Ticket/We Shall Vote 16 to 1." The appeal of this gem lies in its shape, a coin of the day complete with a reeded edge. Not quite as exciting is a smaller clear glass flask from the same campaign (Ill. 158). Four inches in height, it shows McKinley surrounded by the inscription "Gold Standard/No

157. Bryan bottles from the 1896 campaign. A McKinley bottle similar to the one on the left is known.

158. McKinley and Hobart (on the opposite side) are pictured on this small clear glass flask. A similar flask may exist for Bryan and Sewell.

159. Cleveland flasks. At the left is a barrel flask on which a rooster is faintly visible; at the right is a pumpkinseed flask. (The outline of Hendricks' head on the opposite side is seen to the left of Cleveland's bust.)

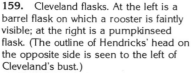

Split Dollars/McKinley"; on the opposite side are a bust of Hobart and the inscription—pretty hoary, even by 1896, but still in use today—"Prosperity and Protection/Hobart." Lucky indeed is the collector who owns the pair.

There are two very elusive Cleveland flasks (Ill. 159). The first, in the uncommon pumpkin-seed shape, was issued in clear glass in 1884 by a Pittsburgh glasshouse. This flask bears a high-relief bust of Cleveland on one side and his running mate, Thomas Hendricks, on the other, but is otherwise unadorned. A similar flask depicts the Republican candidates, James G. Blaine and John A. Logan. Both of these 6¾-inch flasks have unusually long necks that are easily broken. The second, and more interesting, Cleveland flask is molded in the shape of a slightly convex barrel with staves and straps in low relief. On the front is a tiny rooster; on the back are oval busts of Cleveland and his running mate Adlai Stevenson (grandfather of the 1952 and 1956 Democratic nominee). Above the busts is inscribed "Our Choice"; below is "Cleve and Steve/November 8th 92/March 4th 93." This scarce item is known in two sizes, 6 inches and 9 inches, and in two colors, aqua and amber. It makes a superb addition to an inaugural collection.

Collectors should also be aware of flasks bearing paper labels. These date from the 1896 campaign through 1912 and are known for all major party candidates, plus Teddy Roosevelt as the nominee of the Bull Moose party in 1912. Labels are multicolored or red, white, and blue; they depict either the presidential candidate alone or with his running mate. Most flasks are clear, but occasionally a dark amber one turns up. A 1904 example in clear glass pictures the Democratic nominees Parker and Davis on a label inscribed "Our Favorites/Whiskey." An 1896 label pictures a very young William Jennings Bryan and the inscription "Our Choice." This flask, by the way, has an aluminum screw-on cap, suggesting that it might originally have contained cologne.

Plates and Containers

SANDWICH GLASS. This name automatically calls to mind the lovely pressed glass produced by the firm known as the Boston and Sandwich Glass Company on Cape Cod in the mid-nineteenth century. Although other glasshouses, notably the New England Glass Company in Cambridge and certain midwestern glassworks, also produced fine pressed glass designs, it is as Sandwich products that the exquisite cup plates and "industry" bowls, which are political collectors' particular interest, are usually thought of.

Ruth Webb Lee, one of the greatest authorities on American pressed glass, always argued that the little cup plates, from 2⅜ to 3⅝ inches in diameter, were used to hold the handleless cups of the early nineteenth century while the diner sipped coffee or tea from the saucer into which he deliberately poured the beverage to cool it more quickly. For a short period of time, perhaps from the late 1820s to the 1850s, glass cup plates were undoubtedly popular on American dinner tables. Collectors have been grateful almost ever since.

Most cup plates were made in clear glass, but some patterns are known also in various shades of blue, green, amethyst, red, and opal. All colored varieties range from scarce to extremely rare; political collectors will generally have to be satisfied with clear glass examples.

Of the many known cup plate patterns only two are of interest to political collectors—busts and log cabins. Needless to say, both those patterns are also in great demand by collectors of historical glass. Most of the busts and all of the log cabins were produced in connection with the 1840 and 1844 campaigns. There are two scarce bust designs of George Washington that were probably issued for the centennial of his birth in 1832. Two cup plates portray William Henry Harrison, one simply a variation of the other; it has "President-1841" added, which suggests it may commemorate his inauguration or his death. The greatest number of bust cup plates portray Henry Clay (Ill. 160)—at least ten are known, eight with a very young profile facing left and two with an older profile facing right. These last two were probably issued during the 1832 campaign. They are quite scarce, and are generally considered to be of superior workmanship to the eight varieties issued during the 1844 campaign, which are distinguished chiefly by their rim design, type of lettering, diameter, and variations in floral arrangement. Two or three of the 1844 design show up fairly often, and so collectors should have no trouble finding examples. Look also for the "Washington George" cup plate. It has a bust facing right that is very similar to the 1844 Clays, and totally unlike the two Washington cup plates mentioned at first.

160. Sandwich cup plates and industry bowl: William Henry Harrison is depicted at the upper left and Henry Clay at the lower right.

At least fifteen varieties of the log cabin pattern are known. Like the 1844 Clays, they are distinguished by such variations as the presence or absence of a cider barrel, a liberty pole, a flag, or a plain or fancy rim design. Perhaps three varieties show up frequently, including the one variety that has lettering.

Reproductions of historical cup plates have been made at least since the early 1920s; a few of the 1844 Clays are the most frequently copied ones. Most fakes are easily detected! Hold the plate in the center between thumb and forefinger and lightly tap the edge—a pleasant ring should sound if the plate is a nineteenth-century one. Fakes with scalloped rims tend to have rounded edges on the scallops, and often the glass is unnecessarily thick. There will also be minute design variations from the original.

Little is known about the "industry" bowl shown in Illustration 160, so-called because a factory with a smoking stack forms part of the rim design, except that four varieties exist—two made by the New England Glass Company and two by the Boston and Sandwich glass firm. Plain or scalloped rims are the major design variation. The bowl measures 6¼ inches across, and in addition to the factory the rim depicts a farmer with horse and plow—repeated once—and a three-masted ship under full sail. A large log cabin motif occupies the center of the bowl. The industry bowl is "lacy"—i.e., it has a background of delicate stippling that creates an attractive lacelike appearance. Collectors will be more likely to find an example with a scalloped rim than a plain rim.

LATER NINETEENTH-CENTURY ISSUES. Plates, tumblers, sugars, creamers, frosted glass, crystal glass, milk glass—there is something from this period for every collector.

Until further production was halted by the federal government in the early 1890s, coin glass was a popular pattern on American dinner tables. Patterns exactly duplicating the coin of the realm were etched with hydrofluoric acid. They had a frosted appearance, which contrasted pleasantly with the surrounding clear glass. The same technique was applied to a few patterns of political glassware. There are two plate designs, as well as a few tumblers and pedestal busts (which will be discussed later). Each plate pattern is, in my opinion, one of the more impressive examples of nineteenth-century historical glassware. From the 1884 campaign there is an 11-inch circular pattern known as Classic; each plate bears a frosted portrait of the presidential nominee or the vice-presidential nominee of both major parties. (The set of four was appraised recently at a Sotheby Parke-Bernet auction for $600.) None of these plates shows up very often, but no one plate seems to be scarcer than another. The second design also dates from the 1884 campaign. It is 11½ by 8½ inches—and comes in a paired set. On each plate are frosted portraits of either the Democratic or Republican presidential nominee and his running mate set within a rectangular frame bordered with stippled ivy leaves. A handle at each side enhances the general appearance. The same design was also used in the 1888 campaign, but the plates were made without handles and in a slightly small-

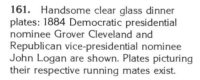

161. Handsome clear glass dinner plates: 1884 Democratic presidential nominee Grover Cleveland and Republican vice-presidential nominee John Logan are shown. Plates picturing their respective running mates exist.

er size—9½ by 8½ inches. Perhaps the 1888 variety appears a bit more often on the market than the 1884 variety. Both varieties were made by Gillinder and Sons of Philadelphia and are signed by the sculptor, a very uncommon feature indeed and evidence of the manufacturer's high regard for his product.

A few other plates, although not of as superior design as the frosted pieces, are nevertheless very desirable. An oval 1912 Teddy Roosevelt design in clear pressed glass measuring 10¼ by 7¾ inches is the most easily obtained. Surrounding a profile of Roosevelt are a spread eagle above and crossed clubs below (remember "Walk softly and carry a big stick"?); to the left, a hunting knife and a shotgun; to the right, crossed rifles and a Rough Rider hat. Between these four symbols of Roosevelt's career are cavorting teddy bears. A hard-to-find set of oval platters (11¼ by 8 inches) from the 1908 campaign portrays Taft and Sherman and Bryan and Kern in low relief. The portraits on the Taft platter are separated by a spread eagle and the "GOP" elephant; below are the candidates' names and the inscription "Our Candidates." The Bryan platter is the same, except that a rooster is shown instead of an elephant. Both these are difficult to locate. Several clear glass plates that are superior in material and pattern are not too difficult to obtain. Some of them were probably made by McKee and Brothers of Pittsburgh. On an 1880 issue James Garfield is depicted in profile surrounded by a wide border of stars. On an 1896 issue, in two diameters, 7 inches and 9 inches, William McKinley is depicted within a shield and a wide border of stars; below is the inscription "Protection and Prosperity." Possibly Garfield's and McKinley's opponents—Winfield Scott Hancock and William Jennings Bryan, respectively—are depicted on similar plates, but I have not seen any.

Tumblers with political themes exist in considerable variety and number from about the 1880 through the 1908 campaigns (Ills. 162 and 163). Portraits of both the

162. Thick glass tumblers picturing William McKinley and Ulysses Grant on the bottom surfaces. Similar glasses are known for Garfield, Hancock, Cleveland, Blaine, B. Harrison, and Bryan.

163. High-quality thin glass tumblers of this type are known from at least 1892 through 1912. The designs are lightly etched.

164. A Heisey glass sugar with a bust of William J. Bryan; a similar sugar pictures William McKinley.

party nominees seem to appear as often as of the presidential nominee only. Most often found are tumblers with an etched portrait. Much more difficult to obtain are those with a raised or an intaglio bust of the candidate in the bottom. Bottom-bust tumblers seem to be of presidential candidates only. Several depicting Ulysses S. Grant are quite possibly memorial pieces or issued in connection with Grand Army encampments. Among other containers similar to tumblers are Heisey clear glass mugs with domed covers and low relief portraits of McKinley or Bryan (Ill. 164). These are well made and designed, and are among the very few of the better political glass pieces of the period that are relatively easy to obtain. More often than not, these mugs turn up without their covers—mugs with covers intact command higher prices.

A pair of handsome 6¼-inch hand-blown goblets in clear crystal glass dates from the 1872 campaign. Each goblet bears a medallion profile, on opposite sides, of the presidential and vice-presidential nominees, Republicans Ulysses S. Grant and Henry Wilson and Democrats Horace Greeley and B. Gratz Brown. This pair (Ill. 165) is among the very few ceramics and glass issues from the 1872 campaign, but—sadly—it is extremely rare, although the Grant/Wilson goblet may show up slightly more often than the Greeley/Brown one.

165. The rare Grant and Greeley goblets. Bust outlines of their respective running mates can be seen on the opposite sides.

166. A matched pair of light amber cups showing Cleveland and Harrison and their running mates from the 1888 campaign; this pattern also exists in clear glass. A similar cup shows James Garfield and Abraham Lincoln—the "martyred presidents" theme.

MILK GLASS.   Among political collectors, milk glass is the most underrated collectible glassware. Milk glass pieces of superior quality have a soft sheen; some have a touch of iridescence that adds to their attractiveness. There is a good variety of political milk glass that, with few exceptions, is fairly easy to acquire.

Plates are the most common form, some of them intended to be hung on the wall. In that category is the famous (among milk glass collectors) Lincoln plaque (Ill. 167). An extremely high relief bust of Lincoln is centered in an oval shaped by an open pattern of split rails, complete with a textured surface. The issue date of this piece is debatable. Because of the way Lincoln's hair is parted and the presence of a beard, some authorities attribute it to the 1864 campaign. But the centennial year of 1909 is an equally likely issue date. Either way, a collector is lucky to have one at all because it is a very difficult piece to find. Other wall plaques are known for Garfield, Cleveland, Benjamin Harrison, McKinley, Bryan, Parker, and Theodore Roosevelt. Some of these have a ridged reverse with holes for looping the hanger; others are holed in the upper rim.

Most such plates seem to have been issued in pairs, especially from the 1896 through the 1908 campaigns. Two examples are noteworthy. A strikingly designed pair from the 1900 campaign has deep-set photographs of Bryan and McKinley framed in gold-leaf borders and openwork rims. The gold leaf has flecked off some of these plates that appear on the market—but they do not appear often. A very political-looking pair from the 1908 campaign portrays front-facing busts of Bryan and Taft with a rim design of spread eagles and stars. Curiously, the Bryan plate is often found with considerable iridescence, and both plates have been found with traces of red and blue paint and gilding, though rarely.

Milk glass collectors consider hand-painted pieces eminently desirable. The 7-inch hand-painted Lincoln plate (Plate 16) is one of the finest and rarest pieces of presidential glassware, and in my opinion ranks near the top of the list of choice pieces of political Americana. It could conceivably have been an 1864 campaign issue, as by that time Generals Grant and Sherman were certainly popular in the North and it would have been appropriate to portray the three heroes together. Perhaps just as desirable, however, are the attractive Bryan (Ill. 168) and McKinley pitcher and tumbler sets from the 1896 campaign, which are decorated tastefully in a pink and green wild-rose design surrounding a black transfer portrait of the candidate. I have never seen either pitcher (the Bryan pitcher is illustrated in Belknap, p. 78), but the tumblers show up occasionally. These sets are made of thin, almost translucent, milk glass, a rarity in itself.

167.   This Lincoln milk glass wall plaque is sometimes found with traces of brown paint.

168.   William Jennings Bryan is shown on a translucent milk glass tumbler from the 1896 campaign.

Modern Political Glassware

There is a considerable variety of modern political glassware consisting mostly of water glasses, ashtrays, flasks and whiskey bottles, and a few plates. Many issues commemorate inaugurations, and these often picture the new president and the new first lady. Red, white, and blue decals and simple silhouette outlines are the basis of most designs.

Far and away the most spectacular modern piece (Ill. 169) is a finely engraved British-made crystal goblet that commemorates both Franklin D. Roosevelt's first inauguration and the repeal of Prohibition. Above a bust of Roosevelt are crossed flags enclosed within a wreath and a spread eagle; below is the inscription "Fiat/1933." On the opposite side are two facing birds (jays?), a cluster of grapes and leaves, and the inscription "Repeal of the 18th Amendment." An inscription around the rim reads "Franklin D. Roosevelt/32nd President of the United States of America/Inaugurated March 4th 1933." Inscribed around the base is "Asst. Sec. of the Navy 1913–1920/Gov. of New York State 1929–1933." A very busy goblet, but unlike much other modern political Americana, it is an aesthetically pleasing and altogether handsome piece. There is also a fine and very heavy 7¾-inch lead crystal vase with his etched portrait that commemorates Dwight Eisenhower's first inauguration in 1953.

169. The finest modern glass piece with a political theme: This crystal goblet (somewhat distorted in the photograph) commemorates both Franklin Roosevelt's first inauguration and the end of Prohibition.

170. Although it is not evident in the illustration, these figural bottles of Generals Scott and McClellan are nearly jet black.

171. Political figural bottles are seldom found in such fine condition as this Cleveland one. A similar Harrison figural bottle is known.

The Roosevelt goblet and the Eisenhower vase are the only truly outstanding modern pieces, but this dismal situation should not keep the collector from adding other modern pieces to his collection. For example, there is a 1936 clear glass cup and saucer with an etched portrait of the Republican nominee Alfred M. Landon; both pieces are inscribed "Elect Landon/Save America." Presumably the country had to be saved from Roosevelt, for in that same year he had spoken at the dedication of the federal government's recently completed hydroelectric project operated by the Tennessee Valley Authority. An interesting bottle commemorating this new venture into public ownership of an energy source is an aqua calabash-type one with a relief bust of Roosevelt, an eagle and shield, and "1936"; on the opposite side is a dam with water flowing, a hand clutching a bolt of lightning, and "TVA." It seldom appears on the market.

Beyond searching for the elusive pieces described here, collectors may want to assemble a collection of water glasses and other tumblers. Such a collection *must* include a clear glass mug bearing a caricature of George McGovern and the inscription "Shakey's Pizza Parlor."

Glass Novelties

FIGURALS. These are bottles made in or to resemble human or animal shapes. Bottle collectors give high priority to figurals, and so political collectors must expect to pay high prices. Late nineteenth-century figurals were usually mold blown of very thin glass

so that all crevices in the mold would be filled; hence, very few bust figurals have survived. More recent figurals such as Avons and Beams were produced in limited amounts. Either way, political figurals are hard to find; when one is found, treasure it.

The earliest political figurals that I am aware of were produced by a tonic manufacturer during the Civil War. These rare figurals are 6-inch pedestal busts of Generals George McClellan and Winfield Scott (Ill. 170) in black or deep amethyst. Probably other Union notables were so immortalized also. Possibly a bit easier to find are a few clear glass figurals from the campaigns of the 1880s, notably busts of Garfield, Cleveland (Ill. 171), and Harrison, ranging in size from 6¾ to about 10 inches. Authorities agree that these figurals were cologne bottles. The cork-closed opening is either at the top of the bust or at the bottom; in the latter case a small wood frame was employed as a stand. Smaller bust figurals of McKinley, Bryan, and Teddy Roosevelt are also known.

There is a fair variety of George Washington figurals commemorating the 1876 centennial (Ill. 172) and the centennial of the first inauguration, in 1889. The variety collectors are most likely to see is a 10½-inch clear glass military pedestal bust inscribed on the base "Simon's Centennial Bitters/Trade Mark"; it is also known in aqua. This has been reproduced many times; the most ubiquitous copy is a 4-inch cobalt bust with a screw top that was made about 1940.

A few animal figurals are also available. Among them are GOP elephants in amber, both horizontal and vertical format, that were probably issued during the 1888 campaign. They are fairly easily obtained. From recent campaigns there are the garish Avon and Beam bottles and the paired elephant and donkey figurals issued by the Wheaton Glass Company for the 1968 campaign. They are quite well designed. The Democratic issue, which measures 6 by 7 by 2 inches, is light green; on each side it bears a circular insert with a relief profile—Hubert Humphrey on one side and Edmund Muskie on the other. The Republican issue in light amber, which has reliefs of Richard Nixon and Spiro Agnew, is similar.

172. A Washington figural bottle associated with the 1876 centennial; copies exist in the same and in different sizes and colors.

MISCELLANEOUS GLASS NOVELTIES. Toothpick holders in the form of Benjamin Harrison novelty hats were issued most often in clear, amber, or milk glass, but some were made of brass, tin, or porcelain. When William Henry Harrison's grandson became the Republican nominee in 1888, Democrats introduced a campaign song entitled "His Grandfather's Hat"—it's too big for Ben. Republicans countered with "The Same Old Hat"—it fits Ben just right. As a result of this amusing incident in the 1888 campaign, a variety of novelty beaver hats were produced measuring no more than 3 inches in height and inscribed, usually, "The Same Old Hat" and less often "His Grandfather's Hat." They are charming pieces, and with patience it is possible to build a representative grouping of them, perhaps to accompany a collection of convention and campaign hats, a subject to be discussed in Chapter 7 (Ill. 266).

On the subject of hats, the milk glass Uncle Sam hats from the 1908 campaign should be mentioned. These red and blue striped novelties were actually candy banks. The openings were fitted with slotted metal disks bearing paper labels picturing Democrats Bryan and Kern or Republicans Taft and Sherman. The disks must be present in order to identify these banks as political.

Another interesting category of political glass, one that has been ignored by many collectors, is the paperweight—a prosaic household item ordinarily, but not so when there were presidential candidates to publicize. Probably the earliest campaign issue is an 1868 thick round weight with a military bust of Ulysses S. Grant in chalk or plaster enclosed in a thick glass cover. From the 1896 through the 1908 campaigns there are handsome clear glass five- or six-pointed star weights with very high convex centers depicting the presidential and vice-presidential candidates and colorful patriotic backgrounds (Ill. 175). These weights are made of very thick glass with gilt decorated points. More commonly found are sepia photograph weights in the shape of a rectangle or a circular disk with a photograph of the candidate pasted on the bottom. The photograph is very often faded. These weights measure about 1 inch in thickness and 2 by 4 inches, or 3 inches in diameter. Also available are memorial weights. A contemporary one picturing Abraham Lincoln is very well done, and there are also the lovely, and very expensive, modern Baccarat sulphide weights in rich ruby, emerald, sapphire, and other colors.

But the prize political paperweight is a 7½-inch clear, solid glass figural of Teddy Roosevelt in safari costume returning from a hunting trip (Ill. 176). In one hand he holds his rifle; slung over his shoulder is a very dead lion whose head lies on the base at the back of the weight. Above Teddy's pith helmet is a knob. This is a very clever piece and obviously the result of careful workmanship.

From the 1888 and 1892 Harrison and Cleveland campaigns there are frosted

173. This small berry dish commemorates Democrat John Davis's nomination for the presidency in 1924; it shows up more often than many of his campaign buttons.

174. A black glass candy dish; the illustrations around the border are gilded, which makes a rather striking combination (1968 campaign).

pedestal busts in heights up to 9 inches. Lindsey (see Bibliography) illustrates one such Harrison bust on an 11-inch black glass column (p. 332). From the 1880 campaign there is a milk glass shaving mug, the only political shaving mug I know, of an unusual shape in that it includes a holder for the brush (Ill. 178). This mug bears a relief portrait of James Garfield and has a blank reverse; another variety pictures Mrs. Garfield on the reverse, and it is reputed to exist in clambroth glass also.

To conclude this brief discussion of political glass novelties, I must mention three delightful little gems from the 1840 campaign. First are two approximately 1¼-ounce bitters bottles in the shape of cider barrels. One is 2¼ inches by 1¼ inches, and sits horizontally. On one side is the inscription "Tippecanoe Extract"; on the other side, "Hard Cider." The other, about the same size, stands vertically; it has raised barrel bands and a cork closure—there is no inscription. The most desirable of the three is one of the choice pieces from the 1840 campaign. This log cabin cologne bottle (2½ by 2 by 2½ inches), with silvered brass neck and glass stopper, is made of very heavy clear pressed glass, and is scarce (Ill. 179).

175. This paperweight has a multicolored picture of the 1904 Republican candidates; a similar paperweight pictures the Democratic candidates.

176. The best political paperweight depicts Teddy Roosevelt. Its clear glass and sparkle do not show well in the illustration.

177. Frosted glass pedestal busts: James Garfield at the left and Benjamin Harrison at the right. Similar busts exist for candidates through the early 1900s.

179. A cologne or perfume bottle from the 1840 Log Cabin campaign (much enlarged in this illustration).

178. The rare Garfield milk glass shaving mug, unusual in that it has a separate holder for the shaving brush.

7
Political Textiles

179A. This ribbon commemorates President Taft's visit to the Alaska, Yukon and Pacific Exposition held in Seattle in 1909. It measures 14¼" × 5¼"!

MANY COLLECTORS do not appreciate political textiles. With the exception of campaign ribbons, the varieties of collectible textiles are limited. Some political textiles, especially banners, take up considerable display and storage space. An equally serious drawback is the lack of information: Scholars and antiquarians have generally neglected the study of American textiles both as a part of our social history and as an art form. The literature dealing with historical American textile prints is nearly nonexistent. Not until the recent publication of Herbert Collins's *Threads of History* was there an authoritative study of the many early textiles depicting American patriotic, presidential, and various social themes and subjects. Nor was there a comprehensive study or catalog describing and locating some of the many, and often magnificent, campaign parade banners that were so much a part of the nineteenth-century electioneering. Today we still lack scholarly studies and cataloging of the wonderful array of campaign ribbons and ribbon badges, which were as popular with voters in their time as campaign buttons are with modern voters. Unlike collectors of historical American china, glass, and paper, who have a large body of research available to them, collectors of political textiles must depend almost entirely upon their own knowledge and instincts.

But there are certain advantages in this overall situation. First, prices are not well established in this low-demand market; hence fine and often rare textiles can be bought cheaply. Second, the subject of political textiles, including campaign ribbons, is so unexplored that there is a fine opportunity for some collector to publish a definitive study. Third, there is the chance to assemble a collection that, for depth and breadth, would be matched only by the holdings of the Smithsonian Institution. Certainly few collections of the scope possible in this area currently exist in private hands.

By and large, political textiles are indeed the untouched sleeper in our hobby.

Political Ribbons

But political ribbons are not "untouched"; indeed, they are almost as popular with collectors as are campaign buttons. For the serious collector of political, or campaign, ribbons, there is a wide variety to choose among, with several areas of specialization, and it is possible to build a distinctive and valuable collection.

179B. Another bit of proof that political Americana shows up in the most unexpected uses!

(Courtesy of Kenneth Hosner.)

180. Typical Harrison campaign ribbons. At the left Harrison is pictured with Washington and Lafayette (who was greatly admired by many Americans). The middle ribbon is an early example of a campaign artifact with a local tie-in; the ribbon on the right depicts "The Hero of Tippecanoe" in a heroic pose and reminds voters of his "humble" origins.

THE EARLY SILKS.   The earliest campaign ribbons, used from 1800 to about 1864, were made usually of silk or silklike material and less often of cotton or linen. These early silks were meant to be used as bookmarks, which is why so many of them are found today in sharp and nearly pristine condition. Naturally, both the kind and extent of damage to a campaign ribbon affect its value: Small tears, creases, pinholes, stains, and fading are the most common flaws.

Almost all ribbons from this period have lithographed designs in black; a few have drawn designs and a few, all rare and all from the 1860 campaign, bear prints of Brady photographs. Most of the early silks were issued in white or cream cloth; occasionally in light shades of green, orange, blue, and red; very seldom in dark colors; and rarely in several colors. Other multicolored designs probably exist, but I know of only one example, the Henry Clay silk, which is shown in Plate 4.

There must be well over 150 designs marking William Henry Harrison's candidacy in 1840; perhaps almost as many were issued for Henry Clay during his three campaigns (but most Clay ribbons date from the 1844 campaign); and perhaps a dozen each mark the campaigns of Martin Van Buren, Zachary Taylor, James Polk, and James Buchanan. Among candidates for whom the fewest ribbons are known are Franklin Pierce, Winfield Scott, Lewis Cass, Andrew Jackson, and John Quincy Adams—each of these candidates is represented by probably no more than five or six different designs, and Adams by only two or three ribbons. There are also a small number of rather crudely drawn designs associated with Thomas Jefferson, James Madison, and James Monroe, but all are extremely rare and seldom appear on the market. At the other end of the period are perhaps as many as fifty different Lincoln designs, many of which are not particularly difficult to find—but because the subject is Abraham Lincoln, they tend to be priced accordingly.

The large variety of Harrison designs makes Harrison ribbons ideal for a specialized collection. On many of them the Hero of Tippecanoe is pictured as a fearless general, or compared with Washington and Lafayette (Ill. 180). One favorite ribbon among collectors pictures Harrison, a log cabin, a spread eagle, the Bunker Hill monument, and a boot, with "Lynn" below. This ribbon was worn by Harrison supporters from that Massachusetts city, noted for its shoe factories. Martin Van Buren ribbons (all designs

181. Henry Clay is likened to Moses on the Mount on one ribbon; he is honored by wagoneers, or "cartmen," on the other. The Know-Nothing ribbon was used, I believe, in a suburb of Philadelphia.

are scarce) frequently picture him in an heroic standing pose accompanied by such forgettable inscriptions as "The Working Man—He is to Society what the main-mast is to the ship."(A similar example depicting Henry Clay is pictured in Illustration 181.) Clay portrait ribbons bear such stirring inscriptions as "The People's Welfare My Reward" or "Fearless Friend of His Country's Rights." An effusive burst on another ribbon portrays him as "His Country's Friend in the Hour of Danger/Pride of America/The Champion of Her Liberties/Poor Man's Friend/Advocate of Our Principles." The rhetoric on ribbons from later in the period tends to be more restrained; most ribbons merely picture the candidate and list a few of his accomplishments or selections from the party platform or perhaps a brief quotation indicative of his patriotism or sincerity.

One ribbon, however, from this later part of the period—issued during the 1856 campaign in support of the Democratic nominee, James Buchanan—is, in my opinion, the most interesting of all the early silks. It is especially notable because it so well portrays the issues of that campaign and the political symbols of the day as well (see Ill. 184). At the top of the ribbon stands a noble stag, "Old Buck," fearless and resolute. He is "coming" to save the country from the Republican nominee, John Frémont, who would "free niggers." (Frémont's name gave rise to the Republican campaign slogan "Frémont and Freedom." Democrats reacted with such puns as "Frémont and Free Love," "Frémont and Free Niggers.") Freed slaves would run off to the Rocky Moun-

182. Scott is pictured on an 1852 ribbon with the names of several of his victories in the Mexican War; Tyler was our first "accidental president" (ribbon, c. 1841); Cass hailed from Michigan, a long way from the sea in 1848; Polk was a strong supporter of statehood for Texas during the 1844 campaign.

183. These Fillmore, Taylor, and Frémont ribbons were used in Connecticut and Massachusetts communities. Clay is pictured with Theodore Frelinghuysen, his running mate in 1844.

184. The 1856 campaign issues are graphically dramatized in this scarce ribbon supporting James Buchanan.

tains, the territory explored by Frémont, "The Pathfinder," and establish black enclaves, thus denying white Americans free homesteading privileges. The "National Candidate" is former President Millard Fillmore, now the candidate of the Native American, or Know-Nothing, party; he will carry but one state (Maryland) in the forthcoming election despite his scattershot approach, as represented by the pepperbox pistol. Fillmore and his cohorts will sail by Salt River, which was a nineteenth-century euphemism for political oblivion, on a "black birder," a slave runner. A remarkable ribbon. But I have not been able to learn the meaning of the "plug organs" mentioned in the next to last line of the ribbon, and I would appreciate hearing from readers and learning of a citation.

For their part, the Know-Nothings themselves had an interesting variety of ribbons—about twenty-five different designs were issued by this party during its short-lived existence. The ribbons are usually headed "Native American Party" or "American Republican Party"; members preferred to be called "Natives." Many of the ribbons picture George Washington, whom the Know-Nothings idealized because of the oft-quoted remarks in his Farewell Address about the "dangers of foreign entanglements" and the need to "beware of foreign influences." Some ribbons bear the name of a city or town, or even a city ward such as "Third Ward/Spring Garden," "First Ward/Moyamensing," or "First Ward/Kensington." In fact, many ribbons from this period carry names of localities down to the smallest villages, something for collectors to consider. As an example, I was born and raised in Salem, Massachusetts, and so have searched for ribbons and other political artifacts that are associated with the Witch City. Given the extent and variety of political artifacts that were, and are, commonplace across the American landscape, collectors should be able to construct novel historical interpretations of their own hometowns in terms of political artifacts. Perhaps a Know-Nothing ribbon or two might become a part of a "hometown" political collection. But be advised that most Know-Nothing ribbons are quite scarce, although a certain six or so show up fairly often and can be purchased for under a hundred dollars each.

As might be expected, Lincoln campaign ribbons are extremely popular and command prices out of proportion to their availability. Most Lincoln designs date from the 1860 campaign, and usually they bear drawn copies of Brady and Hesler photographs of Lincoln. A few of the 1864 ribbons picture a bearded Lincoln; others use the standard 1860 portraits but substitute Andrew Johnson's name or portrait for Hannibal Hamlin's. (Hamlin was Lincoln's running mate in 1860.) The single most desirable Lincoln ribbon is an attractive 1860 silk bearing Brady photographs of Lincoln and Hamlin (Ill. 185). This ribbon is part of a set of four, representing each of the four teams of candidates in the 1860 campaign: Lincoln and Hamlin for the Republicans, Stephen Douglas and Herschell Johnson for the Democrats, John Breckinridge and Joseph Lane for the Southern Democrats, and John Bell and Edward Everett (the other speaker at Gettys-

185. The famous Brady set from the 1860 campaign. *Left to right:* John Breckinridge and Joseph Lane; Stephen Douglas and Herschell Johnson; John Bell and Edward Everett; Abraham Lincoln and Hannibal Hamlin.

burg) for the Constitutional Unionists. The four ribbons are superb examples of Brady's portrait photography on silk and must be considered among the very finest of all political Americana artifacts. For persevering collectors the set of four is a prize indeed.

From the same era a few silks associated with the Confederacy are known. One example is an exact copy of the Stars and Bars and bears the names of President Jefferson Davis and Vice-President Alexander Stephens. The most interesting Confederate ribbon (Ill. 186) is a rather complicated affair that was probably worn during the Confederacy's only presidential inauguration: A 1-inch-diameter albumin photograph of Davis is mounted on a 2¼-inch-diameter blue silk ribbon rosette. Inscribed below the photograph is "The Right Man in the Right Place/Our First President/Jeff Davis"; the rosette, in turn, is mounted on a dark blue or, less often, light red ribbon.

STEVENGRAPHS AND OTHER EMBROIDERED RIBBONS.

Among the most desirable of all political ribbons are the multicolored and aesthetically appealing embroidered designs issued by European and American manufacturers in the 1860–1896 period.

186. The finest known example of a Confederate political ribbon.

Foremost among these "embroideries" are the ribbons issued by the Thomas Stevens Company of Coventry, England. There are two types of Stevengraphs of interest to political collectors: (a) bookmarks, all of which have a pointed lower edge and tassel, and are identified with the mark "T. Stevens/Coventry" on the back of the point; (b) portrait silks, which average 4 by 2½ inches in size and carry no identifying mark. The earliest bookmarks picture Ulysses S. Grant, and since most of these Grant designs are dated "1865," we can assume that they were issued during the last months of the war or shortly thereafter. Although Grant Stevengraphs were issued before Grant decided to seek the presidency in 1868, collectors associate them with the 1868 campaign. There are four attractive Grant bookmark designs, plus two variants, ranging in size from 5½ by 1¾ inches to 9½ by 2⅛ inches, all with tassels. Each of the four designs shows the same three-quarter outward-facing bust of Grant, and he is ranked either as lieutenant general or general. The design of the largest ribbon includes a spread eagle and an oval wreath surrounding the portrait. A variant of this design has the added inscription "President of the United States of America," suggesting that the original design was reissued to commemorate his inauguration in 1869. The smallest ribbon is inscribed in part "Vicksburg/Fort Donelson" along with his inspiring words, which appear on many Grant campaign artifacts, "I Shall Fight It Out on This Line If It Takes All Summer." A variant of this ribbon substitutes "Shiloh" for "Fort Donelson."

One Stevengraph is associated with Democrat Horatio Seymour, Grant's opponent in the 1868 campaign, and the former wartime governor of New York. Seymour is another of those "most forgotten" candidates for the presidency for whom relatively few campaign artifacts exist. We are fortunate to have one showpiece Seymour item to accompany the ferrotypes and medalets from his campaign. The Seymour Stevengraph is 6½ by 1¾ inches and, as can be seen in Illustration 187, provides the essential information. The colors are black, red, and blue on silver—an attractive combination.

Abraham Lincoln is represented by one striking Stevengraph and a variant. The design is similar to the largest Grant design and quite possibly was issued as a companion to it—perhaps to commemorate the Union's victory or Lincoln's second inauguration in 1865. The variant marks his death, and is about an inch longer in order to accommodate an added inscription at the top and "The Late Lamented President Lincoln" below the portrait.

Perhaps five or six bookmarks honor George Washington. All were issued during the 1876 centennial and possibly for the centennial of his inauguration in 1889. The designs are attractive; although they are not campaign related, these bookmarks merit a place in a ribbon collection.

Stevens portrait silks are difficult to identify because the company name is not im-

187. The Hancock ribbon was made by a Swiss weaver; the Seymour one is a Stevengraph; the Cleveland ribbon was manufactured by a Connecticut company.

188. A grim-faced Lincoln is pictured on this French-made 1860 ribbon; the attractive border is embroidered in several colors.

printed. Portrait silks manufactured by the Stevens Company were attached to card mounts when originally issued. Identification and sometimes titles were printed on the card mounts. There are only five silks (that we can be certain about), plus two variants, portraying American subjects: Ulysses S. Grant, Grover Cleveland, Frances Cleveland, Benjamin Harrison, and George Washington. Silks picturing the presidents have a common design consisting of a red, white, and blue shield and crossed flags surmounted by a spread eagle. The silk picturing Mrs. Cleveland has a spray embroidered tastefully in white, purple, and green threads below the portrait. The card mount accompanying this silk reads "Mrs. Cleveland/Queen of 60 Millions of Free People." The Grover Cleveland and Benjamin Harrison designs issued in 1887 and 1892 respectively are known with and without facsimile signatures below the portraits. The Grant silk was probably issued sometime during the 1880s. The Washington silk was first issued in 1888 and was reissued later for the Columbian Exposition in Chicago in 1893. For collectors of political trade cards, there is a bonus: Those silks picturing President and Mrs. Cleveland are known mounted together on a card mount that carries an advertisement for Allen Ginters's Richmond Straight Cut cigarettes.

A fairly large number of embroidered ribbons made by American and other European manufacturers are also of interest to political collectors. Just a few examples will be mentioned here. First in point of time and scarcity are two 1861 European designs, each of which portrays a rather grim-faced Lincoln. One is an undistinguished black and white design of French origin. The second is an outstanding addition to any collection (Ill. 188): Above Lincoln's portrait is a spray of lavender flowers, a shield and an eagle, and a scroll inscribed "Union For Ever"; below is a green spray and "A. Lincoln/President." This ribbon is dated 1861 and was issued by a Swiss weaver, possibly to commemorate Lincoln's first inauguration. Other candidates, through the 1892 campaign, are pictured on a colorful variety of ribbons, a few of which are almost exact duplicates of small Stevens bookmarks picturing British subjects of the period. The United States Badge Company of Pittsburgh and B. B. Tilt and Son of Paterson, New Jersey, are among the better-known ribbon manufacturers of the day. P. W. Turner and Son of Turnersville, Connecticut, are known for their beautiful jugate ribbons from the 1880 and 1884 campaigns. Most ribbons—but not all—issued by these manufacturers will carry their name on the back at the top or bottom. Some Tilt issues simply say "Trade Mark." Of particular interest to collectors are the smallest and the largest American designs. Look for small, neatly embroidered 1892 designs, 3½ by 1½ inches, with tassels, that picture Grover Cleveland, or Benjamin Harrison, and the White House (U.S. Badge). Perhaps the most striking Tilt design (other than a Washington design to be discussed shortly) is a large Lincoln commemorative issued in two varieties during the 1876 centennial. The major differences are in length—11¾ and 13 inches—and in the inclusion of a minor quotation on the longer ribbon. Both are striking red, white, and blue designs dominated by a selection from Lincoln's Second Inaugural Address below his portrait.

FRINGES AND TASSELS.   This section could not be given any other title. Ribbons in the period from 1868 to 1904 are distinguished by their elaborate designs and decorations, their large size (imagine a ribbon 13 inches long hanging from your lapel!), and the liberal use of metallic thread in the form of tassels and fringe—perhaps with the inscription in metallic thread also. Many of the ribbons of this period are fancy affairs indeed, and when we consider the colorful variety of embroidered designs as well, it is clear that collectors have a remarkable opportunity to assemble a specialized collection of interesting and colorful examples of political Americana. Nor should the plain and fancy bar clasps from which many ribbons are suspended be overlooked: spread eagles, engraved floral and geometric designs, and on one 1880 Garfield ribbon a bar clasp in the shape of a canal boat that recalls Garfield's boyhood job as a tow boy (one who walked or rode the mules that pulled canal barges).

Because of the considerable amount of political activity that occurred in cities, villages, and hamlets everywhere in the last part of the nineteenth century, there are virtually hundreds of ribbons available for collectors. They can be found marking state and national conventions, presidential inaugurations, candidate appearances at rallies and parades, candidates' association with the Grand Army of the Republic, and various special events along the campaign trail. There is a particularly interesting array of McKinley "pilgrimage" ribbons, many of which are not difficult to locate (Ill. 189). During the 1896 campaign thousands of citizens traveled in specially scheduled railroad trains to Canton, Ohio, to hear their champion say a few words from his front porch. Of course every visitor had to have a ribbon to commemorate the great occasion. While McKinley was conducting his "front porch" campaign, his opponent, William Jennings Bryan, was crisscrossing the country by train in the nation's first whistle-stop campaign. There are a few ribbons, all scarce, associated with this event that set the precedent for Harry Truman's similar, and successful, campaign in 1948.

188A.   A local stalwart ready for the parade. His fringe and tassel is truly impressive — even on his hefty frame!

189.   Examples of McKinley "pilgrimage" ribbons.

190. These are 1920 ribbon badges marking presidential notification ceremonies.

191. Despite the defiant raccoon and slogan, the Mulligan Letters scandal did hurt Blaine's candidacy in 1884. Note the stain caused by mounting tape at the bottom of the ribbon.

Also of interest to collectors are ribbons worn by members of notification committees. Until Franklin Roosevelt ended the custom in 1932, when he appeared at the Democratic National Convention to deliver his acceptance speech in person to the delegates, elected convention representatives would repair to the home of the successful nominee to notify him formally that he was his party's choice for the White House. The custom is still followed today, but it is a meaningless affair, often consisting simply of a brunch with the nominee and a few politicians from the party's inner circle. Because notification committees usually numbered between fifty and a hundred persons, related ribbons do not show up frequently, but with patience a fine representative collection can be assembled (Ill. 190).

Collections can also be made of the ribbons of special interest groups. Such ribbons were usually worn in local campaign parades and rallies and might have been worn by just a few or by many marchers. Here are the names of a few such groups:

Businessmen's Republican Club (1892)
British Isles American McKinley Club (1896)
Corbin Sound Money Club (T. Roosevelt, Connecticut, 1904)
Harrison and Morton Machinist Club (1888)
Employees of Otis Steel for McKinley (1896)
Commercial Travelers McKinley Club (1896 and 1900)
Jewelers' Taft and Sherman Club (1908)
The Princeton University Hawk Club (McKinley, 1896).

There were undoubtedly many more groups, and finding their previously unknown ribbons always brings a certain excitement to the hobby.

It is impossible to describe all the fringes and tassels favored by collectors, but here are a few of my own favorites. First is a 13-inch-long embroidered beauty that commemorates the inauguration of Grover Cleveland and Adlai Stevenson in 1893 (Plate 4). The color illustration does not fully bring out the rich shades of red, brown, and orange that dominate this ribbon. Note that both historic symbols of Tammany Hall are pictured, the Indian from the Hall's earliest years and the tiger—the famous Tammany Tiger—a symbol used dramatically by Thomas Nast when Tammany Hall was the subject of some of his most vitriolic cartoons. Note also the finely detailed view of the Capitol dome and, surmounting the whole affair, a well-made brass shell eagle clasp. Fortunately this ribbon turns up fairly often on the market.

On one of the more unusual ribbons of the period (Ill. 191), from James G. Blaine's campaign in 1884, a raccoon thumbs its nose; below is the inscription "Ohio/Don't Care/a Damn/for the/Mulligan Letters. /Three Cheers/and a Tiger/for/Blaine." The "Mulligan Letters" referred to a series of events involving Blaine, which began with his securing favorable congressional legislation for railroads and in particular for his railroad president friend, Warren Fisher. At Blaine's request, Fisher's bookkeeper, James Mulligan, returned to Blaine certain incriminating letters regarding the legislation that Blaine had written to Fisher. Blaine thereupon denied any wrongdoing. But other letters surfaced later that directly incriminated him. The resulting scandal hurt his "hopeful" candidacy in 1876 and 1880 and was an important factor in his loss to Grover Cleveland in 1884. This ribbon is another example of why collectors must be knowledgeable about American political history. ("Three cheers and a tiger" was, I believe, a college fraternity cheer of the period.)

Other favorites of mine—actually a grouping of ribbons—are the beautifully colored embroidered jugate designs picturing major party candidates from the 1876 through the 1888 campaigns. These beauties were manufactured by American and German firms; when found in perfect condition, they will have bright, vivid colors.

What should be evident by now is the fact that fringes and tassels exist in a profu-

Plate 1. A miscellany of campaign artifacts. **Left row:** an anti-Prohibition button, 1932; necktie picturing 1936 Republican nominee Alfred M. Landon; an 1896 cologne bottle depicting Democratic candidate William Jennings Bryan. **Top center:** metal serving tray with large portraits of 1908 Republican candidates William H. Taft and James Sherman and smaller pictures of previous Republican candidates. **Bottom center:** an uncommon 1884 campaign poster picturing Grover Cleveland and Thomas Hendricks. **Right row:** an 1860 paper lapel "ribbon" (note misspelling of "Abraham"); a 1964 campaign button for Lyndon Johnson; a rare 1856 campaign flag banner for the first nominees of the Republican party, John Frémont and William Dayton.

Plate 2. A selection of classic campaign buttons: the 1896 "hobby" pair is at the middle center; note the Maxfield Parrish figure pictured on the Taft button at the lower left (this adds to the button's value). A similar button has a portrait of William J. Bryan.

Plate 3. A selection of buttons from the "golden age"; note the third-party buttons and the paired set in the third row.

Plate 4. Colorful ribbons and ribbon badges, **left to right:** Henry Clay, 1844 campaign; Washington commemorative, 1876 Centennial; Tammany Hall issue marking Cleveland's second inauguration in 1893; Grant Stevengraph. Note the McKinley and Roosevelt ribbon badge below the Tammany ribbon.

Plate 5. **Puck** cartoon satirizing James G. Blaine, "The Plumed Knight," attempting to regain his lost reputation only to find that the armor no longer fits.

Plate 6. **The Lost Bet,** Joseph Klir's colorful print (1893) of one election result. The scene is set at what is now the corner of West 12th Street and Roosevelt Road in Chicago.

Plate 7.   Lincoln cartoon, Currier, 1860.

Plate 8.   Benjamin Harrison appears rather ill at ease behind a pair of unlikely looking farm horses on this superb political advertising poster, c. 1888.

Plate 9. Eugene Debs and Ben Hanford: campaign poster of the American Socialist party in 1904.

Plate 10. Currier campaign posters. **Left:** George McClellan and George Pendleton, 1864; **right:** Lewis Cass and William Butler, 1848.

Plate 12. A window decal from the 1920 campaign. A similar decal pictures Democratic nominees James M. Cox and Franklin D. Roosevelt.

Plate 11. What Republicans stood for and opposed are vividly illustrated in this attractive 1900 campaign poster.

Plate 13. Andrew Jackson copper luster creamer, c. 1824 or earlier.

Plate 14. This Wedgwood Etruria pitcher commemorates either James A. Garfield's inauguration or his death (both events occurred in 1881).

Plate 15. Franklin Roosevelt is pictured on this plate, one of a set that also included other Allied leaders in World War II.

Plate 16. Lincoln hand-painted milk glass commemorative plate, c. 1863.

Plate 17. A Bryan and Stevenson serving tray from the 1900 campaign. The fact that this tray carries an advertising message adds to its value.

Plate 18. This serving tray from the 1904 campaign pictures Teddy Roosevelt in a characteristic pose.

Plate 20. An outstanding example of an early campaign flag. The nose-thumbing raccoon was a popular party symbol through the 1880s.

Plate 19. A Lincoln campaign banner carried by Wide-Awakes of Belfast, Maine, in 1860.

Plate 21. William Henry Harrison: hand-painted silk banner, 1840.

Plate 22. Polk campaign flag, 1844.

Plate 23. McKinley and Roosevelt umbrella, 1900.

Plate 24. Garfield and Arthur "red" bandanna, 1880.

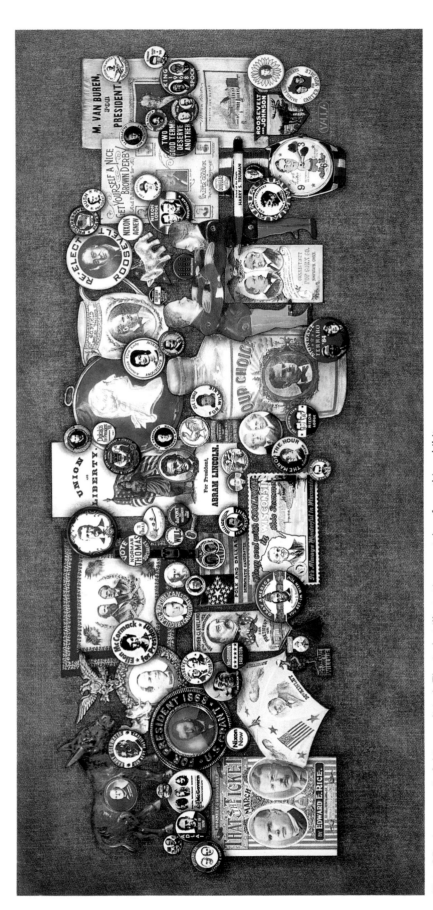

Plate 25. A potpourri of things political. The jacket illustration was taken from this exhibit.

Au·H2O·64

Plate 26. An automobile bumper sticker from the 1964 campaign of Republican candidate Barry Goldwater.

Color photography on the following pages
by Sally Anderson-Bruce

Plate 29. This handsome brooch shows Martin Van Buren, the eighth president. From the 1836 campaign, it also appears in text on page 26.

Plate 30. A glass lantern torch in support of Abraham Lincoln, ca. 1860.

▼ **Plate 28.** This is an appropriate lapel pin for journalist Horace Greeley, from his 1872 campaign. The item also appears in text on page 29 and illustration 49.

Plate 27. George Washington's first inauguration is commemorated by this tankard bearing the inscription "Deafness to the ears and silence to the tongue that will utter a calumny against the immortal Washington/Long live the President of the United States."

Plate 32. Note that Daniel Webster heads the list of "managers" or sponsors of the inaugural ball in honor of the new ninth president, William Henry Harrison.

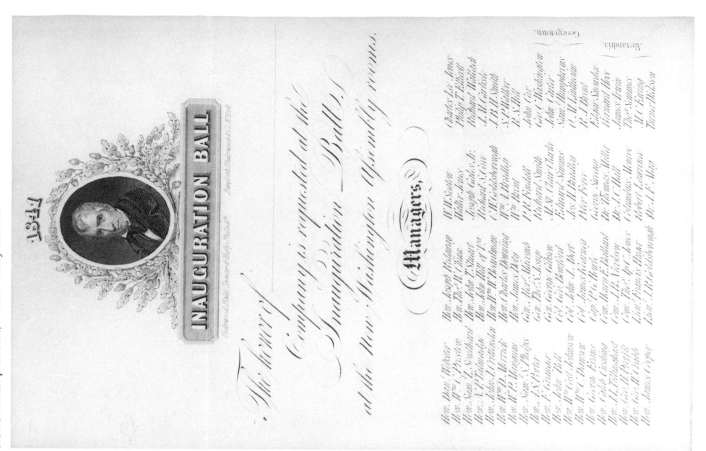

Plate 31. Henry Clay. This bandanna also appears on page 134, illustration 213.

▲ **Plate 34.** Zachary Taylor "Old Rough and Ready," rode his victories in the Mexican War right into the White House in 1848. This pin also appears in text on page 26, illustration 38.

Plate 33. Even though the spelling is wrong, the intent is right, in this hand drawn broadside protraying James Polk and George Dallas (for whom the city in Texas was named) as fearless navigators of the ship of state in 1844 campaign.

Plate 35. Franklin Pierce, the Granite State's favorite ▶ son, was the compromise winner on the Democratic side in 1852. See also page 73 in the text, illustration 107 for

▼ **Plate 38.** Paper letters and figures cut from an English hunting scene combine in a very effective poster supporting John C. Fremont, the first candidate of the Republican Party, and his wife Jessie, in 1856. See text page 61, illust. 93.

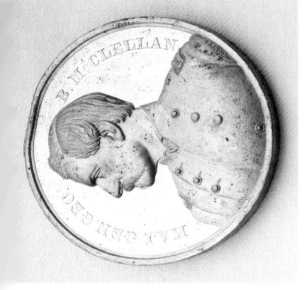

period. This one featuring General George McClellan, the Democratic nominee in 1864.

Plate 36. French caricaturist Jules Renard portrayed Lincoln as a notary public holding forth at the bar of Washington's Kirkland Hotel, ca. 1863.

Plate 39. This American Eagle is unable to keep the fragile shell of democracy intact as slimey and loathsome creatures emerge to form the Confederacy.

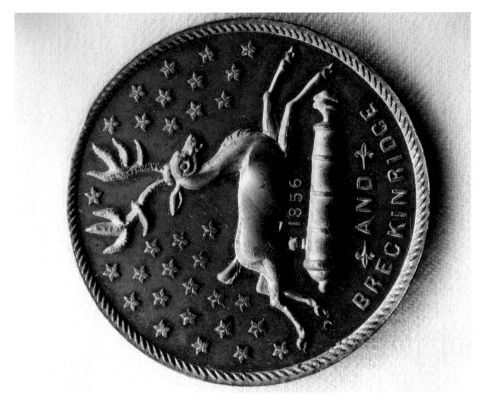

Plate 41. The rebus design on this medal advocates the
Democratic candidate James Buchanan in 1856.

Plate 40. Printmakers Currier and Ives portray George
Washington greeting Abraham Lincoln upon his elevation
to the American pantheon in 1856.

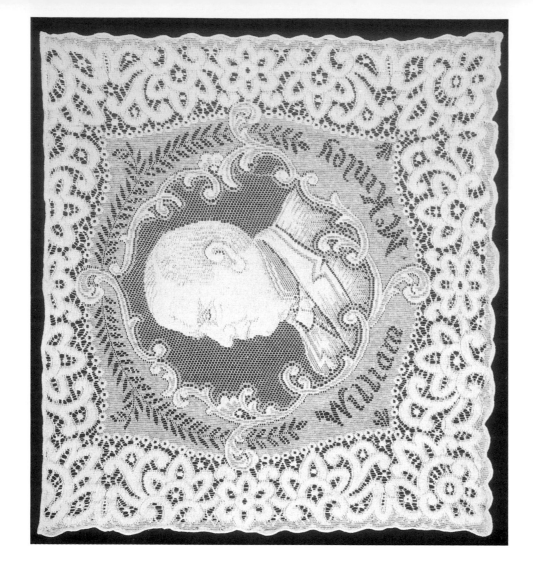

Plate 42. Top left, President William Howard Taft on a tin cookie pan, 1908. This item also appears on text page 96, illustration 137. While at the bottom left, Cartoonist Bill Mauldin used his G.I. character "Willie" to support Adlai Stevenson in 1952. At the right is an unusual piece of lacework which was the result of a lot of hard labor by an apparent ardent supporter of William McKinley, the twenty-fifth president.

Plate 44. Though he was quite an able politician, Governor Horatio Seymour of New York was no match in the presidential campaign against Ulysses S. Grant in 1868.

Plate 43. A pensive Lincoln is pictured on this 1864 campaign badge. See the text page 28, illustration 45 for another example.

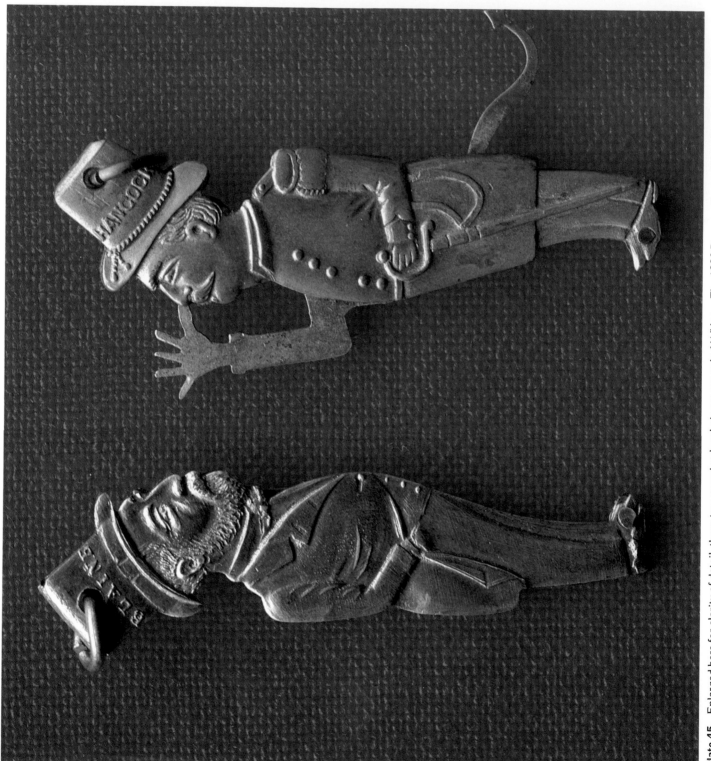

Plate 45. Enlarged here for clarity of detail, these two amusing lapel pieces are only 1½″ long. The 1880 Democratic candidate Winfield Hancock thumbs his nose at James G. Blaine, the Republican candidate in 1884. They are further illustrated in the text on page 30, illustration 52.

Plate 45. This wooden noise maker was made for Grover Cleveland's 1892 campaign. It also appears on text page 151, illustration 254.

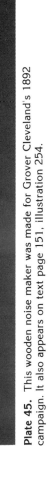

Plate 46. The broom was used symbolically ▶ by candidates who centered their campaigns on cleaning up corruption. Nothing ever seems to change when it comes to campaign themes does it.

Plate 49. A selection of humorous buttons critical of Franklin Delano Roosevelt and his third campaign for the presidency in 1940.

Plate 48. A selection of gold and silver bugs reflected the great economic controversy of [...] illustrations 53 & 54.

Plates 50. and 51. Theodore Roosevelt's popularity is reflected in this variety of objects: Top left, is a teddy bear lapel pin; Bottom left, is a campaign button indicating his recent military career; Above, is a fine example of a bandanna commemorating his receipt of the Nobel Peace Prize for having mediated the Russo-Japanese War.

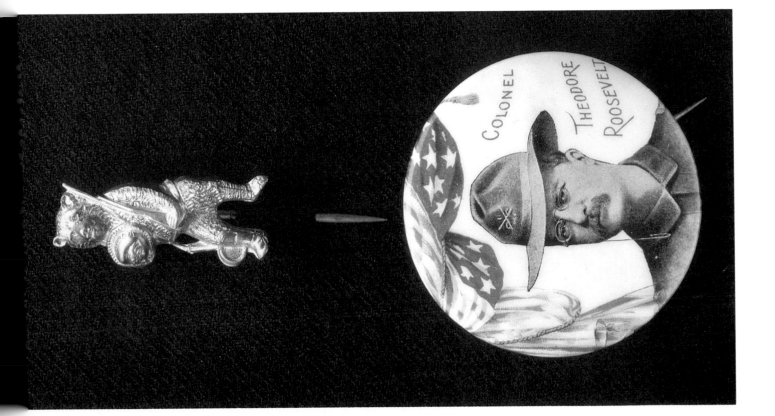

Plate 53. The lapel badge at the right features the 1888 presidential campaign candidates ▲ Benjamin Harrison and Levi Morton. This badge is also shown in the text on page 6, illust. 10.

Plate 52. Below are shown two fine examples of lapel pins, the elephant with glasses obviously for the Republican candidate in 1964, Barry Goldwater. The other is the "famous" PT-109 boat which 1960 Democratic candidate John Kennedy captained during WWII.

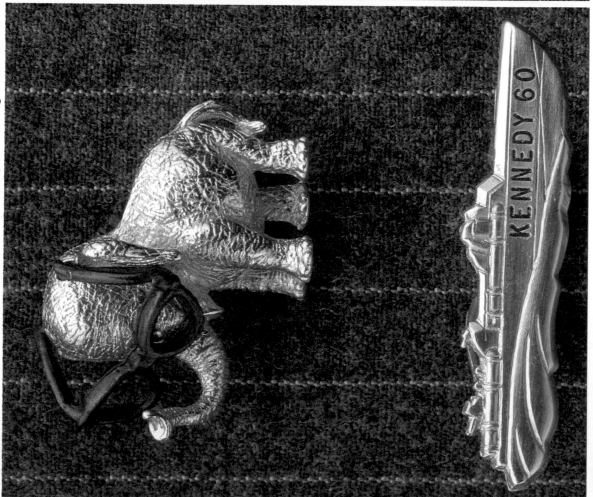

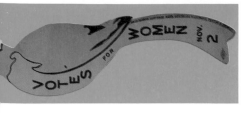

Plate 55. ▲ At the left, a nice example of a lapel tab from the Progressive "Bull Moose" Party, 1912. On the right, a colorful blue and yellow window hanger from a Massachusetts campaign of 1915. The bandanna below carries the hoary slogan "sweep out the rascals" while showing a rooster, the Democratic Party's symbol before they changed to the donkey. This item is also shown on text page 134, illustration 215.

Plate 54. ▲ Above, President Cleveland is portrayed in a statesman-like pose on an 1892 campaign bandanna. While below, ▼ these equestrian rosettes, ca. 1884, feature Republican nominees James G. Blaine and John A. Logan (the founder of Memorial Day).

Plate 56. Another Currier & Ives print portrays Lincoln's victory over his 3 opponents through a baseball setting. This cartoon is thought to be the first use of baseball terms to describe a political event.

THE NATIONAL GAME. THREE "OUTS" AND ONE "RUN".

Entered according to act of Congress in the year 1860, by Currier & Ives, in the Clerk's Office of the District Court for the Southern District N.Y.

Plate 57. Some recent and some very recent campaign buttons. Most of these are quite readily available and may be obtained throughout the 'society of collectors'.

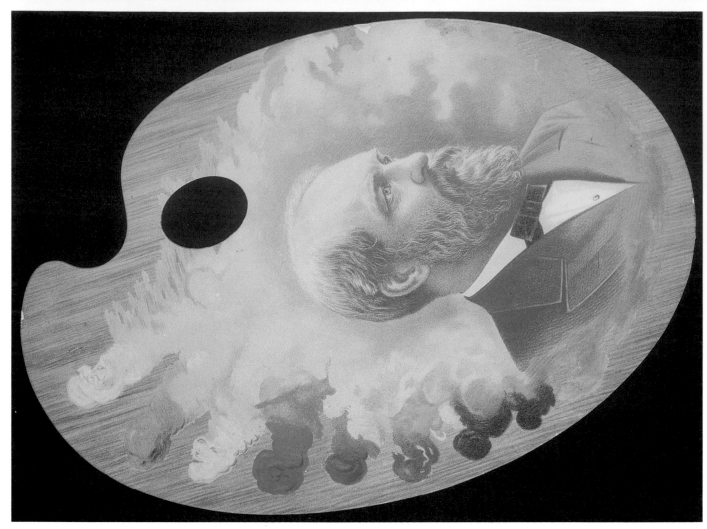

Plate 59. This palette-shaped tea company trading card features a very nice picture of James A. Garfield, ca. 1880. This item also appears on text page 56, illustration 88.

Plate 58. This poster illustrates how "showbiz" personalities are often used to aid in one effort or another. In this case, that of Cesar Chavez and his California Grape Workers and a fund raiser held at Carnegie Hall in 1968 featuring the group Peter, Paul and Mary.

Plate 61. James Madison, the Father of the Constitution, is portrayed on a contemporary medal.

Plate 60. Surrounding the earliest medallic likeness of George Washington are brass and copper buttons commemorating his first inauguration in 1789.

CAVING IN, OR A REBEL "DEEPLY HUMILIATED".

Published by Currier & Ives 152 Nassau St N.Y.

Lincoln battles with Jefferson Davis,

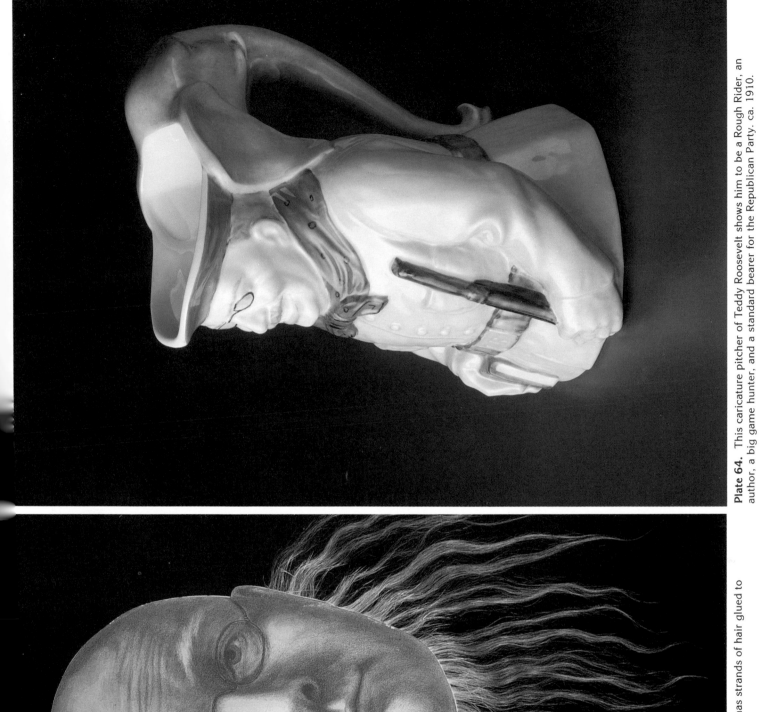

Plate 64. This caricature pitcher of Teddy Roosevelt shows him to be a Rough Rider, an author, a big game hunter, and a standard bearer for the Republican Party. ca. 1910.

Plate 63. This fan, which pictures journalist Horace Greeley, has strands of hair glued to the back of it. A somewhat grotesque appearing item.

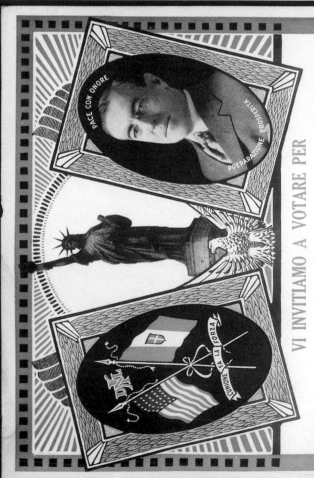

Plate 65. A 1916 campaign placard designed to attract the ethnic voter.

Plate 66. The nation did indeed "Keep cool with Coolidge", electing him by a large majority in 1924. He followed Warren Harding, the handsome Republican senator from Ohio, whose administration was plagued by scandals. ▲

Plate 68. Various major and third party candidates are shown in this collage of campaign paraphenalia. Note also, top right, the example of the rooster as the symbol on the Democratic Party's presidential campaign winners Wilson and Marshall inaugural badge from 1913.

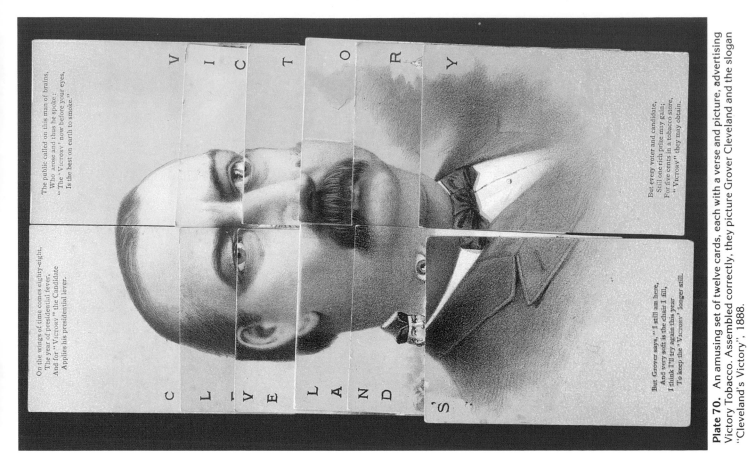

Plate 70. An amusing set of twelve cards, each with a verse and picture, advertising Victory Tobacco. Assembled correctly, they picture Grover Cleveland and the slogan "Cleveland's Victory", 1888.

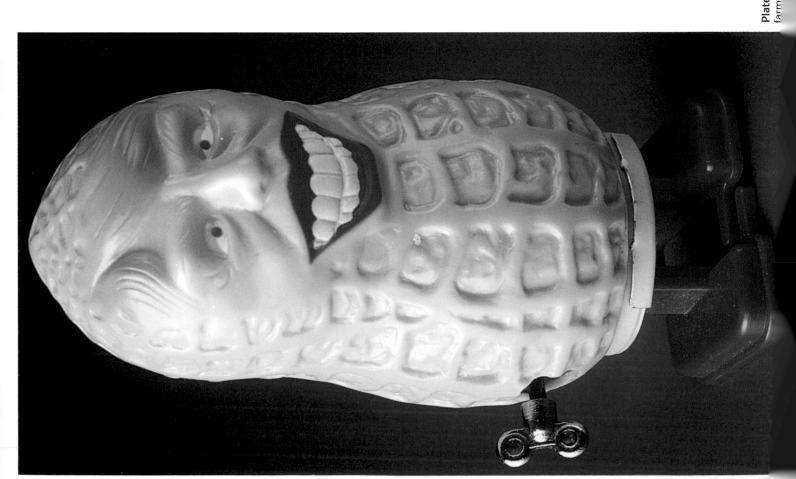

Plate 69. This wind-up caricature toy was made for the campaign of former peanut farmer Jimmy Carter in his 1976 run.

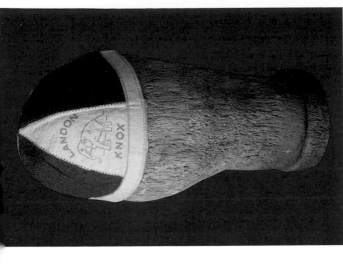

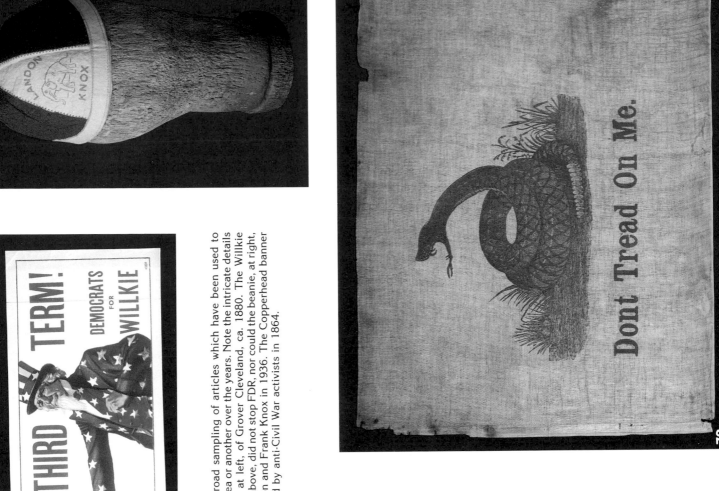

Plate 71. A broad sampling of articles which have been used to promote one idea or another over the years. Note the intricate details in the carving, at left, of Grover Cleveland, ca. 1880. The Willkie window decal, above, did not stop FDR, nor could the beanie, at right, elect Alf Landon and Frank Knox in 1936. The Copperhead banner below was used by anti-Civil War activists in 1864.

Plate 72. A capering President Andrew Jackson celebrates an indemnity of 25,000,000 francs from France as all the world watches, 1836.

Plate 73. This collage of buttons from several recent and not so recent campaigns are representative of the kinds of buttons which formerly played a large part in voter recognition of the candidates with a clever use of the candidate's name (see the Landon button, 2nd row, left), or some clever use of another means of identifying the candidate (such as the WILL- key example). It appears that future elections will rely more heavily on the electronic media now available to the candidates to search out and lock on to the prospective voter rather than these time-worn 'relics' from the 1916-1940 era.

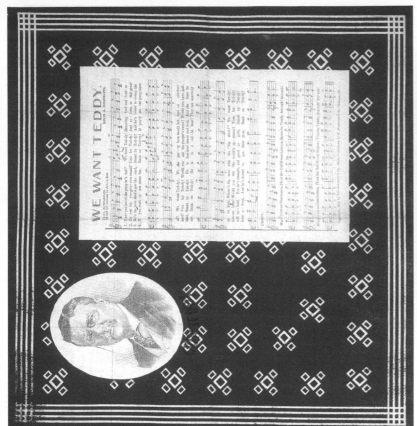

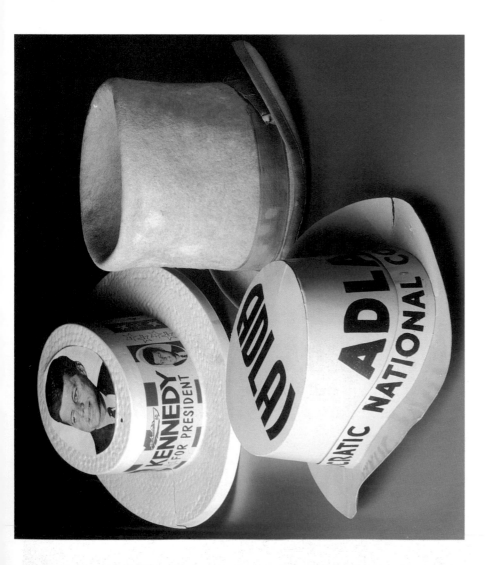

Plate 74. It's not official until the hats are in the ring! These typical samples are from recent campaigns (paper and plastic), while the 'high-top' felt version is from Benjamin Harrison's effort of 1888 or 1892. Other items of apparel and cloth have long been used as campaign paraphenalia and more of the same will surely be available in the years ahead.

Plate 75. ▲ (Un)conditional (S)urrender Grant was the nation's hero when he was elected in 1868, but proved to be one of the least effective. Above, ▲ the election of 1896 is illustrated on these campaign buttons, while to the right, ◀ are buttons from the most corrupt election in American history, that being during our ▲ Centennial year, 1876, when Republican Rutherford B. Hayes defeated Democrat Samuel Tilden.

Plate 76. ◄The 1976 campaign is represented by the row of buttons at the left. The bottom one is also referenced on text page 37, illustration 64. the middle grouping of buttons spans the campaigns from 1972 to 1984. Nixon really did have something to hide didn't he. At the top right, third party candidates are not relegated to some dark corner in the history books as witness this sampling of contemporary campaign buttons, 1968-1976.

THE FULL DINNER PAIL

SMASH CAPITALISM

VOTE COMMUNIST

EQUAL RIGHTS AMENDMENT

Equality of rights under the law shall not be denied or abridged by the United States or by any state on account of sex.

WE MUST RATIFY BY 6/30/02

New York Chapter

Plate 78. These are some very nice examples of campaign lanterns which were popular during the late 1800's. The Dinner Pail is from 1896 election, while the paper accordian lamp was used in 1880. The two glass examples at the bottom are from 1884 and 1864 respectively.

Plate 77. ◄ A recent 'campaign' item from the NOW New York Chapter. Top left, An American Communist Party campaign poster from the early 1950's. Above, are shown two examples of the many kinds of personal apparel items which have been suitably inscribed with the candidate of choice. Note also, the garters which show similar support.

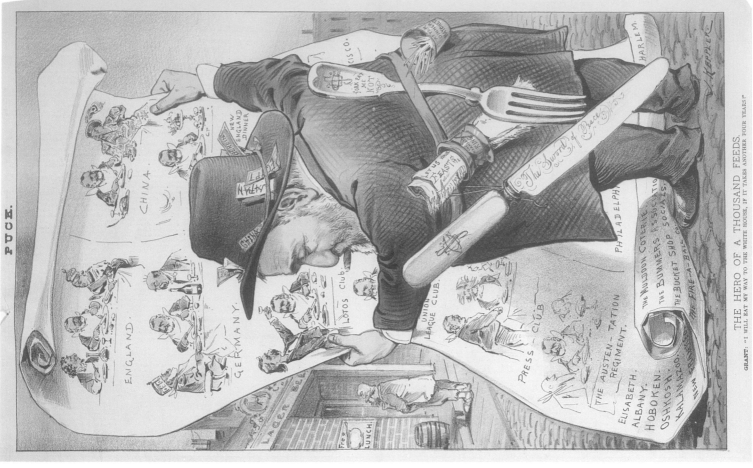

THE HERO OF A THOUSAND FEEDS.
GRANT: "I WILL EAT MY WAY TO THE WHITE HOUSE, IF IT TAKES ANOTHER FOUR YEARS!"

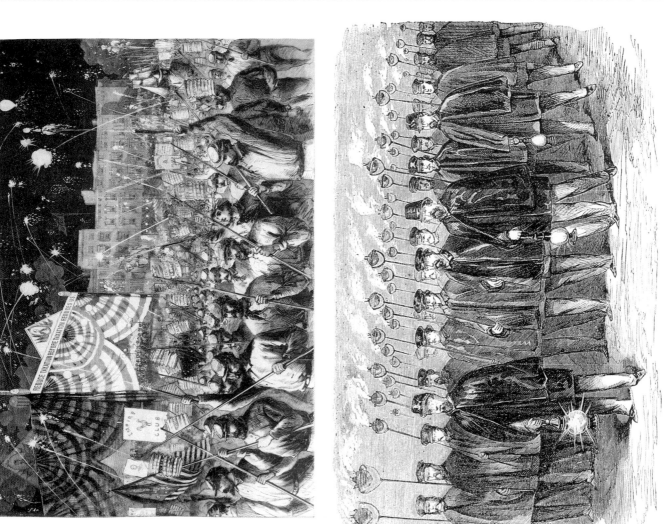

PROCESSION OF THE WIDEAWAKE CLUB OF HARTFORD CONN., ON THURSDAY, JULY 27.—FROM A SKETCH BY OUR SPECIAL ARTIST

Plate 79. Above. A properly orchestrated torchlight parade was a crowd-pleasing extravaganza during most of the campaigns of the 1860-1896 eras. TV has replaced most of this type of activity. **Plate 80.** At the right, *PUCK* cartoonist Joseph Keppler satirizes former president (U.S. Grant's popularity as a dinner guest, 1880.

sion of designs and subjects. Like few other categories of political Americana, many of these ribbons are a challenge to research-minded collectors. Tantalizing puzzles are posed, as the following examples suggest. On a large light blue ribbon (Ill. 193) is the inscription "Joel Parker/Association/Newark, N. J./Inauguration/of/Grover/Cleveland/March 4th 1885" together with a picture of Joel Parker, one assumes. So—who was Joel Parker? On an 1892 Cleveland ribbon is the no-nonsense inscription:

> I am a Democrat
> It is a good Ticket
> We will Carry the State of New York
> I do not know of any Democrat Who will
>   cut the Ticket
> Cleveland will be Elected
> I was for [David] Hill for the Nomination
> I Live in Troy.

Do you suppose its wearer was tired of answering, or was he attempting to forestall certain inevitable questions that always seem to be asked at political conventions?

On a handsome maroon ribbon with the lettering and design woven in raised silver metallic thread is the inscription "Anti-Cobden Club/Philadelphia"; in the center is the monogram "A/C" enclosed within a keystone; heavy metallic fringe hangs from the lower edge. What was so important about Mr. Cobden, probably in 1888, that warranted an imposing ribbon weighing several ounces?

RIBBONS HONORING GEORGE WASHINGTON. Earlier, I mentioned 1876 centennial and Know-Nothing ribbons that bear Washington's portrait. These two examples are merely a hint of Washington's popularity as a subject on nineteenth-century ribbons. The centennial of his birth in 1832 was the occasion for an outpouring of silks eulogizing him for his presidency, his statesmanship, his military prowess, and his association with the Marquis de Lafayette. Among the more interesting of these are the ribbons issued by various occupational groups such as tobacconists, cartmen, and drapers. Washington is also pictured on a few scarce ribbons issued by the Whigs to mark the founding of the party in 1834 (Ill. 194). Collectors should be aware of another embroidered Washington 1876 centennial ribbon; the quality of its color, weaving, and design compares favorably with the Washington Stevengraphs. This ribbon, 13 inches in

194. Washington commemorative ribbons: At the far left and right are 1832 centennial pieces; an occupational ribbon is second from the left and a Whig party ribbon second from the right.

length, was made by the Phoenix Manufacturing Company of Paterson, New Jersey; it is illustrated here (Plate 4) on its original card mount. A near copy of the Phoenix ribbon was issued in a smaller version and in a slightly different design during the 1976 bicentennial, but the modern ribbon is an inferior piece of workmanship.

Many of the Washington ribbons are fairly easy to locate, and since there is no great demand for them, they can be found at reasonable prices.

MOURNING RIBBONS. Mourning ribbons (Ill. 195) are often campaign ribbons with the addition of a black border and an appropriate sentiment. But a good many are original designs. These ribbons are also known as memorial ribbons because they were worn at community-level memorial exercises that customarily followed the death of a president in the nineteenth century. Mourning ribbons are a most underrated collecting topic, although there has recently been a flurry of interest in them.

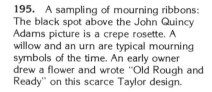

195. A sampling of mourning ribbons: The black spot above the John Quincy Adams picture is a crepe rosette. A willow and an urn are typical mourning symbols of the time. An early owner drew a flower and wrote "Old Rough and Ready" on this scarce Taylor design.

Ninety percent or more of all mourning ribbons were issued during the nineteenth century. Probably well over a hundred and fifty mourning ribbons commemorate presidents' deaths, from William Henry Harrison's in 1841 to Warren G. Harding's in 1923. There is a smattering of ribbons, usually with attached picture buttons, commemorating the deaths of more recent presidents and also-rans.

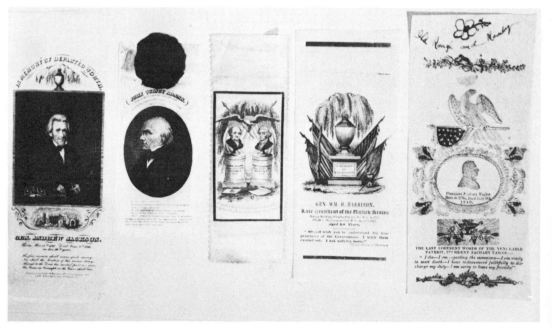

Among presidents before Lincoln, there are more ribbons commemorating Harrison's death than for all other presidents and also-rans combined. Ribbons marking Henry Clay's death are a distant second. Lincoln's death is marked by a great many different designs, which is no surprise: Hundreds of federal and state government offices arranged for employees to wear ribbons during the mourning period (Ill. 196). He is also well represented by mourning cards and similar paper ephemera. A few ribbons are known that mark the deaths of Andrew Jackson and Zachary Taylor, but John Quincy Adams is represented by just one known mourning ribbon. For presidents in the post-Civil War era the largest number of ribbons commemorate the deaths of Ulysses S. Grant and William McKinley; fewer ribbons mark James A. Garfield's death, and perhaps only one or two mark the deaths of other presidents and also-rans of the period. Note that three "martyred" presidents, all dying from assassins' bullets, four popular generals, and two men (John Quincy Adams and Henry Clay) who were held in considerable esteem by the public long after their runs for the presidency dominate nineteenth-century mourning ribbons. If mourning ribbons exist for James Polk, Franklin Pierce, Martin Van Buren, and the Founding Father presidents, they are very rare and seldom seen.

The one exception to that statement is an exception indeed. Both John Adams and Thomas Jefferson died on July 4, 1826. Three known mourning ribbons, all bearing portraits of the two presidents, commemorate the occasion. The one that is most likely to appear on the market, and the most interesting design of the three, depicts both men on pedestals with an eagle, draped flags, and a weeping willow above. Below is the inscription "Together they laboured for our Country, together they have gone to meet their reward." Unlike most mourning ribbons, the Adams/Jefferson ribbons are quite valuable because of the fact that related political artifacts for these two presidents are extremely rare—hence, anything at all associated with them is eagerly sought after. Needless to say, the three ribbons are rare.

The most unusual mourning ribbon from the early period is a Zachary Taylor issue. It is unusual for two reasons: 1) the bust of Taylor, the design, and most of the lettering are embossed; 2) the ribbon is gold gilt, red, and blue on white waxed cotton cloth. To the best of my knowledge, embossing and gold gilt combined with red and blue do not appear on any other mourning ribbon, nor on any campaign ribbon, of the period. Hence this ribbon is rated very highly even by collectors who are not otherwise interested in mourning ribbons. Surrounding a small centered gilt bust of Taylor is an elaborate oval frame surmounted by a draped flag and a spread eagle. Below a funerary urn are the general's last words—which we can safely assume come partly from the ribbon-maker's imagination:

> I die—I am expecting the summons—
> I am ready to meet death—
> I have endeavored faithfully to discharge my duty—
> I am sorry to leave my friends!

Spoken like a true soldier. But the last words attributed to William Henry Harrison are what we should expect of a president on his deathbed:

> I wish you to understand the true
> principles of government. I wish
> them carried out. I ask nothing more.

Fortunately the custom of printing "last words" on mourning ribbons seems to have died out by the time of Lincoln's death in 1865. What we now find printed on ribbons from the later nineteenth century are such treacly phrases as "Our Fallen Hero" (Grant), "He Fell a Martyr to the Cause of Justice and . . . Liberty" (Garfield); "Our Mar-

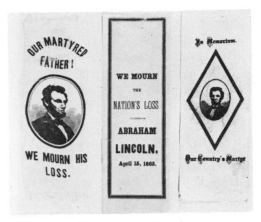

196. A few of the many varieties of Lincoln mourning ribbons, many of which are easily obtained.

196A. Typical examples of later 19th century mourning ribbons.

tyred Father" (Lincoln). Of special interest are those ribbons recalling the deceased president's military service. These ribbons, issued by the Grand Army of the Republic upon the deaths of Grant, Garfield, and McKinley, carry such sentiments as "In Memory of Our Departed Comrade" and "We Mourn a Fallen Comrade."

RIBBON BADGES.   Perhaps this is the best place to discuss the differences between ribbons and ribbon badges (Ill. 197). Ribbons are simply cloth strips. Ribbon badges

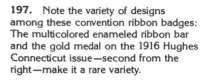

197. Note the variety of designs among these convention ribbon badges: The multicolored enameled ribbon bar and the gold medal on the 1916 Hughes Connecticut issue—second from the right—make it a rare variety.

are ribbons with an added attachment, usually a medal or a celluloid button, mounted directly on the ribbon or suspended from it. Most collectors use the simple term "badge" to include all varieties of ribbon badges. From the 1880s through the 1920s, especially, a considerable variety of ribbon badges all marked the same political events as ribbons. By the latter part of the period ribbon badges had almost completely replaced ribbons in popularity. Although a few ribbons have been issued for modern campaigns, they are generally of poor quality and hold little attraction for collectors. But ribbon badges, particularly those worn by delegates to national party conventions, have a good deal of appeal.

Delegates' badges can be acquired fairly easily; scarcer issues in gold or silver, which were worn by high party officials, are particularly desirable. Recently, inaugural badges, especially those worn at inaugurations in the years 1884–1904 (the most interesting variety were worn in that period), have become popular. Some collectors are content to assemble a representative grouping of inaugural badges; others attempt to build a reasonably complete collection from particular inaugurations. This second type is possible because the members and staffs of inaugural committees wore a standardized design that differed only in the name of the subcommittee that was printed on the ribbon: platform, choir, parade, public comfort, press, fireworks, and perhaps a dozen or more others.

197A. A magnificent black and cream silk mourning ribbon-badge with a brass wire rim frame and glass enclosed photograph.

Campaign Banners

There is something intensely political about campaign banners. No nineteenth-century political event was complete without a banner draped over a balcony, strung across a convention hall, or mounted above a rostrum. Nor is it possible to imagine a campaign parade without colorful banners waving above the heads of the marchers.

Many banners of the pre-Civil War era were made by local partisans to honor candidates and to publicize their messages. The artwork on homemade banners was usually amateurish, but the colors were bright and the messages direct. The candidates' faces wore wooden expressions, but the homely symbols on the banners were familiar, even to illiterate voters: plows and log cabins, spread eagles and laurel wreaths, and, during the 1840 campaign, the first apparent political use of "O.K." Many locally made banners were unique—one-of-a-kind items—and unless they were preserved by museums or historical societies they are gone forever. From contemporary accounts we know of the existence of many banners that have since vanished, as did the Henry Clay parade banner (described later).

Campaign banners from elections following the Civil War are more abundant, and because most were made by firms specializing in the production of campaign accessories they tend to be similar in size, shape, and design. Nevertheless, there are many eye-catching examples worth collecting.

Banners continued as a fixture in party headquarters and in campaign parades through the 1930s, but as campaign parades also waned in popularity, banners were supplanted by paper posters, which were cheaper to print and could be produced in larger numbers. Where once a large banner would have been a cynosure of interest in a headquarters, today a large paper poster or two and many smaller paper posters line the walls.

HEADQUARTERS BANNERS.   These were made usually of satin, silk, linen, or various lightweight cotton weaves that were not intended to be used constantly out of doors. In early campaigns, the banners were hand painted, stenciled, or printed—or designed in combination—with whatever materials were at hand. They were hung in prominent locations in the local party headquarters or, as was a common practice in later campaigns, were mounted on the inside of a headquarters storefront window.

As Herbert Collins points out in his book, many locally made banners from the 1824–1864 period rank with the best examples of American folk art in other media. The examples described in the following paragraph are unique, but this fact should not discourage collectors from the search. Very likely there are similar banners lying long forgotten in barns and attics.

One superb hand-painted example in silk (Plate 21) depicts a log cabin, a deer, and foliage, with an artfully painted spread eagle above. The unknown artist's succinct inscription "W.H.H./O.K." suggests admirably the voters' enthusiastic acceptance of William Henry Harrison's candidacy in 1840. An 1860 John Breckinridge cotton banner pictures a large printed eagle in black, with stars cut from red and blue felt and pasted on. In a local Connecticut historical society, there is an 1840 Harrison design painted on two separate cloths sewed back to back. (This banner is illustrated in Washburn's article; see Bibliography.) Several examples of locally made banners are displayed in the Abby Aldrich Rockefeller Collection in Williamsburg, Virginia, and in the Smithsonian Institution; certainly many state and local historical societies possess at least one or two.

198.   A design similar to this 1868 Grant–Colfax banner bears the names of the 1860 Southern Democrats' nominees John Breckinridge and Joseph Lane, but with the addition of felt stars.

199. Banners of local interest, such as this 1896 banner used in West Hartford, Connecticut, have a special appeal for collectors.

Also of interest from the same period are banners carrying slogans. These were made from cheap cotton cloth and had messages painted or stenciled on in black. Slogan banners were a common campaign fixture until the end of the century. Note the 1896 slogan banner "West Hartford/Solid/for/Sound Money," in Illustration 199; naturally the cloth is dyed gold.

By the 1880s political banners were being produced commercially by such leaders in the field as New York's Cobb Campaign Manufacturing Company (Ill. 236) and the American Banner Company of Saint Louis. A few homemade banners from this period are known; they can be distinguished from commercial banners by their less sophisticated artwork and lack of a finished appearance.

Designs on commercial banners were standardized by this time, and the messages tended to reflect a party's national concerns. Manufacturers offered a limited choice of designs for each party's candidates. Frequently the background design was the same, and the banners differed only in the picture of the candidate and the message. If a message was sufficiently vague, such as "Peace, Prosperity, and Progress" or "Freedom and Equality," then only the candidates' pictures would be different. Because of this design standardization, it is possible for collectors to acquire matching pairs of banners. Sometimes party workers could order commercial banners bearing a message of local interest such as "The Garfield Republican Club of Trenton, N.J." and "The Blaine and Logan Marching Club/Cleveland, Ohio." Most banners were grommeted for suspension and neatly stitched and hemmed, and though impressive enough, many lacked the imaginative individuality characteristic of banners from earlier campaigns. But some of these later banners are eye-catchers and superb examples of late-nineteenth-century political graphic art.

I cannot describe twentieth-century headquarters banners as favorably. By the time of the First World War hand-painted banners had disappeared entirely, and silk and satin (if used at all) were generally restricted to smaller political textile artifacts. Nearly all modern banners were then manufactured in various cotton weaves, particularly broadcloth; also popular was the unattractive but durable oilcloth. Machine-printed designs on broadcloth, of which the 1912 Bull Moose party banner shown in Illustration 200 is an example, were fairly inexpensive and could be hung on a wall, suspended by wires, or attached to a staff. Oilcloth banners such as the 1928 Al Smith one in Illustration 201 could be rolled into compact cylinders and used at other times. Also, posters made of transparent or opaque polyethylene made their first appearance during the 1952 campaign.

200. A gleam in the eye of the bull moose adds to the graphic quality of this scarce 1912 banner.

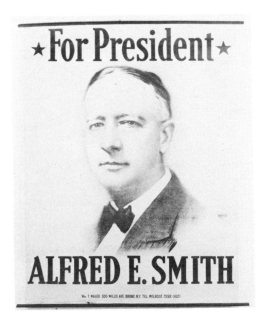

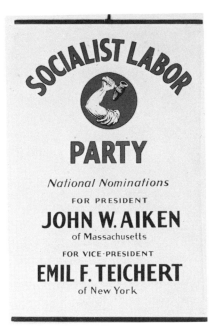

201. The Smith oilcloth banner measures about 5 by 2½ feet; the third-party oilcloth banner, somewhat smaller, dates from the 1936 campaign.

By the 1930s headquarters banners were almost an extinct political species. A few banners are known from the 1932 campaign and several varieties of 1936 red, white, and blue Roosevelt and Landon banners made from a heavy open-weave cotton appear on the market quite often (Ill. 202). But 1936 was the last campaign year in which headquarters banners were used to any extent. A very few 1940 Willkie banners are known, and a few name banners such as "Truman for President" also exist. The choice is generally poor, however, although there is always the hope that somewhere there exists a handsomely designed modern banner adorned with a candidate's picture and a message of local interest. It is not impossible to imagine.

PARADE BANNERS. Obviously, nostalgia is a factor in the collecting of presidential Americana, and in my opinion that feeling is nowhere stronger than it is for campaign parade banners. Unfortunately, they seldom come on the market, nor are there many in the collections of historical societies and museums. As we read manufacturers' advertisements for later nineteenth-century banners, we can see how attractive they were; many are similar in design and style to the tasseled and fringed campaign ribbons from the same period. Such banners were suspended from long wooden staffs either by a brass chain or thick gold cord; attached to each side were brass or silvered brass tassels and sewn along the lower edge and sometimes the sides was a heavy metallic fringe. More elaborate banners included an overlapping flap, which was also adorned with tassels and fringe.

Parade banners from earlier campaigns could be just as elaborate. Indeed, some must have been magnificent creations. I can do no better, in fact, than offer this lengthy description, taken from a contemporary newspaper account, of a banner which was carried by supporters of Henry Clay in an 1844 Whig parade in Baltimore (Ill. 203). This banner, over six feet square, had recently been awarded the "Grand Prize" in a campaign parade. It was made up of two beautifully colored satin panels—the front in "delicate lead" and the back in "Manzarine" blue. A centered portrait of Clay on the front panel was shown against a backdrop of a shield supported by a figure representing Agriculture with a sheaf of wheat to one side; the opposite side was balanced by a figure representing Commerce, together with cotton bales. Surmounting the shield was a spread eagle and a background scene consisting of a factory, a spinning wheel, railroad cars, and sailing ships. Below each allegorical symbol were cornucopias and under Clay's portrait was the motto "In All Assaults Our Surest Signal." On the banner's blue satin reverse each state's coat of arms was depicted, the whole arranged in the form of a

202. A large red, white, and blue heavy cotton banner used in the 1936 campaign. It is typical of several such banners that also picture Alf Landon.

203. A contemporary newspaper illustration of a beautiful Clay banner that was carried in an 1884 Baltimore campaign parade. *Courtesy Becker Collection, Smithsonian Institution.*

wreath. Below the wreath was the motto "The Union, Our Strong Defense; to Foes Impregnable, Priceless to Friends."

The frame was equally magnificent. The top bar was carved in the shape of a bow with raised fruit and flowers carved along the surface. At each end eagles supported the blue satin panel and a much smaller overlapping panel in crimson satin damask. Above the whole was a copper and gilded fasces. The staff was described as having been cut from an ash by Henry Clay himself at Ashland, his home in Kentucky. We will never see that banner's like again.

What with the nineteenth-century passion for campaign parades there must have been thousands of banners. Perhaps none was so striking as that Clay banner, but certainly many were worth preserving. Some are known to be in the collections of museums and state and local historical societies and in the Smithsonian Institution holdings; perhaps a few others are privately owned—but that seems to be it. Because so many of these banners were bulky and difficult to store they were ignored; thus they deteriorated beyond recovery. Others were so badly weather damaged that repairs were impossible. Nineteenth-century parade banners appear on the market so rarely that it is difficult to mention a price range for them, as is also true of better headquarters banners from the same period.

But some campaign banners do appear fairly regularly in auction catalogs and sales lists. Many of these banners are aesthetically pleasing and historically significant; they deserve a favored place in collections of political Americana.

FLAG BANNERS. All flag banners are potentially museum pieces—and most of them are in museums today. Examples in fine or better condition seldom show up on the market; when they do, auctioneers and dealers can be excused if they describe these banners in somewhat exaggerated terms. All flag banners are variations of the national flag; they were used in campaigns from 1840 to about 1900. Because flag banners are essentially political advertising, they as well as other "defacing" uses of the national flag were outlawed by Congress at the turn of the century.

Flag banners range in size from about 12 by 8 inches to about 48 by 24 inches. They are usually exact copies of the national flag, but with an incorrect number of stars, and most bear a picture of the candidate superimposed on the stripes or on the field. Some banners are known with the blue field in the upper right rather than the upper left, and others exist in a vertical format rather than the customary horizontal one. Neither variety, however, makes a difference as far as value or rarity is concerned. Most flag banners were commercially made, although a homemade version turns up occasionally—and that fact does add to the flag's value.

There are perhaps a dozen different designs marking William Henry Harrison's campaign in 1840 and almost as many marking Henry Clay's 1844 campaign. But there are probably no more than three or four designs each to mark the campaigns of James Polk (1844), Zachary Taylor and Lewis Cass (1848), Franklin Pierce and Winfield Scott (1852), and James Buchanan and John Frémont (1856). Abraham Lincoln is well represented on flag banners, a bonus for Lincoln collectors. In fact, there are probably more known Lincoln banners from the 1860 campaign than there are known banners for the other three candidates combined. Lincoln banners from the 1864 campaign, however, are much scarcer. Flag banners marking both of Lincoln's campaigns probably outnumber those from Harrison's campaign, but because the subject is Lincoln, any of his banners would likely be valued at twice the price, or more, of a Harrison banner. On a few 1860 Lincoln flag banners his given name is sometimes misspelled as "Abram" (Ill. 204); that spelling does not add to the banner's value.

Flag banners from post-Civil War campaigns are known in a few designs for all major party candidates through 1900. No design seems to be a great deal scarcer than another. But, as is also true of other artifacts associated with their campaigns, flag banners marking the campaigns of Horatio Seymour (1868), Horace Greeley (1872), Rutherford Hayes and Samuel Tilden (1876), and Winfield Hancock (1880) seldom appear on the market. Surprisingly, in view of the abundance of other artifacts associated with his campaigns, flag banners marking Benjamin Harrison's two campaigns in 1888 and 1892 are quite scarce. Thus, if collectors are to acquire a flag banner or two from the 1868–1900 period, they will most likely have to settle for either Ulysses S. Grant, James A. Garfield, Grover Cleveland (particularly the 1884 campaign) (Ills. 205 and 206), James Blaine, William McKinley, or William Jennings Bryan banners.

203A. Paper flag lapel pins from the 1884 campaign.

Although flag banners picturing a candidate are more popular with collectors, I much prefer slogan banners. Portrait designs carry the usual "For President . . ." A few William Henry Harrison designs both picture "Old Tip" and carry slogans such as "The Hero of Tippecanoe"; but slogan banners always carry a message of historical interest. Among the more unusual banners with such messages are several used in Henry Clay's 1844 campaign. On one of these a raccoon with his thumb to his nose sits atop a large red, white, and blue striped ball (Plate 20). (Thumbing one's nose is, of course, a highly

204. Only a few examples of this 1860 flag banner are known.

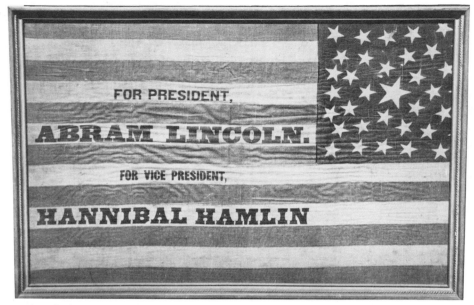

205. A design very similar to this 1880 Garfield banner pictures George Washington standing beside his horse.

206. Other candidates of 1880s campaigns are pictured on similar flag banners.

expressive derisive gesture; a nose-thumbing raccoon suggested Republicans' reaction to their critics. A raccoon preceded the elephant as the symbol of the Republican party, and its portrayal in this pose was common on Republican campaign artifacts; note its use, also, on the Blaine ribbon discussed previously.) The ball is inscribed "The Little Red Fox Is Quite Unlucky/Clear the Track for Old Kentucky/Let Us Rally for Clay and True Frelinghuysen." Above the raccoon is printed "The Same Old Coon." The fox is former President Martin Van Buren, who, in 1844, was the nominee of the Free-Soil party; now he is welcome to join the Whigs in defeating his erstwhile Democratic party. Theodore Frelinghuysen, Clay's running mate, was a true stalwart who was loyal to the Whig cause.

The raccoon was actually a continuation of the log cabin theme. The "same old coon" was a reminder to voters that Whig principles had not changed. An 1844 campaign song ran, in part, "High on a limb/that same old coon was singing to himself this tune/'Get out of the way, you're all unlucky/Clear the way for Old Kentucky.'" And "Old Kentucky," of course, was Henry Clay himself. A similar slogan flag banner pictures a raccoon lying on top of a large barrel marked "Hard Cider"; above is the inscription "The Same Old Coon." Should voters still be unable to make the connection between

THE SAME OLD COON

HARD CIDER

HENRY CLAY AND FRELINGHUYSEN

207. This silk Clay banner is one of several varieties with a similar stars and stripes pattern, but with different pictures or slogans.

hard cider and a raccoon, a tiny log cabin was pictured beneath the barrel as a further reminder (Ill. 207).

Flag banners are among the great showpiece artifacts in political Americana. Examples from earlier campaigns seldom come on the market, and those from later campaigns appear only a bit more often. I know of no comprehensive collection of flag banners, but the Warren Lincoln Library and Museum in Fort Wayne, Indiana, owns an outstanding collection of banners picturing Lincoln and the other candidates in the 1860 campaign. The Illinois State Historical Society owns a number of Lincoln banners and the Smithsonian Institution has a representative grouping from most campaigns.

MISCELLANEOUS BANNERS. There are just two kinds of banners to discuss here, the largest and the smallest.

Among the largest campaign banners were the huge canvas ones that were attached to rope netting and suspended across America's Main streets during campaigns from about 1876 to 1928 (Ill. 208). Pictures of candidates and all inscriptions were painted on canvas strips or squares, in duplicate, and attached to both sides of the netting. Street banners measured up to 30 by 27 feet; they are almost impossible to find today. There is an 1892 Harrison and Reid banner in the University of Hartford collection. Other outstanding large banners are housed in the Smithsonian Institution collection: a Van Buren pennant-shaped banner 25 feet in length that probably dates from the 1836 campaign; an 1864 Lincoln and Johnson design; and two street banners, one picturing 1884 Republican candidates James G. Blaine and John Logan, and the other, William H. Taft and James Sherman.

I should also mention the small window hangers, which are, as Illustration 209 suggests, almost exact miniature copies of street banners. Since the same illustrations appear on both sides of these hangers, and a salesman could hardly haul a street banner from one potential customer to the next, it is possible that these hangers were salesmen's samples. Whatever their intended use, they do not show up very often.

Older readers may remember the small red and white banners bearing one or

208. Taft and Sherman are pictured on the large banner here spanning a street in Westerly, Rhode Island; scenes like this were familiar in the campaigns of the 1870–1912 period. *Courtesy Maxson Collection.*

209. Similar examples of this 1896 window hanger or salesmen's miniature of a street banner picture Bryan and Sewell.

more blue stars that hung in house windows during the Second World War. These banners indicated that one or more members of the household were serving in the armed forces. Similar banners picturing Franklin Roosevelt or Wendell Willkie were popular during the 1940 campaign. These political window banners were made of rayon acetate, and ranged in size from 5 by 9 inches to 9 by 14 inches; they were suspended with gold cords and tassels. Probably twenty or more different designs were manufactured for both candidates combined; they bear such slogans as "Win With Wilkie," "We the People Want Willkie," and "God Bless America/Franklin Roosevelt/Our Next President."

Most designs, for both candidates, show up often at auction and on sales lists. They can be purchased for a few dollars each.

Bandannas

Second to ribbons in popularity among collectors is the considerable variety of textiles with political subjects known collectively as bandannas. This category includes textiles intended primarily to be worn about the person or, as was the case with bandannas from early campaigns, framed and hung. In nineteenth-century usage, bandanna meant any textile that served as a head covering, or as a handkerchief, or as an all-purpose cloth for the workingman. In later times the word also came to include scarves. Regardless of their purpose, bandannas were generally square.

EARLY BANDANNAS. The earliest bandannas were decorative rather than functional. Many from the pre-Civil War campaigns are found in contemporary frames, and as often as not are faded or water stained. Although bandannas commemorating patriotic and historical subjects are known from the earliest years of the Republic, the first bandannas picturing presidential candidates were probably used in Andrew Jackson's first campaign in 1824. His routing of the British at New Orleans in 1815 and his successful Florida military campaign in 1819 made Jackson a national hero and an obvious candidate for the presidency. Cotton bandannas picturing a youthful Jackson are extremely rare. Some Jackson bandannas, equally rare, are made of silk, such as the example in Illustration 210; the design of the framed bandanna is typical, as is the inscription—"Major General Andrew Jackson/The Hero of New Orleans."

Bandannas marking the 1840 Log Cabin campaign show up on the market more often than those from any other campaign in the pre-Civil War era. Almost all these ei-

210. Two examples of silk bandannas honoring Andrew Jackson's leadership at the Battle of New Orleans. The one at the left carries a likeness of Jackson that bears little resemblance to the more accurate picture of him on the other bandanna.

211. Campaign symbols and scenes depicting his military prowess surround an equestrian portrait of William Henry Harrison on an 1840 campaign bandanna.

212. Stirring battle scenes of the Mexican War make up for General Taylor's decidedly unheroic expression on an 1848 campaign bandanna.

213.   A sunburst and wreath of oak leaves frame Henry Clay on an attractive 1844 red, white, and blue campaign bandanna.

214.   The original thirteen colonies and "1776" are highlighted on a scarce Know-Nothing bandanna, c. 1850s.

215.   The brooms and the rooster on this 1888 Democratic bandanna add to its graphic appeal.

ther picture a bust of William Henry Harrison or have him astride a long-legged prancing steed. In the latter designs the "Hero of Tippecanoe" is attired in a handsome uniform with his sword upraised, seemingly ready to charge off into glorious combat. Both designs are bordered with simple geometric or floral patterns. The designs most desired also illustrate Tippecanoe battle scenes or the log cabin motif. Probably the equestrian designs are somewhat more difficult to locate than the bust designs.

Fewer bandannas are known that mark "Old Rough and Ready" Zachary Taylor's campaign in 1848. The designs are similar to the Harrison designs, although the Taylor busts are usually larger. The equestrian designs and a few of the bust designs are bordered with Mexican War scenes. A few bandannas mark Henry Clay's three attempts at the presidency (Ill. 213); most, if not all, of them date from the 1844 campaign. As far as I know, there are no Clay equestrian designs (although he is portrayed that way in a Currier print). What we find are large busts of Clay, which are bordered with various agricultural, commercial, and maritime scenes. There are probably a few Pierce, Cass, Scott, Frémont, and Buchanan bandannas in existence, but like the two or three known designs picturing Abraham Lincoln, they are virtually unobtainable.

Most Harrison, Taylor, and Clay bandannas are squares measuring from 19 to 24 inches, printed in red, blue, brown, or black inks on cheap unbleached cotton cloth. A few bandannas were dyed pale blue or pink; they are very scarce and bring higher prices. But all political bandannas from these campaigns are hard to find, especially in good condition, so consider yourself lucky to own even one—in any condition.

"RED" BANDANNAS.   Campaign bandannas declined in popularity during the Civil War. Bandannas picturing Grant and McClellan were in similar pattern to those picturing Lincoln; all were more likely issued for reasons of patriotism than for use in political campaigns.

There was, however, a revival of interest in campaign bandannas during the 1880s. All campaigns from 1880 through 1900 were dominated by economic issues, especially issues related to domestic tariffs, employment and wages, and working conditions in factories. During this twenty-year period the American Federation of Labor became an important spokesman for skilled labor, the first great strikes and sometimes violent confrontations between labor and management occurred, and workingmen's heroes such as Eugene V. Debs rose to national prominence. The campaign literature of the day is full of articles, cartoons, and speeches comparing American and British working conditions and wages, or arguing the merits of raising or lowering tariffs, or praising the virtues of American workers. (As every collector should know, "A Full Dinner Pail" was a Republican rallying cry during the 1896 and 1900 campaigns.) Labor had become a force to be reckoned with in national politics, and workers now represented sizable blocks of votes to needy politicians. Thus was born one of the most appropriate vote-getting devices ever used in American political campaigning—the "red" bandanna.

As a symbol of the honest workingman and of respect for the dignity of labor, as politicians might have put it, there could not have been a better choice. The red bandannas were so named because, as Plate 24 shows, bright reds dominated the patterns. These bandannas became the symbol through which both major parties identified with the working class. What better way for a politician to show his allegiance to labor principles than to display casually a bright red bandanna in his pocket. Senator Allan Thurmond, Grover Cleveland's running mate in 1888, was called the Knight of the Red Bandanna because he was seldom seen without one. There were even campaign songs about red bandannas. Republicans satirized Thurmond and his red bandanna with such songs as "Cleveland's Vice" and "The Free Trade Banner." But Democrats could always counter with "Wave High the Red Bandanna."

Red bandannas usually average about 22 inches square and picture the candidate either alone or together with the vice-presidential nominee. Most designs have a floral or geometric background, or perhaps a simple border and an inscription above and/or below the portraits. Typical slogans on Republican bandannas are "Protection to Home Industries," "Rights of Workingmen," and "Protective Tariffs." Some frequently used slogans on Democratic bandannas include "Free Trade," "Tariff Reform," and—naturally—"Rights of Workingmen." The majority of the bandannas were issued during the 1888 campaign. Somewhat fewer patterns were issued for the 1884 and 1880 campaigns and even fewer for the 1892 and 1876 campaigns. After 1892 the variety of bandanna patterns decreases sharply; a few of the same patterns were still in use during the 1896 and 1900 campaigns, but red was no longer the dominant color.

Generally, red bandannas picturing Republican candidates are a bit easier to locate than those picturing Democratic candidates. Bandannas picturing Grover Cleveland and Benjamin Harrison will turn up more often than those for other candidates, but Cleveland and Harrison designs from the 1892 campaign are considerably scarcer than designs picturing the same candidates from the 1888 campaign. The 1880 bandannas with Winfield Scott Hancock show up far less often than those with James A. Garfield. Bandannas used by both parties during the 1876 campaign rarely appear on the market (Ill. 217), and those from this campaign that also include a centennial motif such as a portrait of George Washington together with the party nominees' pictures are especially desirable.

Some collectors try to acquire matched pairs from a campaign—i.e., bandannas that differ only in the candidates' pictures, since this is the way many bandannas were made and distributed by manufacturers. Bandannas from the various Harrison and Cleveland campaigns that also picture their respective running mates are especially important because this is often the only way that those can be attributed to the correct campaigns.

Most reds can be purchased at reasonable prices, although rarer and more attractive designs are likely to be expensive. But the prices of all these bandannas are likely to rise, as there has been recent growing interest in them.

Not all bandannas from the 1876–1900 period are dominated by the color red. Among these designs is an otherwise undistinguished matched pair used in the 1888 campaign consisting simply of a border with the repeated slogan on the appropriately colored cloth: "Red Hot Democrat" or "True Blue Republican." There are also a small number of bandannas with designs printed on white cotton cloth, but unless there is some unusual feature about these—attractiveness or rarity, for example—collectors will not value them as highly as the reds. There is, however, one white cotton bandanna that must be considered among the best examples of all later nineteenth-century campaign bandannas. This 1888 Harrison design (Ill. 219) pictures an eagle sheltering in a nest three eaglets representing "Protection/Civil Service Reform/Reduction of Surplus," which is inscribed below the scene. The bandanna is printed in black, red, and purple and bordered with chain-linked stars, each representing a state of the Union. Fortunately it shows up on the market occasionally.

LATER BANDANNAS. Twentieth-century political bandannas are generally well designed and colorful. Only a few designs were used in campaigns before the Second World War. None seems to be particularly scarce, and a few, such as a matched 1928 silk pair with large sepia portraits of Al Smith and Herbert Hoover, are collectors' favorites. Today bandannas are used as kerchiefs and scarves, and most are made of synthetic fabrics. Candidates' pictures seldom appear on modern bandannas; more popular are patterns with donkey or elephant motifs, or a candidate's name repeated in differently shaped and sized letters, or a repeated slogan such as "Nixon's the One."

The 1952 Eisenhower bandanna in Illustration 224 is an example of one of the better modern designs; it is colored red, white, and blue, as are most other modern bandannas. It is, however, a pleasant change that in campaigns since 1968 bandannas in other color combinations are known. Notable among these is a white kerchief used

216. A typical 1888 Republican slogan, a log cabin, and a cavalry scene recalling Harrison's role in the Civil War adorn this handsome red and black bandanna.

217. An outstanding example of combining the theme of the 1876 centennial with pictures of candidates in that year's campaign.

218. The 1880 Hancock and English bandanna is notable for the contrast it offers in the styles of beards.

219. The superior design of this bandanna makes it highly regarded by collectors.

220. The perennial Republican slogan and William McKinley adorn an 1896 dark blue bandanna. A similar bandanna pictures William Jennings Bryan.

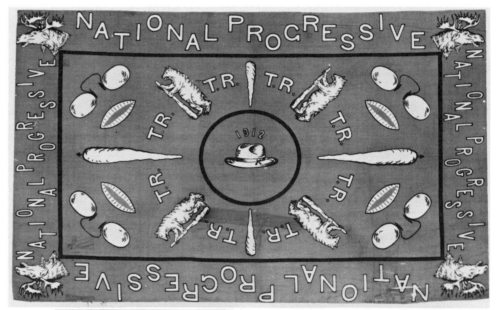

221. An uncommon blue and white Parker and Davis bandanna; its design is typical of campaign bandannas from the early 1900s.

222. Some of the symbols associated with Teddy Roosevelt are amusingly illustrated on this red, white, and black silk 1912 Bull Moose bandanna.

223. A silk bandanna similar to this one pictures Herbert Hoover.

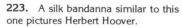

224. Dwight Eisenhower is pictured on a 1952 bandanna, one of the few modern ones that pictures a candidate.

225. Both these Stevenson name bandannas probably date from the 1952 campaign.

226. Two well-designed examples of bandannas used in recent campaigns.

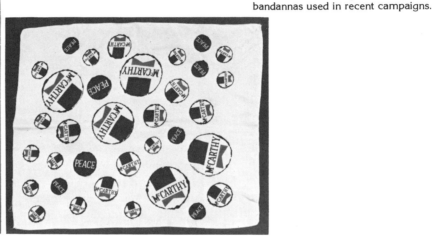

during presidential hopeful Eugene McCarthy's campaign in 1968; on this kerchief appear blue and green copies of McCarthy campaign buttons (Ill. 226). Several 1972 McGovern designs are also quite attractive. One design in beige (Ill. 226) depicts a blue outline map of the United States and the slogan "come home America come home" repeated several times within the map. Another design in beige, red, and black bears repetitions of "George McGovern for President/Truth, Peace, Unity."

Modern bandannas are well worth collecting. There is a good variety to keep one interested, and the subject is so seriously underrated by collectors that prices could not be any lower than they are at present.

Campaign Chintzes

Textiles consisting of long runs of cloth are known more familiarly as yard goods. Those printed with historical subjects were popular from about 1780 to 1880, although the large majority of patterns portrayed subjects associated with the earlier years of the Republic, perhaps through 1850. The most commonly used cloth was bleached or unbleached cotton, which was cut into different sizes and made into such homely objects as coverlets, drapes, cushion covers, and furniture protectors. Many of the earlier patterns are highly prized by collectors of American textiles for the subjects portrayed, such as scenes from the Revolutionary War and the War of 1812, the signing of the Declaration of Independence, scenes of Mount Vernon, the attack of the frigate *Philadelphia* in Tripoli Harbor, battles fought by the U.S.S. *Constitution* ("Old Ironsides"), and agricultural and commercial scenes. Subjects of interest to political collectors include An-

227. An early chintz depicting America presenting Washington and other of her "illustrious sons" at the altar of Liberty. (Cloudy area at the left is a water stain.)

228. This handsome chintz commemorates Andrew Jackson's first inauguration in 1829.

drew Jackson and the Battle of New Orleans, the log cabin motif in several patterns, Zachary Taylor and Mexican War scenes, and several patterns commemorating George Washington. Later political subjects, from the last quarter of the nineteenth century, include depictions of Ulysses S. Grant, patterns linking Washington with the 1876 centennial celebration, and a very limited number of patterns used in campaigns of the 1880s and the 1890s.

All such historical textiles with political subjects are known to collectors as campaign chintzes, although many patterns were dyed in just one color and were not glazed, like true chintz. But campaign chintzes they nonetheless are to political collectors, so that is the term we will use here. Campaign chintzes are often found mounted in contemporary frames; framed or unframed individual pieces (swatches) vary in size from a few inches square to about 2 by 3 feet. Still larger pieces appear occasionally on the market, but because they are so difficult to frame and occupy so much wall space, they are unacceptable to most collectors. Since swatches are cut from larger pieces, the edges of campaign chintzes are likely to be frayed; even ragged edges are acceptable provided the cuts do not intrude too deeply into the pattern.

EARLY CAMPAIGN CHINTZES.   George Washington is the subject of the earliest campaign chintzes (Ill. 227), most of which were probably printed on the occasions of his first inauguration in 1789 and the centennial of his birth in 1832. Several patterns from the earlier period depict him being crowned with laurel by Columbia, as Britannia and Marianne stand admiringly by, or being pulled in a chariot as angels trumpet overhead, or standing majestically with a scroll (presumably the Constitution) in his hand. A popular smaller pattern from the 1832 centennial shows Washington, scenes from his life, and a quotation from his Farewell Address. All Washington chintzes are scarce and tend to bring high prices because of the added competition from textile collectors. Washington patterns are usually found in deep colors, notably rust, brown, and blue, but the inaugural patterns are usually printed in brown, red, or purple on buff-dyed cloth.

Perhaps the earliest truly campaign chintz is a handsome pattern that commemorates Andrew Jackson's first inauguration in 1829 (Ill. 228). This pattern consists of busts of Washington, John and John Quincy Adams, Jefferson, Madison, and Monroe, and an oval bust of Jackson. Inscribed around the border of Jackson's portrait is "President of the United States from March 4th 1829 to Supreme Commander of the Army & Navy"; below the portrait is inscribed "Andrew Jackson/Magnanimous in Peace/Victorious in War." All portraits alternate with a large spread eagle and a ship of the line under full sails. A particularly large example, in light blue and measuring 51 by 34 inches, is in the University of Hartford collection. This pattern is also known in pink and in light brown. Collectors should know that Jackson portraits from only this pattern appear occasionally on the market neatly mounted in modern frames. Because Jackson campaign artifacts are so much in demand, this cut swatch always brings a respectable price. But a scarce and valuable textile has been butchered. In the interests of historical accuracy and personal integrity, collectors should be patient—the parent pattern does come on the market occasionally.

Several different patterns, all with floral backgrounds, are known from the campaigns of William Henry Harrison and Zachary Taylor. The Harrison pattern that collectors are most likely to see pictures Harrison in civilian dress together with a log cabin. Patterns more difficult to obtain include Harrison in the familiar "general" pose—i.e., the candidate with his sword raised high and astride a prancing steed; others picture Harrison standing in front of a log cabin receiving a visitor—or simply show a log cabin with a barrel of cider nearby. The butchering of the Jackson chintz mentioned earlier is repeated with a particular Harrison chintz: Watch for a small modern-framed swatch, usually in brown, depicting Harrison within an oval wreath and with a surrounding floral pattern.

Zachary Taylor chintzes from the 1848 campaign exist in almost as many patterns as the Harrison chintzes. Apparently all Taylor patterns picture the general and Mexican war scenes; most are variations of the "general" pose. The one exception to that pose is very odd: Taylor is depicted in civilian dress sitting sidesaddle and looking for all the world like an English country gentleman viewing his estate (Ill. 229). Solid reds or browns dominate the Harrison chintzes, although a few patterns are dyed in such combinations as brown and orange or blue, brown, and orange. Most Taylor chintzes are multicolored with blue, brown, and orange predominating; a few have an added touch of green. Harrison and Taylor campaign chintzes appear frequently on the market, and because there is not a great demand for them among political collectors, it is possible to build a fine collection at reasonable cost.

LATER CAMPAIGN CHINTZES. Patterns from the post-Civil War era are almost nonexistent. Only two campaigns, 1872 and 1880, seem to have anything to offer— and the 1872 patterns are not impressive. On those from 1872, General Grant's historic words written for his acceptance of the Republican Party nomination in 1868 are quoted: "Let us have peace." The pattern, and the few variants of it, consists solely of the quotation printed repeatedly in straight lines on brown and rust-colored cloth. The pattern is quite common, and for some reason is found usually in small swatches measuring no more than 12 by 10 inches. Collectors have been known to use this chintz as a mounting surface for Grant ferrotypes and medalets, but neither the chintz nor the lapel pieces are enhanced by that practice.

The pattern of the 1880 campaign chintz is a superb design. It exists in a matched pair that pictures either Republicans James Garfield and Chester Arthur (Ill. 230) or Democrats Winfield Hancock and James English in a vertical format. Each portrait is enclosed in a wreath and has shields to each side and crossed flags below. Along each edge of the Garfield/Arthur pattern is a line of scrolls: On one edge the scrolls are inscribed "Union For Ever"; along the opposite edge they are inscribed "Equality of All Men." Similar inscriptions appear on the scrolls in the Hancock/English design. Both chintzes are red, blue, and black. Neither design appears on the market very often, but the Hancock/English design appears to be the scarcer of the two.

MISCELLANEOUS POLITICAL TEXTILES. The most interesting textiles in this category are quilts bearing a few or many campaign ribbons sewn to the upper surface. Such quilts are sometimes called crazy quilts; although they are smaller than bed-size quilts, political collectors may find them too large to display easily. Nevertheless, they

229. Zachary Taylor is pictured both as a dashing general and as a benign elder statesman in this pair of 1848 campaign chintzes.

230. A fine example of later nineteenth-century political textile design. A similar example pictures Hancock and English.

are worth knowing about. These quilts seem to date either from the 1840 Log Cabin campaign or from campaigns in the 1880s. The older ones are always found adorned with William Henry Harrison campaign ribbons; an outstanding quilt from that campaign is in the collections of the Smithsonian Institution. Political quilts from the 1880s are often found with an added campaign bandanna or two plus ribbons commemorating the 1876 centennial and maybe a few Grand Army of the Republic encampment ribbons—together with campaign ribbons. No two campaign quilts from this period are ever quite the same, which is what makes them an interesting subject for the political collector.

Also of interest to some collectors are square or rectangular tapestries, measuring up to 4 feet on a side, which picture candidates from the 1896, 1900, and 1904 campaigns, and perhaps a few later campaigns as well. These tapestries are made of heavy embroidered cloth, with fringe on all sides; they were woven in dark shades of brown, olive, orange, and occasionally a few primary colors. Tapestries picturing Teddy Roosevelt and scenes from his life show up often and are popular with collectors. McKinley tapestries may be as common, but Taft (Ill. 231) and Parker designs appear to be more difficult to locate. Most tapestries were probably used as card table covers or piano throws.

231. This Taft tapestry is known in several sizes ranging from about 12 by 9 inches to about 4 by 2½ feet.

231A. One of the reasons why political Americana can be so exciting to collect!

8

Collecting Political Novelties

231B. This delightful caricature candle is a British product. Note the cruise missle instead of a six-gun in the holster.

POLITICAL NOVELTIES are fun to collect, and the variety available may be overwhelming to the beginning collector. Novelties with political themes are related to so many aspects of American life that we can never be sure of how complete a collection may be. It is impossible to collect all the novelties, but it is possible to form a quite unusual collection according to a collector's interest and taste. In fact, one can be assembled fairly easily because there are so many novelties to choose among. Some kinds of novelties are scarce, of course, but many more are not; thus there are many themes or categories around which a collection can be organized. Whatever in political campaigning strikes one's fancy, or appeals to his sense of humor, or gives the collector a nostalgic pause is probably represented by some campaign novelty.

Novelties range from the trivial—bubble gum cigars—to the historically and artistically significant—folk art in tin, wood, and other materials. They range from the very small—a Taft toy 1 ½ inches high—to the very large—a seven-canister platform torch mounted on a pedestal 8 feet in height. They can be described as bizarre, whimsical, imaginative, homely, childish, primitive, banal, tasteless, or simply entertaining. Some novelties produced a flame, some "walk," others make a noise of some kind, and still others need simply be admired. A few are expensive, but most are not.

I know of just a few collections of campaign novelties, and most of them emphasize the always popular torchlights. But there is so much more to collect. Consider this chapter an exploration into a facet of the hobby that perhaps has more to offer beginning collectors than any other.

Accessories for Campaign Parades

More than any other nineteenth-century political event, campaign parades best conveyed the excitement that politicking could inspire among voters. Some parades were spectacular affairs. According to the November 1, 1896, edition of the *Brooklyn Daily Eagle,* well over 100,000 partisans marched for McKinley and Hobart in New York City's "Sound Money" parade. Broadway was a "mass of blazing color," the newspaper reported, as hundreds of marching groups, with canes, banners, and other

231C. Ready for the parade! This youngster sports one 1896 McKinley and Hobart campaign ribbon.

232. The *New York-Illustrated News* printed this sketch of Wide-Awake groups marching in Hartford, Connecticut, during the 1860 campaign.

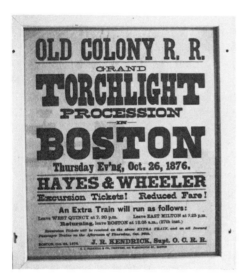

233. An 1876 broadside advertising a Hayes and Wheeler torchlight parade in Boston.

marching paraphernalia, sang such rousers as "We'll Hang Billy Bryan from a Sour Apple Tree." But most campaign parades, especially those held in the earlier part of the century, were decidedly local neighborhood events staged in honor of candidates for community and state offices. Those held at night were called torchlight parades in recognition of the homemade and, later, commercially made torchlights that would become the dominant feature of campaign parades as the century progressed.

For many voters in rural communities, a torchlight parade was often the highlight of a campaign—and in some communities the parade may well have been the social event of the year. For city voters, especially in the latter part of the century when railroads provided excursion cars or trains to bring large groups of marchers to parade sites, a torchlight parade was the occasion for a noisy and riotous celebration. Such parades were enlivened by fireworks, bands, marching groups in splendid uniforms, and an imaginative—if incautious—use of fire. On view somewhere in the procession would be the candidate(s), marching on foot or waving his hat from a specially decorated carriage. Torchlight parades advertised candidates, but they also provided first-rate entertainment for spectators.

The earliest torchlight parades publicizing candidates for public office probably began in the 1830s—the first campaign torch was patented in 1837, according to Herbert Collins in his pioneering study of the subject (see Bibliography). They were undoubtedly an outgrowth of traditional local parades that celebrated the nation's birthday or honored Revolutionary War veterans. Parades during this period were simple affairs. A candidate might be escorted into town by the volunteer fire company, each member resplendent in broad-brimmed leather hat, jacket, and pantaloons. Some members pulled an artistically decorated hand pumper and others carried speaking trumpets or torchlights. Also on hand would be local "persons of prominence" (as one contemporary spectator described them), including an aged Revolutionary War hero or two, the clergy, and the local capitalists, plus an assortment of children and dogs. The candidate would address his audience from the steps of the town hall, or outside the town tavern—and sometimes inside it—or, in more genteel communities, from the pulpit of a prominent church. In some areas it was the custom to place flaming barrels of pitch along the parade route.

By 1860 torchlight parades were a widespread campaign event. But they were not yet the intricately planned and elaborately staged affairs that they would become in the last quarter of the nineteenth century. The link between the simple parades of earlier campaigns and the ambitious demonstrations of later ones is a Hartford, Connecticut, marching group who called themselves the "Republican Wide-Awakes of Hartford!" (Ill. 232). This group of young men was probably the first body of uniformed voters organized specifically to march in campaign parades. The occasion for the formation of the

Hartford Wide-Awakes, as they became more familiarly known, was Abraham Lincoln's visit to Hartford in March 1860. Local supporters formed themselves into a company organized along military lines, dressed themselves in ordinary business suits but added kepis and capes, and staged a welcoming torchlight parade. Their success was immediate. By the time of Lincoln's victory the following November, there were hundreds of Wide-Awake groups in existence in most eastern and midwestern states. Lincoln later gave the Wide-Awakes considerable credit for helping him gain his party's nomination and for his subsequent victory. The Hartford Wide-Awakes and other Wide-Awake groups throughout the country continued to march in Republican campaign parades through at least 1904.

By the time of Lincoln's second campaign in 1864, and in every campaign through the early 1900s, uniformed marching groups—who often competed against one another in marching maneuvers and military bearing—were a standard parade feature. As we can judge from advertisements of campaign accessories manufacturers (Ill. 236), a new industry generated by the popularity of uniformed marching groups helped torchlight parades to become elaborate and highly competitive affairs. Simple homemade torchlights gave way to mass-produced torchlights, which were sometimes artfully shaped into imaginative designs. There were hand-held glass lanterns, paper Japanese lanterns, parade canes, wooden spears and shields, and whistles and other noisemakers. Because of the competition between manufacturers and the popularity of torchlight parades, political Americana collectors can choose among a considerable variety and quantity of parade equipment. Since much of this equipment is metallic, many campaign parade items have survived in reasonably good condition. Even a parade uniform comes on the market occasionally. It is still possible to assemble fine collections of torches, lanterns, and canes, although a collection consisting of a wider range of representative parade accessories would be more interesting.

With marchers and their accessories in proper positions, how might the parade itself have appeared—perhaps in 1888, the peak year for torchlight parades? A parade could easily last two or three hours; it often began or ended with a spectacular fireworks display. Miniature cannon up to 3 feet in length sounded highly satisfying reports and volcano tubes and wagons showered streams of sparks onto marchers and spectators alike. ("Volcanoes" was the name originally given to firecrackers packed with damp gunpowder that hissed and sparked when ignited. Metal volcano tubes were carried by a few marchers, and volcano, or "fireworks," wagons, which must have been awesome sights, were often the greatest crowd-pleaser of all.) Other wagons, suitably decorated in bunting and banners, carried local dignitaries or perhaps one of those marvelous cornet bands that were so popular in the 1880s and 1890s. And, consistent with a century-old tradition, spectators may have seen a smartly attired volunteer fire company or two pulling antique hand pumpers, curiosities now, perhaps decorated and newly painted for the occasion. Nearby would be their colleagues atop horse-drawn engines, on parade but ready for any emergency. Riding high above it all were plain and fancy banners brightly illuminated by the light of a thousand torches.

Among the marchers in a torchlight parade would be boys too young to vote who were paid a few cents to carry a torch. Splendidly uniformed marching groups tried to outdo one another with well-executed drills and complicated manuals of arms with their awkward—and flaming—torchlights. Other members of a group waved their canes or lanterns in prescribed patterns. Civil War veterans, usually self-titled "The Boys in Blue," were a standard parade unit beginning with the 1868 campaign, when veterans marched for Ulysses S. Grant. Also in the line of march were business and professional groups, each member wearing an appropriate ribbon in his lapel. A highlight of McKinley parades during the 1896 campaign, in the period when Americans were first discovering the pleasures of bicycling, was a group called the National Wheelmen for McKinley and Hobart Club. Members of this group would pedal through various parade maneuvers while mounted on regular-size bicycles or on high-wheel "boneshakers." I

234. The cover of this Wide-Awake song sheet pictures an officer of that organization.

235. A framed Wide-Awake membership certificate. Below the busts of Lincoln and Hamlin are pictured Wide-Awake uniforms, an officer's on the left and a private's on the right.

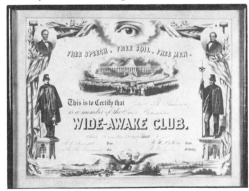

do not know if they rode in night parades with torches mounted on their bicycles.

Despite their hoopla, their extravagance, and their color, the historical significance of torchlight parades is best symbolized for collectors by the artifact that gives these parades their name—torchlights.

TORCHLIGHTS. Originally patented in 1837 as a simply made affair, the torchlight evolved into a creative example of folk art and imaginative commercial production. Torches are divided into two categories, canister and figural. Canister designs, which are the more common, consist generally of four parts: (1) an oil reservoir, or canister, which contained the coal oil used in earlier campaigns or the kerosene used in later campaigns; (2) a holed cap through which fuel was poured; (3) a few inches of cotton wick (some canister torches have a separate cap hole); and (4) a wire frame or strap for suspending the torch from a broom pole, thus enabling it to swing. Some torches are found nailed directly to a pole by means of a socket soldered on the bottom, but that difference is not a factor in determining value or rarity. Canister torches with one wick, or burner, are more common than those with two wicks. Torches with three or four burners, the maximum, were attached to speakers' platforms rather than carried; they are called platform torches, and the few designs known are all scarce. Occasionally an 1860 three-burner design consisting of a canister set on its long axis and a separate cap hole comes on the market. I know of a seven-canister platform torch mounted on an 8-foot sapling; it is attributed to the 1840 campaign and is probably unique.

236. A small sampling of the kinds of parade uniforms and related accessories available in the 1870–1900 period.

237. A selection of torchlights. At the upper left is a double-swivel torch used by the Hartford Wide-Awakes; at upper center is a scarce 1860 torch set on a horizontal axis; at lower right is an 1888 Harrison hat torch; a ballot box torch is at lower center. The other torches are standard designs that show up fairly frequently on the market.

During the 1880s small single-burner brass or nickel-plated hat torches were in use (Ill. 239). These canister torches were attached to metal receptacles on parade hats by means of spring wires. Hat torches are less commonly found than most hand-held torches, but are not particularly scarce. Rifle canister torches are also of considerable interest to collectors (Ill. 241). On these the handle rather than the torch is the attraction; handles in the shape of muskets were carved either from single lengths of wood or from two lengths and joined by means of metal rings. This was the type of torch used by marching groups for their manual-of-arms performances. Rifle torches were probably first used during the 1860 campaign, but most known examples date from campaigns in the 1880s. Although they appear on the market less often than most other torch designs, a rifle torch is highly desirable in a collection. If only a single representative torch is to be put in a political collection, I would much prefer that example to be a rifle torch.

What attracts most collectors to campaign torches is the imaginative figural designs, some of which are genuine American folk art. Early figural torches, like early campaign banners, are spontaneous expressions of campaign fervor. The unusually refined design in the shape of a defiant eagle and the cylindrical torch with an attached tin silhouette of a rooster are superb, and rare, examples of political folk art in tin from the pre-Civil War era (see Ill. 242).

Although figural torches from later campaigns lack the homely appearance of the rooster torch, many are nevertheless striking designs and would be showpieces in any collection of political Americana. Because they were more difficult and time consuming to make, figural torches used in later campaigns (and, in fact, early figural torches also) are found far less often than the canister type. Also, as Herbert Collins has documented in his monograph on campaign torches, some figural designs patented in the 1860–1890 period apparently were either manufactured in very small numbers or

238. This large platform torch holds slightly over one gallon of fuel.

not manufactured at all. Among the designs of which no examples are known (which is not to say that none exist) is an 1884 torch in the shape of a pinecone, presumably intended for use by supporters of the Republican nominee James G. Blaine, a former Maine congressman. Collins also illustrates patent drawings of torches intended for use in the 1888 campaign that were designed in the shape of a "C" for Cleveland and an "H" for Harrison. Among other unusual figurals known only by their patent drawings are an 1888 design in the shape of a human bust and an 1896 design in the shape of a sheep. The appearance of any of these torches on the market would be an epic event in the history of the hobby.

At least as many other figural torches are available to collectors. The designs most likely to be found are a six-pointed star, an ax, a beaver hat, and a glass globe. Star torches were probably used in the 1860 and the 1864 campaigns; some examples are found painted in red, white, and blue, and frequently their points are weak at the joints. But do not reject a star torch for that reason—it will be a long time before you see another one. Ax torches (Ill. 243) date from the 1884 campaign and are the scarcest of the designs described in this paragraph. They are associated with James G. Blaine, who was nicknamed "The Plumed Knight" (Democrats called him "The Continental Liar"), and are another example of the variety of Blaine campaign artifacts with that theme. It should be noted that all known ax torches are associated with Blaine; none can be attributed to Lincoln's campaigns. Torches in the shape of a beaver hat were carried in Benjamin Harrison parades in 1888 and probably in 1892. They were meant to encourage voters to identify Harrison with his grandfather, William Henry Harrison of illustrious

239. Hat torches from the 1870–1880 period. The type on the right is sometimes found with a burner cover. (It is missing from this torch.)

240. An unusual hat torch, probably used between 1848 and 1860.

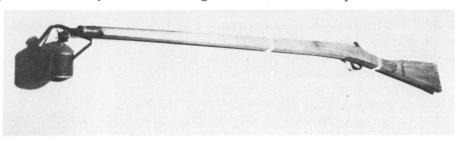

241. A typical rifle torch.

242. Figural and portrait torches. *Left to right:* A rare 1888 torch picturing Benjamin Harrison on one side and Levi Morton on the other; rooster torch, c. 1850s (white area on the neck and head is light reflection); eagle torch, 1840–1860 period; star torch, 1860s.

243. The design of this ax torch permits it to be carried over the shoulder rather than held upright, the usual position for torches.

244. Hand-held lanterns. The name "Clay" is part of the punched-hole design on the 1844 lantern at left. The 1900 McKinley lantern at right is one of several types. (It has been lined with white paper to highlight the slogan.)

memory. Known examples are painted in either black, gold, or, less frequently, copper; they are found attached to poles either by a wire arrangement or by a pole socket soldered to the bottom of the torch. What is so surprising about glass globe torches is the fact that so many have survived intact and unbroken into modern times. The patent title of these torches, which first appeared during the 1880 campaign, is "The Ballot Box Torch" (Collins, 28). They consist of a glass canister globe contained within upper and lower supports that are joined by vertical posts at each corner (see Ill. 237). The more desirable examples will have the patent title or a variant painted on the glass, or perhaps "Garfield & Arthur"; the author has seen examples of both. But consider yourself lucky to own a ballot box torch—with or without an inscription. The star, hat, and ballot box torches are valued at over $400 each, but ax torches are likely to cost more.

Condition, of course, is an important factor when purchasing a torch. A torch should be relatively free of rust; at least some of the original paint, if it had any, should be evident; painted inscriptions, such as "Hurrah for Lincoln" (as on an example in the Smithsonian Institution collection), should be reasonably whole. The value of a torch is also lowered if a hole cap or other part is missing, if there are deep dents, or if the torch is in a generally battered condition. Whole canister torches, including hat torches, in acceptable condition should sell between $75 and $200. Platform torches and rifle torches, with both rings present and the wood in reasonably good condition, will cost over $450 apiece. Figural torches in acceptable condition will go higher.

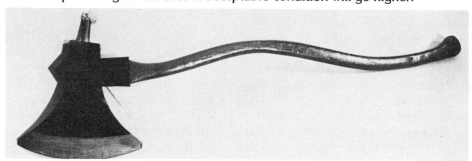

LANTERNS AND OTHER LIGHTING DEVICES. The imagination and mechanical ingenuity evident in the construction of torchlights is also evident in the interesting variety of other lighting devices used in parades and other nineteenth-century political events. Lanterns were made of wood, tin, glass, and paper in various combinations, and considering the fragility of some designs, a surprisingly large number have survived in collectible condition. A few varieties of glass lanterns include attachments for mounting them on poles, but because such attachments seem almost afterthoughts in the total design, we shall treat these as lanterns.

A very early example of a campaign lantern is a locally made and probably unique tin Revere-type design 16 inches in height dating from the early 1840s (Ill. 244). This lantern consists of a punched-hole star pattern with "Clay" punched on the door and a soldered candle socket inside. A somewhat similar punched-hole patterned lantern from the 1856 campaign is inscribed "Fillmore/Donelson" on the door. Very likely other examples exist, from even earlier campaigns, in the collections of state and local historical societies.

But campaign lanterns were not in widespread use until the 1860s. Designs in that period consisted of three- or four-sided metal forms containing inserted glass panels (Ill. 245). Most panels were covered with black and white pasted-on prints depicting a candidate and/or a painted slogan or nickname such as "Old Abe" or "Little Mac." Some panels were left transparent and others were painted in wide horizontal or diagonal red, white, and blue bands. These lanterns were carried either by a wide-looped strap or a thin but strong wire. Campaign lanterns from the 1860s are scarce; 1864 designs seem to show up a bit more often than 1860 and 1868 designs. Lanterns bearing a color print of the candidate, especially of Lincoln, are prized very highly.

245. A three-sided glass-paneled 1864 campaign lantern picturing Lincoln (from a February 1861 photograph by Alexander Gardner) and a slogan; the third panel is blank. Four-sided examples with glass panels are known.

246. *Above left:* An 1884 railroad-type lantern with a deep blue glass chimney marked "Cleveland & Hendricks"; *right:* an 1864 three-sided glass-paneled lantern picturing George McClellan.

Lanterns used in later campaigns were made up of fuel reservoir, an air vent, a wick, and a sturdy wire frame containing a glass globe. Most globes were transparent but a few are known with deep blue or red glass. Candidates' names were painted or stenciled on the globes in black or gold gilt. Many of these lanterns are quite similar to railroad lanterns, and a distinction is not possible if the names are obliterated. All too many glass campaign lanterns from the 1870s through the 1890s come on the market with inscriptions so badly rubbed as to be hardly legible. Obviously, a lantern with its inscription reasonably complete, and with all parts intact, will command a higher price—certainly well over $300.

It is a wonder that any paper campaign lanterns have survived at all! However, some are not particularly difficult to find, probably because they were never used. All examples that we have seen show no evidence of smoke discoloration or holes caused by heat or candle wax. The worst damage is likely to be tears or separations along the folds. There are three types of paper campaign lanterns: (a) expandable hexagonal designs, which were supported by an interior thin spring-wire frame and were popular in campaigns from 1872 through the 1880s; (b) accordion-pleated designs supported by cardboard disks at top and bottom, which were first used in the 1860 campaign and continued in use through the 1870s; and (c) collapsible square lanterns supported by a permanently attached but collapsible thin wire frame, which seem to have been used only during the 1860s campaigns and are seldom seen today.

247. This six-paneled Grant expandable lantern (1872) includes bucolic scenes of home and countryside.

Expandable lanterns (Ill. 247) are "opened up" by inserting the collapsed wire frame into the paper shell and pushing the wooden knobs at each end of the frame toward each other (one knob serves as the candle holder); the frame expands, thus filling out the paper shell. This type of paper lantern is the most politically informative of the three. One or two panels will depict one or both party nominees, two or three panels may carry appropriate slogans, and there will be geometric or floral patterns on the remaining panels. Many expandable lanterns are printed in black and red on heavy, deep yellow paper; when expanded, they measure about 22 to 24 inches in diameter. The designs most frequently found date from the 1888 campaign and are more likely to picture Benjamin Harrison than Grover Cleveland. The Harrison lanterns are usually decorated with a log cabin scene and the slogan "Tippecanoe and Morton Too!"—another reminder to voters of William Henry Harrison—and "Protection," a further reminder of Harrison's support for domestic tariffs. Expandable lanterns used in other campaigns

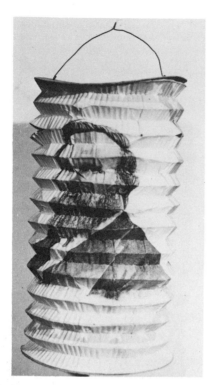

248. Rutherford Hayes and William Wheeler are pictured on an 1876 accordion-pleated campaign lantern.

249. An oil lamp in pink Bristol glass.

show up less often than those from 1888; occasionally an 1872 Grant lantern on white paper comes on the market, but very rarely do we see any picturing Greeley, Hayes, Tilden, Garfield, and Hancock. Since there are two parts to expandable lanterns, there is more to consider when purchasing one. Small tears or separations along the folds of the shell are acceptable, but the frame must be complete—all wires and both knobs present—if the lantern is to operate properly. Harrison lanterns in good or better condition will start at about $350; all others will be priced higher, perhaps to $600 each for scarce examples in mint condition.

The accordion type (Ill. 248) has a tin candle socket attached to the cardboard bottom disk and a wire hanger hooked to the top disk; this type folds flat when not in use. These lanterns are made of white crinkled paper on which the designs are printed in black, red, blue, or brown inks. Several 1864 Lincoln lanterns are printed in three colors. Unlike the other types, accordion lanterns—especially Lincoln designs—are often found in faded condition. Designs from the 1870s tend to have kept their bright colors because the inks had improved in quality. Besides fading, accordion lanterns will often have separated pleats—a condition that requires considerable skill to correct, thus reducing their value further. Accordion lanterns in acceptable condition will sell from $300 to over $500 each, depending upon the condition and the candidate pictured; Lincoln lanterns particularly command a higher price.

The collapsible paper lanterns I have seen are made of heavy prefolded newsprint and carry a candidate's picture and/or a slogan in black. The paper shell was fitted permanently to a thin wire frame, about 9 inches on an edge, which was hinged at the joints, thus allowing the lantern to collapse, or fold flat. The whole construction was so fragile that very few lanterns of this type have survived. Acceptable condition means primarily that the lantern folds properly and the paper cover and design are almost complete. Perhaps between $450 and $700 would be a fair price.

Before discussing the cleverly constructed transparencies, I should mention the interesting 1896 McKinley tin novelty lanterns. Many of these were manufactured in the shape and approximate size of the round tin dinner pails typical in that day (Ill. 244). When the candle was lit, a punched-hole slogan such as "McKinley & Hobart/A Full Dinner Pail" was illuminated. Like the red bandannas, these lunch- or dinner-pail lanterns are an excellent example of a happy union between campaign theme and campaign artifact. There are probably a half-dozen or so different designs that are characterized chiefly by a top cover or lack of one and the particular slogan. All these lanterns, including two or three varieties used in the 1900 campaign, are fairly scarce and will sell for between $350 and $600 whenever they appear on the market.

Transparencies are so seldom seen that they are unknown to many collectors. These ingenious lighting devices were apparently used in campaigns from the 1860s through the 1890s and were both locally and commercially made. A transparency consisted of a light wooden frame onto which a cloth cover was stretched and secured; cutout cloth letters and portraits in contrasting colors were pasted on the stretched cloth. The whole construction was then attached to a two- or three-burner torchlight, thus creating a rather colorful effect when illuminated. Transparencies found today will be either three- or four-sided, with a side measuring from about 17 inches to as much as 30 inches. A three-sided example in the Smithsonian Institution collection pictures Lincoln with appropriate slogans. A four-sided example in the University of Hartford collection spells out a historically informative message—with blue, orange, and purple letters—in support of Ulysses S. Grant:

> Indiana for Grant & Colfax/The People's
> Choice;
> United States Grant/I Am For Peace
> Taxpayers Want Peace;
> Democracy Sold Out Cheap/Gone Down

With Rebel Colors Flying
Seymour and Blair Uniform/Aristocracy/
Blair Rebel Champion.

Here Democratic candidates Horatio Seymour and Francis Blair are accused of selling their principles in order to gain southern votes—hence they are no longer democrats (with a small "d") but aristocrats like their newfound allies. And that is only part of the interpretation.

Condition and rarity are the factors to consider when purchasing a transparency—should the occasion ever arise! The torchlight need not be present but the cloth and frame should be complete and the message reasonably intact, with perhaps just a few damaged letters. I have never known a transparency to come on the market, so it is impossible to establish a price range. Whatever price buyer and seller can agree upon would seem to be the only norm.

A few other kinds of lighting devices are also known, all of which are fairly scarce. The largest examples in this category are platform lanterns. These can measure up to 17 inches or more in height and perhaps 11 inches on a short edge. I know of a four-sided example in those dimensions consisting of a wooden frame, three transparent glass insert panels, and one glass panel painted in red, white, and blue diagonal bands with· "Grant" in the center. Also of interest are oil lamps depicting political subjects. Almost all these apparently date from campaigns in the 1880s and 1890s; they usually have an etching of one or both party nominees on the chimney. Rarer still are oil lamps in which the base rather than the chimney carries the political theme. An example is a pink Bristol glass base bearing the hand-painted inscription "Harrison 1892" (Ill. 249). An example with a transparent glass base in the shape of a log cabin turns up occasionally, but whether it dates from the 1840 campaign or the 1888 campaign is debatable; a variant is dated 1860.

250. A glass chimney from the 1888 campaign is decorated with a likeness of Benjamin Harrison and flags in sepia. A similar chimney pictures Grover Cleveland.

PARADE CANES AND NOISEMAKERS. In my talks about political campaigning I always hold a parade cane while speaking. It can be used as a pointer or as an attention getter. It helps in evoking images of bygone political events, and it provides a good starting point for a talk as well. Collectors and noncollectors alike are fascinated by the sight of what can be done with an ordinary walking stick. Parade canes have either wood or metal shafts and run to about 33 inches in length; they were used in campaigns from about 1868 to 1912.

The type of parade cane most popular with collectors is known as a bust or effigy cane because the head is formed in the likeness of a candidate (Ills. 251 and 252). The bust head was hollow-cast in brass, silver, tin, pewter, or lead; the result was invariably an amazingly accurate likeness. A brief inscription and perhaps an eagle or shield were placed below the bust. The bust canes most likely to be found portray Cleveland, Harrison, Blaine, McKinley, or Bryan. Canes with heads in the likenesses of Grant and Taft show up occasionally, but those with the likenesses of other candidates rarely appear on the market.

Second in popularity to bust canes are functional and decorative novelty canes. Functional designs include horn and torchlight canes. Horn canes—the type I use in my public talks because its horn makes a rather pleasant-sounding honk—are made entirely of tin. One type has an actual small horn soldered to the shaft; another has a blowhole about three-quarters of the way up the shaft and a convex head with a series of 1/4-inch holes around the base of the head. Horn canes were most in use from the 1896 through the 1904 campaigns (Ill. 253). Possibly torchlight canes were used as early as the 1884 campaign, although the examples that I have seen were probably used in the 1892 and the 1896 campaigns. These canes are also made entirely of tin; the wick and the fuel reservoir are revealed by unscrewing the top of the head. Torchlight canes are attributed to the proper campaign by means of the paper label usually

251. An assortment of canes. *Left to right:* McKinley, 1896; Grant, 1868; Harrison, 1888; a Blaine "Plumed Knight" cane, 1884.

252. Hand-carved Lincoln bust canes, all probably dating from the 1909 centennial period.

253. Tin novelty canes from the 1896 campaign. The cap of one torchlight cane has been removed to show the wick; the horn cane is the variety most likely to be found.

picturing the party nominees pasted on the shaft just below the head. The value of both horn and torchlight canes is less if the horn does not sound, large segments of a paper label are missing, or the cane has a generally battered appearance.

The most interesting decorative cane has a head formed in the shape of a knight's helmet with a long plume. This cane marks the 1884 campaign of "The Plumed Knight," James G. Blaine. The head is hollow cast in either lead or pewter, and has rather small overall dimensions. It is not scarce. Other decorative designs that come immediately to mind are an all-wood anti-Prohibition cane (to be described in a later chapter), a 1928 cane with a hollow transparent celluloid head containing a pair of dice (sometimes the head will carry the inscription "Hoover Wins"), and an all-metal invalid-type cane. This last one was manufactured for the 1932 campaign in support of Franklin Roosevelt, and although well intended, it called attention to Roosevelt's inability to walk unaided. It is believed to have been withdrawn from use by the manufacturer, an action that probably explains why it rarely comes on the market today. There are a few other novelty canes, including a rather undistinguished peanut-head design issued in 1976. One thin wood-shaft-type cane with brass head in the shape of an elephant or donkey is fairly easy to obtain.

Bust, torchlight, and horn canes will be valued at $150 and up; bust canes made in brass or silver will cost more than those with the same likenesses made in the other metals. With the exception of the invalid-type cane, which can be quite expensive, decorative canes can be purchased for under $300.

Despite their obviously widespread use, campaign noisemakers do not show up on the market very often, but neither is there much demand for them. However, these few horns, whistles, rattles, and ratchets do provide the collector with an opportunity to add some uncommon campaign items to his collection. Rattles are the earliest example of noisemakers that I know of. Typically all tin, they consisted of a canister about half the size of a modern quart fruit-juice can, and contained a few pebbles; the handle was up to 10 inches in length. Candidates' names were painted or stenciled on the side of the canister. The two campaign rattles I have seen are both cumbersome artifacts—but I can testify to their loudness!

Horns date back at least to the 1860s and probably earlier. Nineteenth-century examples are apparently all made of tin and bear stenciled candidates' names; 10 inches to about 20 inches seems to be the normal length, although a few horns 5 or 6 inches in length are also known. Examples from later campaigns, perhaps through the 1920s, are made of heavy cardboard and usually depict one or both party nominees. Whistles are the most elusive campaign noisemaker. One example likely to be of interest to collectors is an 1888 4-inch wooden piece that bears multicolored paper labels picturing Harrison and Morton; it is called "The Campaign Bugle."

Ratchets are the most interesting type of campaign noisemaker because of their fairly complex mechanism. The few nineteenth-century examples (I do not know of any from twentieth-century campaigns) that I have seen are made of polished hardwood and consist of a frame, handle, toothed wheel, and a pawl or taut catch, which engages the wheel when the frame is rotated. The design most likely to turn up—even though very seldom—will be one or both of a matched hardwood pair from the 1892 campaign. These ratchets (Ill. 254) picture Grover Cleveland or Benjamin Harrison, each with his respective running mate, on multicolored paper labels. The Cleveland ratchet, 14 inches in length, includes selections from his speeches along with the nominees' pictures. The Harrison ratchet is 16½ inches long; one end of the frame is shaped like a beaver hat, and the chief inscription is "One Good Term Deserves Another." (This slogan, which was so popular in later campaigns, especially Franklin Roosevelt's, may have been used for the first time in 1892.)

The Cleveland and Harrison ratchets are valued at about $100, but probably all other noisemakers are worth less, unless they have an uncommon feature, such as an association with Lincoln.

Smoking Accessories

Like some other collecting categories in political Americana, the artifacts that were used with tobacco and snuff range in quality from the superbly crafted to those perhaps only a notch above tacky. Since there is no great demand for them, it is possible to build a comprehensive collection in this category, even though the scope of material is narrow compared to that of parade accessories. The general collector should attempt to acquire a few representative pieces, most of which are fairly easily found and reasonably priced.

SNUFFBOXES AND CIGAR CASES. Every general collection should have a campaign snuffbox, but campaign cigar cases are so scarce that few collectors have ever seen one let alone owned one. Both were in popular use before the Civil War. Snuffboxes picturing political subjects span the period 1824 to about 1880; cigar cases with similar subjects seem to have been in use only during the 1840s and 1850s.

The snuffboxes of most interest to collectors are made of papier-mâché (Ill. 255)

254. The vice-presidential candidates are pictured on the opposite sides of these 1892 campaign ratchets.

255. Papier-mâché snuffboxes. The Jackson box probably dates from the 1824 campaign or earlier; William Henry Harrison is pictured on an 1840 box; and the box picturing Van Buren, Jackson, Webster, and Clay is an 1844 issue.

and range in diameter from about 2 to 3½ inches and in depth to about ¾ inch. They are enameled in black, have paper transfers decorating the covers, and are finished with several coats of lacquer. A few examples surface fairly regularly, and if it was not for their high cost—perhaps $500 to $1,200 each—this category could be well represented in general collections. The cover illustrations on most papier-mâché snuffboxes depict their subjects against deep yellow (almost tan) or deep orange backgrounds, but a few scarce varieties are known that have an illustration on the base also and/or bear a multi-colored portrait of the candidate.

The earliest papier-mâché snuffboxes with political themes bear youthful busts of Andrew Jackson, which helps to date these examples from his 1824 campaign and earlier. All Jackson designs are scarce. Snuffboxes picturing William Henry Harrison turn up more often than those picturing Jackson—but one of the finest and rarest of all papier-mâché varieties has a multicolored bust of Harrison on the cover and a striking black and gold scene of the Battle of the Thames on the base. We can take as typical of Harrison snuffboxes, however, an example from my own collection that depicts Harrison in civilian dress below the slogan "Harrison and Our Country's Welfare." Fewer examples are known portraying other candidates of the period: Several examples picture Zachary Taylor (including a multicolored one) and Henry Clay; even fewer picture Martin Van Buren, Daniel Webster, and James Polk. Snuffboxes with portraits of Winfield Scott, Franklin Pierce, and Lewis Cass may also exist; if so, they are exceedingly rare. My favorite papier-mâché snuffbox—which is relatively easy to obtain—pictures Andrew Jackson, Daniel Webster, Henry Clay, and Martin Van Buren together. If one cannot afford to buy individual snuffboxes that depict these candidates, then this snuffbox is a more than acceptable substitute.

255A. This papier mache snuffbox pictured Rutherford Hayes and William Wheeler on opposite sides. The tin snuffbox with an attached movable disk picturing Garfield and Hancock rarely appears on the market.

255B. Blaine never made it to the White House and he is remembered as a rather unscrupulous congressman.

At least one papier-mâché snuffbox from the post-Civil War era is known. It dates from the 1876 campaign; it is 2⅛ inches in diameter and is rather crudely done. Embossed busts of Rutherford Hayes and William Wheeler are pictured on the top and bottom respectively. This snuffbox seldom appears on the market.

Other snuffboxes with political subjects were made of tin or pewter. The earliest example I know of is oval in shape, made of pewter, and bears an embossed log cabin scene that indicates its use during the 1840 campaign. A similarly shaped tin snuffbox from the 1868 campaign pictures Ulysses S. Grant. The 1840 snuffbox comes on the market occasionally, but the Grant snuffbox seldom does. Perhaps the rarest design known from later campaigns is an 1880 rectangular tin container lithographed in black and red with a ¾-inch oval hole in the cover and above it the inscription "Our Next President"; beneath the cover is a circular disk bearing photographs of James Garfield and Winfield Hancock and their respective running mates—each candidate's picture appears successively in the cover hole when the disk is rotated.

Collectors should be aware of a few commemorative snuffboxes honoring George Washington. The one most likely to be seen is made of tortoiseshell and is 3¼ inches in diameter. The cover of this French-made beauty (c. 1832) has an inserted brass shell embossed with a profile of Washington encased in a convex glass top. A small oval papier-mâché variety—probably issued during the 1820s—depicts Washington and the Marquis de Lafayette in profile on a 1-inch silvered copper medalet, which is inserted in the cover. Other papier-mâché varieties picture Washington on the more usual deep orange transfers. Some Washington snuffboxes are not especially scarce and can be had at a reasonable price.

Political cigar cases may have been used from 1840 to about 1852. Some collectors, however, do not believe these cases were originally intended to hold cigars, but rather business or calling cards. Some contain a removable cardboard insert that could, one assumes, hold cards; in other cases the inserts are not removable, and so cards would fall out very easily. All examples that I have seen expand to about ⅝ inch, which is space for a good many cards—or for a few cigars.

These cases (whatever their purpose) measure about 5 by 3 inches, and fold flat. Those I have seen are beautifully crafted of two thin wood strips joined together by means of a pleated leather fold to make a pocket into which the cigars—or cigarillos—are tucked. One wood strip (or side) bears either a black and orange portrait transfer or a hand-painted multicolored portrait, plus a slogan or message and perhaps an eagle. The other, the back of the case, is enameled in deep brown or black. Several coats of lacquer give the cases a hard shell-like surface.

Probably no more than a dozen or so different cigar-case designs exist. At least five—all hand-painted—picture Zachary Taylor (Ill. 256). Henry Clay, William Henry Harrison, and James Polk are each represented by two or three designs—with both transfer and hand-painted decoration.

Because these attractive artifacts so seldom appear on the market, it is difficult to establish values—perhaps $350 to $650 would be a fair starting price.

POLITICAL PIPES.   Here is another of those subjects where political collectors can expect competition from outside their hobby. Pipe collectors rate political pipes very highly—and for good reason. Many have the bowl shaped like the bust, or effigy, of a candidate, and one rare variety bears a rebus message. Several of the bust designs would be prizes in any pipe collection, and at least one example should be included in a political collection. Political pipes portray candidates beginning with William Henry Harrison in 1840 and extending to Franklin Roosevelt in 1936—and there may be more recently distributed examples of which I am unaware. Some pipes are made of either white clay or meerschaum; others are briar.

One of the earliest designs—it comes on the market regularly—has an uncommonly tall and narrow clay bowl bearing an embossed head of Henry Clay. Meerschaum bust designs depicting Franklin Pierce, Millard Fillmore, and Zachary Taylor seldom appear. I know of no Lincoln pipes used during his campaigns. A French-made white clay bust-design pipe depicting a bearded Lincoln crowned with a laurel wreath (sometimes found with traces of green paint) was probably issued in 1909 to mark the centennial of his birth. It should not be mistaken for an 1864 issue.

A very rare political pipe (Ill. 257), with certainly the most intriguing design of all, is an 1880 glazed mustard-colored rebus design in clay touting Winfield Hancock: Mounted at the junction of the stem and the bowl are an open hand and a young

257. A rare 1880 Winfield S. Hancock rebus puzzle pipe.

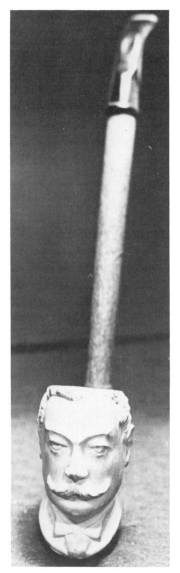

256. These 1848 cigar or card cases depict General Zachary Taylor in heroic poses; part of the inner container and the pull tab are shown on the one at left.

258. A French-made clay pipe with a bust of William Howard Taft; this pipe and the Bryan mate to it are the ones collectors are most likely to see.

rooster; "Our Next President" is inscribed on the stem. A label assures us that this rare gem is "warrented to color like meerschaum." An attractive matched pair of clay pipes from the 1888 campaign has embossed busts of Cleveland and Harrison, respectively, on the bowls. On the opposite side of the Harrison bowl is a spread eagle and shield; the stem is inscribed "Protection for American Labor." The Cleveland pipe also has an eagle and a shield—and a very early locomotive depicted below! The stem of this pipe is inscribed "A Public Office Is a Public Trust." Both these surface occasionally, perhaps the Harrison design a bit more often. Bust pipes from later campaigns are represented by several that were French-made in white clay, probably issued during the 1900, 1904, and 1908 campaigns. These depict William McKinley, William Jennings Bryan, Theodore Roosevelt, and William Howard Taft (Ill. 258). All of them are marked "Gambier A Paris" and carry a sequence number, which suggests that each design may have been

259. Effigy pipes depicting the two Roosevelts.

manufactured in a limited "edition" of 2,000 or 2,500 copies. These pipes appear on the market more frequently than any other design or variety. If a general collector wishes simply to add a political pipe or two to his collection, then these are the pipes to look for. Scarcer McKinley and Bryan meerschaum and clay bust-designs used during the 1896 campaign are known. The Bryan examples are especially scarce.

The two Roosevelts are represented by several bust designs (Ill. 259). At least four different ones depict Teddy—in clay, meerschaum, and briar—with and without his Rough Rider hat. One or another of these shows up frequently, and probably additional designs that are unknown to me also exist. Franklin Roosevelt is represented by a well-executed briar bust that is known in both large and small bowls. This design, which was probably used in 1936, is marked "Bruyere/Superieure/Made in France"; it appears on the market only occasionally.

Political pipes will range in price from less then $200 to perhaps more than $500 for the 1880 rebus type and the 1888 Harrison and Cleveland designs sold as a pair. Normal "browning" of a pipe is to be expected and, in fact, adds a touch of authenticity. But certain conditions can detract from a pipe's appearance and value: Clay pipes are sometimes found extremely soiled; they are difficult to clean because the clay is so porous. The bowls of meerschaum pipes are likely to be chipped from heavy use, but if the bust is intact slight chipping should not seriously affect the value. A well-used pipe is good evidence of either its original owner's regard for a favorite pipe or his admiration for a particular candidate—or both; so treat these pipes appreciatively.

OTHER CAMPAIGN SMOKING ACCESSORIES.   Perhaps the most remarkable feature of other campaign smoking accessories is their low cost. Every artifact described in this section can be bought at under $350 and most of them at under $200. Foremost among these accessories is a matched pair of cast-iron matchboxes made in the likenesses of Horace Greeley and Ulysses S. Grant, which were distributed during the 1872 campaign. As Illustration 260 implies, these matchboxes were intended to hang beside the stove or the fireplace to hold a small supply of matches. Both are scarce and *reproductions do exist* (see Chapter 11). From modern campaigns there is a good variety of matchbook covers with illustrations of candidates and slogans to choose among.

A novelty cigar adds a humorous touch to a political collection. These cigars date at least from 1904 and usually picture a candidate on a colorful band. Look also for long

260.   A matched pair of iron matchboxes from the 1872 campaign. The matches were stored in Greeley's "Quaker" hat and Grant's military cap.

thin cigars encased individually in glass tubes within specially made wooden boxes. Each box and cigar label will say either "Roosevelt" or "Landon." The most interesting cigar-related artifacts are cigar boxes. Some of these date from the 1880s and have colored pictures of candidates either on the outside or inside of the cover. Other boxes simply have candidates' names or an appropriate slogan. The ones most likely to turn up picture Franklin Roosevelt. Collectors should remember that several presidents have been pictured on cigar-box labels, including the earliest presidents, so it is difficult to attribute a particular box to a particular campaign. Perhaps the most unusual cigar box is a scarce double-cover one that has sepia lithographed portraits of 1884 Republican nominees James Blaine and John Logan inserted into frames on the underside of the covers (Ill. 262). Although not strictly campaign related, a cigar-band dish (Ill. 263) makes an interesting addition to a collection. For a while in the early 1900s, it was a fad to paste many different cigar bands over the entire outside of shallow, clear glass bowls so that the colorful bands showed through the glass and could be viewed from the inside of the bowl. A felt covering was glued over the bands on the outside to protect them. Such dishes made up of cigar bands picturing only presidents appear on the market occasionally. They generally sell for quite modest prices.

261. An iron matchbox similar to this 1888 one for Cleveland is known for Benjamin Harrison.

262. This 1884 double-cover cigar box shows James G. Blaine and John A. Logan, the portrait cards being inserted in the undersides of the covers. The cards often show up on the market without the box, as do similar cards picturing Grover Cleveland and Thomas Hendricks, a fact that suggests the existence of a similarly constructed cigar box for those candidates.

Cigarette packages and lighters date from campaigns in the 1930s. The most attractive lighters are slim multicolored 1956 designs picturing Dwight Eisenhower and Richard Nixon. An equally attractive nickel-plated brass lighter from the same campaign pictures Adlai Stevenson and Estes Kefauver (Ill. 264). From the 1964 campaign there are very small lighters with attached brass medalets depicting Barry Goldwater and Lyndon Johnson. Also available are several slogan lighters—e.g., "H.H.H." and "Nixon's the One!"—and miniature lighters in the shapes of donkeys and elephants. The most frequently found cigarette packages picture Stevenson and Eisenhower; George McGovern and Richard Nixon are pictured on cigarette boxes used during the 1972 campaign.

263. A cigar label dish, representative of a fad popular in the 1900–1912 period.

Hats and More Hats

Before the subject of campaign hats is too casually dismissed, consider, please, the role of hats in American political history. For many Americans, impressions of national political party conventions must include delegates wearing hats, delegates throwing their hats in the air, and delegates bedecked with buttons, ribbons—and a crazy hat. The type of hat we most often see at political events is a broad-brimmed white plastic skimmer that is decorated with a wide red, white, and blue band. That hat is the bland descendant of a fascinating assortment of campaign hats, many of which have done their bit to popularize causes and candidates. One of our earliest political symbols is the liberty cap (the French *bonnet phrygien*), a reminder of the cap placed on the end of a long pole to serve as a rallying site for the Sons of Liberty. Political parties used the

264. Tobacco-related artifacts. The Wilson cigar dates from 1912; the Eisenhower and Stevenson lighters were used in the 1956 campaigns.

265. A carved wood Liberty cap surmounting a 5-feet, 4-inch alderman's staff; attached to the staff is a silver plate inscribed "Edward Rowe/Ald 7th Ward/ 1857."

liberty cap symbol on their campaign artifacts through the 1850s (Ill. 265). We know what a politician means when he says "his hat is in the ring." Cartoonists dramatized Abraham Lincoln's height by exaggerating the height of his stovepipe hat. As symbol and as metaphor, hats reach deeply into American politics.

Adorning a hat with some kind of device to denote its wearer's political loyalties precedes the actual use of hats for campaign purposes. Supporters of Thomas Jefferson pinned red, white, and blue rosettes, or cockades, to their tricorns, and supporters of John Adams did the same with brown and black cockades in the 1796 election. Members of New York City's Tammany Society were known as bucktails because of their habit of attaching deer tails to their hats; as the Bucktail party the Tammany Society successfully opposed DeWitt Clinton's bid for the presidency in 1812. We know also that supporters of Daniel Webster wore black top hats with small white ribbons pinned to the crowns. The coonskin hat was a favorite Whig party symbol during the 1840s —Henry Clay's followers are believed to have worn such hats in his 1844 campaign. It is entirely fitting that the most American of hats, the coonskin, was also probably the first genuine campaign hat.

Hats were the trademarks of several candidates. Horace Greeley's broad-brimmed white Quaker hat and his habitual clasped hands-behind-his-back pose were sights so familiar to voters that an 1872 lapel pin in the shape of clasped hands and a hat carried no other identification. Benjamin Harrison's beaver hat was his chief symbol in both his campaigns. An assortment of miniature hats made in different materials and several campaign songs as well popularized his candidacy. Al Smith and his brown derby were an inseparable combination during the 1928 campaign—a song from that campaign was titled "Get Yourself a Nice Brown Derby and Fall in Line for Al." Teddy Roosevelt and his Rough Riders are a part of American folklore; it is possible to assemble a full-sized Roosevelt collection that would include only artifacts depicting Teddy with his Rough Rider hat. Franklin Roosevelt wore his "lucky" fedora throughout his four campaigns; that much-beaten-up hat is now on display in the Roosevelt Museum at Hyde Park. To a lesser degree, we associate Barry Goldwater and Lyndon Johnson with cowboy hats. A coonskin hat was the trademark of presidential hopeful Estes Kefauver in the 1956 Democratic primary campaign.

So campaign hats are serious business. They are an important means for getting candidates and voters to identify with one another. Few candidates can ever hope to become so clearly and easily identified by voters as those mentioned above, but hats as symbols are a necessity for every candidate, even without a special association. A green and white knitted ski hat with a large pom and a picture of Jimmy Carter is evidence of that fact!

MINIATURE BENJAMIN HARRISON HATS. Among the more unusual artifacts used to popularize Benjamin Harrison's 1888 and 1892 campaigns were a number of miniature beaver hats (Ill. 266) produced in transparent and colored glass, milk glass, terra-cotta, porcelain, papier-mâché, and macerated currency (see page 168). These novelties range from occasionally found to extremely rare. The larger ones in glass and china were probably intended to serve as toothpick holders; those in other materials were probably decorative only.

A major problem for collectors is distinguishing the genuine glass and china hats from the similar hat-shaped toothpick holders. The only certain identification is the slogans "His Grandfather's Hat" or "The Same Old Hat"—or simply "Harrison" inscribed on the hatband of a few designs. Others can be identified, but with considerably less certainty, by means of a hatband and buckle around the crown, a feature not commonly found on the ordinary hat-shaped toothpick holder. Harrison's beaver hat, like Greeley's Quaker hat, was such a familiar sight to voters that no further identification was necessary. So we are left with a problem. Hat novelties in other materials sometimes have a painted "H" or "H & M" (for Harrison and Morton) or "Harrison" on

266. Miniature Benjamin Harrison novelty hats: The inscribed ones are made of milk glass and clear glass; the unmarked hats are the same kinds of glass, but they have metal brims. (For another example, see Ill. 290.)

the crown. Those hats not inscribed can likely be considered Harrison-related simply because it is difficult to imagine them serving as toothpick holders and on the same table with a family's best glass and tableware.

Despite the problem that they pose for collectors, these delightful miniature hats deserve a place in a general collection as well as in a specialized collection of campaign hats. And, obviously, further research is needed. Inscribed glass and china varieties are valued at between $125 and $250; unmarked varieties are valued at under $100. Inscribed and unmarked varieties in other materials would perhaps be priced from $75 to $175.

DELEGATE HATS.   Some campaign hats are colorful, some are campy, and a few are simply uninteresting. But delegate hats are something else! Perhaps zany describes them best—and certainly they are unique, for no two examples are ever the same. In the many moments of boredom that occur at national conventions some delegates pass the time by adorning their ordinary campaign hats with buttons, ribbons, balloons, stuffed animals, name stickers, and whatever other political objects are available. The results can be awesome indeed as the delegates try to outdo one another. The relatively subdued example shown in Illustration 267 was put together by a Connecticut delegate to the Democratic National Convention in 1960. Attached to this woven straw hat are one straw donkey, forty-four picture and name buttons in five different designs (including a rare 1956 picture design reading "John F. Kennedy for Vice President" with "Vice" scratched out!), and thirteen name and slogan ribbons in four different designs.

I would like to say that every collection should have a delegate hat. But they are very difficult to locate. They are usually so fragile that they seldom survive convention week, and if one does, then packing it safely for the trip home becomes a chore that some delegates prefer to avoid. Should a hat be brought home intact, it is likely to become a treasured memento of an exciting few days in a delegate's life—hence, not easily parted with. I myself waited ten years for the delegate hat described above before I could add it to my collection. So be patient; delegate hats do surface occasionally.

267. This "creation" was made during the 1960 Democratic National Convention.

MORE CAMPAIGN HATS.   So many campaign hats do come on the market, and so often, that an interesting collection can be built. Rather than describe in detail all the kinds of hats that are available, the list below gives the names of the candidates with whom each category of hat is most associated. With the exception of the first type valued at $200 to $350 each—all sell for much less than $150 and some for just a few dollars each.

Felt "beaver" hats: As is evident in Illustration 268, these hats contain large interior paper labels picturing Cleveland and Harrison and their running mates.

Parade hats: There is an interesting assortment in this category; among the most desirable are copies of Teddy Roosevelt's Rough Rider hat, torchlight kepis, and simple marching hats carrying a candidate's name.

Cowboy hats: The usual kinds come in woven straw and molded felt, and are associated primarily with Barry Goldwater and Lyndon Johnson.

Beach hats: These come with floppy or visored brims: Nixon, Humphrey, Johnson, Goldwater, McCarthy, and Kennedy.

Painters' caps: Eisenhower, Nixon, Kennedy, and Stevenson.

Children's beanies: Cox, Landon, Franklin Roosevelt, Truman, Stevenson, and Eisenhower.

Crew hats: Plain and multicolored; Goldwater, Johnson, Kennedy, Nixon, Humphrey, and George Wallace.

268. Felt beaver hats used during the 1892 campaign.

269. Modern campaign hats. In the foreground are baseball, ski, and overseas caps; in the background are a plastic skimmer, a slot and tab, a beanie, and a crew hat with a multicolored plume two feet in length.

270. When folded another way, this 1896 paper hat, which was distributed by a Boston newspaper, would picture William McKinley.

Baseball caps: Nixon, McGovern, Humphrey, Stevenson, Eisenhower, and Wallace.

Cardboard hats: There are several different shapes that have been distributed at national conventions since 1948; the hat is formed by cutting along dotted lines and inserting tabs; the names and slogans are preprinted.

Skimmers: White plastic with shallow crowns and wide brims. This variety has been in use at national conventions since 1952 and is associated with all major party candidates and many hopefuls.

"Straw" skimmers: Similar in design to white plastic skimmers, but made of light yellow Styrofoam with a surface textured to resemble straw; probably the single most commonly used campaign hat today.

Miscellaneous varieties (all exist in limited numbers):

Yarmulke: satin design with inscription "I Like Ike"; possibly one exists for Stevenson also.

Navaho high-crown felt hat: McGovern.

Coonskin cap: Kefauver ("Kefauver for President" is printed on the inside).

Ski hat; knitted: Carter.

There are probably well over two hundred different hats represented on this list, most of them are fairly easy to locate.

271. The always popular Tammany bank.

Children's Toys

Every collection needs a few political toys—if for no other reason than to bring a light touch to the hobby, which we sometimes take far too seriously. Some of the toys described here appeal to our sense of humor and our sense of the ridiculous. And there is always the appeal to the spontaneous delight and uninhibited enjoyment we had as children and, we hope, have not lost. Once having seen political toys, it is impossible for us ever again to take seriously politicians who have been immortalized in them.

Unfortunately, many of the toys described here do not show up very often. Some varieties were apparently manufactured in limited amounts, and because collectors have shown little interest in the subject, scant effort has been made to find them. Political toys, therefore, are an important sleeper, and, with a few exceptions, their prices are uncommonly low—certainly well below $250 for many varieties.

One of the more expensive toys is the Tammany mechanical bank that was distributed during the 1872 campaign (Ill. 271). The bank gets its title from its presumed reference to Boss Tweed and other corrupt Tammany Hall politicians of the period. This bank operates by placing a penny in the seated politician's upraised hand; the weight of the penny drops the arm to a slot—the politician's pocket—and as the penny falls into the bank, the politicians nods a "thank you." The Tammany bank is well known to mechanical bank collectors and is rated by them as fairly easy to obtain and valued at between $450 and $600, depending upon the completeness of its original paint and its operating condition. One other mechanical bank may be of interest to political collectors. This one, called "Teddy and the Bear," is valued at a much larger amount than the Tammany bank. Although not as specific in its political connotation as that bank, the Teddy and the Bear bank should be of interest to collectors of Teddy Roosevelt ephemera.

Also of interest are a few nonmechanical, or still, banks. By far the most unusual example is a squatting figure of General Benjamin Butler with frog's legs. Butler, a controversial Union army general during the Civil War and later a Massachusetts congressman, was governor of that state when he was nominated by the Greenback party to carry its standard in the 1884 campaign. Members of this party advocated more liberal use of paper money, hence referred to themselves as Greenbackers—but the mostly hostile press called them frogbacks, or simply frogs. The bank was intended, I assume, for the Greenbackers to save their silver dollars against the day when paper money would have destroyed the nation's economy. On the bank, Butler's right arm is inscribed "Bonds and Yachts for Me"; his left arm is inscribed "For the Masses." Presumably the inscriptions suggest what Butler would do with all those greenbacks that he wanted to see in circulation; "yachts" refers to Butler's ownership in those years of the famous racing yacht *America*.

Other still banks worth looking for, all of which sell for under $100, are two different Teddy Roosevelt varieties: a small one, 4 by 2½ inches, in the shape of a bear and inscribed "Teddy," and a similarly small head and torso bust of Roosevelt in his Rough Rider uniform. Also of interest are painted red, white, and blue milk glass Uncle Sam hats from the 1908 campaign, which are discussed in an earlier chapter, and different plastic donkey and elephant-shaped varieties dating from the 1930s to the present.

Benjamin Butler is also represented by a rare animated walking doll made by the Ives and Blakeslee Toy Company probably in the early 1880s. This marvelous toy has a stiff body and a head molded in the likeness of General Butler; it is costumed in a simple khaki uniform. It "walks" by means of jointed legs and tiny rollers on each foot; power is provided by a well-made clockwork mechanism. The same toymakers produced a similar animated doll in the likeness of Ulysses S. Grant in the late 1870s or early 1880s. Grant is portrayed seated in a chair, with his legs crossed, alternately puffing on a cigar and moving his head as smoke is inhaled and exhaled through a small opening in his mouth. This rare toy would be an eye-catching centerpiece in a collection of tobacco-related political artifacts. Grant's cigar is another campaign symbol that collectors should know about; like Horace Greeley's Quaker hat, Grant's cigar was a familiar image to voters in the early 1870s. An 1868 Grant campaign song, "A-Smoking His Cigar," pictured the General as a steadfast leader:

> When volley thundered loudest peal
> Along the front of war,
> The General calmly viewed the field
> A-smoking his cigar.

Consider yourself fortunate indeed to own either one of these ingenious toys. And, by the way, a walking Ives doll in the likeness of Samuel J. Tilden is also known.

There is one modern animated walking toy that is a match in quality for the Butler and Grant dolls. This toy is a remote-controlled, battery-powered elephant made by the Linemar Toy Company, probably in 1952 (Ill. 272). The toy is guaranteed to bring forth squeals of delight whenever it is demonstrated—from schoolchildren especially—as I can testify. As the elephant walks and waves its trunk, a tiny red bulb on the tip of the trunk glows. A red blanket on its back and a yellow celluloid flag pin attached near the tip of the trunk are both inscribed "I Like Ike." It is possible that the blanket inscription and the flag pin were added after this toy left the factory. The toy is well made; it has a gray velvet cover, and measures 10 by 6 inches. It should be considered a "must" piece in a general collection.

272. The "walking" elephant manufactured by the Linemar Toy Company, probably about 1952. The battery pack is at right.

Few collectors will ever see the Butler or Grant dolls, but several less expensive dolls are more easily obtained. The most important dolls in this group are made in the likeness of Abraham Lincoln; many were probably produced between his assassination in 1865 and the centennial of his birth in 1909. Examples that I have seen have a homemade appearance and are quite possibly unique. Clothing style and cloth are typical of the later nineteenth century, as are the molded papier-mâché heads. The Lincoln dolls shown in Illustration 273 stand 10 and 13 inches respectively; the smaller of the two has a tiny pearl attached to the watch chain.

Several modern dolls show up occasionally: Most desirable is a matched pair of 1960 stuffed dolls with wood composition caricature heads in the likenesses of John Kennedy and Lyndon Johnson. These dolls are dressed in business suits and stand 21½ inches. Similar dolls fashioned in the likenesses of Dwight Eisenhower and Douglas MacArthur are dressed in military uniforms and probably date from the 1948–1952 period.

Collectors should also be aware of the interesting variety of board games with presidential themes. "Presidential Election," c. 1892, is a Parker Brothers product in which the object is to move a player's chosen candidate into the White House ahead of

273.   These Lincoln dolls were probably made during the 1909 centennial period.

274.   A modern political board game.

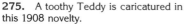

275.   A toothy Teddy is caricatured in this 1908 novelty.

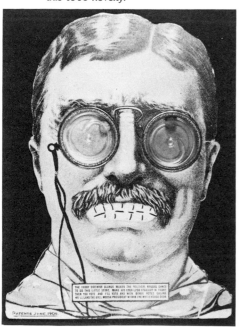

other candidates. The game is played with cards listing electoral and popular votes, different colored wooden playing pieces, and a suitably marked board. A more recent, and humorous, board game is called "*Just For Kicks New Frontier*" (Ill. 274). Again, the object of the game is to reach the White House first. This game consists of a board, two different sets of cards, and playing pieces in the shapes of a P.T. boat, a guided missile,

a football, and a bottle of Scotch. One set of cards, "Boners," carries political goofs such as "You photographed Teddy in Bermudas/trade in your camera for a sketchbook," "You didn't recognize Lyndon at a recent cocktail party/read *Who's Who in Texas,*" "You were seen cheering for Yale at a football game/plead insanity." The other set of cards is called "Apple Polish" and carries such messages as "Should a shrine to the PT-109 be built at Ellis Island or Alcatraz?"; "You painted a pennant on the wall of the Senate men's room [but] Bobby will clear it with the painters' union," and "You have volunteered for the Peace Corps in Massachusetts [so] take trinkets to the natives."

Several block, or tile, games are also available. An early example involves a conflict between President Benjamin Harrison and his Secretary of State James G. Blaine (the 1884 nominee of the Republican party); by moving the tiles in a certain way, Blaine does or does not retain his Cabinet position. A similar, and matched, pair from the 1928 campaign are titled "Hoover Wins!/Prove It" and "Smith Wins/Here's How."

Some other toys worth knowing about: The first is a heavy cardboard picture silhouette of Teddy Roosevelt facing outward (Ill. 275), which contains two shallow tin cups for eyes with a small metal ball in each. The directions for using this toy are amusing:

The Teddy sidewise glance makes the political bosses dance.
To do this little stunt, makes his eyes look straight out in front.
Then you vote and I'll vote, and with other votes galore,
We'll land the Bull Moose President within the White House door.

There are also Taft roly-poly figures with a weighted base; at least two different ones are known: a papier-mâché figure of Taft attired in a tuxedo, which stands 5¼", and a celluloid example, which is colored in black, green, and tan and stands 1½ inches. Look also for clear or lightly colored glass marbles containing sulphide busts of Teddy Roosevelt, William Jennings Bryan, William McKinley, William Howard Taft, or possibly Alton Parker. Sulphides range in diameter from 1¼ to perhaps 2½ inches, and all varieties are considered scarce to rare by marble collectors. In my own collection, I value at $150 a 1¾-inch clear glass example with a sulphide of Teddy Roosevelt (Ill. 277). Chipped or cracked sulphides bring substantially lower prices. Another delightful motion toy is a hand-carved example depicting Grover Cleveland and Benjamin Harrison locked in what appears to be mortal combat. As Illustration 279 indicates, the figures swing to and fro and arm wrestle as they are jounced up and down on the end of a wire.

The toy shown in Illustration 278 defies attribution, although it probably dates from the 1868 campaign. In a glass-enclosed wooden bowl, 3 inches in diameter and 1¼ inches deep, Ulysses S. Grant is depicted as a full-length, uniformed figure; projecting from a fixed torso are his head and four limbs that are attached to the torso by means of tiny—almost hairlike—springs and touches of wax. When the bowl is moved—even slightly—the figure "jiggles" in a random fashion. I can only guess that this incredibly fragile piece is a satirical allusion to Grant's alleged drunkenness during the Civil War, but perhaps a collector can offer another explanation. I know of only a few examples, and because of its delicate construction I marvel that any have survived at all.

276. Taft roly-polys in papier-mâché and celluloid.

277. Besides this sulphide Teddy Roosevelt marble, a similar example is known depicting William McKinley; possibly marbles containing sulphides of William J. Bryan and Alton Parker exist too.

278. A curious anti-Grant novelty; the figure is shown in a typically limbs-askew position.

279. This delightful toy depicts Cleveland and Harrison arm-wrestling their way to the White House.

Political Automotive Accessories

Almost from the time that they first appeared on American roads, automobiles have been a necessary feature of campaigning. The first use of campaign artifacts on automobiles seems to date from the 1920 campaign—or maybe earlier—with small window decals bearing the names of Warren Harding and Calvin Coolidge. By the 1928 campaign a variety of political artifacts made specifically for automobiles were in common use.

Although bumper stickers are the most common type of political accessory—some collectors have several thousand different ones—many collectors consider license plate attachments more desirable (Ill. 280). These were either screwed to the license plate or attached to another part of the bumper. Attachments are known in a variety of shapes and designs, many quite colorful; in size, most duplicate exactly the length of license plates but vary in width from about 3 inches to wider than a plate itself. Some attachments are reflectorized, such as a 1936 example that says in red and white "Roosevelt Is Good Enough for Me." Others are shaped irregularly: Look especially for a small, brightly colored one caricaturing a jayhawk—the Kansas state bird—which

280. Typical license plate attachments.

281. An oilcloth spare-tire cover from the 1932 campaign.

282. These Roosevelt clocks are typical examples. The one at the top also depicts presidential adviser Gerald Johnson and Secretary of Labor Frances Perkins. The clock at the bottom depicts Roosevelt at the wheel of the ship of state. Both were prizes in a 1930s punchboard contest.

$10.00 2-CANDLE LAMP CLOCK
SPIRIT OF THE U. S. A.

$10.00 BEAUTIFUL ELECTRIC ROOSEVELT CLOCK

says simply "Landon." Also of interest is an example made from molded fiberboard depicting gilded busts of Uncle Sam and Franklin Roosevelt, which is inscribed "Drive Ahead with Roosevelt."

Some collectors are interested in the special license plates issued by the Washington, D.C., city government, which are valid only for the duration of an inauguration period. All plates are numbered to a limited amount, are colored red, white, and blue, and were probably first issued for Harry Truman's inauguration in 1949.

The only other political automobile accessory of general interest is spare tire covers (Ill. 281). All examples seem to date from 1924 through 1940, and are scarce; they are valued at about $250 to $500 apiece. These covers are made of oilcloth and have a wire frame and sets of strings for securing the cover to the spare tire. Better examples picture a candidate, but others carry a simple slogan such as "Re-Elect Herbert Hoover." For the political collector who is also an antique car buff, having a political tire cover is a bonus; what better way to add a light touch to an old automobile! Collectors who wish to build a specialized collection of political automobile accessories may be interested in acquiring cotton fender pennants, most of which seem to date from the 1920s and 1930s; unless an example is found with its metal clamp (for attaching to a fender), they are easily mistaken for small hand-held banners.

With the exception of spare-tire covers, political auto accessories can be purchased for considerably under $200.

Collectors' Choice

I mentioned at the beginning of this chapter that political novelties touch upon many areas of American life. Here is a descriptive list of more novelties that suggests how pervasive that relationship is. Each category described here is worth collecting, but most have attracted only a few collectors so, with some exceptions, prices tend to be relatively low.

CLOCKS, WATCHES, AND WATCH FOBS. Most clocks are figural designs portraying Franklin Roosevelt in a variety of poses. These were popular giveaway premiums and punchboard prizes in the 1930s; they are generally made of cast metals, their maximum dimensions being perhaps 13 inches high and 9 inches wide at the base. The clock faces are about 4 inches in diameter; some face designs have automated hands, such as a fisherman moving a ship's wheel or a hand moving a cocktail glass (celebrating the end of Prohibition). The clocks are variously inscribed with "The Man of the Hour," "A New Day/A New Deal," "At the Helm of the Ship of State," and other similar slogans. Perhaps a dozen or more different designs can be collected; Illustration 282 pictures typical examples. Other clocks of historical significance are nineteenth-century shelf or mantel varieties, frequently made by master clockmakers, which include reverse paintings on glass. These paintings depict log cabin scenes, primitive portraits of candidates, and patriotic scenes with candidates' names. They are among the very best of all campaign artifacts and, unfortunately, are beyond the means of many collectors.

A few pocket and wrist watches are also known. The earliest pocket watch with a political theme known to me is an 1896 silver-plate design with "William McKinley/The Nation's Choice" inscribed on the reverse. One of the great rarities in the entire field of political Americana is a pocket watch from the 1920 campaign that pictures Democratic nominees James Cox and Franklin Roosevelt on the face. It is not only very rare but also very expensive. Probably a design picturing Warren Harding and Calvin Coolidge also exists. A pocket watch with a green and white face picturing Jimmy Carter and Walter Mondale was issued during the 1976 campaign. This same design also was issued in red, white, and blue to mark Carter's and Mondale's inauguration.

The only wristwatches I know of, although additional designs most likely exist, are a number of caricature examples picturing Richard Nixon, Spiro Agnew, George Wallace, and Goerge McGovern that were distributed during the 1972 campaign. The Nixon and Agnew designs were reissued during the Watergate scandal with different caricature faces, so it is sometimes difficult to distinguish those issued during the campaign from the Watergate issue.

Many of us regret the passing of the watch fob as a standard article of men's jewelry. Wristwatches are often hidden under shirt cuffs, but the pocket watch with its gold or silver chain or leather-strap fob was there for all to see. An old-time collector writing in a hobby publication some years ago remembered how carefully he saved his pennies in order to buy his first "dollar watch"—meaning pocket watch—and how thrilled he was with the fob that came with it (see Bibliography: Piercy, pp. 9–11). No man or boy felt properly dressed without a fob displayed for all to see. A fob gave a feeling of wealth and importance to its wearer, Piercy wrote, as well as indicating the direction of one's loyalties, his occupation, and his preference in political parties and candidates.

Most fobs are made in irregularly shaped metal designs, but a few consist of a celluloid button attached to a leather strap or simply a leather strap with a printed inscription. A very few fobs are rather elaborate nickel-plated brass or pot metal designs consisting of three or four irregularly shaped segments linked together by tiny brass chains. One segment always depicts the candidate and/or an inscription; a second may depict a donkey or elephant, and the third and fourth segments usually depict the White House and the Capitol—although a Teddy Roosevelt fob is decorated with scenes of the Panama Canal. Political watch fobs were most popular from the 1900 campaign until well into the 1920s, but a few fobs from later campaigns are known. Probably over 70 percent of all political fobs were distributed during the 1908 campaign; at least 125 different ones from this campaign are known, and fobs associated with Taft apparently far outnumber those associated with Bryan (Ill. 283). Other fobs of note are a matched pair from the 1920 campaign with embossed busts of Cox and Roosevelt and Harding and Coolidge. They come in brass and nickel-plated brass and are quite popular with collectors.

CLOTHING. I can merely suggest what clothing is available. There is not an extensive variety, but quite a few examples are known within some of the available categories. Neckties, for example, exist for many candidates from 1888 on; each tie, of course, is typical of its period. There are four-in-hands, bow ties, and bolo ties. The peak period for political neckties was from the 1930s through the early 1960s.

There were red, white, and blue suspenders for Franklin Roosevelt; also for Dwight Eisenhower—saying "Support Ike," naturally—as well as web belts, buckles, stockings,

283. A selection of watch fobs. *Top:* A 1908 brass silhouette of Taft. *Left to right:* A rare all-celluloid 1912 Bull Moose issue; a 1904 brass tag with celluloid inserts of Roosevelt and Fairbanks; a 1908 brass padlock-shaped tag inscribed "The Lock to the White House/Bryan Holds the Key"; a 1908 Taft celluloid button attached to a leather strip.

283A. A traditional Democratic slogan highlights this chain-linked segmented pot metal watch fob picturing 1904 nominee Alton Parker.

including anklets, and nylon hosiery from the 1952 campaign. As is evident in Illustration 284, the nylons are inscribed "Madly for Adlai" and "I Like Ike." Note also that each stocking has a frilly red, white, and blue garter from which a tiny white elephant or donkey is suspended. Also available are women's work gloves, aprons, vests, head and wrist bands, and T-shirts (Ill. 285). In fact, I would not be at all surprised to see jogging gear with appropriate slogans appear during future campaigns!

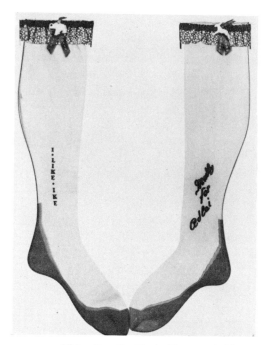

284. Novelty silk stockings, probably from the 1952 campaign.

285. Children's and adults' T-shirts picturing state, local, and national candidates and/or slogans are known from at least the early 1960s. T-shirts will continue to be a popular novelty in future campaigns.

286. Possibly a unique 1888 Harrison and Morton parade jacket made up from campaign bandannas.

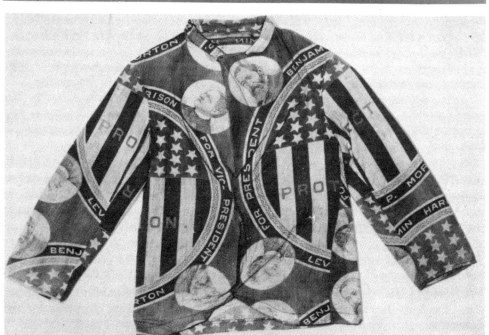

COLLAR BOXES. These date from the days when detachable collars were a necessary part of a gentleman's wardrobe. Collar boxes with political subjects (Ill. 287) are made of wood and are about 5 inches square and 4 inches deep. The hinged cover bears a deeply incised portrait of either a party's presidential or vice-presidential nominee and is always found in a deep rich-looking brown. Covers were made of a pliable material consisting of ground wood or sawdust and dark brown coloring, with shellac as a bond; the mixture was molded in dies and hardened. The result is similar in hard-

ness and appearance to the fancy daguerreotype cases popular with an earlier genera-
tion. These collar boxes seem to be associated only with candidates from campaigns of
the 1880s, with 1880 examples showing up most frequently. The price range is $100 to
$250.

FANS.   The fan is another artifact we associate with political conventions. Political
fans evoke images of tired, perspiring delegates futilely seeking relief from the midsummer humidity in the cavernous convention halls. Democrats were as much relieved to
depart steamy Madison Square Garden in August 1924 as they were relieved at the
nomination of John Davis after a record 103-ballot marathon that lasted two weeks.
The most common variety of fan is simply an irregularly shaped piece of cardboard
with either a wooden handle or a thumbhole. One of the earliest cardboard fans pictures Horace Greeley in silhouette; a wide fringe of false hair around the top of the fan
gives it a bizarre look. This 1872 fan is scarce and expensive. But most cardboard fans
that date from the 1912 campaign until after the 1930s are abundant—and very inexpensive. Folding fans are the other variety. All designs known to the author are scarce,
and the multicolored example (Ill. 288) is no exception: This shows Republican 1892
(or 1896) hopefuls— Benjamin Harrison, William McKinley, Chauncey Depew, John
Sherman, Levi Morton, and Thomas Reed—in standing poses exhorting a crowd of voters. The reverse pictures a seated Columbia, an eagle and shield, the Capitol, and the
White House. Interestingly, this particular fan carries the printed advertisement of a gro-
cer on Mackinac Island in Michigan; presumably, it was distributed to his customers.

287.   Chester Arthur is pictured on an
1880 collar box with a gutta-percha
cover.

288.   Most fans are similar to the 1920
Harding and 1944 Roosevelt examples
shown here. Folding fans are unusual,
and this 1896 example is also quite
scarce.

JACKKNIVES.   Here is another category of considerable interest among collectors.
There are two types of political jackknives: 1) those with celluloid handles depicting one
or both party nominees on one side and a patriotic scene on the other; 2) those with
handles covered with a brass shell depicting embossed busts of a candidate on one
side and perhaps his running mate or a patriotic scene on the other. Jackknives date at
least as early as the 1900 campaign and possibly earlier. Examples from early campaigns will range in value from $100 to $250 or more, depending upon which
candidates are pictured. Modern examples sell for under $100.

JEWELRY.   It is too bad that this category is so underrated by collectors because there
is an interesting variety of earrings, tiepins and clips, bracelets, necklaces, brooches,
rings, and collar pins that are well worth investigating. Although much of this material
might be classed under the heading of junk jewelry, many pieces, especially those in
wood, chrome, and enamels, are typical of the jewelry fashions of their period. But the
prices are low and there are plenty of examples to go around. Look especially for wood
lapel pins in the shape of a donkey or an elephant from campaigns of the 1930s and
1940s. More recent designs include bracelets with attached cutout letters spelling a
candidate's name; lapel pins in the shape of John Kennedy's World War II ship PT-109

(Ill. 289); cloth lapel pins and brooches showing sequined elephants; cowboy pins and earrings from the 1964 Goldwater and Johnson campaign; a copper derby pin for Al Smith; peace dove coat pins for George McGovern; brass earrings, tie tacks, and lapel pins in the shape of a peanut for Jimmy Carter; and my favorite—a well-made brass lapel pin in the shape of an elephant wearing black plastic glasses, from the 1964 campaign. Illustration 289 merely hints at what is available.

Campaign jewelry is fun to collect. A considerable variety is available, and most pieces sell for well under $75.

289. A selection of campaign jewelry. *Far left:* At the top of the illustration are "Adlai" and Kennedy P.T. boat lapel pins; below them are a Goldwater elephant and a Nixon rhinestone coat pin, and at the bottom is a Kennedy bracelet. *Top center:* A McCarthy coat pin made from Scrabble tiles and an uncommon wood Willkie lapel pin; below are lapel pins in the shape of a shovel (Willkie), an eagle (F. D. Roosevelt), and a red glass heart (Eisenhower). *Far right:* A Nixon necklace.

MACERATED CURRENCY FIGURES. Here is a collecting oddity that has its own following and is also a favorite with some political collectors. Macerated currency was a term applied by the United States Treasury Department to paper money that was unfit for further use and was therefore redeemed by the Department. Old paper money was pulped, or macerated, then mixed with a paste solution and molded into the shapes of Washington, D.C., buildings, busts and profiles of presidential candidates, Uncle Sam hats, and similar patriotic subjects (Ill. 290). To the uninitiated, macerated currency figures look like pieces of dirty old cardboard all stuck together. But on the underside of a figure there will be a small label that indicates the dollar amount of the currency—$3,000, $15,000, and so on that is contained in that figure. The value of a figure is enhanced if its label is present and if most of the original paint—some figures were painted—is present. Although a particular figure may be scarce, examples of political macerated currency appear fairly often on the market. Prices will reach to $100 for examples in excellent condition.

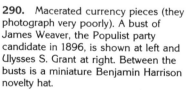

290. Macerated currency pieces (they photograph very poorly). A bust of James Weaver, the Populist party candidate in 1896, is shown at left and Ulysses S. Grant at right. Between the busts is a miniature Benjamin Harrison novelty hat.

PENNANTS. A 1920 Socialist party pennant picturing Eugene V. Debs sold recently for over $200. That price, however, is far out of line because of the subject—with a few such exceptions most pennants sell for under $50. Pennants picture candidates (Ill. 291); mark conventions, inaugurations, and the place names of a candidate's stops along the campaign trail; or carry names and/or slogans. Probably pennants were first used during the 1896–1904 campaign period. They are in abundant supply, so it is fairly easy to build a comprehensive collection.

PENS AND PENCILS. There seems to be an infinite assortment of political wooden and mechanical pencils and of ink and ball-point pens. They have long been favorite political giveaways. The earliest campaign pencil known to me is a simple brown one marked "Tilden and Hendricks," and the earliest pen I know of is a red, white, and blue one with a celluloid handle picturing Teddy Roosevelt. As would be expected, mechanical pencils are the scarcest artifacts in this category. The earliest apparently date from the 1936 campaign and picture Franklin Roosevelt or Alfred Landon. A red, white, and blue example bearing a Truman slogan (Ill. 292) sold recently for $65, an uncommonly high price for any political pencil or pen and not at all typical.

292. A mechanical pencil from the 1948 campaign.

291. Four examples of the many political pennants available to collectors. Note the matched pair picturing Roosevelt and Landon with their running mates.

POCKET MIRRORS. These little mirrors have been a fairly common feature of campaigns since the 1920s, and maybe even earlier. Political mirrors are simply campaign buttons with a mirror back rather than a pin or wire back. Some political mirrors picture candidates, but more desirable examples will have such statements as "Will the Person on the Other Side Please Vote for Calvin Coolidge" (or whomever). Mirrors with uncommon or scarce celluloids will bring very high prices, just as those celluloids would if pins were attached instead. Prices, therefore, can range from a few dollars for mirrors from recent campaigns up into the hundreds of dollars for certain earlier issues.

PHONOGRAPH RECORDS. Of most interest to collectors are early 78s and the few known cylinder recordings containing words spoken by candidates themselves—I think Benjamin Harrison speaking when he was president in 1889 is the earliest cylinder recording of a president's voice. Other subjects of interest include Will Rogers commenting on presidents and politics, inaugural and campaign speeches, and campaign songs. Nor should collectors overlook modern long-playing recordings such as Vaughn Meader's satire of the Kennedys, Raymond Massey reading selections from Abraham Lincoln's writings and speeches, narrated histories of the presidency, and collections of campaign songs.

RAZORS. These are the early single-edge straight razors that were in common use before the invention of the safety razor. A good straight razor is a finely crafted product. Despite the heavy use that these razors received, the blades are generally sharp and rust free, and the celluloid or bone handles will at most have slight splits or chips. This is fortunate for political collectors because it means that razors bearing political inscriptions or busts on the blade and inscriptions on the handle are likely to be quite legible and otherwise in presentable condition. Razors with political subjects date from about 1840 to 1912 and bear slogans typical of those years: "Old Tippecanoe," "Rough and Ready," "General Grant/The Union Forever." Busts of candidates with and without running mates appear on these razors, as do busts of presidents in connection with a historic event such as Teddy Roosevelt and a Panama Canal scene. Look also for razors commemorating the 1876 centennial, which will have etched busts or standing poses of George Washington with such inscriptions as "Father of His Country" and "Champion of Liberty." Political razors usually sell for between $200 and $450, and at least one should be a part of a general collection.

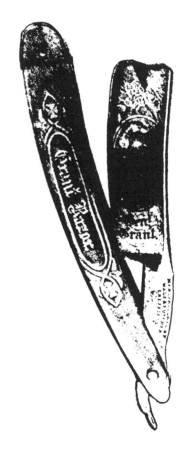

291A. This embossed razor is both a perfect collectors' item and a humorous reminder that Grant himself could have shaved more often.

SEWING KITS. These are small cloth kits or paper packets intended for voters' purses or coat pockets. Sewing kits were in fairly common use in campaigns from 1928 on, although an example from an earlier campaign occasionally turns up. The kits consist of a few tiny spools of thread and two or three needles, with a printed political inscription somewhere on the outside of the container or packet. A packet with a good-sized assortment of needles only and bearing portraits of Herbert Hoover and Charles Curtis appears frequently. Most kits can be purchased for under $60.

SPOONS.   A small variety of teaspoons have political themes; most were issued as souvenirs of presidential inaugurations, but a few bear a candidate's bust and an appropriate slogan. We do know of a silver-plated tablespoon bearing a relief bust of Grover Cleveland, which probably dates from the 1892 campaign, and other similar spoons must certainly exist. Teaspoons that are part of a "presidential series"—i.e., bearing busts of each president beginning with Washington, plus a depiction of a historic event in each president's administration—are of little interest to political collectors. There is not much demand for campaign or inaugural spoons, nor are there many available, so prices are reasonable—perhaps between $50 and $125, but higher for sterling silver examples.

292A. A selection of wonderfully detailed sterling silver political commemorative spoons. The one on the extreme right has a red, white and blue enameled flag.

STATUARY.   This subject might be treated as more than a chapter subsection, so extensive are the variety and number of sculptured artifacts. I include the subject here, however, because of the near total lack of collector interest in it: Greater space is not warranted. Busts of Abraham Lincoln make up the largest group of political statuary. Many of them are products of the "martyr" cult that was popular for some years after his death and enjoyed a revival during his centennial in 1909. Most of these post-assassination busts sell for under $100 each, but Lincoln busts sculptured from life can bring very high prices—into the thousands of dollars. From the viewpoint of political collectors, the most important life bust is the beardless one created by Leonard Volk (1828–1895) in 1860. Volk also did a life mask, about which Lincoln is reported to have remarked when he first saw it: "There is the animal himself" (Holzer and Ostendorf, p. 382). This life mask has been duplicated several times since 1860 in clay, bronze, and plaster, as have been casts of Lincoln's hands done at the same time as the mask. Volk's original pieces are far beyond the means of most collectors, but the later copies can be purchased reasonably.

Most candidates in twentieth-century campaigns are portrayed in statuary. In our opinion the most outstanding example is Jo Davidson's handsome life bust of Franklin Roosevelt done in 1934 (Ill. 294). Davidson is better known among political collectors for his superb medals commemorating Roosevelt's 1941 and 1945 inaugurations. The 1934 bust is cast in bronze and is most often found in a size about 6 inches in height and mounted on a marble or aluminum base. The size of these copies—the larger original is in the Roosevelt Museum at Hyde Park, New York—suggests that they were distributed at party fund raising affairs, or given in return for certain levels of contributions, or perhaps sold at local party headquarters. The copies sell for under $100 and should represent political statuary in a general collection.

Other sculptured pieces to look for, although none have any artistic merit, are small—up to about 5 inches in height—head and shoulder busts of Herbert Hoover, Al Smith, and Eugene Debs in silver-colored base or pot metal. Similarly lacking in merit are smaller bronzed pot-metal busts of Debs, who is portrayed in his convict uniform. (Debs was imprisoned during World War I for his pacifist statements against American involvement, but he was later pardoned by President Harding.) The Debs busts are quite expensive, up to $300 or more, but the Smith and Hoover busts and similarly sized pot-metal busts of McKinley, Roosevelt, Taft, and other candidates sell for far less. Remember, frosted glass busts and figural glass bottles can be classed as statuary; they too are suitable in such a collection.

292B. The author worked in this store during his high school years, but, sorry to say, these nice spoons were long gone by then.

THREAD BOXES.   Despite their prosaic purpose, these artifacts are among the most desired of all political Americana. They date exclusively from the 1824 and 1828 cam-

293. One of the John Rogers parlor sculptures that were so immensely popular in the latter decades of the nineteenth century. This example is titled "The Council of War"; it was probably issued in 1873. It is one of three variants, all of which are distinguished chiefly by the position of Secretary of War Stanton's hands in relation to Lincoln's head.

294. A small version of Jo Davidson's bust of Franklin Roosevelt is shown here along with a Hoover bust in zinc casting.

295. Soap sculptures from the 1896 campaign. Shown here are a bust of William McKinley and a baby. The baby is often found with an attached tag reading "My Papa is Voting for McKinley [or Bryan]." Soap babies are usually contained in a one- or two-compartment box; the cover of one such box is illustrated.

paigns of Andrew Jackson and John Quincy Adams. Most were probably imported from France and usually made of rainbow-colored cardboard with gilt paper edging. On the inside of each hinged cover is a glass-enclosed picture of Jackson or Adams; on the outside is a pincushion that bears such inscriptions as "Jackson and No Corruption," "Adams and Liberty," and "People's Choice." Illustration 296 shows two varieties: The rectangular one is about 5 by 3 by 1½ inches; the square one is about 4 inches on a side by 4 inches deep. A third example (not illustrated) is rectangular in shape but has convex sides. Plain colored boxes in light green or blue are also known. These gems seldom come on the market; when they do, a price between $900 and $1,500— or higher— is not uncommon.

TRAYS.   Collecting metal serving trays, especially those advertising Coca-Cola and ale and beer, has become a popular hobby in recent years. Political collectors can ex-

296. Thread boxes. The pincushion on the John Quincy Adams box at left is inscribed "The Great Statesman"; the glass-enclosed portrait of Jackson is the one most often seen.

297. A Nixon umbrella or parasol from the 1960 campaign.

298. This rare and possibly unique carved wood wall decoration bears a picture of Martin Van Buren; it dates from the 1836 campaign. The stylized globe and eagle suggest a Pennsylvania origin.

pect stiff competition for the beautifully colored and generally uncommon serving trays that picture candidates from about 1896 to 1904. Perhaps twenty to thirty different designs are known: Teddy Roosevelt seems to be depicted most often and Alton Parker the least. The trays shown in Plates 17 and 18 are typical examples: The tray picturing William Jennings Bryan and Adlai Stevenson (grandfather of the 1952 and 1956 Democratic nominee) was apparently issued by an Athol, Massachusetts, cigar company during the 1900 campaign; Teddy Roosevelt is pictured as a Rough Rider in a dramatic equestrian pose. William Howard Taft and his running mate James S. Sherman are pictured on a 1908 tray (Plate 1), one of the most pictorially informative of all campaign artifacts, and—fortunately for collectors—this tray turns up more often than any other tray. Small coaster or tip trays very similar to the Taft and Sherman serving tray also appear frequently; the large and small trays should be treated as a pair. In good condition the Taft/Sherman serving tray sells for well under $250; the Roosevelt tray sells nearer to $500; the Bryan/Stevenson tray sells for closer to $650 because of its advertising tie-in, an uncommon feature on serving trays with political subjects. Condition is a very important factor with these trays: Scratches, scrapes, flaking, and dents will lower the value considerably.

UMBRELLAS. These are among the hobby's conversation pieces (Ill. 297). Umbrellas with pictures of candidates and patriotic symbols were used almost entirely in the 1896—1904 campaign period. Because of their wood, wire, and cloth construction, few from that period exist in sound operating condition. That situation, plus a consistently high demand for early umbrellas, means selling prices of $450 and up. A few umbrellas, especially from the 1896 and 1900 campaigns, are known with handles in the likeness of either William McKinley, William Jennings Bryan, William Howard Taft, and possibly Teddy Roosevelt. These effigy heads are similar to those on marching canes from the same campaigns; they could well have been made from the same molds. These kinds of umbrellas are also scarce.

"Collectors' Choice" does not end with umbrellas. Here are additional novelties with political themes. Although generally not as high in collector interest as the novelties discussed in greater detail, they are all eminently collectible: artificial flowers, bottle openers, bubble gum cigars, change purses, combs, feathers, hatpins, letter openers, money clips, playing cards, pot holders, powder compacts, sunglasses, tape measures, thimbles, and trivets. The prices are reasonable.

298A. Women's Suffrage Movement, circa 1915.

298B. While his Socialist Party counterpart Eugene Debs garnered nearly 920,000 votes in 1920, Socialist Labor nominee William Cox managed barely 32,000.

9

Movements, Causes, and Personalities

298C. A fine example of a Communist Party campaign poster, 1932.

298D. The always popular and quite scarce Rough Rider stillbank.

THERE IS CONTINUING interest among collectors in material associated with the great social and political events that are so much a part of political campaigning. With the exception of the temperance-prohibition movement, which has related material dating at least as far back as the 1840s, most of the material discussed in this chapter is of later nineteenth-century and twentieth-century origin. A few "cause" artifacts are quite expensive, but most can be found for under $50 and many modern cause buttons sell for under $5. Because of these low prices many younger collectors get their start with cause material; I have seen several well-planned and informative collections that were assembled by high-school students.

Collectors tend to be more interested in groups and personalities operating on the fringes of a movement—in particular, any movement to the left of the political center. One reason for that preference, I think, is the fact that fringe groups (e.g., the Black Panthers, Young Socialist Alliance, the National Women's party, and Students for a Democratic Society) have readily accepted militancy as a necessary step in achieving their purposes—a position that may give such groups a romantic appeal to some collectors. Also, some members of fringe groups are superb polemicists; over the years they have disseminated interpretations of social and political problems that are likely to sound novel or heretical to many Americans. And certainly there is a large amount of sympathy among collectors for the underdog. It is true, also, that cause material sometimes demonstrates the persuasive and hortative dimension of politicking as well as, if not better than, much material issued by the major parties. Beginning collectors should note that some of the causes discussed in this chapter were or are, in one way or another, linked to third parties, notably the American Communist party, the different Socialist parties, and the Prohibition party. If a collector expects to assemble an informative cause collection, then third-party material must be included.

Earlier cause material, generally from before 1900, consists in large part of paper items such as broadsides, leaflets, pamphlets, and posters; recent material is dominated by buttons. I would guess that over four thousand buttons have been issued since

298E. Consider collecting anti-American protest posters.

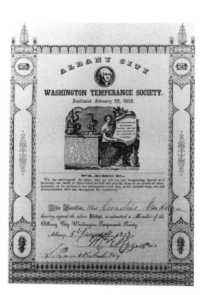

298F. An elaborate but otherwise quite typical temperance pledge card.

the early 1960s in support of student and antiwar protest activities, radical militants, and the feminist movement. When we add related paper material as well, then a person could be kept quite busy collecting only examples of what has been issued during the past twenty years. Also included, of course, should be material associated with the Equal Rights Amendment, civil rights for blacks and other minority groups, environmental concerns, abortion, and nuclear power—all are political issues. There is a lot out there waiting to be collected.

Because of their unconventional beliefs and behavior, certain specific personalities associated with different causes are unusually attractive to collectors. Victoria Woodhull and George Francis Train were born protestors whose life-styles and beliefs were beyond the comprehension of most Americans of their day. They would have been more at home in the 1970s rather than the 1870s, when they were most active. Despite several election defeats Ben Butler—who generally operated within the political mainstream—always bounced back, more rambunctious than ever. Butler, Woodhull, and Train: Each thumbed his nose at the Establishment and got away with it. Naturally, the three of them are highly popular with collectors.

Cause material is wide open to collecting. Both temperance and early labor material have been largely ignored by collectors, as has been protest literature from the 1920s and 1930s. Because militant publications and similar ephemera were frequently perceived by authorities as inflammatory or otherwise un-American, much of it was confiscated and destroyed, and so digging out such material can be a challenge. Since cause collecting itself is on the fringes of the hobby, there is considerable potential for building outstanding collections. Depending upon what it emphasizes, a well-planned and representative cause collection may in time prove to be quite valuable.

The Temperance-Prohibition Movement

Since collector interest in cause material depends largely on the specific amount of material that is available to collect, the temperance-prohibition movement makes a good specialty because it seems to offer more varied material than all other causes and movements put together. Possibly the major reason for the abundance of this material is the fact that the temperance-prohibition movement was a national concern for almost 150 years, and for most of that long period collectible material was issued. The subject is rich in cartoons, broadsides, songsters, tracts, leaflets, ribbons, medalets, and buttons. A few pieces of early china also have temperance themes. Because the movement was based primarily in rural America, its underlying values and assumptions are in sharp contrast to those of the other movements discussed in this chapter, most of which were centered in America's cities. Even a cursory comparison of temperance-prohibition material with material from later militant labor groups, for example, indicates how wide the latitude is for personal expression in this country.

The first temperance groups were probably organized in the early 1800s. From that period to 12:01 A.M. on January 21, 1920, when the Volstead Act became the law of the land, the temperance-prohibition movement caught up five generations of Americans in a force that at one time or another was a cause of bitter divisiveness in thousands of communities; was a major source for the development of the women's rights movement; dominated thinking in several state legislatures and ultimately in Congress; and generated more nonsense than all other movements combined. The existence of prohibition during the 1920s was an important factor in the rise of national crime syndicates and in Al Smith's defeat in 1928, but his opposition to Prohibition undoubtedly helped Franklin Roosevelt win the White House in 1932.

The movement began first as temperance—or moderation; evolved into anti-temperance—or total abstinence; and with the passage of the Maine Law and its several revisions, beginning in 1846, temperance became prohibition—the legal banning of

299. Currier and Ives dramatized both sides of "The Question" with this pair of multicolored prints titled "The Drunkard's Family" and "The Happy Family."

299A. Father Theobald Mathew (1790-1856), the widely popular champion of Irish American sobriety, is pictured on this later commemorative ribbon.

liquor importing and selling, first in a few states and later in the nation. The pattern can be noted in the focus of anti-liquor groups at different times in the nineteenth century: In 1833 the American Temperance Union became the first national group formed to fight the "Demon Rum"; in the early 1850s Father Theobald Matthews founded his Total Abstinence Society for the purpose of keeping Irish immigrants sober and industrious; in 1869 the Prohibition party was organized, and in 1872 the party nominated its first candidate—James Black—for the presidency.

The temperance-prohibition movement, like most other movements in American history, attracted its share of visionaries, humane reformers, fanatics, chronic viewers-with-alarm, eccentrics, and charlatans. The hundreds of organizations spawned by the movement produced tens of thousands of publications, which were distributed to every corner of the country and to every social class. Melodramas such as "Ten Nights in a Bar Room" and "The Drunkard" were small-town staples well into the twentieth cen-

300. Possibly the best cartoon associated with the temperance movement, this multicolored one was drawn by Charles Jewett in 1839. Death, astride a rampaging boar (a symbol of drunkenness), kills children, violates the Bible's teachings, and breaks state laws. Lookers-on cheer the boar or bemoan his devastation. At the upper left the Devil praises the boar's progress.

301. Mottoes of the early temperance movement adorn this creamer, which is part of a tea set that probably dates from the 1830s. Other temperance themes on ceramics are known.

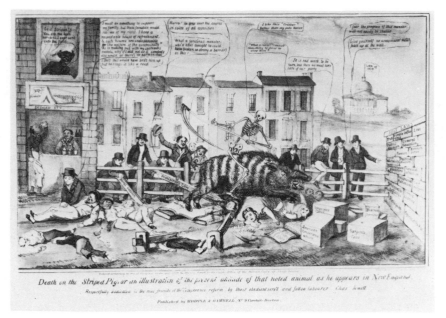

tury. The movement was a major factor in the enormous success of the patent medicine business, and, indeed, from the 1870s on—when its militancy intensified—whenever a Wet pointed out that cause and effect, there was a Dry ready to zap him. From the early 1900s on, a Wet or Dry plank was an important difference between the Republican and Democratic platforms. Increasingly, how a politician stood on "The Question" was a factor in his subsequent election or defeat. Democrats seemed to spend more time at their state and national conventions refereeing intraparty squabbles between Wets and Drys than they did in nominating candidates for office.

The artifacts available to collectors as a result of all that activity can be divided into several categories: personalities, temperance organizations, the Prohibition party, and anti-prohibition material.

THE PERSONALITIES. Far and away, the personality of most interest to collectors is the Kansas saloon-smasher Carry A. Nation (Ill. 302). Although she is ridiculed today, she was a tragic figure. Like many other women who became deeply involved in the movement, she had experienced firsthand the horrors of alcoholism: a grandfather who insisted on giving his grandchildren a daily tot of rum and a young husband who died an alcoholic, leaving her pregnant. Carry Nation "smashed" her first saloon in 1899 in the Kansas town of Medicine Lodge, but she became nationally known when she was jailed briefly for smashing up saloons in Wichita, a notoriously wet city in what was a dry state. In time she traveled the lecture circuit and published a small tabloid newspaper, *The Voice,* and similar forms of self-serving publicity, including her autobiography *Carry Nation: A History of Her Life.*

302. Carry Nation is pictured in a typical pose on the cover of one of her more popular publications.

What most attracts collectors, however, are lapel pins in the shape of a hatchet, which she sold as a fund raiser. Although she smashed her first saloon with stones wrapped in newspapers, she soon began using a hatchet. It was the hatchet in combination with her bellicose personality that made her a national figure. There appear to have been about six varieties of the hatchet lapel pin: four in brass and two in cast iron (Ill. 304.) The most interesting iron miniature is looped and is 3¾ inches in length. One side has a bust of Carry facing outward and the inscription "1901/Ax of All Nations"; the handle is inscribed "Cut Out the Whiskey." The reverse of this pin advertises a Detroit stove company. The brass lapel pin that is most easily obtained is 1 inch in length. Mounted to a stickpin, it is inscribed "Carry A. Nation" on the handle. The most attractive brass hatchet pin is a shell with an attached mother-of-pearl blade bearing a tiny centered rhinestone. The handle is also inscribed "Carry A. Nation." A similar pin has a

THE TEMPERANCE CRUSADE—WHO WILL WIN?

303. Only one of the saloon habitués seems responsive to the entreaties of the temperance ladies in this 1870 newspaper illustration of a "pray-in."

303A. This silk ribbon was issued by a Philadelphia temperance group and is a fine example from the earlier years of the temperance crusade.

pearl in place of the rhinestone. These pins sell for about $100 each, but they are not common, either in taste or availability. The iron pins and other brass varieties are in the $25 to $75 range.

There were other, and more important, personalities in the movement than Carry Nation, but few ever matched her short-term influence. Among the other temperance-prohibition personalities that collectors should be aware of—excluding Prohibition party candidates for the moment—are Frances E. Willard, energetic co-founder and early leader of the Women's Christian Temperance Union and later a power in the women's suffrage movement; Francis Murphy, the "Apostle of Gospel Temperance (Ill. 305)," one of the many reformed drunks to achieve prominence in the movement and popularizer of the phrase "Dare to Do Right," which appears in later Prohibition party campaign material; Timothy Shay Arthur, the Horatio Alger of temperance, best known for his "Ten Nights in a Bar Room" and similar potboilers; and Bartholomew Clough, ham actor and brilliant lecturer. These personalities are not the most important in the movement, but certainly collectors will find them well worth looking into.

304. Temperance movement lapel devices. Shown here are cast-iron and rhinestone axes along with an Anti-Saloon League button at right center, a Home Defender button (W.C.T.U.) in the bottom row, and other buttons with pro- and anti-Prohibition slogans.

305. Reformed drunk Francis Murphy is pictured on the cover of this temperance songster, a typical piece of temperance ephemera.

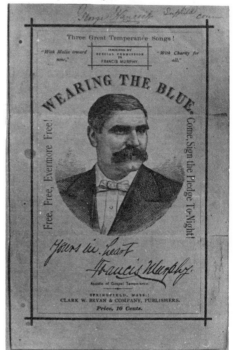

306. Note the differences between the Know-Nothing ribbon on the left and the Washington Temperance Society one on the right.

THE ORGANIZATIONS. It is impossible to list all the organizations that flourished in the movement between 1800 and 1920. Every community seemed to have some kind of group, as did every state, and with the founding of the American Temperance Union a sense of national direction and purpose was achieved. I have singled out four organizations. All four exerted considerable influence in their day, and all four distributed a good-sized variety of collectible material.

Washington Temperance Society (better known as the Washingtonians). This had its beginnings in a Baltimore tavern in 1840 when a number of the habitués took the pledge after hearing a local temperance lecturer. In pyramid fashion, each member was required to bring a potential member to meetings; soon two member teams were circulating throughout the eastern states preaching the virtues of temperance. Eventually the Washingtonians added a ladies' auxiliary (the Martha Washington Society, naturally), a juvenile division, newpapers, and a variety of other publications. What makes the Washington Temperance Society particularly interesting is its emphasis upon attracting members of the working class to its cause—in effect, reformed drunks were converting drunks. The Washingtonians started what was to become a new direction in the movement: less leadership from educated upper-class advocates and more from uneducated workers. In fact, the reformed drunk waxing eloquent about his downfall and rejuvenation on the lecture circuit became a standard feature of the movement. One such convert, John Woolley, was the Prohibition party's nominee in 1900.

The Washingtonians staged parades with thousands of participants. Marchers were usually organized into divisions in terms of their occupations. Most of the banners carried in these parades have long since vanished, but collectors can obtain ribbons, many of which are additional examples of the early silks described in Chapter 6. The Washingtonian ribbon may picture a water fountain and some implement indicating its wearer's occupation. Another kind of ribbon collectors should be especially alert for pictures George Washington. The emergence of the Washington Temperance Society and its subsequent popularity coincided with the spread of the Native American party, the Know-Nothings, who had also adopted George Washington as its symbol. Ribbon manufacturers often used the same portrait and framing design and simply added the appropriate wording for each organization. The pair of ribbons pictured in Illustration 306 show differences collectors should be aware of. The same floral border design and paean to Washington's greatness are evident on both, but one ribbon shows also a water fountain and the date of a Washingtonian parade in Boston; the other ribbon shows a winged female figure bearing a scroll reading "beware of foreign influence," a standard inscription on Know-Nothing material.

Washingtonian ribbons picturing George Washington show up on the market much more frequently than occupational ribbons. But because of low demand both kinds sell in the $30 to $75 price range. Other Washingtonian material rarely appears on the market.

The Cold Water Army.   This group, which calls to mind the thirteenth-century Children's Crusade, was most active during the movement's shift toward advocation of total abstinence and the "discovery" of water as a substitute for the "Demon." The Cold Water Army was founded by the Reverend Thomas Hunt in 1836 as an outgrowth of his weekly visits to Sunday schools. The Army was the first, and the most interesting, of several juvenile temperance groups that were active in the nineteenth century (Ill. 307). Probably several hundred thousand children took the pledge before the Army's demise during the 1870s:

307.   This cotton banner measures about 4½ by 3½ feet; the letters, border, and fringe are blue.

> We, Cold Water Girls and Boys,
> Freely renounce the treacherous joys
> of Brandy, Whiskey, Rum, and Gin;
> The Serpent's lure to death and sin:
> Wine, Beer, and Cider we detest,
> And thus we'll make our parents blest;
> *"So here we pledge perpetual hate*
> *To all that can Intoxicate."*

We cannot know how many children actually kept their vow as they matured, but we do know that equating the innocence of children with the purity of water was a master stroke. If children could enthuse over a glass of water, then so could their elders. From this time on, total abstainers would refer to themselves as "cold waterers," who assembled at cold-water conventions with cold-water men and women. The best-known cold-water zealots were President and Mrs. Rutherford B. Hayes. Lucinda, the First Lady of the land, was known as "Lemonade Lucy" because of her refusal to serve liquor in any form at White House functions. A member of her husband's Cabinet once described a White House party as one at which water flowed like champagne.

Cold Water Army artifacts usually picture water fountains together with the following verse, which appeared on ribbons worn by members in temperance parades or at pledge meetings:

308.   One of the best examples of a Cold Water Army pledge card because of its illustration, verse, and biblical citations.

> Give us to drink the crystal stream—
> Pure, sparkling, healthful, fine;
> And this shall ever be our theme,
> "Away, away, the wine."
> Then pledge us in the cooling draught,
> Away with wine, away.

Collectors should look for pledge cards; the example in Illustration 308 is just one of several types. Also of interest are small brass buttons, ⅝ inch in diameter, which display a spread eagle and the inscription "Cold Water Army." One variety has the eagle above the inscription, and the other has the eagle centered with the inscription surrounding it. Also available are such paper ephemera as song sheets and songsters (booklets), broadsides, and tracts containing horrendous stories about the evils of drink. All Cold Water Army material can be bought for under $125.

The Anti-Saloon League. The members of this organization can be considered the shock troops of the temperance-prohibition movement. The Anti-Saloon League

308A. A fine example of an Anti-Saloon League postcard; ca. 1910.

was founded in the 1890s during a time when the movement seemed to be moribund. Under the aggressive leadership of its first director, Howard Hyde Russell, and his successor Wayne Wheeler, the League became a powerful propaganda force for prohibition. Some authorities, in fact, believe that the League was more instrumental than the Prohibition party in securing passage of the Volstead Act. League members were efficient and flexible opportunists: They were able to command large blocs of votes at local and state levels; a paid staff maintained the national operation and supplied lawyers and instructions for harassing taverns. The League's own publishing house, The American Issue Publishing Company, produced hundreds of titles in the form of circulars, tracts, broadsides, and songsters under such titles as "The Saloon Must Go" (the League's motto), "The Saloon or the Boys and Girls," "The Home vs. the Saloon—Which Will It Be?" Local no-license campaigns (attempts to deny the license renewals of taverns) were flooded with literature—and buttons—picturing a young boy or girl and the slogan "Vote No for My Sake." The League's fundamentalist small-town tenor enabled it to picture cities as cesspools of Wet political corruption, inhabited by women and children who were exposed to the cruelties of drunken husbands and fathers. Richmond Hobson, a Spanish-American War naval hero and an ardent Dry, coined the term "Flying Squadron" for the groups of League activists who went from city to city giving speeches, dramatic presentations, and generally loudly condemning Wet social and political activities.

Material bearing League subjects and slogans is easy to obtain. Most often found are the no-license buttons mentioned above: They are ⅞ inch in diameter and have rims of different colors, commonly red, blue, green, or brown. One of the most striking designs of all cause buttons is that of a colorful League issue picturing a boy and a girl and the national flag with the slogan: "The Real Issue/The Saloon or the Boys and Girls." This button is known in two diameters, the easily obtained 1¼ inches selling for about $50 or less, and the scarcer 1½ inches selling for about $125. There are a few Flying Squadron buttons and buttons with such slogans as "Vote Dry for My Sake" or "Support No License"; these sell for under $20. Also available are postcards, envelopes, and letterhead stationery bearing those slogans, which sell for about $10 each.

The Women's Christian Temperance Union. The WCTU is important to collectors primarily because of its remarkable co-founder and second president, Frances E. Willard. The organization was formed as the result of the women's militant temperance crusade that swept midwestern states in the early 1870s. Thousands of women held prayer meetings in front of taverns—and sometimes inside them; in jails, after they had been arrested; and in the halls of state legislatures. Under Willard's energetic leadership, beginning in 1879 and lasting until her death in 1898, the WCTU became a highly effective women's organization. It is still in existence.

Willard was a prolific writer, a fine platform speaker, and—from the collecting viewpoint—a major link between the temperance-prohibition and women's rights movements. She was an "exalter of women" who was convinced that only when women had the vote would national prohibition become a reality. In her view, each WCTU member had both year-round and lifetime responsibility of agitating for the Dry cause *and* for female suffrage. Women were "home defenders" and the stabilizing force in family life, a belief that is evident in the WCTU's motto, "For God and Home and Native Land." The organization's symbol was a white rose and ribbon. A few buttons are known picturing that symbol; in fact, one of the scarcest Prohibition buttons, which was issued in support of Herbert Hoover during the 1928 campaign, pictures a white ribbon and is inscribed "WCTU/Vote for Hoover." It is valued at about $60.

Unfortunately, little collectible material is associated with Frances E. Willard other than the usual paper ephemera. Some Prohibition party tickets are known with the heading "Prohibition/Home Protection Party"; they were motivated by a brief alliance she formed with the Prohibition party in 1882. A fairly common ¾-inch sepia lithographed button was issued many years after her death, probably for the WCTU's

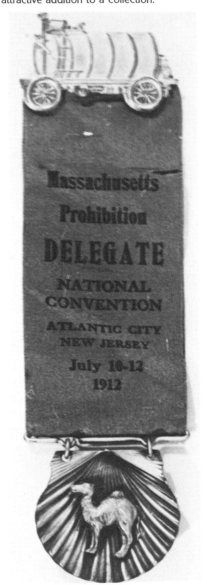

309. Prohibition party buttons. With the exception of the 1896 Joshua Levering button, second from top in the left row, all these buttons and badges were used in twentieth-century campaigns.

310. The ribbon bar in the shape of a water wagon, the camel in the scallop shell, and a Lincoln quotation on its back make this fine delegate badge an attractive addition to a collection.

fiftieth anniversary in 1924. A handsome aluminum medal, 2 inches in diameter, marking the dedication of the WCTU's Chicago headquarters in the 1890s depicts Willard with co-founder Matilda Carse. I believe that a few additional buttons exist picturing Willard; they are probably memorial issues from the late 1890s or commemorating the WCTU's fiftieth anniversary. All this material should sell for well under $50.

The Prohibition Party. Members of the modern Prohibition party are proud of the fact that their party has entered a nominee in every presidential campaign since 1872, a record for third-party longevity. The party's best year was 1892, when it amassed 270,000 votes, but over the years it has averaged under 100,000 votes. Its success in earlier years was helped considerably by its alliances with the Anti-Saloon League, the WCTU, and similar organizations. From its national headquarters in Denver, the party today operates an active membership network and issues a newsletter and similar publications, which are available to collectors for a donation.

The Prohibition party was founded in 1869 by representatives from several temperance groups, including the Right Worthy Grand Lodge of Good Templars and Gerrit Smith's Anti-Dramshop party. Political material is known from every campaign, but—as might be expected—the availability of the material ranges from easily obtained to extremely scarce. Lapel artifacts used in the 1872, 1876, and 1880 campaigns are practically nonexistent. From 1884 on, medalets, shell badges, studs, and campaign buttons (Ill. 309) exist in sufficient numbers so that collectors should be able to acquire at least one example from most campaigns.

Among the more interesting Prohibition party candidates for the presidency is John St. John (Ill. 311), who, through a combination of circumstances, gained a sufficient number of New York State votes in 1884 to help deny that crucial state to Republican James G. Blaine, thus giving Grover Cleveland a very narrow victory overall. Also of interest to collectors is John G. Woolley, the presidential nominee in 1900, and one of the last reformed drunks to achieve prominence in the party. His campaign song, which he himself sang at his public appearances, was called: "Then and Now"; it borrowed the music of "My Old Kentucky Home." Here are the first verse and chorus:

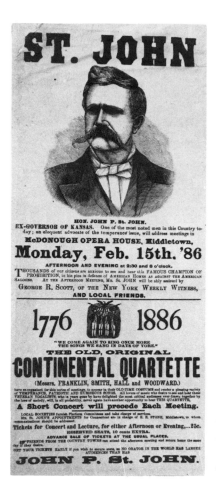

311. John St. John, the Prohibition party's 1884 nominee for president, was an outstanding platform speaker.

They sing sweet songs on the little village green
At evening when labor is done;
No fear of want, no thought of ill or wrong,
For there's plenty there for everyone;
But soon there comes to this lovely little spot
The drinkman with whiskey and beer,
And the song dies out, the drunken brawl begins
And there's pain and grief where once the cheer.

Chorus:

Cast your vote, my brother,
Oh, cast your vote today,
The saloons must go with poverty and woe
Cast your vote, my brother, while you may.

Stuart Hamblen, the party's nominee in 1952, was a singing cowboy and rodeo performer. He wrote his campaign song, "It's No Secret What God Can Do," which—for a brief while—was on radio's "Hit Parade," the first gospel song ever to reach that pinnacle of popular music. Campaign material associated with Woolley and Hamblen and other party presidential nominees through 1956 appears most often as buttons; these sell from $75 to about $300. Buttons picturing candidates from 1920 through 1936 are particularly scarce, and should bring prices of over $150 each. Buttons and other material picturing candidates after 1956 are fairly easily obtained and sell at most for $15 or $75 each.

Prohibition party lapel artifacts from the late nineteenth-century campaigns can be quite expensive. Shell badges are valued in the $200 to $500 range; ribbons are fairly scarce and valued at $250 to $500; medalets are more common—especially those issued for the 1880 campaign; most are priced under $75. Paper material is generally inexpensive, although spectacular examples, such as a colorful John Woolley poster that recently sold for $500, can go high. Convention and delegate badges usually sell for under $100, although an unusual delegate badge such as is shown in Illustration 310 would probably sell for very much more.

Temperance Numismatics. This topic is almost totally ignored by collectors; therefore most of the medalets discussed here can be bought cheaply. Interesting varieties of medalets were issued by different temperance organizations throughout the nineteenth century. The type collectors are most likely to come across are pledge pieces; they range up to 1¾ inches in diameter and were made, as were most other temperance issues, in different metals. Common designs on the front depict a man drinking water from a well (Ill. 312), a bust of George Washington, an upturned cup, different allegories representing prosperity and virtue, and a young child. Reverses of all these designs contain a pledge in one wording or another. Other temperance medalets bear such inscriptions as "Touch Not, Taste Not, Handle Not the Unclean Thing" and "To the Cause of/Temperance/Ten Dollars/To/King Alcohol/Not One/Cent." Another type commemorates the passage of New York State's Prohibition law in 1854. (It was later vetoed by Governor Seymour.) One of these reads: "Dedicated to the Rum-Soaked City of New York"; another includes a pledge to eschew tobacco also—"I'll Never Use Tobacco in Any Form/Tobacco Leads to Idleness, Poverty, Strong Drink, Vice, Ill-Health, Insanity, and Death." A few types—all very scarce—were issued by the Washington Temperance Society; they depict various occupations.

ANTI-PROHIBITION MATERIAL. So much of the temperance and prohibition material is determinedly serious and humorless that it can be a relief to add anti-prohibition material to one's collection. Some material of this kind is a tongue-in-cheek celebration of repeal—or predictions of repeal—of the Volstead Act. Our favorite example is a novelty cast-iron and aluminum bartender set made in the likeness of Mr. Dry, cartoonist

312. Temperance medalets. *Top row:* Anti-Prohibition medalet showing Mr. Dry; a dramatic design in white metal depicting a snake emerging from the drunkard's glass; Cold Water Army medalet. *Bottom row:* Reverse of a copper issue (a similar design appears on the creamer in Ill. 301); a brass "King Alcohol" medalet with a bust of Washington on the opposite side; and perhaps the most commonly used design showing a man drawing a bucket of water from a well.

Rollin Kirby's classic caricature of prohibition (Ill. 313). This amusing artifact is housed in a silk-lined box shaped like a coffin. The hat contains a corkscrew, the legs and feet form a bottle opener, and the midsection is a whiskey shot container in the shape of a beer barrel. This piece does not show up very often; it sells for under $150. Also of interest to collectors is a novelty cane with a wooden head shaped like a beer barrel; just below the head is a small goblet bearing a label inscribed "1933" (Ill. 314). Another label

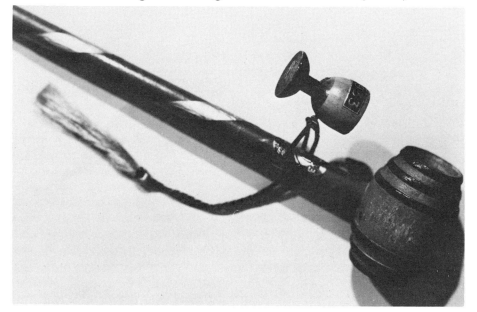

313. A "Mr. Dry" bar set shown in its coffin-shaped and silk-lined box. The set was apparently made before 1933—the year in which the Volstead Act was repealed—because that date is not printed on the cover label.

314. A 1933 wood cane marking the end of Prohibition.

elsewhere indicates that this rather scarce cane was distributed at the Chicago World's Fair in 1933. Equally amusing are cast-metal mantel clocks with illustrated and animated faces. The face on one pictures a bartender shaking a cocktail mix; another pictures a cocktail party scene with a moving arm holding a martini glass. Both varieties sell for under $200. Anti-prohibition material also includes what must be the largest glass container with a political theme known to collectors—a goblet, or beer "schooner," that is 10 inches high and holds 2½ quarts (Ill. 315). A number of humorous decals celebrate the return of the Demon; a skinny camel, symbol of the Prohibition party; Mr. Dry swinging from a gallows; a donkey and an elephant standing over a keg of beer; several tipplers; a few bars of "How Dry I Am," and other decorations. This item does

315. Perhaps the most humorous anti-Prohibition artifact. It bears eight different illustrations.

316. *Puck*'s idea of what would happen if a woman got the vote.

not show up very often, but because of the low demand for anti-prohibition material it can be bought for under $100.

Perhaps a bit more serious are ceramic beer mugs that picture Franklin Roosevelt in profile and a shield, along with a slogan indicating the repeal of prohibition. These mugs, which range in height to about 4½ inches, appear on the market quite often. A shot glass of superior quality is also easily obtained; on it is pictured a kicking donkey with the inscription "Happy Days Are Here Again." Mugs and shot glass sell for under $20. There is also a fair-sized variety of buttons with such slogans as "We Want Beer," "Repeal the 18th Amendment," and "Vote Yes on License." Buttons with more interesting designs picture a mug of beer and are inscribed "No Beer/No Work"; other buttons bear suspended miniature beer mugs or tankards. And there are a few metal and celluloid studs in the shape of beer mugs with large heads of suds. Most anti-prohibition buttons sell for under $15.

Remember, too, that one of the very finest examples of political glassware, described in an earlier chapter, is the crystal goblet issued to commemorate both Franklin Roosevelt's inauguration and the repeal of prohibition (Ill. 169).

The Women's Rights Movement

Although the American women's rights movement has a history dating at least from the Seneca Falls, New York, convention in 1848, most collectors are interested nearly exclusively in the period of militant protest from 1910 to 1920. In those ten years occurred the great suffragette parades, mass arrests, forced feeding and other brutalities inflicted upon suffragettes, determined heckling of politicians inside the Capitol itself—and the founding of militant women's groups.

A FEMALE SUFFRAGE FANCY.

THE NATIONAL WOMEN'S PARTY.   By 1900, the two major women's organizations, the American Woman Suffrage Association and the National Woman Suffrage Association, were joined in a rather shaky union. For several reasons the new organization, now called the National American Woman Suffrage Association, remained relatively sluggish in the face of what some members saw as a need for direct confrontation with authorities, if ever the franchise was to be won. In 1907, Harriet Stanton Blatch, daughter of Elizabeth Cady Stanton, founded the Equity League of Self-Supporting Women. (It became the Women's Political Union in 1910.) In 1913, Alice Paul and Lucy Burns, co-leaders of NAWSA's Congressional Union Committee, split with the parent organization over the proper degree of activism. From this rupture came Paul's and Burns's National Women's party, perhaps the most militant protest group of its day and a worthy predecessor to the future National Organization of Women.

Paul and Burns had observed firsthand how the courage of the British militant Emmeline Pankhurst and her daughters in the face of considerable and often brutal opposition helped change the British government's attitude to suffrage. The two women decided to adopt the Pankhurst strategy of direct confrontation. The resulting tactics of their National Women's party would be repeated again in the 1960s, but for other purposes: picketing and chaining themselves to the White House fence; waving banners and heckling in Congress, and above all—from the collector's viewpoint—the mass demonstrations and parades.

It would probably be futile to argue whether NAWSA or the NWP had the most direct influence on President Wilson and Congress in effecting the change in attitude that reached its climax in the passage of the Nineteenth Amendment in 1920. But by concentrating their strategy of protest at the national level (i.e., in the nation's capital)—rather than limiting their efforts to state and federal legislatures, as was NAWSA's policy—the National Women's party undoubtedly hastened the arrival of woman suffrage.

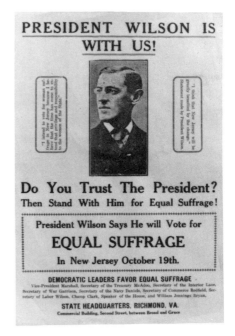

316A. Despite the positive impression created by this broadside Woodrow Wilson only very reluctantly came out in support of women's rights.

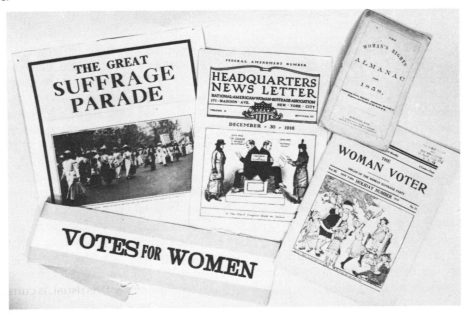

317. A suffragette miscellany: a broadside, typical publications, and a white, yellow, and black parade sash.

SUFFRAGE MATERIAL.   This material was issued over a short span of years—from 1910 to about 1920. Most of the artifacts described here sell for under $300, but a few novelty items, such as umbrellas, sell for more. Buttons and pennants are the most often found collectibles. The buttons range in size from about ⅝ inch to larger and more desired diameters up to 1¾ inches; the selection of buttons illustrated is typical. Several pennants in different designs are available; they are made of either yellow and black felt or purple, green, and white felt—both combinations of colors were used by women's groups. Most pennants simply say "Votes for Women" (Ill. 317), but others

carry, in addition, a state name or a symbolic design. More difficult to locate are sashes, arm and hat bands, umbrellas, pocket mirrors, sewing kits, and such seldom seen humorous items as the green felt Christmas stocking inscribed "Ask Santa to Bring a Vote for Mother" (Ill. 318). Collectors will have better luck with paper ephemera; a good variety is available of leaflets, pamphlets, broadsides, and postcards—some of which are serious and some mildly satirical. This kind of material shows up fairly often and sells at low prices. But the periodicals, especially the NWP's *The Suffragist*, broadsides, and newspapers published by the different suffrage groups, seldom appear—hence they are priced higher, perhaps in the $75 to $250 range.

318. Santa Claus is pictured on the opposite side of this felt stocking.

319. There is an excellent variety of pro- and anti-suffragette postcards. Both these cards are fairly scarce.

ERA MATERIAL.   The National Women's party published its "Declaration of Principles" in 1922. It was the opening gun in what has become a long battle for adding an equal rights amendment to the Constitution. In 1923 the first ERA bill, the Mott Amendment, was submitted to Congress, where it was promptly rejected. Both actions widened the gap between the NWP and NAWSA's successor, the League of Women Voters, which was beginning to view its mission as educational and its stance as nonpartisan. Although the NWP lobbied extensively through the 1920s and 1930s for an equal rights amendment, educated women tended to reject it by joining the League or similar groups such as the American Association of University Women and the Association of Business and Professional Women. It was the resurgence of political and social protest in the 1960s that led to the National Women's party reincarnation (in a sense) as the National Organization of Women. NOW's immediate acceptance among college students and faculty, plus shifts of attitude among members of the League of Women Voters and other women's professional groups, provided a base strong enough to get an equal rights bill through Congress in 1973. The Equal Rights Amendment fell short of ratification by just a few states, but the subject, as usual, is currently embroiled in controversy—which is where the matter now stands.

319A. Canvas tote bag used in a New York City ERA rally.

For collectors, the current controversy over ERA, along with the existence of activist women's groups, means an abundance of material. So far as I know, few collectors are making serious efforts at assembling a representation of ERA material and other material related to these groups' concerns. Probably well over three hundred buttons, many with colorful and imaginative designs, have been issued during the past few years. There is also a rich variety of paper material, an occasional cloth banner, and several publications. A good representative collection of the twentieth-century women's movement should include ERA material. It is inexpensive and easily obtained.

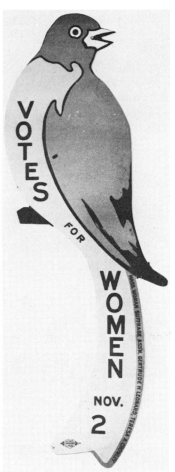

320. Collectors have a high regard for this colorful tin window hanger that was issued by a Massachusetts women's group.

321. Representative historic and modern buttons. The bright yellow ribbon badge is an important addition to a suffragette collection; the Healey button is a Los Angeles issue from the late 1960s; Frances "Sissy" Farenthold lost a Texas gubernatorial contest in the mid-1970s; the *anti*-suffrage button is representative of such material, which should be included in a suffrage collection.

322. Examples of ceramics associated with the women's suffrage movement. Other patterns are known.

TWO EARLY FEMINISTS. Victoria Claflin Woodhull (Ill. 323) is the most overlooked and ignored feminist in the entire nineteenth-century's women's movement. She was a forceful speaker, a superb organizer, a polemicist, a journalist, an intellectual, and a social nonconformist—and certainly the most hated and feared woman of her day. Thomas Nast's cartoon picturing her with horns and clawed devil's wings and holding a broadside inscribed "Free Love" expresses a typical contemporary opinion of her. Her outspoken advocacy of sexual freedom for women and her aggressive willingness to defend her iconoclastic viewpoints at first endeared her to the women's movement. She was the first woman ever to argue the cause of woman suffrage before a congressional committee. Eventually, however, her outrageous opinions and flamboyant life-

VICTORIA C. WOODHALL.
CANDIDATE FOR THE
PRESIDENCY OF THE UNITED STATES

323. A rare 1872 campaign poster.

324. One of the most desirable of all campaign newspapers; the ticket on the front page adds to this copy's value.

325. Satirical Woodhull and Lockwood novelties. Note the misspelling of Lockwood's given name.

style proved to be too much for other suffragists—so Woodhull continued to plead for woman suffrage in her own way.

In 1872, Woodhull and her sister, Tennessee Claflin, started a newspaper, *Woodhull & Claflin's Weekly,* with funds gained from successful Wall Street investments and financial support from Commodore Vanderbilt. Woodhull used the paper as a vehicle for publicizing her bid for the presidency. In the same year, with Frederick Douglass as her running mate, she organized the Equal Rights party, although in her newspaper she always called it the "Cosmo-Political Party" (see Ill. 324). And, of course, there was a campaign song—"Victoria's Banner":

Hark the sound of women's voices
Rising in their might;
'Tis the daughters of Columbia
Pleading for their right;
Flock around Victoria's banner,
Wave the signal still;
Brothers, let us share your freedoms
Help us and we will.

There is no record of how many votes the Equal Rights party received.

In the fall of 1872, Woodhull published a harsh attack on the Reverend Henry Ward Beecher, member of a famous family, a well-known lecturer, popular preacher at Brooklyn's Trinity Episcopal Church, and president of the American Woman Suffrage Association. Her publicizing of Beecher's adulterous affair with the wife of Theodore Tilton, popular journalist and women's rights supporter, and her strident coverage of the trial that followed, eventually resulted in her being arrested several times on obscenity charges brought by the morality crusader Anthony Comstock. She was acquitted on each occasion, but her influence in the women's movement was about over; by 1877 she was settled in England, where she later married a banker and became active in the British women's movement.

I have illustrated an intriguing paper artifact apparently related to the Woodhull-Beecher-Tilton-Comstock affair (as newspapers of the day called it), but cannot attribute it positively (Ill. 325). The 4- by 2½-inch card pictures a standing ballerina, with the inscription below "Don't Expose Me." When the paper skirt is lifted, Henry Ward Beecher is revealed. The ballerina is probably Victoria Woodhull, but perhaps a collector can provide additional information.

Political material associated with Victoria Woodhull and her Equal Rights party is nearly impossible to find. A small lapel pin containing a sepia albumin photo is known, and several cartes de visite with different poses. Copies of *Woodhull & Claflin's Weekly* do not turn up very often. Nevertheless, despite the scarcity of Woodhull-re-

lated material, collectors of women's movement artifacts need to know of her existence. She is too important in the history of the movement to be ignored.

Belva Ann Lockwood was a teacher, lawyer, ardent espouser of world peace, early supporter of political rights for women, and the first woman ever to practice before the United States Supreme Court. Her political and social beliefs were close to Victoria Woodhull's, but Lockwood's calm and understated style was in sharp contrast to her contemporary's flamboyance.

Lockwood and other suffragists founded the National Equal Rights party in 1884 as a vehicle for publicizing woman suffrage. In that year she was nominated by the party as its candidate for president. The party published a newspaper, *Equal Rights,* through which the members sought debate with presidential candidates of the major and other minor parties. Lockwood ran again for the presidency in 1888, but not so enthusiastically as she had in 1884. She was now increasingly involved in her law practice. (On her business cards was the slogan "For Equal Civil and Political Rights.") Her greatest contribution to the women's rights movement was her drafting of suffrage amendments for presentation in state legislatures and her involvement in framing the law that gave women equal property rights with men in the District of Columbia.

Lockwood political material is almost as scarce as Woodhull material. Besides copies of *Equal Rights,* two other Lockwood artifacts are known. The first is a campaign ribbon, which is so unusual that collectors occasionally do not recognize it. It bears a rebus puzzle: a bell, a "V," a padlock, and a block of wood—and nothing else (Ill. 326). Two varieties are known, differing only in the size or shape of the objects pictured—$700 is the current price for either one. Even scarcer than the rebus ribbons is a small multicolored card bearing a full-length figure of Lockwood with a movable paper skirt. When the skirt is lifted, a crouching figure of Ben Butler thumbing his nose is revealed. I am uncertain of the allusion here, but would guess that Butler, a well-known champion of woman suffrage and one of the most criticized figures of the day, is portrayed as a coward hiding under a woman's skirt. However, I do not know the significance of the statement on the card: "But Don't Give It Away." Perhaps a collector can provide enlightenment. So far as I know, this artifact has never appeared on the market; I would estimate its value at about $250. A ticket titled "National Equal Rights Party" and picturing Lockwood and her running mate Marietta Stow is also known.

Other Protest Groups and Personalities

The National Women's party was not alone in the rough treatment its members experienced at the hands of public authorities in the early decades of this century. Actually, for nearly fifty years, from about 1890 to the early 1930s, one protest group after another challenged public authorities, particularly at the federal level, to live up to constitutional guarantees. Large-scale demonstrations, passive resistance, jailings, and frequent confrontations between militants and local authorities set the precedent for similar kinds of activities that would occur during the 1960s. Many members of these earlier protest groups lived on the fringes of American society. A good many were foreign-born and non-English-speaking; others were refugees from urban slums, and many were unskilled laborers in occupations that were generally rejected or ignored by the craft-centered American Federation of Labor.

This period is particularly rich in protest material—obviously so in the case of suffrage material—although until recently collectors had made slight effort to unearth it. Protest groups of this period frequently attracted to their ranks well-educated "rebels" who could write or paint—as did artist Ben Shahn, for example—with flair and passion. Although every group discussed in this chapter is essentially a protest group, political collectors tend to make some fine distinctions: To them, protest groups in this period are made up of minority members who, because of their sex or race, or ethnicity, or occupation, are abused, exploited, or discriminated against by legally constituted author-

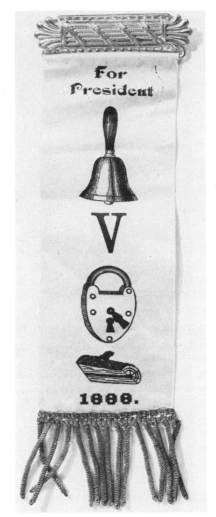

326. A Lockwood rebus puzzle ribbon; a similar ribbon is known from the 1884 campaign. *Courtesy Harris Collection.*

ity—with the full weight of the law, and sometimes public sentiment—behind it. In a word—underdogs. The flamboyant quality in word and picture of some protest material in this period makes the subject all the more appealing to collectors.

A sizable group of "cause" collectors confine their attention to twentieth-century movements. I know of several superior collections that have been assembled with luck and patience. A newsletter to keep cause enthusiasts informed is published quarterly (see Bibliography); cause material generally moves well at political Americana shows. Although suffragette artifacts and material associated with the radical labor movement tend to sell for higher prices than most other protest material issued in this century, that situation should not deter a collector from starting a cause collection. There is ample material for most budgets and most interests.

The groups discussed in the following pages are those that have proved most attractive to collectors. For beginners, it is perhaps best to collect cause material in general—i.e., representative material from many protest groups. If the collector restricts himself to a group or two, the potential material will be either skimpy, as is true of Sacco and Vanzetti material, or redundant. For example, two thousand peace buttons from the 1960s that all say much the same would be more an accumulation than a collection. A good protest collection will be as diverse as the subject itself.

THE WOBBLIES. In our school history texts we read about the growth and development of American labor unions, particularly as mirrored in the history of the American Federation of Labor and later of the Congress of Industrial Organizations. Other than a sentence or two, few textbooks mention the long struggle of unskilled workers for union recognition, workers who often found themselves rejected by and sometimes allied against the A. F. of L. Many of these workers were employed in lumbering and mining in the north central and western states and in eastern textile factories.

Their champion was the Industrial Workers of the World—the I.W.W.—whose members gloried in being "workstiffs" and "bindlebums"; they are better known to history as the "Wobblies." Their official song was "Solidarity Forever," but the Wobbly spirit is better represented in a song written by one of them, "Hallelujah, I'm a Bum!"

326A. One of a series issued by Labor Union pioneer Terence Powderly. Some cards vary in the position of and the border design of Powderly's picture.

327. Labor and social protest buttons. In the middle is a scarce double or button-on-button (the only example I know of). The Mesabi strike issue and the Scottsboro picture buttons are at right in the top row. The vertical row at extreme left contains labor martyr buttons from the World War I period. The Ettor & Giovannitti issue at far right is the only known picture button for these Wobblies.

For a few years, from 1908 to about 1920, the I.W.W.—under its brilliant leader, William "Big Bill" Haywood—fought, often successfully, against the exploitation of workers by industries that relied upon unskilled laborers. Wobblies viewed the labor-management relationship as a class struggle between an exploited working class and gluttonous capitalists. Because many of their beliefs seemed communistic and otherwise un-American to public officials, the Wobblies were harassed constantly throughout their short history. The "foreign" names of many of the members and their pacifist leanings in this period of rampant xenophobia also made them favorite targets of authorities.

Jailings on trumped-up charges and circumstantial evidence were commonplace, and in one case which attracted national attention—that of Joe Hill—there was an execution by a Utah penitentiary firing squad. Swedish-born Joe Hill, whose real name was Haggstrom, is better known to collectors as the "Troubadour of the Discontented"; he composed numerous protest songs, many of which eventually appeared in different editions of *The Little Red Book,* a paperbound book of Wobbly songs that is a real prize to own today. Joe Hill is in the same musical tradition as Woody Guthrie and Pete Seeger. During the 1960s he became a popular hero with student protest groups—and that is how he tends to be perceived by collectors today.

Wobblies saw themselves as living in fiery times, locked in combat with employers—the enemy—whom Wobblies always referred to as "the Iron Heel." Collectors are attracted to the I.W.W. cause because of the material that was issued as a result of the constant clashes between that organization and the industrialists. In that connection, Arturo Giovannitti and Joseph Ettor, Wobbly leaders in the famous Lawrence, Massachusetts textile strike of 1912, are a popular subject (Ill. 328). Other I.W.W. strikes for which related collectible material is known occurred in Paterson, New Jersey, in the Mesabi iron ore region of northern Minnesota, and at different locations in Oregon and Washington. Any Wobbly who was imprisoned or otherwise harassed by authorities was considered a martyr of "class oppression" by his comrades. Thus, collectors will note such expressions as "A Martyr to the Cause" or "Their Only Crime Is Loyalty to the Working Class" (Ettor and Giovannitti) appearing on some buttons and in the literature.

Perhaps a dozen or so different I.W.W. buttons and lapel studs are known. The most interesting usually picture a Wobbly behind bars. A black and white design with that scene is inscribed "We're In For You/You're Out for Us." A scarcer 1¼-inch black, white, and red button issued during the Mesabi strike pictures four Wobblies behind bars, and has the inscription "Don't Let the Steel Trust Incarcerate These Men for Life." There are several buttons picturing I.W.W. leader William Haywood that turn up occasionally, as does a brass red-and-black-enameled lapel membership stud depicting a gilded globe with the initials "I.W.W."

Generally, Wobbly material is hard to find. Collectors will see buttons more often than literature. The lack of literature is not too surprising. Much I.W.W. material was seized and later destroyed by the United States Department of Justice during the World War I era, and in the early 1920s additional material was lost when the I.W.W. headquarters was burned. Nevertheless, Wobblies liked to write, and the voluminous amount of information they disseminated cannot all have been destroyed by federal agents and fire. Somewhere, it seems to me, long forgotten caches of Wobbly ephemera may still exist. Finding them is a particularly fine challenge for the cause collector.

SACCO AND VANZETTI.   The story of Nicola Sacco and Bartolomeo Vanzetti has been told many times since their execution in 1927. Their trial for allegedly robbing a bank truck and killing a guard in an eastern Massachusetts town was a cause constantly in the headlines during the 1920s. Although a few pamphlets are known in university collections, there is very little available on the market for collectors. Most must be satisfied with two lithographed buttons, each an inch in diameter and bearing the same design, but with different wording and color combinations. Both buttons picture Sacco

327A. Wobblies had a knack for coming-up with memorable slogans as is evident with this 1918 songbook.

328. This postcard was distributed in the Lawrence, Massachusetts, area during the great textile strike.

and Vanzetti. One button is red, black, and white, and is inscribed "Life and Freedom for Sacco and Vanzetti"; the other is red, white, and blue, and inscribed "Remember Labor's Martyrs/Sacco and Vanzetti." One button seems to be no scarcer than the other; the usual price range is $150 to $250, depending upon condition. (A reminder: Lithograph buttons scratch easily.)

COXEY'S ARMY. Jacob S. Coxey was a retired army general who, in March 1894, "marched" with his army of unemployed farmers on Washington, D.C. Coxey and his followers were one of the first groups to do this, thus helping to establish a practice that today is almost a monthly event and no longer worth getting excited about. But, in 1894, official Washington did get excited. Coxey was arrested for trespassing on the White House lawn, and some marchers in his army of "commonwealers," as they called themselves, were attacked by police and jailed. Collectors are most likely to find a paper lapel "ribbon" picturing Coxey and giving a statement of his beliefs (Ill. 329). A small tin stickpin containing a paper insert picture of Coxey with the admonition "Keep Off the Grass" is also known.

THE SCOTTSBORO BOYS. The Scottsboro Boys were one of the great causes of the early 1930s. The "Boys" were nine young black men who were convicted (by an obviously bigoted Alabama jury) of raping two white prostitutes. Their cause became a crusade among northern liberal groups. None of the men was executed, but all spent some time in jail—one of them, nineteen years. Their main legal and moral support was provided by the International Labor Defense, an organization of the American Communist party. So this cause is also of interest to collectors of American Communist party material. Several buttons exist, most of which were probably issued by the I.L.D. Unlike most other material related to groups described in this section, *all* Scottsboro buttons bring high prices, ranging from $75 to over $200 each. The only known picture button (Ill. 327) depicting the nine young men is extremely scarce and desirable—it sells for $500 to $800!

BLACK HISTORY. The history of black Americans in this country begins with the arrival of the first slaves. For collectors, however, black history begins with the Abolitionist movement. Newspapers—especially copies of William Lloyd Garrison's *The Liberator*—material associated with Frederick Douglass and Sojourner Truth, and with the few black congressmen during the Reconstruction period up to the advent of Jim Crow, are the chief attractions from the nineteenth century. Black history material not

329. Jacob Coxey widely publicized his provocative political slogan "Keep Off the Grass"—as on this 1894 paper lapel "ribbon."

330. The center decoration on this plate (attributed to Josiah Wedgwood, c. 1790s) is thought to have been done by the black British artist Richard Pease. It was a symbol used extensively by abolitionist groups on both sides of the Atlantic. Other early ceramics picturing abolitionist themes are known.

I Sell the Shadow to Support the Substance.
SOJOURNER TRUTH.

331. Despite the many hundreds of these fund-raising cards that Sojourner Truth must have sold, examples seldom come on the market.

332. A grotesque statuette, indeed, but desirable nevertheless.

specifically political in nature, such as slave bills of sale, broadsides advertising slave auctions, early accounts of their slavery written by former slaves, material associated with the Underground Railroad and the Fugitive Slave Law, is all certainly collectible. From my viewpoint, such material is not strictly political—but perhaps a well-rounded collection dealing with black Americans in politics would "fit" better into this kind of broader historical context. How wide and deep a collector wants to go is a personal decision.

From the latter part of the nineteenth century, collectors should seek an example of Sojourner Truth's famous fund-raising studio card with its memorable statement: "I Sell the Shadow to Support the Substance" (Ill. 331). Collectors will also be interested in a bisque china statuette of Sojourner Truth. This grotesque figure (Ill. 332) was probably made about 1912, many years after her death. As is evident, she was an ardent supporter of women's rights (her famous "Ain't I a Woman?" speech in 1851 is, in my opinion, an American classic), but because of the gaping mouth and the overall "apish" appearance of this statuette, I believe it to be a deliberately racist and sexist caricature. The statuette, one of the more important cause artifacts, sells for about $250.

Frederick Douglass is represented by a few cartes de visite, the Sulphur Bitters advertising card (Ill. 333) and copies of his newspaper *The North Star*. I have seen cartes de visite of Hiram Revels and B. K. Bruce, who were United States senators from Mississippi between 1870 and 1881, and there were also a few black congressmen from southern states during the Reconstruction years who will be of interest to collectors; the first northern black congressman was Oscar de Priest in 1928. Also of importance to a political black history collection is James Ford, vice-presidential nominee of the American Communist party from 1932 to 1940.

Modern black history political material dates generally from the early 1960s and can be considered part of the civil rights movement. Some material was issued locally for such mayoralty candidates as Carl Stokes of Cleveland, Senator Edward Brooke of Massachusetts, and Congressman Charles Diggs of Michigan. Material issued at the national level is typified by Eldridge Cleaver's Black Panther organization and the Peace and Freedom party, which issued a number of attractive buttons for the 1964 and 1968 campaigns. Buttons and literature distributed during the emancipation march in Washington, D.C., August 28, 1963—and the occasion for Martin Luther King's speech "I Have a Dream"—should be included also.

333. Frederick Douglass and his white wife are the butts of racist remarks on this Sulphur Bitters trade card, c. 1880s.

Black history material is a good starting point for novice collectors. There is an abundance of modern material and some earlier material, which is neither especially scarce nor expensive.

The black power movement is a related area. Look for buttons issued by the W. E. DuBois clubs and other black protest groups, buttons picturing Angela Davis and other black militants, and buttons picturing black comedian Dick Gregory, who campaigned, half seriously, for the presidency during the 1960s and early 1970s. Some collectors may want to include buttons related to the 1930s black leader Marcus Garvey, NAACP membership buttons, and Malcolm X material. Remember to include the antislavery medalets described earlier.

334. Representative buttons of black candidates. Clifton DeBerry was the Socialist Labor party presidential nominee in 1964; Paul Boutelle was the vice-presidential nominee of the Socialist Workers party in 1968.

THE STUDENT PROTEST AND ANTIWAR MOVEMENT OF THE 1960s. This is another good starting point for collectors. The best-known student protest groups were Students for a Democratic Society and the Young Socialist Alliance. Although opposition to the Vietnam war was a major rallying focus for those groups and others, student protest groups also militated against what they perceived as rigid university administration, excessive reliance upon nuclear power, and ecological concerns. We will probably never know how many different buttons and paper ephemera were issued between 1963 and 1972, but the area is a happy hunting ground for collectors.

In my opinion, some of the best-designed buttons in modern times were issued in protest against American involvement in Vietnam. The buttons pictured in Illustration 336 merely suggest the interesting and colorful variety that can be collected. There are probably several hundred different ones available. Buttons issued between 1963 and 1966 are valued more highly than later issues—perhaps up to $15 each—because there are fewer of them; the movement had not yet swelled into the mass demonstration of later years. Buttons from the later period sell for under $10.

OTHER CAUSES TO COLLECT. The most notable cause in this category is Cesar Chavez's United Farm Workers. The U.F.W.'S approach to labor-management problems reminds one of the I.W.W.'s style, perhaps because both organizations fought some of their great battles in California's Imperial Valley. U.F.W. material is colorful and easily obtained, and several U.F.W. posters are superb examples of modern political art (Ill. 335). Material associated with this organization is part of a broader subject—viz., the increasing involvement of Hispanic Americans in state and national politics. I think that this subject has considerable collecting potential. Other subjects to consider are American Indian militancy, gay rights, and the different groups that periodically march on Washington, D.C.

MATERIAL FROM ORGANIZATIONS ON THE RIGHT. This subject is discussed last in this section because of the almost total lack of collector interest in it. Perhaps the only exception is the somewhat limited interest in the Ku Klux Klan, which offers the collector a fairly wide assortment of material such as the traditional hood and sheet uniforms, literature, pennants, medalets, and buttons. Generally, however, collectors show little interest in organizations to the right of the American political center. This situation is unfortunate, I think, because some of these groups, like some left-leaning organizations, disseminate unconventional ideas and other information. Look for material associated with Father Charles Coughlin, the "Radio Priest" of Royal Oaks, Michigan, who in his radio talks and his weekly, *Social Justice,* commanded a good-sized following across the country. His diatribes against Franklin "Rosenfelt" and his support of William Lemke, presidential nominee of the Liberty party in 1936, bring him into the field of political Americana. And look for material associated with the Louisiana Kingfisher Huey Long, whose grandiose "Share Our Wealth" program ended with his assassination in 1935. Buttons picturing Long as a presidential hopeful bring high prices.

Among modern organizations, there is material issued by the Young Americans for Freedom, a conservative Republican youth organization; the John Birch Society; and the Conservative Caucus, which operates at both state and national levels. There is material supporting United States involvement in Vietnam; material critical of our ending of control of the Panama Canal; and, as experienced collectors know, a small variety of buttons and literature was issued for various modern and earlier "states' rights" parties, best known of which were the 1948 "Dixiecrats," who actually did take a few electoral votes away from Harry Truman.

335. A fine poster issued by the United Farm Workers of California.

335A. For awhile it was thought that these three "crusaders" would be a serious threat to Franklin Roosevelt's re-election chances in the mid-1930s.

336. An assortment of anti-Vietnam war, or peace, buttons. The 1966 issue in the center is perhaps the scarcest among this group.

336A. A selection of recent protest buttons. All are fairly easily obtained.

336B. Very rare Nast caricature of Benjamin "Beast" Butler.

The Personalities: Author's Choice

Every campaign season seems to flush out individuals who eye the presidency as a platform for fulfilling all kinds of personal dreams. What has always struck me as most interesting about these "candidates" is not so much their platforms—which seldom differ that much from the prevalent ideology of the times—but rather their personalities, their appearance, and how they viewed themselves. Such candidates, I think, have a high sense of mission and a degree of confidence that provides strong motivation for achieving at a level beyond that of most of their peers. Conventional political restraints are too much for them; they are not very good players at the games politicians feel must be played. As a result, men such as Ben Butler and George Francis Train were more often on the fringes of party activity than within it. Both these men were successful in not one but several fields, and both campaigned for the presidency in their own peculiar ways.

Butler and Train are a continuing source of fascination to collectors. It is a truism that the office of the presidency shapes the man, but Benjamin Franklin Butler and George Francis Train would have been decidedly unorthodox presidents. Neither had a chance of ever entering the White House, a fact that deterred them not at all, but I like to think that had they been elected to the presidency, the office would never again have been the same. Butler reminds me of those roly-poly toy figures, such as the one made in the likeness of William H. Taft, described earlier, that rock to all sides but never tip over. Train never harbored any idea that he might be wrong; for him, the presidency would have been a forum for expressing some of the most outrageous beliefs of the day. Collecting Butler and Train material is a diverting and rewarding sideline that will add immeasurably to the quality of a collection of political material from the late nineteenth century.

BENJAMIN FRANKLIN BUTLER.   Butler had a crossed left eye, a droopy eyelid to accompany it, and in later years he carried a magnificent paunch. Those features, plus his unsavory reputation—which was partly undeserved—made him probably the most caricatured public figure between Abraham Lincoln and Theodore Roosevelt. During the 1870s and 1880s, *Puck, Judge,* and major newspapers such as *Harper's Weekly* seemed to publish a cartoon ridiculing him almost every week. Typical cartoons pictured him as a strutting general, a Cinderella, an avenging angel, as Moses, as a housemaid—all testifying that Ben Butler was good copy. He lived most of his life in Lowell, Massachusetts; he was a Democratic congressman and governor, a candidate of the Greenback party for governor and president, a not very successful Union general, and a textile magnate. He was also sympathetic chairman of the House Judiciary Committee, which sat for the first appearance ever of a women's rights group before Congress; a lawyer for every underdog in his day—and author of the infamous General Order No. 28 issued in 1862 when he was military governor of Louisiana. In that edict Butler threatened to treat every New Orleans lady "as a woman of the town plying her advocation" if she continued her contemptuous insulting of Union soldiers. He was called "Beast Butler" for this action, an epithet that stuck with him for the remainder of his life. Shortly after, when he was reassigned, the rumor circulated throughout the South that he left New Orleans with a coffin filled with silver spoons. That explains why collectors will see anti-Butler literature picturing or mentioning spoons.

But Butler knew how to handle such criticism. Collectors should look for round tin lapel ferrotypes bearing an albumin picture of him with a tiny suspended spoon (Ill. 337). Inscribed in the ferrotypes is "The Workingmen's Friend," suggesting that they were used in his gubernatorial and presidential campaigns in the 1878 to 1884 period, when he relied heavily on the votes of Lowell millworkers and other workers across the state. These delightful artifacts sell for about $150 and are fairly scarce. Even scarcer, however, are lapel pieces in the shape of a spoon, the bowl of which contains a sepia-color picture of Butler. Only a very few are known. They are valued currently at about $500. Remember, too, the Butler frog bank discussed previously, certainly the most outstanding artifact associated with him. Not far behind in scarcity is a lightly glazed white ceramic matchbox about 5 inches in height (Ill. 338). On each of the four sides are similar high-relief outward-facing busts of Butler. On the cover is a kepi, signifying his participation in the Civil War. On the surface of the cover is inscribed "Contraband of War/Set Them to Work," Butler's response when, as a general during the war, he was asked what to do with slaves living in territory now occupied by the Union Army. From that time on, freed slaves were called contrabands. Around the rim of the cover is inscribed "A Match for Any One." The pottery mark on this piece is dated in October 1874—which suggests that the box was issued during one of Butler's congressional campaigns. Because of the cover inscription, this choice piece can also be associated with a black history collection.

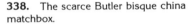

337. Butler lapel devices with the spoon theme (enlarged).

338. The scarce Butler bisque china matchbox.

A considerable amount of paper ephemera is also associated with Ben Butler. Collectors will be most likely to find Greenback party material from the years 1878 and 1884, when he was that party's nominee for governor and president respectively. Look particularly for anti-Greenback paper artifacts in the approximate size of contemporary paper money. Typical examples portray Butler as the callous spender of the people's money, as a destroyer of the gold standard, and as a rank opportunist—which he undoubtedly was. There are probably a dozen or more different designs, some of which are painted in green ink and valued at under $50, as is all the material described in this paragraph. The Greenback party issued a miniature—3 by 1¾ inches—version of a dollar bill, which listed the party's platform. These items are quite distinctive and should be part of a Butler collection. There are also several tickets (Ill. 339) known with differ-

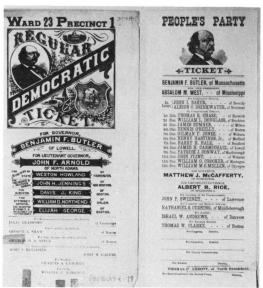

339. Butler is pictured as a candidate for state and national offices on these superb examples of campaign tickets.

ent scenes—those picturing Butler are most desired; all these show up occasionally. He was a favorite subject on advertising cards; in the example pictured (Ill. 340) he sits by himself at a separate tavern table, away from the 1884 major party candidates. A large Sulphur Bitters card (Ill. 341) pictures Butler dancing to the fiddler's tune (played by two Irishmen)—i.e., maneuvering for the party nomination with Samuel Tilden—as other Democratic hopefuls look on. See, by the way, the figure in the doorway: He is a caricature of Irish-American voters, who are depicted in cartoons of that day as whiskered disreputable drunks with pretentions (note the tuxedo).

A few quite valuable ribbons from the 1884 campaign picture Butler alone, or less often, with his running mate, Alanson West. Note that these ribbons often say "People's Party"; the Greenbackers frequently used that synonym to indicate their belief that they were a grass-roots force. This designation appears often in campaigns of the period. Butler ribbons are priced in the $400 to $600 range.

340. Butler and other candidates in the 1884 campaign are pictured on a trade card advertising a brewery. Note the unsavory-looking character in the doorway. He also appears in the following illustration.

341. Ben Butler and Samuel Tilden dance a hoedown while other Democratic party hopefuls look on in this scarce Sulphur Bitters trade card, c. 1880s.

342. A delightful satire of Ben Butler and Absalom West as Cupid and Psyche, portrayed on a studio card.

GEORGE FRANCIS TRAIN.   This man was one of the great nineteenth-century eccentrics. His life was a mixture of solid accomplishments and bizarre events that alternately left his contemporaries awed or amused. His accomplishments: part owner of the clippers *Flying Cloud* and *Monarch of the Seas;* originator of the foreign agent—steam packet service that brought large numbers of Irish immigrants to America; developer of the British steel railway system; organizer of the Credit Mobilier—but not involved in the later scandal; militant defender of the Union in Great Britain during the Civil War; probably America's first foreign correspondent; a millionaire before he was twenty-five. The "Citizen," as he preferred to be called, was prouder of his more adventurous achievements: On a visit to Ireland he spent time in a Dublin jail for inciting the Irish to riot; on a visit to Italy he agitated for the revolutionary Carbonari; in Australia he was convicts' favorite for president of that country; twice he circled the globe—one trip beat Nellie Bly's record and the other was the inspiration for Jules Verne's Phineas Fogg in *Around the World in Eighty Days.*

Train first ran for the presidency in 1864, at which time he said what has since become a classic piece of doggerel about out-of-office politicians:

> Why wax they so exceedingly wroth?
> Their feet are not inside the trough.

The only Train political item from this campaign is a 1- by ¾-inch lapel pin bearing a sepia albumin photograph of him. It rarely appears on the market; the most recent price I am aware of is $300.

Train ran again in 1872. Appropriately enough, some of his campaign literature is dated from Blarney, Ireland, where he sat out much of the campaign season. His campaign literature touted him as "the Man of Destiny/the People's Candidate for President," who was running on a platform which, among other planks, advocated "down with politicians, up with people . . . woman suffrage . . . presidential term [limited to] six years . . . compulsory education in public schools sans Bible . . . ballot to boys of eighteen . . . abolish electoral college . . . hydrotherapy and Turkish baths [for public employees] . . . impeachment of Grant . . ." A fair amount and variety of material are available: The most desired 1872 campaign piece is a 2- by 1¾-inch card bearing his photo (Ill. 343). Occasionally this turns up with "For President" and the date neatly lined out and "Dictator-1873" substituted. Train believed that once he had achieved the presidency, he would become leader in the new era of Psychologic Evolution. Look also for cartes de visite (he frequently autographed them), broadsides, lecture notices, circulars, and flyers on all kinds of subjects. The "For President" card is valued at $200 to $350, but other 1872 material sells for under $125.

The Citizen was a prolific writer, and his actions were always good for newspaper copy. As a result, there is considerable additional material with dates extending into the late 1890s. Of particular interest are cards, about 3 by 2 inches, which were handed out to his admirers. These always bear a handwritten inscription in black ink or blue or red pencil—sometimes on both sides—and are usually signed "Geo. Francis Train." The following inscriptions are typical:

> When Deposits Increase, then $300,000,000
> in 10,000 Banks has been swallowed in McK's
> air ships, "Reign of Terror" will shock Cosmos!
> Mills Hotel/N.Y./Nov. 18 '97 Geo. Francis Train

If that statement is obscure, this one is not:

> Live as I do (on Fruit and Grain,
> One Daily Meal) in sun and air

343. Representative Train items. The broadside is typical of the "Citizen's" style; the three cards all date from the 1870's.

> If you desire to Health, retain [sic]
> And live long life (upon the square).
> Madison Square   Geo. Francis Train

And on this card is a comment that we certainly would not quarrel with: "The autograph of the most sane man in our mad world, N.Y. 21-P.E. 47 Geo. Francis Train." (The date can be translated as the twenty-first day of the forty-seventh year of Psychologic Evolution.) These inscription cards are popular with collectors; hence, they sell from $100 to $250. Since Train was always busy, there are also lecture notices on different subjects, especially about his world tours and his perennial condemnations of whichever party controlled the White House.

George Francis Train is one of the most interesting personalities in American political campaign history. He deserves representation in a general collection.

343A. An uncommon example of the inevitable caricature — puns on Train's name.

10
Protecting Your Collection

A COLLECTOR'S SOURCE of pride in a fine collection of political Americana is its physical appearance. A well-cared-for collection speaks for itself. But along with the pleasure of building a collection comes the need to protect it—and protection is first a matter of prevention. Political Americana is perishable, and so requires care. Artifacts enter our collections showing wear from use in campaigns and occasionally from negligence. Protective measures must be aimed at preventing further deterioration from natural environmental threats or from our own ignorance. In the act of collecting we are—in effect—preserving an unusual aspect of American political history, but we must also protect our investment of time and money. Protecting our collections means, then, not only preventing natural deterioration and possible future damage, but also providing proper storage and taking adequate measures against theft.

Restoration is a further dimension of protecting artifacts. But restoring Americana demands considerable skill and an intimate knowledge of an artifact's material composition. Collectors should tread cautiously in this area.

There are certain precautions that collectors can take, however, to ensure at least minimal safety of their collections. Some of these precautions are a matter of common sense; others require investigating the literature dealing with artifact protection. This chapter will suggest some basic protective measures for collectors to take. But the subject of artifact protection is too complex to be summarized in a few pages. Included in the Bibliography, therefore, are several sources dealing with more specialized measures. I particularly recommend the publications of the American Association for State and Local History (1315 Eighth Avenue, Nashville, Tennessee 37203). Besides Per Guldbeck's exemplary study *The Care of Historical Collections,* the association publishes a large number of leaflets on protecting and maintaining Americana collections, and they are well worth their low cost. The association is geared primarily to the needs of local historical societies, but I have found it quite helpful to me as an individual collector. The books by Per Guldbeck and Frieda Kay Fall contain extensive bibliographies dealing with specialized protective measures. Local libraries are likely to have books on collecting glass, ceramics, bottles, metal artifacts, and paper ephemera that include chapters on protection. The tabloid *Antique Trader Weekly, The Magazine*

ANTIQUES, and similar publications concerned with Americana in general also frequently carry advertisements for books and materials dealing with the subject.

And always remember, before taking the first step in cleaning, repairing, or removing stains and the like, to think about the possible consequences of your action. Under all circumstances, follow the basic axiom of museum curators and restorers—*if in doubt, don't.*

Environmental Concerns

Collectors should be aware of three extraordinary threats to their collections. The first is light, both natural and artificial. The second is dampness. The third is atmospheric pollution.

Natural light is particularly dangerous because the deterioration it causes can be so insidious. Sunlight can be brutal to framed artifacts hanging where they will receive light from southern-facing windows or patio doors. In fact, any wall that is struck by sunlight part of the day should not be hung with paper or textile artifacts. Even artificial light from incandescent bulbs, if it is close enough, can be destructive; and ultraviolet rays from fluorescent tubes as well as from sunlight, when combined with excessive heat and humidity, can accelerate deterioration. Under improper lighting conditions, celluloid buttons, prints, posters, and textiles fade, leather dries up and becomes flaky and brittle, wood splits, and photographic images darken. To avoid—or at least minimize—all these various types of light-caused damage, pay particular attention to the display (and storage) suggestions given later in this chapter.

Dampness in the environment—especially that of a humid summer day—is immediately apparent; dampness on one's fingers and palms is not so evident. Keep your hands dry when touching or handling artifacts; and remember: A normally dry environment is essential for a collection's well-being. Excessive dampness causes mildew and rust, paper sticks or loses its freshness, textiles rot, and corrosion appears on metals. Collectors have to be concerned about extremes of both heat and dryness that can affect their collections over a period of time. Constant heat will suck the normal amount of moisture from the atmosphere, thus subjecting artifacts to some of the same damage that excessive light causes. But unless a house is poorly insulated or not insulated (in winter climates), a normal room temperature range and a relative-humidity range of between 45 and 65 percent are acceptable for most collections.

Atmospheric pollution, the third environmental concern for collectors, is seldom as noticeable as excessive light, heat, or dampness. Soot, dust, and fireplace ashes, for example, can have a corrosive effect on the kinds of artifacts to which I have referred. Simply dusting occasionally, gently washing glass and ceramic artifacts, and keeping at least the most valuable pieces behind glass are usually sufficient precautions for most collections. If, however, your collection is housed in an area with high industrial pollution, or large amounts of moisture from nearby salt water, or the house furnace emits large amounts of coal or oil fumes, then special precautions may be necessary.

PROTECTING PAPER ARTIFACTS. Because many collectors tend to undervalue paper artifacts, there seems to me to be a corresponding tendency to treat them rather carelessly. All paper artifacts need protection, whether they are early broadsides and prints with a high rag content or modern posters and leaflets printed on glossy stock.

Modern paper is made from raw wood containing such various substances as gum, oil, lignus, cellulose, and resins. Depending upon the quality of paper and the combinations and amounts of chemicals added during the manufacturing process, all paper has a certain amount of "acid." The cheaper the paper—shirt cardboard and newsprint, for example—the more acid present. High-grade paper used for fine engraving, etching, and watercoloring, has a low acid content. This distinction is important because acid "migrates." This is why it is not a good idea to use cheap cardboard for backing or matting your good paper artifacts. In time the acid in cheap cardboard will travel, or "migrate," to the artifact; eventually it will "bleed" through to the surface, causing discoloration that will be difficult to remove. I strongly urge collectors to use acid-free materials with their papers and textile pieces. Museums and similar institutions use acid-free stock in various dimensions, thicknesses, and colors, to ensure a level and longevity of protection that cheap shirt and corrugated cardboard and similar stiff stock sold commonly by stationery stores cannot provide. Acid-free stock is somewhat more expensive than ordinary stock, but the protection it provides is well worth the higher cost.

Large prints and posters should be matted and framed. The framing may consist of a glass or Plexiglas covering, a wood or metal frame, and the appropriate acid-free stock, or simply of matting and mounting for temporary protection or exhibition. If an artifact is to be framed permanently, the following are necessary requirements:

1. The subject—print, poster, or broadside—must be separated from the covering by means of an acid-free mat. Matting is necessary in order to protect the subject from moisture that may accumulate on the inside of the covering. The mounting—the stock to which the subject is attached—and the backing are attached directly to the back of the frame.

2. A subject is attached to its mounting with small strips of Japanese rice paper or tissue paper. Do not use common household glues, school pastes, or paper cement—use only rice or wheat pastes (see Bibliography).

3. The backing is either sealed to the frame with pressure-sensitive tape or, better, pasted to the frame.

4. Manufacturers of glass usually include in their inventory kinds of glass that alter the amounts of heat, light, and ultraviolet rays that strike a surface. An alternative to these fairly expensive glasses is the somewhat cheaper Plexiglas. Type UF-1 Plexiglas is clear; type UF-3 is slightly yellowed and a bit more expensive, but it provides better protection than Type UF-1.

Some collectors prefer to dry mount their artifacts. Dry mounting is a process that permanently seals a subject to its mounting under intense pressure. Should improper framing cause damage to the subject, restoration becomes very difficult. Dry mounting is not recommended for valuable and rare artifacts, although it is probably acceptable for modern pieces that exist in large numbers. Lamination is a more elaborate process for protecting artifacts, especially early documents—but it is expensive and should be done only by an expert.

Small paper artifacts can be preserved in a number of ways. I have found it most convenient to use transparent corner mounts to attach subjects to acid-free stock that has been cut to fit three-ring binders. I then insert the mounts into transparent acetate holders punched to fit the binders. Corner mounts and punched three-ring acetate holders are available in stationery stores. There are several sizes of binders and matching acetate holders on the market that are suitable for paper artifacts of larger dimensions. Larger binders and folders ranging up to 24 by 18 inches must be specially ordered, as a rule. Several variations of the standard size, 8½- by 11-inch, acetate folders contain up to nine pockets; although that variety is intended primarily for baseball cards, it is ideally suited for political postage labels and similar small pieces. There are also acetate holders for postcards and envelopes; stiff, imitation-leather-cover holders with transparent acetate fronts; and acid-free file folders and expansion envelopes. All these containers are available in different sizes. Folders and envelopes are especially suited for storing duplicate materials.

Collectors should remember two very important don'ts concerning paper artifacts: a) Never, under any circumstances, attach pressure-sensitive tape (Ill. 344), such as Scotch, masking, or library tapes. directly to an artifact. It can seldom be removed with-

344. What pressure-sensitive tape can do to paper: This scarce 1880 anti-Hancock broadside is permanently damaged.

out taking along some of the paper, and the ugly stains left are difficult to remove. b) Never use metal paper clips or staples. Plastic paper clips are available that do not leave the rust stains caused by metal paper clips.

PROTECTING TEXTILES.　Textiles undergo continuous chemical change; therefore, heat, light, and moisture can be just as destructive to textiles as they are to paper. Fading, rotting, staining, mold, rust, tears, and dirt are conditions that cannot be easily corrected in textiles.

Several techniques can be used for preserving and restoring textiles, but most of them depend upon the nature of the particular cloth. Careful reweaving, attaching textiles to protective nets, and restoring missing portions are tasks best left to experts. Entries concerned with textile restoration appear in the Bibliography for those collectors who wish to pursue the subject further.

Silk is the most difficult cloth to deal with. Like wool, silk is of animal origin, and hence is subject to attack by moths and silverfish. Old silk artifacts are often found with tiny holes; note that condition in the Jackson bandanna in Illustration 210. The most fragile political artifacts are the early silk lapel ribbons that were in common use during the first half of the nineteenth century. These ribbons should be handled as little as possible. I make it a practice to cover ribbons with commercially made, narrow, translucent plastic sleeves, available from coin dealers, which protect them from dust, the perspiration on one's hands, and direct light. Longer silk pieces can be covered with polyester sheets if the artifact is to be matted, or glass or Plexiglas if it is to be framed. Silk campaign flags and banners should never be put up to hang by their own weight; they will tear. Note the tears in the campaign flag in Illustration 206. Once silk threads begin to separate, only an expert can minimize further separation. If a collector chooses to hang a silk artifact, then that artifact must be framed and matted. One method that I have found useful is to secure the textile to its mount with "straps"—i.e., narrow strips of board laid along each edge, to a depth dependent upon the size of the textile, the width of its margins, and the width of the straps. Each end of the strip is secured to the mount; the textile is adjusted so that it lies flat and taut; and matting—and framing—if intended, follow. Use acid-free board. I suggest laminating, especially for fragile silk artifacts that may be used frequently in displays or public lectures.

Although cotton, linen, and man-made synthetics are more resistant to damage than silk, collectors should nevertheless exercise discretion. Fading is a particularly worrisome concern with these fabrics; be particularly attentive to the condition of red bandannas from the 1880s campaigns, cotton bandannas from earlier campaigns, and campaign flags.

Textiles should never be:

1. washed or dry cleaned without knowing which method is safest for the artifact in question, or without having a thorough knowledge of the appropriate techniques and

the properties of cleaning materials (it is better to leave a stain or tear in the artifact than to attempt to remove them in an amateurish manner);

    2. folded; every crease weakens threads, and in time threads break from continuous bending;

    3. directly sprayed with fumigants (spray the storage or display area instead);

    4. subjected to pressure-sensitive tape, metal paper clips, staples, or pins of any sort.

PROTECTING METALLIC ARTIFACTS. Political metallic artifacts are found most often in ferrous metals—iron and iron with a tin surface finish; in cuprous metals, copper and brass especially; and in the "noble" metals, silver and gold. The first thing to say about protecting metallic political artifacts is that if a collector plans to clean them, he must be certain—absolutely certain—that he *wants* to clean them. The damage that has been done to fine and sometimes rare metallic pieces in the name of cleaning is appalling. Bringing a shine to an artifact is seldom the best way to preserve its condition, and shining can, in fact, cause further damage.

    Ferrous Metallic Objects. Iron and iron with a tinned surface rusts. Left unchecked, rust will eventually cause holes to form in iron. Rust, in time, literally eats iron away. Fortunately, few political artifacts are made of cast iron—some nineteenth-century bust plaques and the Tammany mechanical bank come immediately to mind. If surface-level rust is present, one protective measure is to rub with #000 steel wool dipped in kerosene. The kerosene must be removed with white gas or acetone because kerosene itself attracts water, and the potential for further rusting remains if the kerosene is not removed. If an artifact is deeply pitted or seriously gouged with rust holes, then specialized prevention techniques need to be employed by a knowledgeable person.

    Tin torchlights and other tin artifacts deserve special concern. These artifacts are made from sheet iron with a minuscule covering of tin. Tin is relatively resistant to rust, but because torchlights were given hard outdoor use and because their owners later disregarded them, torchlights always seem to be found with some rust. The tin covering was not sufficient to protect the iron base from the elements. Tin objects that are free of rust should be lightly covered with a household or sewing machine oil, or given a silicone spray, and then gently wiped off. If rust is present, apply repeated coatings of lightweight penetrating oil followed by gentle rubbing with #0000 steel wool; finish with an application of machine oil, or silicone spray, and a rubbing. A periodic rubbing with a light oil should ensure against future rust damage. Do not attempt to restore a shine to tin; even when new, tin objects soon lose their shine. We expect to see torchlights showing the results of their hard use, so leave the dents, nicks, and scrapes alone too. Holes and breaks in the metal caused by rusting are sometimes found in the area around the torchlight burner. There is not much that can be done about that condition: A tin patch would detract from the torch's antique appearance, and it is nearly impossible to get at the damage and mend it from inside the canister. Just hope that eventually you will be able to replace a torch that has this kind of damage with a better example.

    Cuprous Metals. Many political artifacts, especially numismatic issues, are made of copper. Bronze, brass, and gun and bell metal are all copper alloys and relatively resistant to rust. But collectors need to be alert for corrosion in cuprous metals— tiny black spots or powdery dark green areas are evidence of corrosion that will spread if not checked. Corrosion cannot be removed entirely, so resist the urge to clean a medalet or other copper or brass artifact. Nothing is more aggravating than to see a medalet that is shiny but lacks the luster of its original state. With the passage of time copper and brass medalets acquire a patina or alteration in the surface finish; this can give a piece a handsome mellow-toned appearance that adds to its value. Never clean any numismatic artifact or metallic lapel piece such as shell badges, studs, ferrotypes, or brooches with polishing paste, polishing cloths, or commercial "dips." Pastes and cloths can be abrasive and may leave microscopic scratches, and the use of dips is deplorable. In my opinion, although liquid cleaning solutions do remove surface dirt, they can also remove the surface finish—the patina—to such a depth that even an artificial "shine" is not possible. Perhaps the best a collector can do with corroded cuprous metal artifacts is to wash them gently—removing any finger rings first—in lukewarm soapy water and dry them with a soft, absorbent tissue paper. Because of possible body oil or perspiration, such pieces should not come into direct contact with the skin; when you must handle them, hold them with the edge between thumb and forefinger, with tissue paper.

The "Noble" Metals. Other than exceedingly rare inaugural medallions, a few inaugural committee badges, and a few equally rare early medalets, gold is not otherwise a popular medium for political artifacts. But silver is popular. Some of the very nicest numismatic issues were minted in silver of different degrees of fineness. Although silver is fairly impervious to corrosion, it is tarnished by sulfuric components in the environment. Tarnish on a political artifact is not objectionable unless the object has become so black as to be nearly unrecognizable. In that case, cleaning should be done by an expert. Silver numismatic pieces should not be polished, buffed, or dipped in an attempt to remove tarnish. Some jewelry firms are using a cleaning method based upon sound waves, which, if nothing else, removes tarnish from tiny crevices in patterned silver. I am uncertain how effective this method is with silver political artifacts, but I do know it should not be used on silver *numismatic* issues. The patina on silver medalets is a beautiful sight to see; iridescent ones of coppery brown and purple sometimes take years to form—but it takes only a few seconds for a well-intentioned cleaning to remove that iridescence forever.

Other Metals. "Silvered," or nickel-plated, artifacts also need special attention. The same view regarding treatment and the same methods that applied to copper, brass, and silver are equally true of plated artifacts. But artifacts of this nature have an additional characteristic of concern to collectors: the electrochemical bonding of silver or nickel to copper bases. Some brass shell badges and copper medalets have microscopically thin silverlike finishes that wear off very easily. Commemorative and campaign spoons, some convention and inauguration badges, and the metallic components on campaign ribbons—fringes and tassels—have slightly thicker finishes, but they too wear off. So—no polishing or dipping. Collectors should also be aware of the characteristics of cast zinc artifacts, which were popular in the 1920s and 1930s, such as the Roosevelt clocks and the cheaply made busts of Al Smith, Herbert Hoover, and Eugene Debs. These had either a silvery look or an obviously artificial dark bronze tone, but the finish wore off quite quickly, and many found today have a rather unsightly "blotched" appearance.

Painted metal artifacts, such as serving trays and license plate attachments, can be protected with a light coat of carnauba wax or beeswax after giving them a quick washing in soapy lukewarm water. (Do *not* let them soak.)

PROTECTING CERAMICS AND GLASSWARE. Breakage is the primary problem with ceramics and glass, and repairing such breakage requires special skills. Several books listed in the Bibliography describe proper restoration techniques. I urge collectors to investigate those sources rather than attempt to make amateur repairs.

Here are a few helpful suggestions for collectors of glass and ceramic artifacts:

1. Ceramic and glass artifacts should be kept in cabinets or under glass—not left standing about on tables, unprotected. For display outside of cabinets, set a delicate glass or ceramic artifact on a wooden base and cover it with a bell jar. These dome-shaped covers are available in different heights and diameters.

2. Use plate holders, which come either to stand freely or to hang on the wall. There are also similar holders for a cup and saucer. All these are widely advertised in na-

tional antiques publications, and are well worth their cost. However, most wall hangers have a spring arrangement on the back, so that they clutch the plate tightly. Therefore, to avoid damage to the edge of a plate, make sure the holder you use is large enough—and be very careful in inserting or removing a plate from the hanger.

3. Be particularly careful how you treat artifacts made of unglazed bisque. Such pieces are especially porous, hence pick up dirt, which in time becomes very difficult to remove. An occasional gentle dusting should be sufficient to keep them clean.

4. Do not display ceramics near radiators or other sources of heat because excessive heat and cold cause expansion or contraction between the body and the glaze, leading to glaze cracks (crazing).

Display, Storage, and Security

Planning a home display is one of the more satisfying aspects of collecting political Americana. There is something to be said for an environment in which one can relax, contemplate, and be surrounded by the happy result of his labors. Some collectors have designed a den or family room around their collection. Others acquire secondhand cabinets and bookcases for housing bulky and fragile artifacts. Still others display their collection in their business offices. A good source of display cases is any local store that is going out of business. Such a store will frequently sell its display cases quite cheaply, and these will probably be in a variety of sizes and styles; small counter cases are especially useful to a collector. Overall, a collector need not have sophisticated carpentry skills in order to house his collection in an intelligent, safe, and aesthetically pleasing manner. Simple shadow box or wall frames and bric-a-brac shelves are easy to make; a combination of floor shelves and cabinets makes a compact arrangement for a limited space. Local libraries have books full of ideas and patterns for constructing furniture at home. Just remember the environmental nature and limitations of your display space, and go to it.

Displaying lapel artifacts properly and safely is always a special concern for collectors. Most collectors use wooden button frames or Riker mounts for housing such artifacts, as explained earlier, but I much prefer coin cabinets. Not only do they take up considerably less space, but they maintain buttons and ferrotypes in total darkness. I simply do not like to see such material exposed to natural or artificial light for very long.

STORING ARTIFACTS.   Storing political artifacts properly should be a concern because they can deteriorate—even in storage—if not protected. Plan your storage facilities as carefully and thoughtfully as you plan your display cabinets, shelves, and other areas. Disregarding the light, heat, and moisture in a storage area can be an invitation to disaster; you should also make sure that your material will be easily accessible. It may be convenient—but it is shortsighted—to wrap artifacts in newspaper and pack them in cartons brought home from the supermarket. Newspaper ink smudges what it wraps, sometimes to a degree difficult to remove. Take the time to study all aspects of the storage problem; it will be time well spent.

Here is a list of storage suggestions. They are based on the assumption that the collector will use acid-free materials—e.g., paper sheets and cardboard containers from which certain acids that are commonly in paper have been removed.

1. If the storage area is damp occasionally, consider using a dehumidifier. At the very least, mount a relative humidity indicator in the area. Adequate ventilation is imperative.

2. Artifacts should be suitably wrapped and packed to avoid breakage, and then stored in boxes, each of which is labeled with a list of its contents.

3. Set boxes on wooden frames rather than directly onto cement floors, which may hold moisture.

4. Store all material in darkness; that means each box or other container should

have a cover. This precaution is especially important for paper and textiles.

5. Prints, posters, broadsides, and textiles should be stored flat. Each piece should be laid on stiff board and covered with a sheet of tissue paper. Large textiles can be rolled loosely, with tissue sheets separating each roll.

6. Do not crowd ceramics and glass in a container. Delicate artifacts should be packed in smaller containers first. Do not pack ceramics and glass with iron or similarly hard or heavy objects.

7. Small paper pieces, such as leaflets and pamphlets, should be stored in appropriately sized polyester holders and placed in folders—then into containers.

8. Place silver artifacts in tarnish-resistant bags; these can usually be bought at local jewelers.

9. Before storing rust-susceptible artifacts, give them a light coating of machine oil or spray them with silicone.

HOME SECURITY.   Probably one sign of a hobby's popularity is the number and frequency of thefts. At least two important collections of political Americana were stolen from their owners' homes in 1978. Political Americana will become increasingly attractive to thieves as prices continue upward. Safeguarding your home is much too complicated a subject to discuss satisfactorily here. I have included several books in the Bibliography that have been useful to me. There are a number of precautions, however, that apply to any valuable collection displayed in one's home. Beyond the obvious importance of keeping display frames, cases, and a storage area locked, and planning for your collection's safety when the house will be empty for a vacation period, certain other measures can also be taken.

1. Thieves read newspapers too. Before your collection is given publicity in the local press, you must decide whether you want your name and address included. Consider, instead, being identified as "a collector from western Massachusetts" or "from the northern part of the state," or some other vague place-indicator. As experienced collectors know, however, this recommendation creates a dilemma: Publicity can bring one the opportunity to add to his collection, as a reader may offer to sell or donate an item he possesses. At the same time, publicity can bring unwelcome visitors to your home.

2. Most thieves are looking for household objects that can be fenced easily. But increasingly, it seems, today's thieves have a sufficiently advanced knowledge of antiques to know what to look for and where to get rid of it. Like it or not, you must consider renting a safe deposit box from your bank. Of course, that solution means that you will not be able to enjoy some artifacts when you want to—but you will be assured, if not guaranteed outright, of more formidable protection.

INSURING YOUR COLLECTION.   Study the problem of insuring with particular care, and arrange to have a meeting or two with your agent so that you can get clear answers to all your questions. In recent years homeowners' policies (and also renters' policies) have become more comprehensive in their coverage. If you maintain an updated inventory—not only a written record but, I hope, in pictures too—then your homeowner's policy may provide the coverage you need. An alternative to coverage under a homeowner's policy is a fine arts policy. This kind of coverage is sold primarily to museums and similar institutions, but some insurance firms will sell fine arts policies to homeowners. A fine arts policy is more expensive than a homeowner's policy, but it can cover all kinds of items—rare china, glass, and gold medals, for example—that the latter is not intended to cover. Some fine arts policies have a "20 percent clause," which means that items added to a collection after the policy is issued are insured up to 20 percent of the total worth of the collection; that clause is particularly important to the collector who is adding constantly to his collection.

A compromise between these two policies is a fine arts rider (sometimes called a floater or an endorsement) to a homeowner's policy. A fine arts rider insures selected artifacts at predetermined values. It is well worth the added cost because your artifacts can be insured at exact value (which you can increase as the market changes), and are not subject to deductible or depreciation allowances, as can be the case with home-owners' policies. Fine arts riders can usually be negotiated; provisions are not so stan-dardized as in homeowners' policies, and hence you have the opportunity to tailor a rider to your specific requirements. These riders can vary in how each insurance firm handles "exclusions" (i.e., kinds of artifacts or damage not covered), the reimbursing for lost, stolen, or damaged artifacts, and the coverage of material added after a rider's starting date. It will pay you to discuss your insurance needs with several firms.

Other points to be aware of, if you are considering a fine arts rider to your home-owner's policy:

1. Artifacts to be covered by a rider must be listed, although less valuable artifacts can often be grouped and listed accordingly. Any anticipated settlement is based on ac-tual cash value of the artifacts—which means you must make periodic appraisals and price adjustments, where necessary, and report your changes to the insurer.

2. The kinds of breakage or other damage that may occur should be described in the policy. (Some companies will not insure against breakage.)

3. Initial coverage under a fine arts rider usually entails your submitting, along with your application, a financial appraisal done by an independent source.

4. Be particularly alert to include coverage for damage to especially fragile objects and for "mysterious disappearance" of artifacts—i.e., those items that disappear but for which theft cannot be proven.

5. The insurer can rightfully insist that you take ordinary—perhaps even extraordi-nary—measures to protect your collection. Such measures might include environ-mental and security precautions such as those discussed earlier in this chapter. Some kind of continuously updated inventory is usually required for coverage, and you should maintain a working inventory, in any case. A photographic inventory is always best—photographs accompanied by accurate descriptions.

6. The question of insuring material that is in your possession while you are on a trip, or that you are displaying at a collectors' meeting, must be resolved too. Consider also the question of insuring material that is in your home but that does not belong to you—material you are holding for trade or purchase.

7. Remember to include in your coverage your reference library, display cases, and other objects used to house or otherwise improve the overall quality of your collec-tion. I think this coverage is worthwhile in view of the high cost of replacing such mate-rial.

MAINTAINING AN INVENTORY.   A thorough inventory stressing accuracy and com-pleteness is essential. If you cannot handle a photographic description, try to maintain a written version. What at first seems a chore becomes a rather pleasant task in time, as you begin to see the written evidence of the scope of your holdings. You are acquiring the "big picture," a view of the totality, which helps you to pinpoint the strengths and weaknesses of your collection and shows you where to add or to dispose. As I said pre-viously, an inventory is often required by insurers, but it is also an essential aid in revis-ing the value of different artifacts as the market changes.

Unfortunately, there is no comprehensive numbering system to designate political artifacts as there is for stamps and for coins. There is simply too much material of too varied a nature to permit easy cataloging. Such an overall system could not be insti-tuted without a large-scale cooperative effort by collectors. There are, however, several numbering systems that collectors use to designate specific kinds of artifacts, and new collectors should familiarize themselves with these.

1. The DeWitt system was devised by J. Doyle DeWitt, a pioneer collector of politi-cal Americana, whose collection is now owned by the University of Hartford. The DeWitt

numbering system applies only to lapel pieces in use between 1789 and 1889, as described and illustrated in DeWitt's book *A Century of Campaign Buttons*. (See the Bibliography for Chapter 3 for further information about this source and those that follow in this discussion.) An artifact may be listed by a dealer or collector as DWWHH 1840-24, meaning "DeWitt/William Henry Harrison/1840 campaign/artifact number 24." "DW" is usually assumed rather than written because his system is so widely used. But DeWitt's book does not include many items discovered after its publication in 1959, and so the phrase "unlisted in DeWitt" often appears in dealers' advertisements and auction catalogs. This reference work is virtually unobtainable; it sells for about $100 whenever it does appear on the market. I wrote a revised and expanded new edition in 1981 (see Bibliography, Chapter 4).

2. The Bristow IPBB system is primarily used with buttons issued since 1896. The letters refer to dealer Richard Bristow's *The Illustrated Political Button Book,* which has gone through several printings since its first appearance in 1971. It is essentially an illustrated checklist and price guide. Bristow uses candidates' initials and a four-digit code to identify campaign buttons. Thus AES0013 is the thirteenth Alfred E. Smith button in a series. Bristow has published other similar checklists, which can be purchased from him.

3. The Hake system was originated by dealer Theodore Hake and is geared to a code used in his three illustrated checklists and price guides. Hake uses a combination of candidate initials, the appropriate campaign year, a four-digit set, and a letter indicating the kind of artifact. The first number in the set refers to one of the three checklists in which an artifact is illustrated and priced; the remaining three places in the set indicate the number of a particular artifact. Thus, WHH1840–3019–B is a William Henry Harrison 1840 campaign bandanna and the nineteenth Harrison piece illustrated in Hake's *Political Buttons, Book III, 1789–1916.* Hake's first two checklists illustrated lapel items from the 1896 campaign on; only the third publication includes material from before 1896.

344A. This colorful red, white and blue window decal is sheer fantasy. It dates, I think, from the mid-1920s.

11
Fantasies and Reproductions

FANTASIES AND REPRODUCTIONS pose an extremely serious problem for political Americana collectors. Hardly a month goes by, it seems, when a collector does not discover a heretofore unknown fantasy or reproduction. The problem is so serious that the APIC maintains a standing committee on the subject and includes updated information in nearly every issue of its monthly publication *The Standard.* The APIC's voluminous and well-illustrated research is available to its members; much information in the following pages is taken from that source. I urge new collectors to begin familiarizing themselves with that research from the very moment they acquire their first campaign artifact.

New collectors should be aware of the Hobby Protection Act, which was passed by Congress and signed into law (Public Law 93 – 167) by Richard Nixon — his last such action before his resignation. Essentially P.L. 93 – 167 calls for imitations of various kinds of Americana to be marked "Reproduction" or with a similar term in a prominent place on the copy, and in a nonremovable manner. But in some cases copies of Americana do appear on the antiques market without such designation — either some manufacturers are unaware of the law or choose to disobey it. Some reproductions of lithographed tin campaign buttons are marked as the law requires, but the information is easily removed and the bared surface repainted. So, although political collectors do have the benefit of the law, that is not a substitute for a sound knowledge about fantasies and reproductions.

The APIC uses the archaic British word "brummagem," meaning a showy but worthless and inferior object, to describe political fantasies and reproductions. The word is so ugly, I think, that it is easily remembered. Political collectors use brummagem to describe the kind of material that is the subject of this chapter, viz., fantasies and reproductions. Such material is often showy and it is worthless, as uninformed collectors soon learn. Well over 90 percent of all fantasies and reproductions consist of pinback buttons. The remainder consists of copies of Washington inaugural buttons, certain medalets, some paper ephemera, and a few novelties.

Generally, fantasies are objects, usually buttons, depicting political subjects that were not used for campaign purposes. Reproductions are copies of artifacts, usually buttons, that actually were used in campaigns. Fantasies and reproductions appear

345. A striking early fantasy badge. It was issued by the National Republican League in 1906 to commemorate the Republican party's fiftieth anniversary. John Frémont was the party's first presidential nominee.

regularly during every presidential campaign season and some pieces appear to be re-issued every four years, although usually under different sponsorship. New collectors should expect no different in future campaigns. Even before the New Hampshire primary in February of a presidential year, we can expect to see fantasy buttons and reproductions of campaign buttons displayed in stores and advertised in national antiques publications.

This material originates from several sources: mail-order houses, business firms promoting a product, button manufacturers, individuals out to profit from the current interest in campaign buttons, even an occasional collector. Illegitimate buttons of one kind or another are found in abundance at flea markets, and they are advertised regularly in some antiques publications.

As already mentioned, not all fantasies and reproductions are produced to deliberately deceive anyone. Some fantasies are distributed by businesses that use buttons with political subjects as a feature of product promotion campaigns; General Motors Corporation, Abbott Laboratories, Kimberly-Clark Corporation, and the American Oil Company are examples. A few years ago a New York State history teacher in a small city ordered a number of buttons for use in a mock election being held by his students; the buttons read "Truman for President." These buttons have been a source of confusion to collectors ever since. They are fantasies, but like the fantasies issued by different businesses for product promotions, no deception was ever intended. They are also fakes, but none of us would know that if we did not know about their origin.

Nor is it easy to define a reproduction. Button manufacturers have been known to increase production of one or more button designs after a campaign is over in order to meet collectors'—or the general public's—demand. Such buttons are called *reruns.* An example: Possibly only 1 or 2 percent of all buttons picturing or naming the 1972 Democratic candidates George McGovern and Thomas Eagleton were actually issued before Eagleton was dropped from the ticket and replaced by R. Sargent Shriver. A deluge of McGovern/Eagleton buttons was produced throughout the campaign and for a while afterward for the sole purpose of profiting from the notoriety. Another example: The lasting affection of many Americans for John F. Kennedy has generated a profusion of buttons picturing him, and they are, flea market dealers assure me, good sellers. A few years ago buttons came on the collector market bearing the names of candidates from the 1940 through the 1960 campaigns, but all looked suspiciously "new." The manufacturer did not claim that the buttons actually had been used in the appropriate campaigns; apparently they had not been "buttoned-up" (decal, pin, and frame all brought together) at the time they should have been. Later, the material was sold to an individual who prepared them properly and then marketed them. The buttons in these three examples are reruns, but are they also reproductions because they were not actually used in a campaign? No one can say. Such examples represent that gray area of fantasies and reproductions that defies solution.

Recognizing fantasies and reproductions is not as easy as it may seem, either. As a first step, new collectors should familiarize themselves with the indispensable APIC research on the subject. Bringing suspect pieces to collectors' meetings is also useful, for experienced collectors can be helpful. Also, at meetings, there usually are many artifacts—especially buttons—on view with which comparisons can be made.

Button Fantasies and Reproductions

POLITICAL BUTTON FANTASIES.   Many fantasy buttons really are showy (though worthless), and they can be appealing to inexperienced collectors. Fantasy buttons are best defined in depth by dividing them into four categories. The first category includes buttons picturing presidents who were in office before there were campaign buttons. The second includes buttons issued by manufacturers as a means of promoting their products. The first category is not a problem for collectors once they are familiar with dates of presidents' tenures and know when celluloid and lithographed buttons were first used. Nor, with a few exceptions, is material in the second category much of a problem. But the exceptions could be deceptive. Examples are the General Motors set and the Red Garter Saloon Coolidge button—both of which I will discuss shortly. The G.M. set is unmarked and the tavern's trademark can be removed and the surface repainted. Generally, however, there has not been a conscious attempt to mislead. But the third category is particularly obnoxious. In it are buttons distributed by mail-order firms for sale in stores, in gift catalogs, and (increasingly) by various hobby publications. The fourth category is devoted to out-and-out fakes. The last two categories are of the most concern: Mail-order houses frequently make extravagant claims for the buttons they sell, and fakes are a deliberate attempt to deceive.

Note, in Illustration 346, the buttons picturing Franklin Pierce and Ulysses S. Grant.

346. The buttons illustrated are near to their actual sizes. The McKinley button at upper left is representative of a small group picturing different presidents issued some years ago by Westinghouse Electric Company. These buttons all have advertising slogans around the lower rim, hence are easily recognized as fantasies. The McKinley button at upper center and the Harding button are out-and-out fakes—both have wide collar flanges (see Ill. 357). *Courtesy Drost Collection.*

I cannot attribute the Pierce button, but the Grant buttons date from the turn of the century and may have been used at a Grand Army encampment. Similar buttons picturing all presidents through William McKinley were distributed as premiums by manufacturers of gum and tobacco products during the same period (Ill. 347). Another prominent example is buttons picturing Abraham Lincoln that were issued during the centennial of his birth in 1909. Quite a few different varieties are known.

Buttons typical of those distributed to advertise a company's product are pictured in Illustration 348. Those shown are all 2 inches in diameter and were issued by General Motors Corporation in 1968 as a feature of a promotional campaign advertising Chevrolet trucks. The buttons appeared originally mounted on a card, as pictured, which carried various messages; the bottom button with the legend "You Can't Beat a Chevrolet Fleet" obviously indicates this set's purpose. If these buttons are found separated from the card, however, then attribution is impossible because there is no marking on any of them. The Eisenhower and Roosevelt (Franklin) buttons are large-size approximations of much smaller common campaign buttons; hence they can be considered reproductions. The Wilson, Kennedy, and Hoover buttons are simply fakes, although they were never intended to mislead.

Seagram Distillery issued a set of nine lapel tabs in the late 1960s. Each tab is about 2 inches in diameter and bears color pictures of Wilson, the two Roosevelts, Eisenhower, and Coolidge, along with two slogans—"A Full Dinner Pail" and "Keep Cool with Coolidge." On the reverse of each tab is the inscription "Vote for Seagram's 7/It's America's Whiskey." Tabs, by the way, are circular or rectangular—or occasionally irregularly shaped—tin lapel pieces that were attached by a projection either folded over

347. A typical set of premium buttons from the early 1900s. All presidents but McKinley were in office before there were campaign buttons, so the McKinley button may be deceptive. *Courtesy Drost Collection.*

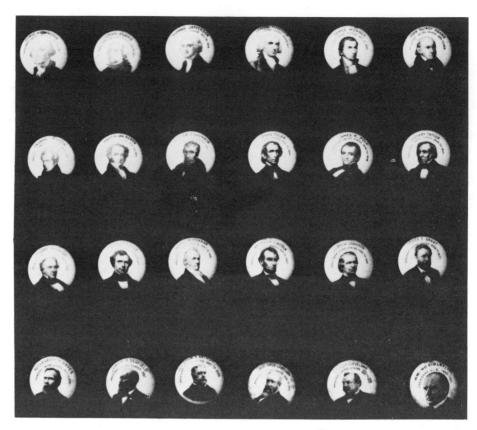

348. The General Motors set. When seen in their original context, these buttons do look more like advertising devices.

349. Representative Seagram Distillery promotional tabs. The company's logo appears on the back of all tabs in the set.

the top of the lapel or put through its buttonhole. Genuine political tabs carrying candidates' names were seldom over an inch in diameter or larger than 1 ½ inches by ½ inch. One of the more amusing examples in this category is a button picturing Calvin Coolidge with the message "Coolidge for President/Red Garter Campaign Headquarters." This button, along with a window decal and several picture cards bearing a similar message, was distributed in 1966 by San Francisco's Red Garter Tavern, a self-styled "banjo bar," as part of a publicity campaign. Again, there was no attempt to deliberately mislead.

Fantasies sold through mail-order firms are usually accompanied by statements suggesting that a buyer is getting "a piece of America's heritage," or "can now wear an authentic copy [sic] of a memorable original." Some firms also include, for an extra dollar or two, a fancy frame decked out in patriotic colors. Most firms include a mixture of reproductions and fantasies in their offerings, but the firm I am listing at this point, Art Fair (or Art Forum), has offered in past years a colorful set of nine celluloid fantasies, each 2 inches in diameter, that was apparently manufactured in a large amount because buttons from this set turn up at flea markets very often. As Illustration 351 points out, only the Taft and Teddy Roosevelt buttons could actually have been used in a campaign, but no originals of these two buttons are known. Collectors should look for the

351. The Art Fair set. Only the Roosevelt and Taft buttons may be troublesome, as the other ones picture subjects in existence before there were buttons.

350. The Crackerbarrel Company's advertisement for their "authentic 'election collection'" that is described as a "rare and remarkable [sic!] keepsake [and] . . . an impressive addition to any home." For an additional fee these buttons were mounted in "walnut finished real wood frames."

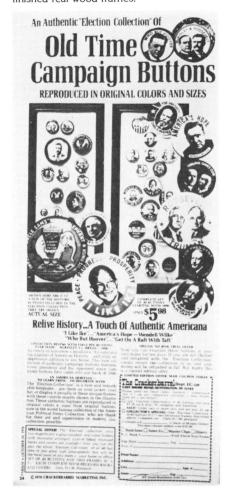

352. Most of these fakes are difficult to distinguish from originals. Originals of the top three center buttons have diameters of 1¼ inches; with the exception of the Wilson, the four other buttons in the top row have been darkened by artificial aging (especially evident on the McKinley-Roosevelt). Originals of the Stevenson-Sparkman are 3½ inches in diameter. Collectors must check the back, general appearance, and the type of collar (Ill. 360) of the other button. Even then, one cannot be sure. *Courtesy Drost Collection.*

inscription, which can be removed, on the bottom of the button: "Art Fair 1967 New York, NY. 10001."

To sum up, there are two kinds of fake buttons—fantasies, which I am discussing here, and reproductions, which are the subject of the following section. Both kinds can be distinguished from originals by using the same criteria. Look carefully at Illustration 352; it pictures a number of fantasy fakes that could pass as legitimate issues.

POLITICAL BUTTON REPRODUCTIONS.   The quality of campaign button reproductions ranges from the obviously fake to a level that defies distinguishing from originals. Many buttons, from the 1896 campaign on, have been reproduced; no major party candidate seems to have escaped being pictured on fakes. Both common and scarce buttons, including a few picturing third-party candidates, ranging in diameter from ¾ inch to over 3 inches, have been copied. There is no discernible pattern, although some originals have been copied more than others.

I have selected for listing here those sets of buttons new collectors are most likely to encounter; many of these fakes first appeared as parts of sets made up of forty different buttons. Sets usually include a few fantasies—i.e., buttons picturing presidents whose administrations occurred before there were campaign buttons. Some fakes appear time and again; and the marking on a button's curl (the part that tucks around the pin)—top or bottom—changes according to the seller. Some buttons are duplicated, therefore, among the sets of reproductions listed below.

A. United States Boraxo Company: a set of twenty-five lithographed buttons described in the company's advertising as "historic campaign buttons . . . authentic full-size, full-color replicas of actual campaign buttons" (Ill. 353). This set was issued in

353. United States Boraxo Company's advertising for their button reproductions and fantasies; note the offer of a velour-covered wall plaque for an additional fee. *Courtesy Drost Collection.*

354. A close-up of the Boraxo buttons. The Grant, Cleveland, Harrison, Arthur, and Garfield buttons are obvious fantasies.

355. The American Oil Company set. All buttons shown are lithographs, but most originals were celluloids.

356. Front and back of button cards that were given by AMOCO gas station dealers to motorists who made purchases. On these cards the buttons are described as reproductions. *Courtesy Drost Collection.*

1972 on the occasion of the company's one hundredth anniversary; the buttons range in diameter from ⅞ inch to 1¼ inches and each is marked "Reproduction" on the bottom curl.

B. American Oil Company: a set of thirty-eight lithographed buttons, 1³⁄₁₆ to 1¾ inches in diameter, many of which are larger than the originals. Each button is marked "A-O-1972-1" (through #38) on the bottom curl (see Ill. 355).

C. Abbott Laboratories: a set of twelve lithographed buttons in different diameters. This set was issued in 1968; "Repro 68" is marked on the upper curl and "Abbott" on the lower curl.

D. Kimberly-Clark (Kleenex Paper Products): a set of thirty-five lithographed buttons issued in 1968. Each button is marked "Kleenex Tissues '68" on the lower curl; diameters range from ⅞ inch to 2¼ inches (Ill. 357).

E. Crackerbarrel (a mail-order firm): a set of forty lithographed buttons picturing

357. The Kimberly-Clark set. Shown here are twenty-nine of the thirty-five buttons in this set. The Crackerbarrel set is exactly the same but includes two added 1972 Nixon and McGovern buttons.

candidates from 1896 through 1972 (the year of issue of this set) (Ills. 357, 358) that range in diameter from ⅞ inch to 2¼ inches. Printed on the back of each button is "Crackerbarrel/Farmingdale, N.Y. 11735/(Reproductions)/Limited Edition." This set contains the same reproductions as the Kimberly-Clark set, but with five additional buttons including two of the 1972 campaign.

F. The Liberty Mint of Teaneck, N.J.: a set of forty-one celluloid buttons (Ill. 359) picturing candidates from 1896 through 1972; each button is ⅞ inch in diameter. Marked on the bottom curl of each button is "© 1972/The Liberty Mint." Individual buttons in this set can be deceptive as the identification does not show clearly.

G. A set of forty-one lithographed buttons picturing candidates from 1896 through 1972: each button is ⅞ inch in diameter. Printed on the back of each button is "1976 Reproduction." Buttons in this set are exact lithograph versions of the Liberty Mint set.

H. Procter and Gamble, Inc.: a set of thirty-eight celluloid buttons was distributed by this company in 1976 as a promotional feature for Bold detergent. Each button has an outer rim composed of red, white, and blue stripes, and is marked "Reproduction by S & B Co. 1976" on the lower curl; diameters range from 1¾ to 3 inches. The coloring and photographic quality of these buttons are poor—they look like fakes.

I. A set of thirteen lithographed buttons, in different diameters, picturing candidates from the 1916 through the 1952 campaigns. Each button is marked "Japan" on the lower curl.

New collectors are urged to examine carefully Illustration 352. It pictures different reproductions that are not parts of sets, but they are distinguished according to the criteria given in the next section.

IDENTIFYING CAMPAIGN BUTTON REPRODUCTIONS.   The following criteria for determining a button's authenticity are, at best, a guide. A button is suspect if just one of these points is met.

1) Many reproductions (Ill. 360) are lithographed copies of original buttons that were issued in celluloid form only. Most buttons in the sets described above are examples.

2) Reproductions frequently appear in different diameters than the originals.

3) Examine a suspect button's photography. Reproductions may lack sharpness of detail; letters may be ever so slightly blurred. Sometimes a reflection of the camera flash is evident on the decal. Perhaps the portrait may be a bit fuzzy.

4) Note the graphic style. Ornate designs are not typical after 1920; plain unadorned designs are not typical before 1920. But, obviously, there are exceptions.

5) Examine the paper decal if the suspect button is a celluloid. Decals in early original buttons have a smooth untextured surface. Decals on some reproductions have a slightly dimpled or grainy surface.

6) Examine the back of a button. Most original buttons, both celluloids and lithographs, have plain unpainted backs; reproductions may have ivory or cream painted backs—but so do some modern originals.

7) Look for evidence of rust. Aged rust looks duller than fresh rust, and may appear in random spots on the back of a pin. Artificially added rust may appear as a large blot in the center or in a uniform pattern around the inside of the rim.

8) Concerning celluloids: Look at the kind of collar, or flange, attached on the reverse to hold the celluloid in place. The collars on original earlier buttons usually are narrow; reproductions will often have a wider collar. This point is helpful in authenticating buttons made before 1960; after that date buttons—originals and reproductions—will have the same kind of wide collars (Ill. 360).

9) On reproductions, the colors may not be in the same combinations as on the originals, or there may be variations in color depth, or perhaps different colors entirely.

10) Look for evidence of touch-up painting on the curl of suspect lithographed buttons. A difference in shade would suggest that a mark indicating the button was a reproduction had been scraped off.

358. The back of each button in the Crackerbarrel set is marked as shown here.

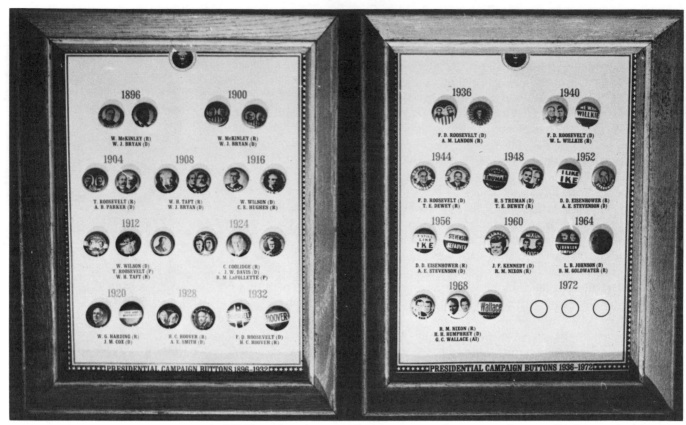

359. The Liberty Mint set mounted in wood frames. The colors of these celluloid reproductions are not as bright, nor are the color contrasts as sharp, as on the originals. These differences are also true of the lithographed reproductions. *Courtesy Drost Collection.*

11) Examine the overall appearance of a suspect button. If a button looks like a fake, it probably is. The Proctor and Gamble set mentioned previously is a good example.

Reproductions of Other Campaign Artifacts

With the exception of campaign and Washington inaugural buttons, reproductions of other political artifacts are not generally a problem for experienced collectors. Copies of other artifacts do show up frequently, but most of these copies are fairly easy to detect once one knows what to look for. As is also true of campaign buttons, there is no discernible pattern. Some reproductions were made recently; others were made during the nineteenth century. Some copies, especially of campaign medalets, show careless workmanship, and other copies are much scarcer than their originals.

Listed and illustrated—where possible—are the reproductions that I know of. By and large, these reproductions are known to experienced collectors; an awareness of their existence should be basic information for new collectors. Undoubtedly other reproductions exist that could be "discovered" at any time, particularly during campaign season.

360. At right is the back of a reproduction; note its wide collar and painted surface (but these conditions are not usually enough for a certain identification). The original at the left has a narrow collar and a random rust pattern.

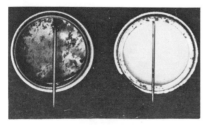

REPRODUCTIONS OF WASHINGTON INAUGURAL BUTTONS. Originals of these buttons are scarce. They are excellent examples of button craftsmanship of the period; and—the major reason for copying—they have an enduring appeal to collectors and noncollectors alike. Possibly the first copies were made in the late 1880s during the centennial of Washington's inauguration in 1889. Copies have appeared sporadically ever since, most recently during the 1976 bicentennial.

Modern reproductions are easily found. Many are sold in gift shops in the form of cuff links or lapel pins, used as magazine subscription bonuses, and sold in museum gift shops. The major characteristic of modern copies is that they are produced usually in silver, lead, or a bright—almost white—brass. The originals are known *only* in copper, deep yellow brass, and pewter.

A. The reproductions most likely to be a problem for collectors are those distributed in the late 1880s by a Philadelphia source. These deceptive copies were cut from brass sheet used by a scales manufacturer; as a result, the reverses of these copies may show one or two numbers or a number of letters. Other copies from this period have thicker shanks (the button loop) than found on originals; or have the inscription on the reverse "Long Live the President" (no original has a reverse inscription); or are struck on early English pennies or colonial Connecticut and Vermont cents. Alphaeus H. Albert, an authority on Washington inaugurals, says that some of these copies appear to have been double struck (which can cause an ever so slight double impression of the image), unlike the originals. Still other reproductions are octagonal in shape; the originals are round. Some of these copies are illustrated in Albert's *Record of American Uniform and Historical Buttons* (see Bibliography).

B. A single reproduction showing the monogram "GW" within an oval. This piece is known in brass and silver, and is marked "Copy" on the reverse. The maker is not known, but it is a modern reproduction.

C. Liberty Village, Flemington, New Jersey (a mail-order firm?): This source offered a set of four different reproductions during the mid-1970s. The same set was offered, also, by American Heritage Publishing Company. Each reproduction is $1^{13}/16$ inches in diameter and is made from brass. An incursed inscription (letters cut below the surface level) on the reverse reads "Repro 74/Liberty Village."

D. Smithsonian Institution. A set of six buttons in sterling silver was issued by this source during the bicentennial year. These buttons, copies of coat and sleeve inaugural originals, come in diameters of $1^{13}/16$ and $1^{7}/8$ inches. They are well identified as reproductions: On the reverse of each copy is an incursed outline of the Smithsonian "castle" and the inscription "Smithsonian Institution/Stieff/Sterling."

E. A very obvious fake is a brass two-piece button with a lacquered finish and an unmarked reverse; it is about $1^{13}/16$ inches in diameter. This copy comes on a card labeled "Majestic Buttons/75¢"; printed on the back of the card is "Continental Merchandising Co., Div. of Kingsport International, Inc., Concord, Calif. Made in Japan."

Collector Donald Ackerman's exemplary criteria for distinguishing authentic buttons from reproductions details what collectors should know. All Washington inaugural buttons were handcrafted; they were punched out of sheets of metal, and the designs and shanks were applied by hand. Originals, therefore, lack a finished look; their edges will be sharp and uneven. (Be wary of any example with perfectly smooth and rounded edges.) All authentic specimens were cut from fairly thin planchets, $1/16$ inch or less, and are not perfectly flat; when viewed from a side, they show a slight irregularity or waviness where the metal has expanded or bent under pressure from the die. Originals will show signs of wear, perhaps minute scratches, or a patina will be evident. Beware of a button that polishes up easily and is smooth and shiny. No originals were cast: Casting marks—pitting and minute specks of metal—lettering with rounded edges or uneven surfaces, or filled letters are evidence of casting. No original was inscribed on its reverse, although the design will sometimes show through.

REPRODUCTIONS OF CAMPAIGN MEDALETS. From the viewpoint of political Americana collectors, reproductions of campaign medalets are not a serious problem. Only a few medalets have been reproduced, and these copies are generally poorly made. Once a collector has seen an original (Ill. 361), spotting the differences in a copy is not that difficult. A few early and rare medalets have been reproduced, which is sufficient reason for collectors to have a basic understanding of how to recognize political numismatic fakes.

There are five basic recognition factors for identifying reproductions of medalets. Any combination of these factors should suffice for a proper identification.

1) Only a very few genuine medalets were issued in lead, but reproductions are often made in that metal. Some lead copies are also gilded or have a silverlike finish, which wears easily, thus leaving minute traces of gilt or unsightly blotches.

2) Examine the surface of a suspect piece—with a magnifying glass, if necessary. Reproductions are often cast poorly: Look for a grainy surface (caused by a sand mold); letters with rounded edges; tiny pits where the metal did not flow; lack of sharpness in an image and other parts of a design.

3) Examine the rim. Some reproductions have seams where the sides were joined together by electrolysis—i.e., depositing a coat of copper, for example, over an impression taken from both sides of a genuine specimen, which is secured to a base metal core—lead usually—and closed, thus causing a seam.

4) Note the diameter: Some reproductions have different diameters from their originals.

5) Note the design: Some reproductions have blank reverses, as do some originals. Others have designs on the reverses, indicating their use in anniversary celebrations of earlier political events. An example is a particular 1860 Lincoln medalet that was reproduced to mark the centennial of Lincoln's first inauguration, but similar reproductions picturing other presidents are known.

The following list of political medalet reproductions is not complete; included here are those copies that collectors are most likely to see. Remember that nearly all nine-

361. The original medalets illustrated here should serve as a basis for comparing with reproductions. Depicted on the reverse of the Clay medalet is a factory, sailing ship, and an inscription—all details are sharply defined.

teenth-century political medalets were well made; their details are usually sharply defined; copper, brass, and silver specimens may be nicely toned with a patina; and I know of no original medalet with a seamed rim. Where applicable, I have included the appropriate DeWitt number as a further aid in distinguishing authentic specimens from their copies. Where possible, each copy is illustrated by an original example (Ill. 361):

Thomas Jefferson (DWTJ1800–1). Originals and copies are 45 millimeters in diameter. Originals are known in bronze, silver, and white metal; known reproductions exist in iron (with a grainy surface), brass, and lead that has been colored brown to give the copy the appearance of a bronze or copper original.

John Quincy Adams (DWJQA1824–1). Originals and copies are 51 millimeters in diameter. Originals are known in silver and white metal; known reproductions exist in iron (with a grainy surface) and brass, and apparently are mates to the Jefferson copies. A brown-colored lead reproduction may exist also.

Henry Clay (DWHC1844–6). A reproduction in the same diameter exists in lead: The bust of Clay is not sharp and letters in the inscription are rounded and somewhat vaguely defined; there are several obvious pit marks and the "N" in Henry is bent. Altogether a crude copy.

Abraham Lincoln (DWAL1860–31). Originals and copies are 34 millimeters in diameter. Originals are known in silver, dark copper, and white metal; copies are in glossy light copper, brass, and a silverlike finish, and they are a millimeter or two thicker than originals. These copies originated in Illinois, I think, and commemorate the centennial of Lincoln's first inauguration.

Samuel J. Tilden (DWSJT1876–6). Originals and copies are 31 millimeters in diameter. Originals exist in copper, brass, and white metal. The known copy exists in white metal, but when compared to an original specimen in the same metal, the differences are apparent: rounded letters, surface blemishes, and a seam around the rim.

Benjamin Harrison (DWBH1888–8). The original exists in several different metals, and all varieties picture George Washington on their reverses. The known copy is poorly made of a base metal—probably lead—has a grainy surface, and is pitted. The reverse is blank.

William Jennings Bryan. A poorly made copy of a silver Bryan dollar, Zerbe 5 (see Bibliography, Chapter 3), is known. The copy is in white metal, has numerous pits, rounded letters, and is a few millimeters smaller in diameter than the original's 52 millimeters.

REPRODUCTIONS OF POLITICAL PAPER ARTIFACTS. There are surprisingly few political paper reproductions, which makes matters easier for collectors. A particular kind of political paper reproduction, which should fool no one and is not intended to deceive, is the variety of campaign posters, prints, and cartoons published for use in elementary and secondary-school social studies programs. Most examples are clearly labeled as facsimiles or reproductions, have an explanatory text on the front or back, and are usually printed on heavy plain or glossy stock that is totally unlike the dull wood- or rag-based paper actually used in early campaigns. These reproductions look like what they are—classroom teaching materials.

But there are a few reproductions of political paper artifacts that can be deceptive. A number of reproduced campaign tickets—perhaps thirty in all—were distributed in the mid-1960s by a Long Island company. These copies picture the candidates, symbols, and slogans used on original nineteenth-century campaign tickets. Copies are known in two sizes, 8½ by 11 inches and 5 by 4 inches. The printing is somewhat indistinct, and some copies have been aged artificially. The chief identifying feature to look for is the letters PHL, which appear somewhere on the upper part of each ticket.

Earlier, I mentioned the fantasy button issued by the Red Garter Tavern in San Francisco. This source also issued four different cards, 3¼ by 2½ inches, and one automobile window decal, picturing Calvin Coolidge, together with the inscription "Keep Cool with Coolidge for President." Printed prominently on each item is "Red Garter—S.F. Campaign Headquarters." Coolidge is also pictured on a red, white, and blue automobile window decal that says "Keep Cool with Coolidge for President/Farrell's Ice Cream Parlour Restaurants." This decal and the Red Garter material are fantasies, in that no such originals exist.

An extremely deceptive reproduction to watch out for is a copy of an admission ticket to the Johnson impeachment proceedings. Originals are popular with collectors, and one can easily buy a copy without suspecting. Visually, the copy is an exact duplication of the original: It is printed in black ink on heavy blue stock and is dated "March 31, 1868." In tiny letters below the lower margin is "Reproduction July 1974," which can be easily cut off. Be wary if you are offered a Johnson impeachment ticket with its lower edge trimmed right to the margin.

REPRODUCTIONS OF OTHER POLITICAL ARTIFACTS.   Collectors need to be aware of a scattering of other reproductions. A copy of an 1872 Horace Greeley cast-iron matchbox is particularly deceptive. The copy can be distinguished from an original in three ways: 1) the bust is attached to its support by wires, but on the original the bust is riveted to its support; 2) the hat has a grainy surface; 3) stamped on the reverse is "LB 77/3"; there are no stampings on originals (Ill. 260). It is very possible that the Grant mate of the Greeley original has also been reproduced.

It was probably some time after 1972 that a number of jackknives with white plastic handles began appearing at flea markets. One variety depicts the Confederate flag, a standing soldier, and a cannon on one side; on the other side is the inscription "'For States Rights'/Vote Thurmond & Wright!/C 1948." The "C 1948" is apparently meant to imitate a copyright date, but the "C" is not circled, as is customary. Two varieties picture George McGovern and Richard Nixon with their respective running mates; a fourth variety pictures George Wallace on one side and the American flag on the other. These last three knives are dated "1972." All examples I have seen are in "like new" condition, and all are fantasies (Ill. 362).

I am unable to illustrate a particular cast-brass watch fob that has been reproduced. Apparently the copies were struck with the original die, thus making it nearly impossible to distinguish them from originals. Raised likenesses of Taft and Sherman are depicted, together with the inscription "Our Choice/Taft & Sherman." The reverse surfaces on copies are perhaps a bit more irregular than are those on the originals.

One of the oddest political fakes—a fantasy, actually—is an opaque white glass beer bottle slightly over 6 inches high. Inscribed in blue and red on the base is "Keep Cool & Keep Coolidge with Near Beer." I have no other information about this bottle except that it appears often at flea markets and brings respectable prices. It seems always to be found in pristine condition.

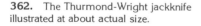

362.   The Thurmond-Wright jackknife illustrated at about actual size.

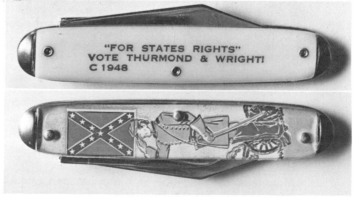

Appendixes
GLOSSARY

These are the terms used most often by political collectors.

Celluloid. Name of a material used on the surfaces of campaign buttons, but a few lapel pins of solid celluloid were used briefly in the 1880s.

Fantasy. Any object depicting a political subject, but not actually used in a political campaign or for another political purpose.

Ferrotype. Term used for a lapel pin with brass or cloth-covered frame containing a tintype photograph of a candidate.

Flasher. Plastic lapel pin, up to 3 inches in diameter, that shows a presidential nominee's picture when tilted one way and the vice-presidential nominee's picture when tilted the opposite way.

Foxing. Stains or spots, caused by dampness, rust, or mold, that appear on paper artifacts, including the decals used on celluloid buttons.

Jugate. Any campaign item picturing a party's presidential and vice-presidential nominees together. Commonly used as an adjective; thus, "a jugate button."

Lithograph. Campaign buttons stamped from tin and in use after 1920 are usually called lithographs. Also, a general term used by collectors when referring to prints, posters, and broadsides.

Medal. In political numismatics, medal is a general term for medallic issues ranging in diameter from 1¾ to about 3 inches. This term is sometimes used instead of medallion.

Medallion. The term for numismatic issues ranging in diameter from about 2½ to over 3 inches. But *medal* is more commonly used by political collectors.

Medalet. Numismatic issues ranging up to about 1¾ inches in diameter. Most political medallic pieces are medalets.

Name button. Celluloid and lithograph buttons bearing one or more candidates' names, as "Stevenson for President" or "Coolidge and Dawes."

Obverse. The front design on numismatic issues or on bottles, flasks, and various other two-sided items.

Pinback. A synonym for modern campaign buttons; it refers to the spring wire in the button back by which the button is pinned to a lapel.

Planchet. A flat metal disk ready for stamping or the engraving of a design.

Reproduction. A copy of a political artifact manufactured after the campaign it purports to represent.

Ribbon. A strip of cloth bearing pictures of candidates or political slogans that could be attached to the lapel. Early nineteenth-century ribbons were also used as bookmarks.

Ribbon badge. A political ribbon to which a medalet or campaign button is attached, or a medallic issue suspended from a ribbon—e.g., many inauguration and convention pieces.

Shell badge. Lapel pin in plain or elaborate pattern bearing a candidate's picture; stamped from thin brass or copper sheets. Shell badges with a moving part are called mechanical badges.

Slogan button. Any button bearing a political expression. Best-known examples are the 1940 Willkie buttons with slogans critical of Franklin Roosevelt, such as "Dr. Jekyl of Hyde Park," "Out Stealing Third," and "No Franklin the First."

Stickpin. A metal or celluloid button with an attached pin as much as 2 inches in length, which is pinned to a lapel or inserted into a necktie.

Stud. A lapel piece with a projection on the back for insertion in a lapel buttonhole.

Tab. Tin lapel piece that is attached by folding the top part over upper edge of a lapel or through the buttonhole.

Three-D. Term designating political artifacts such as glass, ceramics, and novelties that have more than two sides.

Token. A numismatic issue used as a substitute for money. Strictly speaking, a few 1864 Lincoln and McClellan issues can rightfully be called tokens because they were used briefly in place of money during the Civil War. However, through long usage of the term, medalets picturing Andrew Jackson and other subjects that were issued during the 1830s are called tokens; specifically, Hard Times tokens.

White metal. A metallic mixture composed mostly of lead and tin; it was a popular material for nineteenth-century numismatic issues, and was called tin by numismatists in that period. The silverlike sheen of new white metal soon wears off in use, leaving a dull gray surface color.

CAMPAIGN SLOGANS

NO CAMPAIGN WOULD be complete without slogans to rally the party faithful and to create favorable candidate images with voters. Only a few slogans manage to survive elections: Some do so because they are alliterative; others seem pertinent in later campaigns; still others survive because they recall some important event in our historical past. Here are my favorite slogans; most of them could easily provide the nucleus for a small specialized collection.

A Public Office Is a Public Trust. This slogan was taken from a speech given by Grover Cleveland when he was governor of New York. The slogan was used extensively in his 1884, 1888, and 1892 campaigns, and was revived during the Watergate scandal in 1973.

Free Soil, Free Speech, and Frémont. This 1856 slogan is one of the more alliterative in presidential campaign history. It is the best known among several slogans that played on Frémont's name. Democrats countered with a few of their own, one of which—Free Love Frémont—was a coarse allusion to Frémont's illegitimate birth.

The Full Dinner Pail. This 1896 and 1900 Republican campaign slogan called attention to the Republicans' perennial advocation of full employment and prosperous factories. The slogan helped generate an interesting variety of artifacts that would make a fine specialized collection.

I Like Ike. The most succinct slogan ever used. It probably first appeared in the late 1940s, when Dwight Eisenhower was being wooed as a presidential candidate by both major parties. It reappeared in the 1956 campaign as "I Still Like Ike."

Peace, Protection, and Prosperity. This is the hoariest slogan in presidential campaign history. It has been used by both major parties for over a century and half, and shows no inclination of being given the long-overdue burial that it deserves.

Tippecanoe and Tyler Too! One of the best-remembered campaign slogans. In 1840 it re-minded voters of William Henry Harrison's victory over Chief Tecumseh at Tippecanoe Creek, In-diana, in 1811. "Tyler Too" referred to John Tyler, who became the nation's first accidental presi-dent (critics called him "His Accidency") following Harrison's death from pneumonia a month after his inauguration.

Vote the Land Free. The campaign slogan of the 1848 Free-Soil party, whose members were fundamentally opposed to the extension of slavery into the new states and territories. This slogan appears on a few leaflets supporting former president and Free-Soil nominee Martin Van Buren. But collectors know the slogan best as a stamped impression on copper pennies of the day—a decidedly clever idea, to use the nation's currency for political propaganda—at least until Con-gress declared such a practice illegal.

16−1. One of William Jennings Bryan's slogans in the 1896 silver/gold campaign. Bryan argued for a national monetary standard based upon sixteen parts silver to one part gold. Many Republi-can-issued Bryan "dollars" ridiculed this slogan, and the Democrats issued a number of cam-paign shells, studs, and buttons—all of which make a good subject for a specialized collection.

WINNING AND LOSING CANDIDATES

The following listing is intended as an aid for assigning material to the proper campaign. I have included only those candidates who received electoral votes.

A = American party
AF = Anti-Federalist
AM = Anti-Masonic party
CU = Constitution party
D = Democratic party
DN = Northern Democratic party
DR = Democrat Republican party
DS = Southern Democratic party
F = Federalist party
I = Independent
ID = Independent Democratic party
NR = National Republican party
P = Populist party
PG = Progressive party
R = Republican party
STR = States Rights Democratic party
W = Whig party

1789	1792
George Washington	George Washington (F)
and	and
John Adams	John Adams

George Clinton (AF)
Thomas Jefferson (AF)
Aaron Burr (AF)

1796

John Adams (F)
Thomas Jefferson (DR), Vice-President
Thomas Pinckney (F)
Aaron Burr (DR)

1800

Thomas Jefferson (DR)
Aaron Burr (DR), Vice-President
John Adams (F)
Charles Pinckney (F)
John Jay (F)

1804

Thomas Jefferson (DR) and George Clinton	Charles Pinckney (F) and Rufus King

1808

James Madison (DR) and George Clinton	Charles Pinckney (F) and Rufus King

1812

James Madison (DR) and Elbridge Gerry	DeWitt Clinton (F) and Jared Ingersoll

1816

James Monroe (DR) and Daniel Tompkins	Rufus King (F) and John Howard

1820

James Monroe (DR) and Daniel Tompkins	No opposition

1824

John Quincy Adams (DR)
Andrew Jackson (DR)
William Crawford (DR)
Henry Clay (DR)

No candidate had a majority in 1824, and so the House of Representatives chose the president from among the three candidates with the highest number of electoral votes. Clay gave his votes to Adams, thus ensuring Adams's victory. John C. Calhoun received the highest number of electoral votes, from among several candidates, for vice-president.

1828

Andrew Jackson (DR) and John C. Calhoun	John Quincy Adams (NR) and Richard Rush, William Smith

1832

Andrew Jackson (DR) and Martin Van Buren	Henry Clay (W) and John Sergeant

John Floyd (ID)
and
Henry Lee

William Wirt (AM)
and
Amos Ellmaker

1836

Martin Van Buren (D)
and
Richard Johnson

William Henry Harrison (W)
and
Francis Granger

Hugh White (W)
Daniel Webster (W)
Willie Mangum (I)

1840

William Henry Harrison (W)
and
John Tyler

Martin Van Buren (D)
and
Richard Johnson

1844

James K. Polk (D)
and
George Dallas

Henry Clay (W)
and
Theodore Frelinghuysen

1848

Zachary Taylor (W)
and
Millard Fillmore

Lewis Cass (D)
and
William Butler

1852

Franklin Pierce (D)
and
William King

Winfield Scott (W)
and
William Graham

1856

James Buchanan (D)
and
John C. Breckinridge

John C. Frémont (R)
and
William Dayton

Millard Fillmore (A)
and
Andrew J. Donelson

1860

Abraham Lincoln (R)
and
Hannibal Hamlin

Stephen Douglas (DN)
and
Herschell Johnson

John C. Breckinridge (DS)
and
Joseph Lane

John Bell (CU)
and
Edward Everett

Confederate States of America: 1861
Jefferson Davis
and
Alexander Stephens

	1864	
Abraham Lincoln (R) and Andrew Johnson		George McClellan (D) and George Pendleton

	1868	
Ulysses S. Grant (R) and Schuyler Colfax		Horatio Seymour (D) and Francis Blair, Jr.

	1872	
Ulysses S. Grant (R) and Henry Wilson		Horace Greeley (D) and B. Gratz Brown

	1876	
Rutherford Hayes (R) and William Wheeler		Samuel J. Tilden (D) and Thomas Hendricks

	1880	
James A. Garfield (R) and Chester A. Arthur		Winfield S. Hancock (D) and William English

	1884	
Grover Cleveland (D) and Thomas Hendricks		James G. Blaine (R) and John Logan

	1888	
Benjamin Harrison (R) and Levi Morton		Grover Cleveland (D) and Allan Thurmond

	1892	
Grover Cleveland (D) and Adlai Stevenson		Benjamin Harrison (R) and Whitlaw Reid
		James Weaver (P) and James Field

	1896	
William McKinley (R) and Garret Hobart		William J. Bryan (D) and Arthur Sewell

William McKinley (R) and Theodore Roosevelt		William J. Bryan (D) and Adlai Stevenson

	1904	
Theodore Roosevelt (R) and Charles Fairbanks		Alton Parker (D) and Henry Davis

	1908	
William H. Taft (R) and James Sherman		William J. Bryan (D) and John Kern

1912	
Woodrow Wilson (D) and Thomas Marshall	Theodore Roosevelt (PG) and Hiram Johnson
	William H. Taft (R) and James Sherman

1916	
Woodrow Wilson (D) and Thomas Marshall	Charles E. Hughes (R) and Charles Fairbanks

1920	
Warren G. Harding (R) and Calvin Coolidge	James M. Cox (D) and Franklin Roosevelt

1924	
Calvin Coolidge (R) and Charles Dawes	John Davis (D) and Charles W. Bryan
	Robert LaFollette (P) and Burton Wheeler

1928	
Herbert Hoover (R) and Charles Curtis	Alfred E. Smith (D) and Joseph Robinson

1932	
Franklin D. Roosevelt (D) and John N. Garner	Herbert Hoover (R) and Charles Curtis

1936	
Franklin D. Roosevelt (D) and John N. Garner	Alfred M. Landon (R) and Frank Knox

1940	
Franklin D. Roosevelt (D) and Henry Wallace	Wendell Willkie (R) and Charles McNary

1944	
Franklin D. Roosevelt (D) and Harry Truman	Thomas Dewey (R) and John Bricker

1948	
Harry Truman (D) and Alben Barkley	Thomas Dewey (R) and Earl Warren
	J. Strom Thurmond (STR) and Fielding Wright

1952	
Dwight D. Eisenhower (R) and Richard Nixon	Adlai Stevenson (D) and John Sparkman

	1956	
Dwight D. Eisenhower (R) and Richard Nixon		Adlai Stevenson (D) and Estes Kefauver
	1960	
John F. Kennedy (D) and Lyndon Johnson		Richard Nixon (R) and Henry C. Lodge
	1964	
Lyndon Johnson (D) and Hubert Humphrey		Barry Goldwater (R) and William Miller
	1968	
Richard Nixon (R) and Spiro Agnew		Hubert Humphrey (D) and Edmund Muskie
		Geroge Wallace (A) and Curtiss LeMay
	1972	
Richard Nixon (R) and Spiro Agnew (Replaced by Gerald Ford and Nelson Rockefeller)		George McGovern (D) and Thomas Eagleton (Replaced by R. Sargent Shriver)
	1976	
Jimmy Carter (D) and Walter Mondale		Gerald Ford (R) and Robert Dole
	1980	
Ronald Reagan (R) and George Bush		Jimmy Carter (D) and Walter Mondale
John Anderson (I) and Lucey		
	1984	
Ronald Reagan (R) and George Bush		Walter Mondale (D) and Geraldine Ferraro
	1988	
George Bush (R) and Daniel Quayle		Michael Dukakis (D) and Lloyd Bentsen

COLLECTORS' ORGANIZATIONS AND PUBLICATIONS

AMERICAN POLITICAL ITEMS COLLECTORS is the only collectors' society in the political field. The A.P.I.C., which has over eight thousand members, sponsors a large number of local and special clubs—or "chapters"—in all parts of the country. Several standing committees are concerned with reproductions of artifacts, collection insurance, research, and educational services. The organization's major publication is *The Keynoter*, an always well-illustrated quarterly that offers articles and other information supplied by its members.

The A.P.I.C. took a leading role in the passage of the Hobby Protection Act, and continues to be an aggressive pursuer of fraud and misrepresentation within the hobby. Occasionally the A.P.I.C. publishes substantive illustrated checklists of artifacts associated with particular candidates or campaigns. Besides the many frequently held chapter meetings, the society also sponsors a biannual "convention," which is held in a major city.

The A.P.I.C. also underwrites the costs of undergraduate college interns at the Smithsonian Institution's Museum of American History and the University of Hartford's Museum of American Political Life.

Many members of the parent organization belong to one or more local or specialty chapters as well, and some of these publish their own newsletters and host periodic regional meetings or "swap sessions."

Annual dues in American Political Items Collectors is currently $20. Membership information can be obtained from its secretary-treasurer, Joseph D. Hayes, 5922 Hidden Drive, San Antonio, Texas 78247.

Beyond *The Keynoter* and chapter newsletters the most important publications are two monthly tabloids: *Political Collector* (420 Madison Avenue, York, Pennsylvania 17404; subscription $12 per year) and *Political Bandwagon* (1632 Robert Road, Lancaster, Pennsylvania 17601; subscription $12 per year). Both publications tend to be overly oriented toward political button collecting. Nevertheless, both are especially important to beginning collectors, though one should be alert to the occasional extravagant claims made by some advertisers. By an arrangement with the A.P.I.C. the *Political Bandwagon* includes in its pages that organization's monthly newsletter.

Because of my interest in political paper there are two other related collectors' organizations worth investigating. The membership of the Ephemera Society of America is interested in the immense and colorful variety of paper material associated with 19th century lithography in this country and in Europe. The Society holds an annual show, outstanding in the quality of its offerings, in a northeastern state. Superb political paper is always available. A membership with annual dues of $25, can be obtained by writing to Mary McCabe, P.O. Box 224, Ravena, New York 12143.

The Thomas Nast Society is dedicated to the memory of the great cartoonist. It publishes a quarterly journal and hosts an annual meeting in Nast's hometown of Morrison, New Jersey. Those interested can write to the secretary, Lois Densky, in care of the Morristown/Morris Township Library, Miller Road, Morristown, New Jersey 07960.

SOURCES OF MATERIAL

Auctions. A considerable amount of political material gets listed in auction catalogs. Beginning collectors should subscribe to several catalog series because auction prices are a chief means for understanding price trends and arriving at approximate values for one's own collection. Remember, however, that auction prices tend to be a bit higher than sales prices. Each firm or person listed in this section publishes several well-illustrated annual catalogs.

Auctioneers:

Al Anderson, Post Office Box 644, Troy, OH 45373
COHASCO, Inc., Postal 821, Yonkers, NY 10702
Collectors Americana, 10 Lilian Road Ext., Framingham, MA 01701
David Frent, Post Office Box 455, Oakhurst, NJ 07755
Hake's Americana and Collectibles, Post Office Box 1444, York, PA 17405
Dr. Hal Ottaway, Auction Americana, Post Office Box 780282, Wichita, KS 67278
Political Gallery, 1325 W. 86th St., Indianapolis, IN 46260
Rex Stark, 43 Wethersfield Rd., Bellingham, MA 02019
Wilson, Jack, Political/Collectibles Auction, Post Office Box 49271, Austin, TX 78751

Dealers:

Americana Resources, 18222 Flower Hill Way, Suite 299A, Gaithersberg, MD 20879
Lynn Bettman, Post Office Box 1104, Scarsdale, NY 10583
Morton Berkowitz, 316 West 84th St., New York, NY 10024
Robert Coup, Post Office Box 348, Leola, PA 17540
Tom French, 1840 1st Avenue, #102-128, Capitola, CA 95010 (also runs an occasional auction)
Hunter's Vault, Post Office Box 926, Frankton, IN 46044

Dealers. (continued)

Charles McSorley, Post Office Box 21, Closter, NJ 07624
Lois Jacobs, 702 North Wells Street, Chicago, IL 60610
Presidential Coin and Antique Company, 6550-I Little River Turnpike, Alexandria, VA 22312 (also runs political numismatic auctions)
C. Peter Scanlan, 15 Glenwood St., Albany, NY 12203 (specializes in Theodore Roosevelt material)
Mark Suozzi, Post Office Box 102, Ashfield, MA 01330
Nelson Whitman, 11091 Connecticut Avenue, N.W., Washington, DC 20036

VALUE GUIDE

THE POLITICAL AMERICANA market seems to be chronically fluctuating. Better material generally moves upward in value consistently because of the steady demand, although individual artifacts may sometimes sell at prices lower than usual. Commonly obtained material sells at prices more consistent with inflation than with demand, hence moves upward slowly. As a candidate's popularity with collectors waxes and wanes, prices for related material respond accordingly. Knowing how to anticipate future price directions in the political market is a survival technique that collectors need to master.

As the traditionally popular early and modern lapel pieces, which have dominated the hobby for so long, increasingly become priced beyond many collectors' ability to pay, attention is currently turning to the better advertising cards, prints, and cartoons among paper ephemera and the small-size better artifacts among textiles. We can expect price increases for figural torchlights and other better novelties for the same reason. Artificially high prices caused by speculation seem to be a problem associated only with campaign buttons. Collectors should make it a point to read carefully the occasional columns about button prices published in *Political Collector;* they are written by knowledgeable collectors and dealers.

Another problem related to values is the confusion over terms describing the degree of an artifact's availability. "Unique," which means that only one example is known, or that an item is unmatched in quality, is perhaps the most overworked designation. "Scarce" and "rare" are often used interchangeably: *Scarce* artifacts turn up often enough so that they are familiar to most collectors; *rare* artifacts seldom turn up and perhaps are known to just a few collectors. I note that new collectors are especially careless in discriminating between what is unique, rare, or scarce. Probably no more than 5 percent of all political Americana can be considered unique and rare, and perhaps another 10 percent is scarce—which means that 85 percent can be obtained without much effort.

The following value guide is at best an approximation. Scarcity, demand, condition, aesthetic appeal, size, and candidate popularity are the basic factors governing prices. I must emphasize that material listed under the different value categories is arranged according to what collectors of political Americana will pay; collectors in other hobbies may pay more or less for a particular artifact.

ARTIFACTS VALUED AT $150 AND UP.
Scarce and rare mechanical shell badges.
Inaugural medals through 1948 (silver issues through 1956).

Thread boxes.

Ferrotypes picturing a party's presidential and vice-presidential nominees together on the front; the back will have only a pin.

Some classic campaign buttons.

Papier-mâché snuffboxes.

Daguerreotypes and ambrotypes of presidential candidates before 1868.

Figural torches.

Buttons picturing Eugene Debs, James Cox, John Davis, and a few picturing Woodrow Wilson, William Howard Taft, Theodore Roosevelt (1912 Bull Moose), Herbert Hoover, Al Smith, and Franklin Roosevelt—*each pictured together with his respective running mate.*

Figural glass bottle busts.

Washington inaugural buttons.

Campaign flags.

Most campaign ribbons associated with the Founding Father presidents, Andrew Jackson, Abraham Lincoln, Lewis Cass; ribbons picturing Franklin Pierce, Zachary Taylor, William Henry Harrison, Winfield Scott, and James Polk—each pictured with his respective running mate.

Liverpoolware, especially smaller examples.

Colorful campaign posters before 1924.

Lapel brooches from the log cabin era.

Some early historical flasks.

Autographed correspondence and documents associated with early presidents.

Contemporary numismatic issues associated with Thomas Jefferson, John Adams, and John Quincy Adams.

ARTIFACTS VALUED IN THE $200—$800 RANGE.

Parade canes.

Two-burner and some single-burner torchlights.

Scarcer serving trays.

Political pipes.

Stevengraph ribbons.

Some campaign buttons picturing both party nominees before 1940.

Log cabin china.

Parianware.

Ferrotypes picturing a presidential nominee. (The appropriate vice-presidential nominee may or may not be pictured on the back.)

Bryan money.

Larger medalets, to about 1¾ inches, depicting a party's nominees before 1872.

Ceramic pitchers and better designed plates issued in the 1872–1912 period.

Better bandannas from the 1872–1904 period.

Mechanical toys and the better still toys.

Black and white prints and cartoons before 1872.

Campaign flasks after 1876.

Umbrellas in working condition, 1896–1912.

Single-edge razors.

Paper lanterns.

Early sheet music with colorful covers before 1880.

Shell badges with albumin photographs.

ARTIFACTS VALUED IN THE $100—$600 RANGE.

Modern bandannas.

Political almanacs.

Campaign biographies.

Embroidered ribbons other than Stevengraphs.

A few modern buttons.

Toby pitchers.

Inaugural medals from 1960 on (bronze issues from 1952 on; silver Kennedy issue, $125).

Better mechanical and rebus advertising cards.

Single picture buttons from 1896 on.

Nineteenth-century medalets beginning with Jackson issues.

Pennants, 1903–1928.
Early satirical medalets.
Scarcer numismatic commemorative and mourning issues.
Mourning ribbons.
Lincoln memorial ceramics.
Sandwich cup plates.
Better watch fobs.
Portrait tiles.
Political chintzes.

ARTIFACTS VALUED IN THE $25—$100 RANGE.
Most modern cause material, buttons and paper especially.
Campaign newspapers.
Recent numismatic issues.
Ballots.
Modern textiles.
Tickets.
Modern smoking accessories.
Most campaign hats.
Probably 80 percent of all campaign material issued between 1940 and 1976.
Jewelry.
Some watch fobs.
Most protest literature.
Pens and pencils.
Most recent inauguration material.
Most advertising cards.
Puck cartoons.
Some inaugural badges.
Most material associated with state and local candidates.
Most postcards.
Most slogan buttons.

Bibliography

Chapter 1. Campaigning for the Presidency

(Note. *The APPA Standard* was published by the Association for the Preservation of Political Americana. This short lived collectors' organization disbanded in the early 1980s.)

Almquist, Eldon J. and Crain, Chris. *The Political Collectibles of Richard Nixon.* N.p.: the Authors, 1989. Unbound.

Barrone, Michael and Ujifusa, Grant. *The Almanac of American Politics, 1990* (10th ed.). Washington, DC: *National Journal,* 1989.

Boller, Paul. *Presidential Anecdotes.* New York: Oxford University Press, 1981.

Boller, Paul. *Presidential Campaigns.* New York: Oxford University Press, 1984.

Brenner, Walter C. *The Ford Theater Lincoln Assassination Playbills.* Philadelphia, PA: Privately printed, 1937. Limited edition of 137 copies.

Congressional Quarterly. "Members of Congress Since 1789." 2nd. edition. Washington, DC: Congressional Quarterly, Inc., 1981.

Cutter, Robert A. "Presidential Hopefuls, Vice Presidential Hopefuls". A biographical listing. N.p.: the Author, 1988. Unbound.

DeGregorio, William A. *The Complete Book of U.S. Presidents.* New York: Dembner Books, 1984.

Diamond, Robert A. *Congressional Quarterly's Guide to U.S. Elections.* Washington, DC: United States Government Printing Office, 1975 and later dates.

Fischer, Roger. *Tippecanoe and Trinkets, Too.* Urbana: University of Illinois Press, 1988.

Gardner, Bonnie, and Goldberg, Harvey. *The Campaign Items of John F. Kennedy.* 2nd. printing. N.p.: the Authors, 1980. Unbound.

Gardner, Bonnie, Goldberg, Harvey, and Henigan, John. *The Campaign Items of Robert F. Kennedy*, N.p.: the Authors, 1982. Unbound.

Gores, Stanley. *Presidential and Campaign Memorabilia*. Greensboro, NC: Wallace — Homestead Book Company, 1988.

Hudson River Museum. *Packaging Presidents: Memorabilia From Campaigns Past*. Essay by Frederick S. Voss. Yonkers, NY: the Museum, 1984.

Idzeida, Stanley J. *Lafayette: Hero of Two Worlds, The Art and Pageantry of His Farewell Tour of America, 1824-1825*. Hanover, NH: University Press of New England, 1989.

Jamieson, Kathleen Hall. *Packaging the Presidency: A History and Criticism of Presidential Campaign Advertising*. New York: Oxford University Press, 1984.

Keitzer, David I. *Ritual, Politics and Power*. New Haven, CT: Yale University Press, 1988.

Klaptor, Margaret, and Morrison, Howard A. *George Washington: A Figure Upon a Stage*. Washington, DC: Smithsonian Institution Press, 1982.

Kochmann, Rachel M. *Presidents: Birthplaces, Homes and Burial Sites*. N.p.: the Author, 1988.

Kotche, James. *John B. Anderson: Congressman and Presidential Candidate*. N.p.: the Author, 1981. An illustrated checklist of Anderson campaign material.

Maisel, L. Sandy (ed.). *Political Parties and Elections in the United States, An Encyclopedia,* 2 vols. New York: Garland Publishing, 1990.

Marling, Karol Ann. *George Washington Slept Here: Colonial Revival and American Culture, 1876-1986*. Cambridge, MA: Harvard University Press, 1988.

McGerr, Michael. *The Decline of Popular Politics: the American North, 1865-1928*. New York: Oxford University Press, 1986.

McGuiness, Collier, and Sayers, Maria, eds. *American Leaders, 1789-1987*. Washington, DC: *Congressional Quarterly*, 1987.

Post, Robert C., ed. *Every Four Years*. New York: W.W. Norton & Company, 1980.

Reichly, A. James, ed. *Elections American Style*. Washington, DC: Bookings Institute, 1987.

Scriabine, Christine. *The Presidency*. Know Your Government Series. New York: Chelsea House Publishers, 1988.

Southwick, Leslie, comp. *Presidential Also-Rans and Running Mates, 1788-1980*. Jefferson, NC: McFarlane & Company, 1984.

Sullivan, Edmund. "Campaigning American Style." An Essay in the Catalogue of the 14th Annual Mint Museum of Art Antique Show. Charlotte, NC: the Museum, 1980.

Sullivan, Edmund. *Hellbent for the White House*. Edited by Nancy Swain. Stamford, CT: Champion International, 1988.

United States Government Printing Office. *Biographical Directory of the United States Congress, 1774-1989*. Bicentennial Edition. Washington, DC: USGPO, 1989.

Chapter 3. Lapel Devices

Ackerman, Donald L. "The Sulphides." *The APPA Standard*, vol. IV, no. 1, Spring 1977.

_____ . "George Washington Inaugural Buttons . . . The G.W.'s." *The APPA Standard*, vol. III, no. 4, Winter 1976.

Albert, Alpheus H. *Record of American Uniform and Historical Buttons with Supplement*. Hightstown, NJ: the Author, 1973.

Cobb, J. Harold. *George Washington Inaugural Buttons and Medalets: 1789 and 1793*. Privately printed, 1963.

_____ . "The George Washington Historical Buttons." *The Keynoter*, Summer 1964 and Summer 1965.

DeWitt, J. Doyle. *A Century of Campaign Buttons: 1789-1889*. Hartford, CT: privately printed, 1959.

Ford, Marian F. *Project '68: The Presidential Election of 1968 as Seen Through Campaign Pins*. ca. 1968.

French, Tom. *The 1972 Presidential Campaign in Buttons*. Capitola, California: the Author, 1973.

Hake, Ted. *The Encyclopedia of Political Buttons . . . 1896-1972*. New York: Dafran House Publishers, 1974. Updated editions of this book and the following two by Theodore Hake are available from the author at P.O. Box 1444, York, PA: 17405.

Political Buttons: Book II, 1920-1976. York, Pennsylvania: Hake's Americana and Collectibles, 1977.

_____ . *Political Buttons: Book III, 1789-1916*. York, PA: Hake's American and Collectibles, 1978.

Hamilton, Charles, and Ostendorf, Lloyd. *Lincoln in Photographs: An Album of Every Known Pose*. Norman, OK: University of Oklahoma Press, 1963.

Sigoloff, Marc. *Collecting Political Buttons*. Chicago: Chicago Review Press, 1988.

Stoolmacher, Irvin S. "The Greening of America, Jimmy Carter's Use of Campaign Buttons in the 1976 Presidential Campaign." *Practical Politics*, vol. I, no. 3, March/April 1978.

Sullivan, Edmund B. *American Political Badges and Medalets, 1789-1892*. Lawrence, MA: Quarterman Publishers, 1981. A revised edition of J. Doyle DeWitt's *Century of Campaign Buttons, 1789-1889*.

Wagner, Dale. *Presidential Campaign Memorabilia: A Concise History, 1789-1972*. Washington, DC: Public Policy Research Associates, 1972.

West, Richard. "The Willkie, McNary and Chemurgy Button." *The APPA Standard*, vol. III, no. 4, Winter 1976.

Chapter 4. A Treasure in Political Paper

Blaisdell, Thomas C., Jr., and Selz, Peter. *The American Presidency in Political Cartoons: 1776-1976*. Salt Lake City: Peregrine Smith, Inc., 1976.

Brodsky, Vera Lawrence. *Music for Patriots, Politicians and Presidents*. New York: Macmillan Publishing Co., 1976.

Brown, William Burlie. *The People's Choice: The Presidential Image in the Campaign Biography*. Baton Rouge: Louisiana State University Press, 1960.

Bullseye. The Magazine of Editorial Cartooning. Lynbrook, NY (P.O. Box 150); $20/12 issues).

Burdick, J. R., et al. *The American Card Catalogue*. East Stroudsburg, PA: the Author, 1960.

Campbell, Mary and Gordon. *The Pen, Not the Sword*. Nashville, TN: Aurora Publications, 1970.

Cunningham, Noble, Jr. *The Images of Thomas Jefferson in the Public Eye: Portraits for the People, 1800-1809*. Charlottesville, VA: University Press of Virginia, 1981.

Greenhouse, Bernard L. *Political Postcards: A Price Guide, 1900-1980*. Syracuse, NY: Postcard Press, 1984.

Grote, Suzy Wetzel, "Engravings of George Washington in the Stanley DeForest Collection." *Antiques*, July 1977.

Gutman, Richard J.S. and Kellie O. *John Wilkes Booth Himself*. Dover, MA: Hired Hand Press, 1979. Limited edition of 1,000 copies.

Hart, James D. "They All Were Born in Log Cabins." *American Heritage*, vol. VII, no. 5, August 1956.

Holzer, Harold. "In the Image of Lincoln: The Face That Launched a Thousand Collectors." *The Antique Trader Weekly*, February 11, 1975.

_____ . "Lincoln Caricature Collectibles." *The Antique Trader Weekly*, February 7, 1979.

_____ . "Memorial Prints of Washington and Lincoln." *Antiques*, February 1979.

_____ . "Prints of Abraham Lincoln." *Antiques*, February 1974.

_____ . Baritt, Gabor S., and McNeely, Mark, Jr. *The Lincoln Image: Abraham Lincoln and the Popular Print*. New York: *Charles Scribner's Sons*, 1984.

_____ . *Changing the Lincoln Image*. Fort Wayne, IN: Louis A. Warren Lincoln Library and Museum, 1985.

Johnson, Malcolm. *David Claypool Johnston*. Catalog of an exhibition jointly held by the American Antiquarian Society, Boston College, The Boston Public Library and the Worcester Art Museum in March 1970. Published by the author, 1970.

_____ . *Great Locofoco Juggernaut, A New Consolatory Sub-Treasury Rag-Monster: A Cartoon Bank Note* by D.C. Johnston. Barre, MA: Imprint Society, 1971. Contains a fine insert reproduction of Johnston's famous satirical bank note.

Keller, Morton. *The Art and Politics of Thomas Nast*. New York: Oxford University Press, 1968.

Miles, William. *The Image Makers*. A Bibliography of Presidential Campaign Biographies. Metuchen, NJ: Scarecrow Press, 1979.

_____ . *The People's Voice*. An Annotated Bibliography of American Presidential Campaign Newspapers. Westport, CT: Greenwood Press, 1987.

_____ . *Songs, Odes, Glees and Ballards: A Bibliography of Presidential Campaign Songsters*. Westport, CT: Greenwood Press. 1990

Milgram, James W. *Abraham Lincoln: Illustrated Envelopes and Letterheads, 1860-1865*. Northbrook, IL: Northbrook Publishing Corp., 1984.

Murrell, William. *A History of American Graphic Humor: 1747-1865*. 2 vols. New York: Whitney Museum of American Art, 1933, 1938. Reprinted by the Cooper Square Press, 1961.

National Portrait Gallery. *Permanent Collection Illustrated Checklist*. Washington, DC: Smithsonian Institution Press, 1982.

Nevins, Allan, and Weitenkampf, Frank. *A Century of Political Cartoons. . . 1800 to 1900*. New York: Charles Scribner's Sons, 1944.

Oliver, Andrew, ed. *Portraits of John and Abigail Adams*. The Adams Papers, Series IV. Cambridge, MA: Belknap Press of Harvard University Press, 1967.

_____ . *Portraits of John Quincy Adams*. The Adams Papers, Series IV. Cambridge, MA: Belknap Press of Harvard University Press, 1967.

O'Neal, David, compiler. *Early American Almanacs: The Phelps Collection*. Peterborough, NH: the compiler, c. 1978.

Paine, Albert Bigelow. *Th. Nast: His Period and His Pictures*. New York: The MacMillan Co., 1904.

Peters, Harry J. *America on Stone*. New York: Doubleday, Doran & Company, Inc., 1931.

Press, Charles. *The Political Cartoon*. Rutherford, NJ: Fairleigh Dickinson University Press, 1981.

Shaw, Albert. *Abraham Lincoln: A Cartoon History*. 2 vols. New York: Review of Reviews Corporation, 1929.

Silber, Irwin. *Songs America Voted By*. Harrisburg, PA: Stackpole Books, 1971.

Simkin, Colin, ed. *Currier and Ives' America*. New York: Crown Publishers, 1952.

Stauffer, David McNeely. *American Engravers Upon Copper and Steel*. New York: Burt Franklin, n.d. 1960s, reprint. Original edition published in 1907.

Tyler, Ron, ed. *The Image of America in Caricature and Cartoon*. Catalog of an Exhibition Presented by the Amon Carter Museum of Western Art. Fort Worth, TX: the Museum, 1975.

University Microfilms. *An Index to the Presidential Campaign Biographies, 1824-1972*. University Microfilms International, Ann Arbor, MI: 1981.

Weitenkampf, Frank. *Political Caricature in the United States. . . An Annotated List*. New York: The New York Public Library, 1953.

Welling, William. *Collector's Guide to Nineteenth Century Photographs*. New York: Collier Books, 1976.
West, Richard. *Satire on Stone: The Political Cartoons of Joseph Keppler*. Urbana, IL: University of Illinois Press, 1988.
Wick, Wendy. *George Washington, An American Icon: Eighteenth Century Graphic Portraits*. Washington, DC: Smithsonian Institution and the Bana Foundation, 1982.

Chapter 5. Political Numismatics

Baker, W.S. *Medallic Portraits of Washington*. Philadelphia, PA: Robert M. Linsay, 1885. Reprinted by Krause Publications of Iola, Wisconsin, in 1965.
Chamberlain, GA: "Morris Furst: Die Sinker and Engraver." *The Numismatist*, June 1954.
DeWitt, J. Doyle. *Alfred S. Robinson: Hartford Numismatist*. N.p. Hartford, CT: Connecticut Historical Society, 1968.
_____ . *A Century of Campaign Buttons, 1789-1889*. Hartford, CT: the Author, 1959.
_____ . "Election Medals of the Campaign of 1844." *The Numismatist*, June-November 1943. Reprinted by the author, n.d.
_____ . "Medalets of the Presidential Campaign of 1848." *The Numismatist*, November 1948. Reprinted by the author, n.d.
Douglas, Susan H. "George Washington Medals of 1889." *The Numismatist*, May, June, and July 1949.
Dusterberg, Richard B. *The Official Inaugural Medals*. 2nd ed. Cincinnati, OH: Medallion Press, 1976.
Edgar H. Adams' Plates of Lyman Low's Hard Times, Tokens. Lawrence, MA: Quarterman Publications, 1980.
Eidlitz, Robert J. "Medals Relating to Thomas Jefferson." *The Numismatist*, September 1924. Reprinted as a booklet under the title *Medals and Medallions of Thomas Jefferson*, n.p., n.d.
Fuld, Melvin and George. "Medallic Memorials to Theodore Roosevelt." *The Numismatist*, November 1958.
Julian, R. W. *Medals of the United States Mint: The First Century, 1792-1892*. La Cajon, CA: Token and Medal Society, 1977.
Kenney, Richard D. "Early American Medalists and Die Sinkers." *The Coin Collector's Journal*, January/February, September/October, and November/December 1951.
King, Robert P. "Lincoln in Numismatics." Various issues of *The Numismatist* in February 1924, April 1927, and August 1933. Reprinted by the Token and Medal Society in 1966.
Kobbe, Gustave. "Presidential Campaign Medals." *Scribner's*, September 1888. Reprinted by Charles McSorley, Closter, NJ: in 1970.
Levine, H. Joseph. *Collectors Guide to American Presidential Inaugural Medals and Memorabilia*. Danbury, CT: Johnson and Jensen, 1981.
Low, Lyman. *Catalogue of Hard Times Tokens Issued For and Against The United States Bank*. Boston: T.R. Marvin and Sons, 1886.
_____ . *Hard Times Tokens: An Arrangement of Jackson Cents*. New York: Privately Printed, 1900. This title and the previous title have been reprinted several times; reprints of both titles are often found in one binding.
MacNeil, Neil. *The President's Medal, 1789-1977*. New York: Clarkson N. Potter, Inc., 1977.
Mayhew, Aubrey. *The World's Tribute to John F. Kennedy in Medallic Art*. New York: William Morrow and Co., 1966.
Rulau, Russell. *Hard Times Tokens*. N.p.: Krause Publications, 1980. An updated revised study of Lyman Low's early works.
Rulau, Russell, and Fuld, Melvin. *Medallic Portraits of Washington*. Iola, WI: Krause Publications, 1985. An updated and revised edition of Baker's *Medallic Portraits of Washington*.
Snowden, James Ross. *The Medallic Memorials of Washington in the Mint of the United States*. Philadelphia, PA: J. B. Lippincott, 1861.
Sullivan, Edmund B. "Political Numismatics." *The Numismatist*, vol. 93, no. 2, December 1980.
Vermeude, Cornelius. *Numismatic Art in America*. Cambridge, MA: Belknap Press of Harvard University Press, 1971.
Zerbe, Farran. "Bryan Money. Tokens of the Presidential Campaigns of 1896 and 1900—Comparative and Satirical." *The Numismatist*, July 1926.

Chapter 6. Ceramics and Glassware

Belknap, E. McCamly. *Milk Glass*. New York: Crown Publisher, 1949. Contains an illustration of the Bryan water pitcher hand painted with a wild rose pattern.
Heacock, William. "McKinley by McKee." *The Antique Trader Weekly*, February 7, 1979.
Klamkin, Marian. *American Patriotic and Political China*. New York: Charles Scribner's Sons, 1973.
Larsen, Ellouise Baker. *American Historical Views on Staffordshire China*. New York: Doubleday, Doran and Company, 1939.
Lee, Ruth Webb, and Rose, James H. *American Glass Cup Plates*. Northborough, MA: the Authors, 1948.
Lindsey, Bessie M. *American Historical Glass*. Revised and edited by Walter Risley. Rutland, VT: Charles E. Tuttle, 1967. Published originally in two volumes in 1948 and 1950 under the title *Lore of Our Land Pictured in Glass*.

McKearin, Helen, and Wilson, Kenneth M. *American Bottles and Flasks and Their Ancestry*. New York: Crown Publishers, 1979.
Marsh, Tracy H. *The American Story Recorded in Glass*. Minneapolis, MN: the Author, 1962.
Munsey, Cecil. *The Illustrated Guide to Collecting Bottles*. New York: Hawthorn Books, 1970.

Chapter 7. Political Textiles

Christopherson, Katy. *The Political and Campaign Quilt*. Catalogue of an Exhibition at the Old State Capitol, Frankfort, KY: 1984.
Collins, Herbert R. *Threads of History*. Washington, DC: The Smithsonian Institution Press, 1979.
Godden, Geoffrey A. *Stevengraphs*. Rutherford, NJ: Fairleigh Dickinson University Press, 1971.
Goldberg, Harvey. *Kennedy Ribbons*. Clark, NJ: KPIC Publications, 1988. Unbound.
Hornung, Clarence. *Treasury of American Design*. New York: Hary N. Abrams, Inc., 1976. Published in editions of two volumes and two volumes in one.
Lincoln Lore. "United States Flags of Lincoln's Presidential Period." Number 1522, September 1964. Edited by R. Gerald McMurty. Fort Wayne, IN: Lincoln National Life Insurance Company.
Sullivan, Edmund B., and Fischer, Roger. *American Political Ribbons and Ribbon Badges, 1825-1981*. Lincoln, MA: Quarterman Publications, 1985.
Washburn, Wilcomb E. "Campaign Banners." *American Heritage*. vol. XXIII, no. 6, October 1972.
Weiss, Hillary. *The American Bandanna: Culture on Cloth from George Washington to Elvis*. San Francisco, CA: Chronicle Books, 1990.

Chapter 8. Collecting Political Novelties

Ackerman, Donald. "Snuff Boxes." *The APPA Standard* (Journal of the Association for the Preservation of Political Americana), Summer 1977.
_____ . "Thread Boxes." *The APPA Standard* (Journal of the Association for the Preservation of Political Americana), Autumn 1977.
Collins, Herbert R. *Political Campaign Torches*. (Contributions from the Museum of History and Technology.) United States National Bulletin, Paper 45. Washington, DC: Smithsonian Institution, 1964.
Hertz, Louis H. *The Toy Collector*. New York: Hawthorn Books, 1976. Contains illustrations of the Butler and Grant mechanical dolls and the Butler bank.
Holzer, Harold, and Ostendorf, Lloyd. "Sculptures of Abraham Lincoln from Life." *Antiques*, February 1978.
Mullins, Linda. *The Teddy Bear Men: Theodore Roosevelt and Clifford Berrymen*. Cumberland, MD: Hobby House Press, 1987.
Piercy, Elmer. "Watch Fobs." *The Keynoter* (Journal of the American Political Items Collectors), Spring 1970.
Wallace, David H. *John Rogers, The People's Sculptor: His Life and His Work*. Middletown, CT: Wesleyan University Press, 1967. Contains important information about "The Council of War."

Recordings

American Heritage Publishing Company. *The Invention of the Presidency*. 1968, #XB-136.
Audio Archives Enterprises. *If I'm Elected: Actual Voices of Our Presidents and Their Opponents*, 1892-1952. 1952.
_____ . *Election Songs of the United States*. Sung by Oscar Brand, #FH-5280.
_____ . *Moonshine and Prohibition*. 1962, #FH-5263.
Folkways Record and Service Corporation. *Songs of the Suffragettes*. 1958, #FH-5281.
Time, Incorporated. *Sing Along with Millard Fillmore*. 1964.
See also William Miles, *Songs, Odes, Glees and Ballards, op. cit.*, for an extensive listing.

Chapter 9. Movements, Causes and Personalities

PROHIBITION

Feldstein, Albert L. "Prohibition or. . . How Dry I Am." *The APPA Standard* (Journal of the Association for Preservation of Political Americana), vol. III, no. 4, Winter 1976.
Filippelli, Ronald L. (ed.) *Labor Conflict in the United States, An Encyclopedia*. New York: Garland Publishing, 1991.
Furnas, J. C. *The Life and Times of the Late Demon Rum*. New York: G.P. Putnam's Sons, 1965.
Osbury, Herbert. *The Great Illusion: An Informal History of Prohibition*. Garden City, NY: Doubleday and Corp., 1950.
Taylor, Robert Lewis. *Vessel of Wrath: The Life and Times of Carry Nation*. New York: New American Library, 1966.

WOMEN'S MOVEMENT

Atkinson, Diane. *Votes for Women*. Women in History Series. Cambridge, England: Cambridge University Press, 1988.

_____ . *Mrs. Broom's Suffragette Photographs*. London, England: Dick Nishen Publishing, n.d. [1988].

_____ . *Suffragettes*. London, England: The Museum of London, 1988.

Feldstein, Albert L. "The Women's Movement Today." *The APPA Standard* (Journal of Association for Preservation of Political Americana), vol. III, no. 3, Autumn 1976.

Flexner, Eleanor. *A Century of Struggle: The Women's Rights Movement in the United States*. Cambridge, MA: Harvard University Press, 1966.

Gallagher, Robert S. "I was Arrested, Of Course: An Interview with Miss Alice Paul." *American Heritage*, vol. XXV, no. 2, February 1974.

Irwin, Inez Haynes. *Angel and Amazons: A Hundred Years of American Women*. Garden City, NY: Doubleday, Doran and Company, 1934.

Johnston, Johanna. *Mrs. Satan: The Incredible Saga of Victoria Woodhull*. New York: Popular Library, 1967.

Koppelman, Elmer. "Victoria Claflin Woodhull." *The Keynoter* (Journal of American Political Items Collectors), Summer 1969.

Lunardini, Christine. *From Equal Suffrage to Equal Rights: Alice Paul and the National Women's Party, 1910-1928*. New York: New York University Press, 1986.

Lyon, Peter. "The Herald Angels of Women's Rights." *American Heritage*, vol. X, no. 6, October 1959.

Papachristou, Judith. *Women Together: A History in Documents of the Women's Movement in the United States*. New York: Alfred A. Knopf, 1976.

Scott, Anne F., and Andrew M. *One Half the People: The Fight for Woman Suffrage*. The America's Alternatives Series. Philadelphia, PA: J.B. Lippincott, 1975.

Stevens, Doris. *Jailed for Freedom*. Introduction by Janice Law Trecher. Studies in the Life of Women's Series. New York: Schocken Books, 1976.

Tickner, Lisa. *The Spectacle of Women: Imagery of the Suffrage Campaign, 1907-1914*. Chicago, IL: University of Chicago Press, 1988. Authoritative account of the British suffrage movement.

Zophy, Angela Howard and Kavenik, Frances M. *Handbook of American Women's History*. New York: Garland Publishing, 1989.

PROTESTS AND PERSONALITIES

Buhle, Mari Jo and Paul, Georgakas, Dan, eds. *Encyclopedia of the American Left*. New York: Garland Publishing, 1989.

The Cause. Newsletter of American Political Items Collectors Cause Chapter. Edited and Published by John O'Brien, 1200 North Gardner #5, West Hollywood, CA 90046, 1977-.

Dubofsky, Melvyn. *We Shall Be All: A History of the Industrial Workers of the World*. New York and Chicago: Quadrangle Books, 1969.

Dulles, Foster Rhea. *Labor in America: A History*. 2nd ed. rev. New York: Thomas Y. Crowell Corp., 1960.

Foner, Phillip S. *History of the Labor Movement in the United States*. 4 vols. New York: International Publishers, 1947 (3rd printing, 1962).

Litwack, Leon. *The American Labor Movement*. Englewood Cliffs, NJ: Prentice Hall, Inc., 1962.

Okun, Rob A., ed. *The Rosenbergs: Collected Visions of Artists and Writers*. New York: Universe Books, 1988.

Scriabine, Christine and Sullivan, Edmund. *Voices of the Left, 1870-1960*. Catalogue of an Exhibition at the Museum of American Political Life, University of Hartford. Essay by Paul Buhle. West Hartford, CT: the Museum, 1990.

Snow, Richard. " 'American Characters': Joe Hill." *American Heritage*, vol. XXVII, no. 6, October 1976.

Zurier, Rebecca. *Art for the Masses: A Radical Magazine and Its Graphics, 1911-1917*. Philadelphia, PA: Temple University Press, 1988.

THE PERSONALITIES: AUTHOR'S CHOICE

Butler, Benjamin F. *Butler's Book: Autobiography and Personal Reminiscence*. Boston, 1892.

Holzman, Robert S. *Stormy Ben Butler*. New York: Macmillan, 1954.

Russell, Francis. "Butler the Beast?" *American Heritage*, vol. XIX, no. 3, April 1968.

Sullivan, Edmund. "George Francis Train: Citizen of the Republic. *The Keynoter*. (Journal of American Political Items Collectors), Summer 1969.

Thornton, Willis. *The Nine Lives of Citizen Train*. New York: Greenberg Publishers, 1948.

Train, George Francis. *My Life in Many States and Foreign Lands*. New York: D. Appleton, 1902.

Chapter 10. Protecting Your Collection

Cooper, Sydney & Bella Anne. *Home Security Systems,* Springfield, IL: C.C. Thomas, 1989.

Crain, Chris. "Safeguarding Your Collection." *Political Collector,* December, 1978.

Cross, Reva. *China Repair and Restoration.* New York: Drake Publishing Company, 1973.

Fall, Freeda Kay. *Art Objects: Their Care and Preservation.* Washington, DC: Museum Publications, 1967.
_____ . *Handbook for Museums and Collectors.* LaJolla, CA: Laurence McGilvey, 1973.

(Home Security): *Home Security Alarms: What They Do and How They Work* and *Home Security Starts at Your Door.* These pamphlets are available free of charge from Consumer Information Center, Pueblo, CO 81009.

Leene, Jentian E., ed. *Textile Conservation.* Washington, DC: Buttersworth, 1972.

Levin, Thomas. Security: *Everything You Need to Know About Home Security Systems.* Minneapolis, MN: Park Lane Enterprises, 1982.

MacLeish. A. Bruce. *The Care of Antiques and Historical Collections: A Handbook for The Nonspecialist.* Nashville, TN: American Association for State and Local History, 1985.

McDermott, Robert, and Irwin, Theodore. *Stop Thief! How to Safeguard Your Home and Business.* New York: Macmillan, 1978.

Plenderleith, H. J., and Werner, A.E.A. *The Conservation of Antiquities and Works of Art,* 2nd. ed. New York: Oxford University Press, 1979.

Shelly, Marjorie. *The Care and Handling of Art Objects.* New York: Metropolitan Museum of Art, 1987. Distributed by Harry N. Abrams, Inc.

Sloane, Eugene A. *The Complete Book of Locks, Keys, Burglar and Smoke Alarms.* New York: William Morrow, 1977.

Note. For help in locating conservation specialists and firms, collectors should write to the American Institute for Conservation of Historic and Artistic Works, 1400 16th St., N.W., Suite 340, Washington, DC 20036.

SOURCES OF PROTECTIVE AND DISPLAY MATERIALS

Acid-free Paper, Pastes and Mylar Containers: COHASCO, Inc., Postal 821, Yonkers, NY 10702
Hollinger Corporation, P.O. Box 618V, 3810 South Four Run Drive, Arlington, VA 22206.
Light Impressions, 439 Monroe Avenue, Rochester, N Y 14607-3717.
TALAS. Catalogue of the Technical Library Service, 104 Fifth Avenue, New York, NY 10011.
University Products, 517 Main St., Holyoke, MA 01041.

Lamination: New England Document Conservation Center, Abbott Hall, School Street, Andover, MA 01810.

Riker Mounts: Tom Bankard, 1523 Brian Road, Baltimore, MD 21237.

Wood Cases: Indian River Display Case Company, 13706 Robins Road, Westerville, OH 43081.
Vector Inc., P.O. Box 857-PC, Sturgis, MI 49091.

Chapter 11. Fantasies and Reproductions

Ackerman, Donald L. "George Washington Inaugural Buttons: the G.W.'s" *The APPA Standard* (Journal of the American Association for Preservation of Political Americana), Winter 1976.

Albert, Alpheus H. *Record of American Uniform and Historical Buttons.* Bicentennial Edition. Hightstown, NJ: author, 1977.

American Political Items Collectors. "Brummagen, An APIC Project." *The Keynoter,* Fall/Winter 1985. Essential reading.

Spieler, Dave. "Repro Report." *The Political Collector.* A series of articles about campaign button reproductions that appeared in the January, March, April, June, and September 1974 issues.

INDEX

Note: page numbers in italics refer to illustrations or captions.